Real Life
WINDOWS® 95

Real Life
WINDOWS® 95

by Dan Gookin

IDG Books Worldwide, Inc.
An International Data Group Company

Foster City, CA ♦ Chicago, IL ♦ Indianapolis, IN ♦ Braintree, MA ♦ Dallas, TX

Real Life Windows® 95

Published by
IDG Books Worldwide, Inc.
An International Data Group Company
919 E. Hillsdale Blvd.
Suite 400
Foster City, CA 94404

Library of Congress Catalog Card No.: 95-78402

ISBN: 1-56884-483-2

Printed in the United States of America

10 9 8 7 6 5 4 3 2

1I/RR/QY/ZV

Distributed in the United States by IDG Books Worldwide, Inc.

Distributed by Macmillan Canada for Canada; by Computer and Technical Books for the Caribbean Basin; by Contemporanea de Ediciones for Venezuela; by Distribuidora Cuspide for Argentina; by CITEC for Brazil; by Ediciones ZETA S.C.R. Ltda. for Peru; by Editorial Limusa SA for Mexico; by Transworld Publishers Limited in the United Kingdom and Europe; by Al-Maiman Publishers & Distributors for Saudi Arabia; by Simron Pty. Ltd. for South Africa; by IDG Communications (HK) Ltd. for Hong Kong; by Toppan Company Ltd. for Japan; by Addison Wesley Publishing Company for Korea; by Longman Singapore Publishers Ltd. for Singapore, Malaysia, Thailand, and Indonesia; by Unalis Corporation for Taiwan; by WS Computer Publishing Company, Inc. for the Philippines; by WoodsLane Pty. Ltd. for Australia; by WoodsLane Enterprises Ltd. for New Zealand.

For general information on IDG Books Worldwide's books in the U.S., please call our Consumer Customer Service department at 800-762-2974. For reseller information, including discounts and premium sales, please call our Reseller Customer Service department at 800-434-3422.

For information on where to purchase IDG Books Worldwide's books outside the U.S., contact IDG Books Worldwide at 415-655-3021 or fax 415-655-3295.

For information on translations, contact Marc Jeffrey Mikulich, Director, Foreign & Subsidiary Rights, at IDG Books Worldwide, 415-655-3018 or fax 415-655-3295.

For sales inquiries and special prices for bulk quantities, write to the address above or call IDG Books Worldwide at 415-655-3200.

For information on using IDG Books Worldwide's books in the classroom, or ordering examination copies, contact Jim Kelly at 800-434-2086.

For authorization to photocopy items for corporate, personal, or educational use, please contact Copyright Clearance Center, 222 Rosewood Drive, Danvers, MA 01923, or fax 508-750-4470.

 is a registered trademark under exclusive license to IDG Books Worldwide, Inc., from International Data Group, Inc.

Acknowledgments

To God, for creating the world.

To the ancient Phoenicians, for creating the alphabet.

To the Chinese, for creating the printing press (and takeout food).

To Thomas Paine, for creating my country.

To my parents, for creating me.

To Silicon Valley, for creating the mess that makes a book like this one necessary.

(The publisher would like to give special thanks to Patrick J. McGovern, without whom this book would not have been possible.)

Credits

Publisher
Karen A. Bluestein

Acquisitions Manager
Gregory Croy

Acquisitions Editor
Ellen L. Camm

Brand Manager
Melisa M. Duffy

Editorial Director
Mary Bednarek

Editorial Managers
Mary C. Corder
Andy Cummings

Editorial Executive Assistant
Jodi Lynn Semling

Editorial Assistant
Nate Holdread

Production Director
Beth Jenkins

Supervisor of Project Coordination
Cindy L. Phipps

Supervisor of Page Layout
Kathie S. Schnorr

Pre-Press Coordinator
Steve Peake

Associate Pre-Press Coordinator
Tony Augsburger

Media/Archive Coordinator
Paul Belcastro

Project Editor
Rebecca Whitney

Editors
Corbin Collins
Mary C. Corder

Technical Reviewer
Greg Guntle

Production Staff
Gina Scott
Carla C. Radzikinas
Patricia R. Reynolds
Melissa D. Buddendeck
Dwight Ramsey
Robert Springer
Theresa Sánchez-Baker
Megan Briscoe
Maridee V. Ennis
Angela F. Hunckler
Bradley Johnson
Anna Rohrer

Proofreader
Sandra Profant

Indexer
Anne Leach

Book Design
Theresa Sánchez-Baker

Cover Design
Kavish + Kavish

About the author

Dan Gookin considers himself a writer and computer "guru" whose job it is to remind everyone that computers are not to be taken too seriously. His approach to computers is light and humorous, yet very informative. He knows that the complex beasts are important and can do a great deal to help people become productive and successful. Yet Dan mixes his vast knowledge of computers with a unique, dry sense of humor that keeps everyone informed — and awake. His favorite quote is "Computers are a notoriously dull subject, but that doesn't mean I have to write about them that way."

Dan's most recent titles include the best-selling *Word For Windows 6 For Dummies, Buy That Computer!,* and *PCs For Dummies,* 3rd Edition (all published by IDG Books Worldwide). He is the author of the original *...For Dummies* book, *DOS For Dummies.* All told, he's written more than 35 books about computers. Dan holds a degree in communications-visual arts (okay, let's be honest: Art!) from the University of California-San Diego and lives with his wife and four sons somewhere in the Pacific Northwest.

You can contact Dan at the following e-mail addresses:

CompuServe: 73055,1405

Prodigy: PKHG47A

America Online: dgookin

The Internet: dgookin@iea.com

ABOUT IDG BOOKS WORLDWIDE

Welcome to the world of IDG Books Worldwide.

IDG Books Worldwide, Inc., is a subsidiary of International Data Group, the world's largest publisher of computer-related information and the leading global provider of information services on information technology. IDG was founded more than 25 years ago and now employs more than 7,500 people worldwide. IDG publishes more than 235 computer publications in 67 countries (see listing below). More than 60 million people read one or more IDG publications each month.

Launched in 1990, IDG Books Worldwide is today the #1 publisher of best-selling computer books in the United States. We are proud to have received 8 awards from the Computer Press Association in recognition of editorial excellence, and our best-selling ...For Dummies™ series has more than 17 million copies in print with translations in 25 languages. IDG Books Worldwide, through a recent joint venture with IDG's Hi-Tech Beijing, became the first U.S. publisher to publish a computer book in the People's Republic of China. In record time, IDG Books Worldwide has become the first choice for millions of readers around the world who want to learn how to better manage their businesses.

Our mission is simple: Every one of our books is designed to bring extra value and skill-building instructions to the reader. Our books are written by experts who understand and care about our readers. The knowledge base of our editorial staff comes from years of experience in publishing, education, and journalism — experience which we use to produce books for the '90s. In short, we care about books, so we attract the best people. We devote special attention to details such as audience, interior design, use of icons, and illustrations. And because we use an efficient process of authoring, editing, and desktop publishing our books electronically, we can spend more time ensuring superior content and spend less time on the technicalities of making books.

You can count on our commitment to deliver high-quality books at competitive prices on topics consumers want to read about. At IDG Books Worldwide, we value quality, and we have been delivering quality for more than 25 years. You'll find no better book on a subject than an IDG book.

John Kilcullen
President and CEO
IDG Books Worldwide, Inc.

WINNER
Eighth Annual
Computer Press
Awards ≥ 1992

WINNER
Ninth Annual
Computer Press
Awards ≥ 1993

IDG Books Worldwide, Inc., is a subsidiary of International Data Group, the world's largest publisher of computer-related information and the leading global provider of information services on information technology. International Data Group publishes over 235 computer publications in 67 countries. More than sixty million people read one or more International Data Group publications each month. The officers are Patrick J. McGovern, Founder and Board Chairman; Kelly Conlin, President; Jim Casella, Chief Operating Officer. International Data Group's publications include: **ARGENTINA'S** Computerworld Argentina, Infoworld Argentina; **AUSTRALIA'S** Computerworld Australia, Computer Living, Australian PC World, Australian Macworld, Network World, Mobile Business Australia, Publish!, Reseller, IDG Sources; **AUSTRIA'S** Computerwelt Oesterreich, PC Test; **BELGIUM'S** Data News (CW); **BOLIVIA'S** Computerworld; **BRAZIL'S** Computerworld, Connections, Game Power, Mundo Unix, PC World, Publish, Super Game; **BULGARIA'S** Computerworld Bulgaria, PC & Mac World Bulgaria, Network World Bulgaria; **CANADA'S** CIO Canada, Computerworld Canada, InfoCanada, Network World Canada, Reseller; **CHILE'S** Computerworld Chile, Informatica; **COLOMBIA'S** Computerworld Colombia, PC World; **COSTA RICA'S** PC World; **CZECH REPUBLIC'S** Computerworld, Elektronika, PC World; **DENMARK'S** Communications World, Computerworld Danmark, Computerworld Focus, Macintosh Produktkatalog, Macworld Danmark, PC World Danmark, PC Produktguide, Tech World, Windows World; **ECUADOR'S** PC World Ecuador; **EGYPT'S** Computerworld (CW) Middle East, PC World Middle East; **FINLAND'S** MikroPC, Tietoviikko, Tietoverkko; **FRANCE'S** Distributique, GOLDEN MAC, InfoPC, Le Guide du Monde Informatique, Le Monde Informatique, Telecoms & Reseaux; **GERMANY'S** Computerwoche, Computerwoche Focus, Computerwoche Extra, Electronic Entertainment, Gamepro, Information Management, Macwelt, Netzwelt, PC Welt, Publish, Publish; **GREECE'S** Publish & Macworld; **HONG KONG'S** Computerworld Hong Kong, PC World Hong Kong; **HUNGARY'S** Computerworld SZT, PC World; **INDIA'S** Computers & Communications; **INDONESIA'S** Info Komputer; **IRELAND'S** ComputerScope; **ISRAEL'S** Beyond Windows, Computerworld Israel, Multimedia, PC World Israel; **ITALY'S** Computerworld Italia, Lotus Magazine, Macworld Italia, Networking Italia, PC Shopping Italy, PC World Italia; **JAPAN'S** Computerworld Today, Information Systems World, Macworld Japan, Nikkei Personal Computing, SunWorld Japan, Windows World; **KENYA'S** East African Computer News; **KOREA'S** Computerworld Korea, Macworld Korea, PC World Korea; **LATIN AMERICA'S** GamePro; **MALAYSIA'S** Computerworld Malaysia, PC World Malaysia; **MEXICO'S** Compu Edicion, Compu Manufactura, Computacion/Punto de Venta, Computerworld Mexico, MacWorld, Mundo Unix, PC World, Windows; **THE NETHERLANDS'** Computer! Totaal, Computable (CW), LAN Magazine, Lotus Magazine, MacWorld; **NEW ZEALAND'S** Computer Buyer, Computerworld New Zealand, Network World, New Zealand PC World; **NIGERIA'S** PC World Africa; **NORWAY'S** Computerworld Norge, Lotusworld Norge, Macworld Norge, Maxi Data, Networld, PC World Ekspress, PC World Nettverk, PC World Norge, PC World's Produktguide, Publish& Multimedia World, Student Data, Unix World, Windowsworld; **PAKISTAN'S** PC World Pakistan; **PANAMA'S** PC World Panama; **PERU'S** Computerworld Peru, PC World; **PEOPLE'S REPUBLIC OF CHINA'S** China Computerworld, China Infoworld, China PC Info Magazine, Computer Fan, PC World China, Electronics International, Electronics Today/Multimedia World, Electronic Product World, China Network World, Software World Magazine, Telecom Product World; **PHILIPPINES'** Computerworld Philippines, PC Digest (PCW); **POLAND'S** Computerworld Poland, Computerworld Special Report, Networld, PC World/Komputer, Sunworld; **PORTUGAL'S** Cerebro/PC World, Correio Informatico/Computerworld, MacIn; **ROMANIA'S** Computerworld, PC World, Telecom Romania; **RUSSIA'S** Computerworld-Moscow, Mir - PK (PCW), Sety (Networks); **SINGAPORE'S** Computerworld Southeast Asia, PC World Singapore; **SLOVENIA'S** Monitor Magazine; **SOUTH AFRICA'S** Computer Mail (CIO),Computing S.A.,Network World S.A., Software World; **SPAIN'S** Advanced Systems, Amiga World, Computerworld Espana, Communicaciones World, Macworld Espana, NeXTWORLD, Super Juegos Magazine (GamePro), PC World Espana, Publish; **SWEDEN'S** Attack, ComputerSweden, Corporate Computing, Macworld, Mikrodatorn, Natverk & Kommunikation, PC World, CAP & Design, Datalngenjoren, Maxi Data,Windows World; **SWITZERLAND'S** Computerworld Schweiz, Macworld Schweiz, PC Tip; **TAIWAN'S** Computerworld Taiwan, PC World Taiwan; **THAILAND'S** Thai Computerworld; **TURKEY'S** Computerworld Monitor, Macworld Turkiye, PC World Turkiye; **UKRAINE'S** Computerworld, Computers+Software Magazine; **UNITED KINGDOM'S** Computing /Computerworld, Connexion/Network World, Lotus Magazine, Macworld, Open Computing/Sunworld; **UNITED STATES'** Advanced Systems, AmigaWorld, Cable in the Classroom, CD Review, CIO, Computerworld, Computerworld Client/Server Journal, Digital Video, DOS World, Electronic Entertainment Magazine (E2), Federal Computer Week, Game Hits, GamePro, IDG Books Worldwide, Infoworld, Laser Event, Macworld, Maximize, Multimedia World, Network World, PC Letter, PC World, Publish, SWATPro, Video Event; **URUGUAY'S** PC World Uruguay; **VENEZUELA'S** Computerworld Venezuela, PC World; **VIETNAM'S** PC World Vietnam.
05/17/95

Contents at a Glance

Table of Contents

Chapter 14

xvii

Chapter 24

Chapter 25

Chapter 26

Chapter 27

Chapter 28

Chapter 29

Mousy Concepts 527

Chapter 30

Working with Text and Graphics 537

Introduction

Welcome to *Real Life Windows 95,* a book written just for you. This is the unofficial manual, the human being guide-book, a new approach to explaining only what's useful and not rambling on about the rest. I promise to tell you exactly what's important in Windows and what can be cheerfully ignored.

Honestly, Windows 95 is a *massive* program. Even the "complete" reference books — the hefty 1,000+ pagers — only scratch the surface of what the Windows 95 operating system can do. But do *you* really want to know all that stuff?

Of course not! You want to know what's important. You want to know it now. The other stuff? Forget it. Just getting the job done in the quickest way possible is the philosophy of this book. The other stuff, the details and boring technical matter, are all omitted — not even glanced at here. And don't be surprised if, on the way to getting the most from Windows 95, you have a little fun as well. This book educates *and* entertains. Such a deal!

Brazen Assumptions

I'm assuming that you have a computer and that your computer has the Windows 95 operating system installed. That's about all you really need to get started here. This book takes care of the rest.

Although this book does detail the operation of Windows 95, it does not discuss older versions of Windows. In fact, you should forget everything about Windows 3.11 or Windows for Workgroups and concentrate instead on getting your work done in Windows 95 — which is what this book does best.

This book does cover a lot of ground, but some things are not specifically covered here. Primarily, this book does not cover the Microsoft Plus! package, an extension to the things that Windows can do. Also not covered are the Windows Internet connection (which just isn't working as this book goes to press) plus the Microsoft Network, which was bare-bones and utterly dull two months before its doors were officially set to open. Future editions of this book will incorporate these items.

How to Use This Book

My philosophy is simple: Why write a big book about Windows and then litter it with Tip icons telling you what's hot? Instead, inside this book, *everything* is a tip! Still, you need a way to get started, and that usually begins by asking questions.

How Do I . . .?

Every part of this book (and the end of this Introduction) begins with the "How Do I?" section. That's a list of questions and answers plus references to specific spots in this book where you can find more information and maybe a tutorial or step-by-step to work through.

Like Windows, this book makes ample use of graphical figures. Margin figures like the one to the right are scattered everywhere to describe options, offer suggestions, and help you find certain objects on the screen.

Larger figures contain *callouts,* or references within the figures that help you further locate special things as well as complement the nearby text. Figure I-1 shows you how it all works.

Perhaps the greatest bonus in this book is its overdose of cross-references. So many things are related in Windows that it just makes sense to put in references to other spots in the text where the same thing is discussed. If you want to know more about your disk drives, for example, you can look up that information by using the following cross-references:

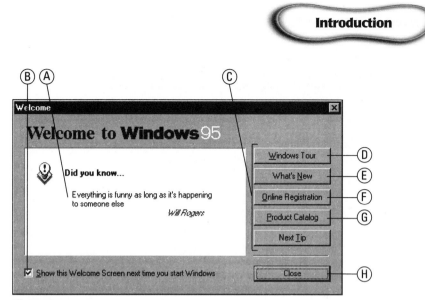

Figure I-1
Now you're finally welcome.
A. Some sorta tip. **B.** Click here to avoid seeing this thing in the future. **C.** You may not see all these buttons displayed. **D.** A waste of time. **E.** Boring. **F.** Don't bother. **G.** Shameless hype. **H.** Bye-bye!

➡ For more information about the types of disk drives in your computer, see Chapter 14.

➡ Chapter 2 covers the My Computer program, where you can graphically examine your computer's disk drives and peek at their contents.

➡ The subject of maintaining disk drives is covered in Chapter 18.

Icons Used in This Book

This book uses the following icons to flag certain items in the text:

A useful suggestion or quicker alternative strategy (though, really, *everything* in this book is a tip).

Something you probably don't want to do.

A tutorial you can try.

When you're told to use one of Windows' menus, the key word is *choose*. So if the text reads "Choose File⇨Exit," that means to pluck out the Exit command from the File menu. You can use either the keyboard or the mouse for this operation (see Chapter 27, the section "Chasing Menus," for more information).

Keyboard commands, though rare, work like this:

Alt+F

This is a key combination. Press and hold down the Alt key, and then press the F key — the same as you would press the Shift key to produce a capital *F*. If more than one key is required in a sequence, it reads like this:

Ctrl+Esc, S, C

Press the Ctrl+Esc key combination, release both keys, and then press the S key and then the C key.

Where to Start?

Every part of this book starts out with some basic "Where do I start?" type of questions. Just mull them over, and you'll get an idea of what's possible in that section. And keep in mind that after you get to where you're going, there are more cross-references that lead you to other, interesting related spots.

To get the whole thing rolling, start off with the following:

How do I...?

Start a program?

There are lots of ways to start a program in Windows, but most often you use the Start button in the bottom left corner of the screen.

➡ Using the Start button is covered in Chapter 3, in the section "Marching through the Start button marsh."

➡ The way a typical program behaves is covered in Chapter 4.

➡ And see Part II, which covers working with programs in depth, including specifics on the freebie programs that come with Windows (Chapter 9) and Microsoft Office (Chapter 10).

➡ Information about starting your computer (and turning it off) is offered right up front, in Chapter 1.

Mess with Windows?

Changing the way Windows works and looks is called *dinking,* and it's a major time-waster. Most dinking is done from the Control Panel, though numerous Properties commands exist all over Windows for massive messing.

➡ Common dinking tasks, such as messing with fonts, adjusting your printer, and networking, are covered in Part IV.

➡ To change the date and time on your computer, see the section "Fooling with the time (Setting the time on your PC)" in Chapter 7.

➡ Changing Windows' look is the topic of Chapter 24.

➡ Also take a look at Chapter 25 for some strange and wonderful stuff.

Work the windows on the screen?

Windows comes with all sorts of gizmos and graphical gadgets to (supposedly) help you get your work done. Intuitive? Maybe. Frustrating? Just about all the time!

➡ See Chapter 27 for basic information about controlling those windows on the screen.

➡ See Chapter 28 for working the intricacies of a dialog box.

➡ Chapter 29 helps you get acquainted with your computer mouse, which is necessary if you ever expect to get any mileage out of Windows.

Play a game?

In addition to being aggravating, Windows offers a choice selection of diversions, including the ever-popular Solitaire game. Not that you ever would. . . .

➠ See Part V for having fun.

➠ Games are covered specifically in Chapter 26.

Part
I

Breaking In to Windows

In this part

- The big picture

- A quick tour of My Computer

- Starting your work

- Use one program, you've used them all

- Places to go, things to see

How do I...?

Look at the files on my computer?

The answer is to look in My Computer — the icon thing that lives on Windows' desktop. Click on the My Computer icon to see the disk drives, folders, and files that live on your computer.

➠ Chapter 2 discusses in detail how My Computer works. Be sure to check out the section "Different Ways to Look at the Stuff in My Computer."

➠ Using My Computer is easier when you display its handy toolbar. See the section "Whip out the toolbar" in Chapter 2.

Start a new something?

Windows has a button named *Start,* but that's not the only place you can go to start your work. It all really depends on what it is you want to start.

➠ If you're starting a document you were working on recently, see Chapter 3, the section "Finding your document lurking in the Documents menu."

➠ If you're starting up a new document, see the section "Taking advantage of the numerous New menu commands" in Chapter 3.

➠ If you're starting a new project (more than one document), see Chapter 3's section "Starting a New Project."

Work Windows applications?

Getting work done is easy in Windows because most applications work alike.

➠ See Chapter 4, the section "Going About Your Business," for a few pointers on carrying out some common application tasks: printing, saving, and so on.

Figure this darn thing out?

Windows has a Help system that is actually quite helpful. It enables you to look up topics and get step-by-step instructions for carrying out specific tasks in Windows and in all Windows applications.

➠ For more information about the Windows Help system, see the section "The Windows Way of Offering Help" in Chapter 4.

Rescue a file I just deleted?

Files in Windows aren't deleted; they're tossed into the politically correct Recycle Bin. From there they can be easily recovered — and without the rotten banana peels and wet-dog smell you get in real recycle bins.

➠ See the section "A quick, odorless peek into the Recycle Bin to restore something" in Chapter 5 for information about snatching back freshly deleted files.

Deal with all this new pop-up menu wackiness?

Windows 95 is loaded with helpful shortcut menus that tend to "pop up" at you whenever you click the mouse's right button (a right-click).

➠ See Chapter 5, the section "The Ubiquitous Pop-up Shortcut Menus" for more information about the shortcut menus and a brief talk on the various Properties dialog boxes that also infest Windows.

The Big Picture

Two things exist to help you and your computer get something done: an operating system and applications programs. And two things are there to get in your way: an operating system and applications programs. Welcome to the world of computer software!

Software is the stuff that controls your computer hardware. It tells the hardware what to do, how to start in the morning, how to get your work done. The whole idea is to put *you* in the driver's seat when it comes to using your computer. And the main program in charge of all that is your computer's operating system: Windows.

Start Your Computer!

You can't get anything done until you turn on your computer. If it's not on already, start it up:

1. Start your computer by flipping on its switch.

   There are actually two switches you should turn on. The first is on the computer box. Flip that one first. Then flip on the switch on your computer's monitor.

Just about every item hanging on your computer has its own switch. If you're going to print, turn on the printer. If you're going to use some other external device — a modem, scanner, external disk drive, whatever — turn on that switch as well.

2. Your computer comes to life.

This step takes a while, depending on how much stuff you have crammed into your computer's innards or hanging on your computer through that ganglia of cables 'round back.

Your computer may beep. It may snort.

Eventually you see the message "Starting Windows 95" displayed on the screen. It's beginning. . . .

➡ If your computer has already come to life and you desire to shut it off, see the instructions toward the end of this chapter in the section "Quitting Windows and Turning Off Your PC."

➡ If you've just started your computer after adding a new piece of equipment — a modem, printer, or some other hardware, for example — see Chapter 23 for information about the software side of that hardware setup.

3. Windows explodes on the screen.

Yeah, yeah, yeah. Windows 95. Hurrah for Microsoft. Let's have another stock split. Whoop-de-doo.

This madness lasts for about 30 seconds, maybe longer, depending on the number of goodies your PC has, whether your PC is shackled to a network, and the phase of the moon. Eventually you are welcomed to Windows, which is covered in the following section.

Save time by turning it all on at once

You can save a great deal of time and hassle by plugging in all your computer gadgets to a power strip. This strip can be purchased at any hardware store, or you can pay more money and buy a "power organizer" type of thing at your computer store. Be sure to look for a power strip that offers surge protection as well as spike protection and other goodies designed to guard your precious electronics from the evils of electricity.

Even more ways to say "start your computer"

Starting a computer is easy. (Having it do what you want it to is the problem.) But to make starting a computer more difficult, the computer whiz kids have come up with a battalion of terms, each of which means "start the computer." Here's a sampling:

Power-up: Geekish for turning on the computer, very nuclear-reactor sounding.

Power-on: Same as power-up, though it doesn't have any weight-lifter attachments.

Boot: Classic computer term for starting a computer, though it refers specifically to starting your computer's main piece of software, the operating system.

Warm boot: Another term for resetting the computer; everything starts over with the power still on.

Cold boot: Resetting the computer, but turning the power off first. The power is off, so you're starting it "cold."

Reset: Interrupts the computer from whatever it's doing and forces it to start all over (a warm boot). Reset only as a last, drastic measure to get control.

Reboot: Another term for reset or warm boot.

Welcome to Windows, Surrender Your Life

One of the problems with Windows is that it prevents you from getting to your work right away. You have to sit there and watch its rah-rah and then wade through two dialog boxes before you get your work done.

➠ You have to use a mouse to use Windows. See Chapter 29 for information about using a mouse if the concept is alien to you or if you just fear rodents.

➠ Understanding what a dialog box is and does is covered in Chapter 28.

Dialog box #1: Log in, mystery guest

The first dialog box you may encounter urges you to log in, to either the Microsoft Network (see Figure 1-1) or just Windows.

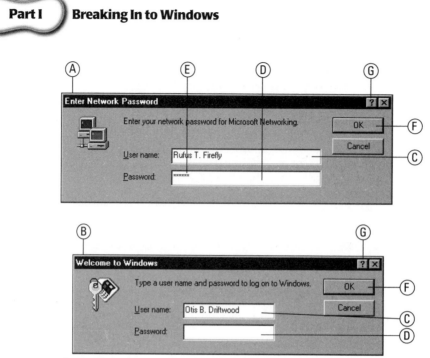

Figure 1-1
The prisoners identify themselves to the warden.
A. You see this one if your PC is networked. **B.** You see this one if you don't have a networked PC. **C.** Type your name here. **D.** Type a password here. **E.** Your password is displayed as asterisks. **F.** Click here to log in. **G.** Click here, and then point and click on any other part of the dialog box to see some pop-up help.

To log in, follow these steps:

1. Type your name in the box labeled User name.

   Type your first and last names or any special code name used to identify you on a network. For example, this is what the Pope types to log in to the Vatican computer:

   John Paul II

   This is what I type to log in to my network — my network code name:

   dang

   Type your first and last names or code word. When you're done, *don't press the Enter key!* Press the Tab key instead.

   If your user name (secret code name) is already displayed in the box, you don't have to retype it; just skip ahead to the next step.

2. In the box labeled Password, type your secret password.

For example, type **none**, which is the password I use at my office.

The password you type isn't displayed; Windows shows you asterisks instead. This is part of its security, so you have to erase the whole thing if you make a mistake. Use the Backspace key.

By the way, passwords can be from one to several characters long. Keeping them short and memorable is always a good idea.

3. It's okay.

After typing your password, click the mouse on the OK button. The dialog box goes away, but Windows remembers who you are.

➧ If you're using a network, it's a good idea to log in every time. Chapter 22 discusses networking aspects of Windows.

➧ Also see Chapter 22, the section "Logging Off and Logging In As Another User" for information about how two or more people can share the same computer.

"But I don't wanna type a name and password!"

There is no real reason to log in to Windows, not if you're the only one using your computer and you aren't on a network. Just click on the Cancel button in the "Who are you?" dialog box. Click. The box goes away.

If more than one person does use your computer, logging in is a way to identify yourself as someone special. That way, Doris can use the computer with her special settings, and Oscar can do the same, each without bothering the other. Or if you're on a network, others on the network can recognize that so-and-so is using a particular computer.

"Uh-oh! Windows doesn't know who I am"

Windows isn't rude to you if you've never typed your name and a password. It merely wants to confirm the password you're using. You see a dialog box, similar to the one shown in Figure 1-2.

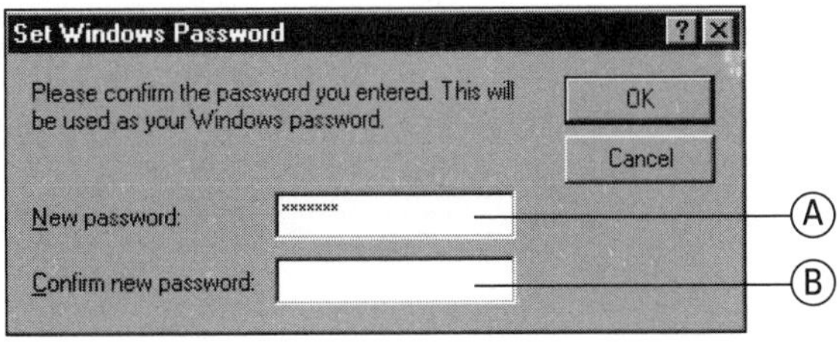

Figure 1-2
Windows wants you to remember your password. **A.** The password you typed already, shown in crypto-asterisk. **B.** Retype the same password here.

The New Password dialog box contains the password you just entered, shown in crypto-asterisk.

1. Type that same password again in the Confirm new password box.

   This is an argument for making brief, memorable passwords.

2. It's okay.

   Click on OK, and Windows will remember you. But it's now up to you to remember your password. Windows demands it every time it starts (unless you follow my original advice and click on Cancel when the box first appears).

"I want to change my password" or "I forgot my password"

If you forget your old password, click on the Cancel button in the log-in dialog box. So much for security.

Windows warns you when you forget your password or type something goofy. A "naughty-naughty" dialog box is displayed, but you can still click on the Cancel button to use Windows.

The only true way around this pickle is to create a new user name for yourself or to just get in the habit of clicking on the Cancel key every time you see that stupid dialog box.

Dialog box #2: Almost there – Windows says hello for the *n*th time

Don't be alarmed if there is a long, scary pause between the what's-your-password box and the Welcome to Windows 95 dialog box, shown in Figure 1-3. You can dawdle here or just click on the Close button to start your work.

➡ If you click on the Close button, you're ready to use the desktop. See the following section.

➡ Sometimes other windows may be open on the screen, which cover all or part of the Welcome to Windows 95 box. To see the Welcome dialog box up front, click on the Welcome button on the taskbar. See Chapter 7, the section "Buttons and Windows Galore," for more information about clicking on taskbar buttons.

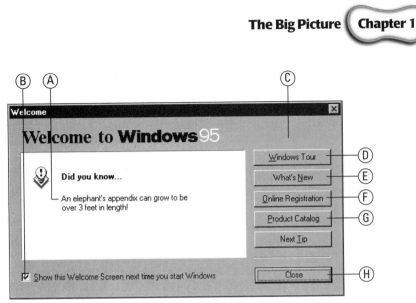

Figure 1-3
Now you're finally welcome.
A. Some sorta tip. **B.** Click here to avoid seeing this thing in the future. **C.** You may not see all these buttons displayed. **D.** A waste of time. **E.** Boring. **F.** Don't bother. **G.** Shameless hype. **H.** Bye-bye!

➡ For more information about using a dialog box, especially filling in various "fields," see Chapter 28.

➡ If you need help using your mouse, see Chapter 29.

The First Stop Is the Desktop

When you operate a car, you sit in the driver's seat. In a plane, the captain and co-pilot control things from the cockpit. In Windows, your center of control is the desktop (see Figure 1-4). That's Windows' front door to everything in your computer, the place where you work, the end result of all the hoopla it took to get the thing started.

As a cockpit, the Windows desktop is disappointing. They do this on purpose. Microsoft figures that too many knobs, dials, and buttons get in your way. The minimalist approach tends to be cryptic, however, so it's an unusual trade-off.

➡ Turn to Chapter 5, the section "Moseying Around the Desktop," for a more detailed drive around the desktop.

➠ You should also note that Figure 1-5 (in the following section) shows what the desktop may look like on your screen. If what you see is different and you want to change it, see Chapter 24, the section "Background Information." (You can change everything about the desktop. It's completely customizable.)

Turning off the "Welcome to Windows 95" thing forever

If you really don't want to be bothered with the Welcome to Windows 95 dialog box, you can turn it off forever. (If you don't do this, you see the box every time Windows starts.) To turn the darn thing off, follow these steps:

1. Click the mouse in the box by Show this Welcome Screen next time you start Windows.

   You can also press the Alt+S key combination to uncheck this item. Press and hold the Alt key, and then tap the S key. Release both keys.

2. The ✔ check mark in the box disappears.

   You're done.

If you want to get the box back, you have to run the Welcome program (which displays the Welcome to Windows 95 box) and put a ✔ check mark back in the little square. See Chapter 3, the section "Running to the Run command to start a program," and type **Welcome** in the box to rerun the Welcome program.

Windows is a GUI, the future of all computing

Back in the early '80s, it was decided that the best way to use a computer was graphically. Things would appear on the screen as graphical images — buttons, icons, pictures, and text — that looked on the screen exactly the way they would print on your printer. This is all part of the graphical user interface, or GUI.

By the way, GUI is pronounced "gooey" as in "geoduck" (look that up if you don't get it!). Personally, I say "jee-yew-eye."

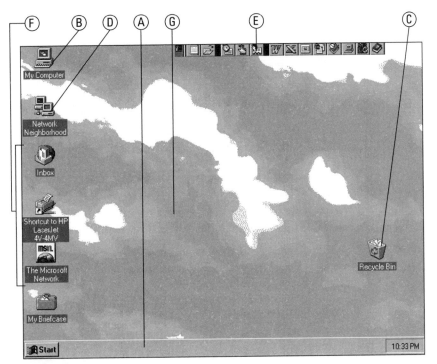

Figure 1-4
The Windows desktop.
A. The taskbar, covered in Chapter 7. **B.** My Computer, uncovered in Chapter 2.
C. The Recycle Bin; see Chapter 5, the section "The Politically Correct Recycle Bin."
(And yes, you can move the icons around if you like.) **D.** Network Neighborhood,
visible only if you're on a network (see Chapter 22). **E.** The Microsoft Office chorus
line/wonder bar, which appears only if you're using Microsoft Office (see Chapter 10). **F.** Other icons, which appear on the desktop as you add them. See
Chapter 17, the section "Bringing Order to the Desktop." **G.** The desktop
background. See Chapter 24 for the details.

The Start Thing, the Heart of Windows

To one side of the taskbar you find the Start button, or Start Thing, as I like
to call it. It's a thing because when you click on the Start button, up pops a
menu full of selections, which lead to even more selections, which lead to
even more selections. It can be pretty unwieldy if you're not careful.

1. Activate the Start Thing by clicking your mouse on it.

   Click your mouse on the Start button. Click.

   You can also press Alt+S whenever you see the taskbar.

   And if you don't see the taskbar on your screen (if something else is covering it up, for example), you can press Ctrl+Esc — the Ctrl (Control) and Esc (Escape) keys together — to pop up the Start Thing's menu.

2. Up pops the Start Thing's menu.

   Several items are on the Start Thing's menu, as shown in Figure 1-5. Each of these items plays some role in working Windows.

Figure 1-5
The Start Thing's menu.
A. Click on the Start Thing to see the menu.
B. These triangles mean that there's a submenu lurking. **C.** Supposedly gives you help in running Windows. **D.** Enables you to run programs by — get this — typing their names in a little box (a primitive concept). **E.** How you quit Windows.

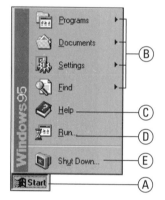

3. Click on the Start Thing button again.

   This step makes the pop-up menu disappear. You can also just click your mouse anywhere on the desktop or press the Esc key. Poof! It's gone.

➡ You need a mouse in order to use Windows. See Chapter 29 for more information about using a mouse.

➡ Configuring and changing the Start Thing is covered in Chapter 6.

What to Do in Windows

Windows doesn't exist for itself. Yes, it does look impressive on the screen. But if you want to impress people that way, turn your TV to PBS and have "Masterpiece Theatre," not a computer, running on your desk. To get the most from a computer, you have to do something. In Windows, there are three things you can do:

✘ You can work.

✘ You can play.

✘ You can dink.

Working is what you do most of the time. Playing is what you do when you should be working. And dinking is what you do when you'd rather be doing anything else.

There's more than one way to say that you're "starting a program"

You don't just start a program, you can also do the following:

✘ Launch an application.

✘ Run software.

✘ Start software.

✘ Run a program.

✘ Launch a program.

✘ Start an application.

✘ Run an application.

Working in Windows

You get your work done in Windows by using various applications, such as Microsoft Word, dBASE, 1-2-3, WordPerfect, whatever software you have. After all the hoopla of Windows starting, you get down to work by running one or more of these programs.

➠ See Chapter 3 for more information about the various ways you can get work done in Windows.

➠ Also check out Part II, "Getting Work Done."

➠ Windows applets, the "free" programs that came with Windows, are discussed in Chapter 9.

➠ See Chapter 10 for a few pointers on using Microsoft Office.

➠ Even if you're stuck using DOS programs, you can get work done in Windows (see Chapter 12).

Playing in Windows

Playing works just like working in Windows. The only difference is that you start a fun program rather than something linked to "productivity."

Windows comes with many fun programs for playing and generally wasting time. There's the ever-popular Solitaire game (which actually made the news as something many companies were thinking of banning as an anti-productivity tool!). And there are other, numerous ways to pass the hours in a fun and graphical way.

To start a game, use the Start Thing to pop up the menu, and then choose Programs and then Accessories and then Games. That's where you find most of Windows' games.

➠ Believe it or not, all of Part V covers having fun in Windows.

➠ The subject of Solitaire is covered specifically in Chapter 26.

➠ Honestly, the best games on your computer will run under DOS. See the last part of Chapter 26, the section "Wrestling with DOS Games," for information about running DOS games in Windows.

Dinking with Windows

Dinking is the art of adjusting the way something works on a computer. If you're a dinker, Windows is paradise. If you hate messing with things, Windows is hell.

Before becoming bubbly with elation or drowning in despair, you should know that there are two kinds of dinking. First comes dinking to get something to work. That's a pain. Then there's dinking just because. You can change the way Windows looks and works all over the place. This can be fun and also an incredible time-waster.

➡ Part IV of this book covers dinking in depth.

➡ Most dinking is done in Windows' Control Panel (see Chapter 20).

➡ Just about everything in Windows has a special control menu attached to it: a shortcut menu. How to use this menu and general information about the Properties command are covered in Chapter 5, in the section "The Ubiquitous Pop-up Shortcut Menus."

Quitting Windows and Turning Off Your PC

When you're done for the day, you have to shut down Windows and turn off your computer. (Of course, there is a school that says leave it on all the time; see the sidebar "Leaving your PC on all the doo-dah day," later in this chapter.)

To shut down Windows and wrap things up, follow these steps:

1. Activate the Start Thing's pop-up menu.

   You do this most quickly by pressing Ctrl+Esc. You can also click on the Start Thing's button if you see the taskbar or press Alt+S. Up pops the menu.

2. Choose the bottom item, Shut Down.

   Don't think that a movie is about to start because the screen dims. Instead, a dialog box appears (see Figure 1-6), giving you various options for putting away Windows.

Figure 1-6
Windows is ready for bed.
A. Click here when you're
done for the day. **B.** Click
here to reboot (a "warm
boot"). **C.** Retreat to the
DOS prompt (quit
Windows). **D.** See Chapter 22, the section "Logging
Off and Logging In As
Another User." **E.** Shut
down. **F.** "I've changed my
mind."

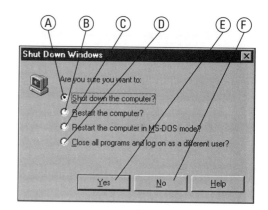

3. Make sure that the option Shut down the computer? is selected.

   Click on that option with the mouse if there isn't a black dot by it.

4. Click on the Yes button.

   Yes, you want to quit and shut down.

   If you change your mind, click on No. Windows returns to normal (more or less).

5. Windows hums. It stirs. It wraps things up for you.

   If you haven't yet saved any documents to disk, you're informed of that now and given a chance to save. Otherwise, Windows hums and stirs some more.

   ➠ See Chapter 4, the section "Saving your stuff," for information about saving your stuff.

   ➠ If someone else on the network is using your computer, you see a warning dialog box displayed. Click on the No button so that you don't shut down your computer and accidentally peeve them. See Chapter 22 for more information about networking.

6. All done.

   The final screen displays the Windows 95 logo and tells you that it's okay ("safe," actually) to turn off your computer.

7. Turn off your computer.

   Flip off the power switch on the computer box and monitor, plus anything else attached to your PC.

8. Get out and get some fresh air.

   ➠ It's not always necessary to quit. See Chapter 4, the section "Done for the Day? To Quit or Put Away," for more information.

It's important when you turn off your computer

Never turn off your computer unless Windows tells you that it's okay to do so. This is the best way to ensure that your computer lives a safe and happy life and that you never lose anything accidentally.

Leaving your PC on all the doo-dah day

Windows takes so long to start that it makes you wonder why anyone would ever bother with turning it off.

The answers are many to the "Should I leave my PC on all the time?" question. On the "definitely not" side are the following reasons:

✗ Leaving your computer on all the time uses more energy, and Al Gore would get mad.

✗ And that ups your electric bill.

✗ And something else I can't think of right now.

On the side of "leave it on all the time," I offer the following reasons:

✗ Your computer uses only a thin slice of your overall energy pie.

✗ Turning your computer on and off can damage the PC's innards. The changing temperature (from hot to cold to hot) stresses the solder points inside your computer, causing them to eventually crack and break. If you leave your computer on all the time, the possibilities of this happening decrease.

✗ Many newer model computers come with "Energy Star" power-saving features, which make it easier on your electrical bill if you just leave everything on all the time.

My advice is to leave your computer on all the time and turn it off only for extended leaves of absence, such as a vacation or long weekend. Otherwise, leave it on all the time. (Also see Chapter 25 for information about the screen saver.)

A Quick Tour of My Computer

Chapter

2

In This Chapter

- Using the My Computer thing
- Looking at stuff in My Computer
- A brief look at the Control Panel and Printers folders
- Looking at files and folders
- Changing the way My Computer displays information
- Using My Computer's toolbar
- The one-window approach to My Computer

My Computer is really Your Computer, the one sitting on your desk right now. The one running Windows 95. What the My Computer icon on the desktop represents is all the stuff on your computer — everything. It's kind of an anchor point for the things you do with your stuff, a way to get at your stuff. Of course, Windows has many programs that do the same thing, from the nerdy Explorer to the disgusting DOS prompt. But of all of them, My Computer (a.k.a. Your Computer) is the best way to see your stuff.

My Computer, Your Computer

My Computer represents all the things inside your computer, the stuff you have stored there. It contains a visual representation of your computer's hard drives, folders, and files, showing you how and where information is stored. This is perhaps the best way to deal with that sort of stuff, though Windows has other ways to display or get at that information as well — which you should cheerfully ignore for now.

➠ The My Computer icon is stuck on the desktop. You can move it around, but you cannot remove or delete it. Just about everything else on the desktop, however, can be rearranged. See Chapter 17, the section "Bringing Order to the Desktop," for more information about icons stuck to the desktop.

➠ You can change the name of the My Computer icon to something else, such as Billy's Computer or Bumples or whatever you want to call it. See Chapter 16, the section "Blessing a File with a New Name," for information about renaming icons (and files).

➠ Another way to view information stored on your computer is with the Explorer, though it's really geeky and even people who *like* computers complain about it. The Explorer is covered somewhat in Chapter 17 and throughout Part III of this book.

Opening up My Computer and looking inside

Open the My Computer icon by double-clicking on it with the mouse. This displays a window on the screen that shows certain goodies lurking inside your computer, similar to what you see in Figure 2-1.

Figure 2-1
My Computer's first window.
A. Floppy drive. **B.** Hard drives lurking in your computer. **C.** The Control Panel (see Chapter 20). **D.** The Printers folder (see Chapter 19).

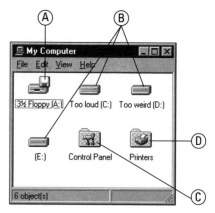

At this stage, you see two types of items: disk drives and special folders. The disk drives represent your computer's disk drives, and the special folders hold two things: the Control Panel and Printers.

➠ The shape and appearance of the disk drives in My Computer depend on what types of disk drives live inside or nearby. See Chapter 14 for more information about the various disk drives in your computer, er, My Computer.

➠ The Control Panel and Printers folders are included in My Computer because they are important parts of your computer, just like the disk drives. Sections covering each of these items appear later in this chapter.

➠ The "serving hand" thing you may see under some of your disk drives is offering the drive up for grabs on the network. That's a *shared* drive. Likewise, a drive that looks like it's connected to the sewer system is a drive on someone else's computer on the network, one that your computer is currently "borrowing." You can find out more about this networking stuff in Chapter 22.

Behemoth (C:) C on 'Koby' (F:)

Opening up stuff inside My Computer

My Computer displays the goodies inside your computer as icons. To see what's inside an icon — a disk drive or folder or whatever — you double-click on it with the mouse, just as you double-clicked on My Computer to open it up.

➠ Opening an icon is done by double-clicking on it. This usually displays a window on the screen, detailing what the icon represents. To close that window, click on its Close button (the ¥ button). If you need to, see Chapter 27 for more information about working with windows.

When you double-click on a disk drive to open it up, a window appears, displaying its folders, and files appear.

(C:)

When you double-click to open up a folder, a window appears, displaying its files and maybe even more folders.

➠ *How* you see the files and folders can vary. See the section "Different Ways to Look at My Computer," later in this chapter.

➠ When you see a file, which doesn't look like a folder or file, you can open it up to see what's inside it as well. However, opening up the file typically starts the application that created the file. See Chapter 3, the section "Starting a Document Instead of a Program," for more information, but also check out the section "Who Knows What Evil Lurks in the Heart of Files?" in Chapter 15.

➠ See Chapter 29 for information about using a mouse and all that double-clicking nonsense.

"Oh, lordy, I have too many windows open!"

It really isn't a problem for several windows to be open at a time on the desktop. The only sin committed, in fact, is one of clutter.

To find a lost window, use the taskbar. All open windows have their names plastered on the taskbar as a button. To go to a specific window, just click on that window's button on the taskbar. To go back to the Projects folder, for example, locate the Projects button on the taskbar and click on it once with the mouse. This brings that window front and center.

If you find the clutter of all the windows too much to bear, organize them by following these steps:

1. Find the taskbar.

   The taskbar should line the bottom of the desktop, like that annoying scroll of stock quotes during the day on "CNN Headline News." If you don't see the taskbar, move the mouse pointer down to the bottom of the screen, and the taskbar should pop right up.

2. Right-click the mouse on the taskbar.

   The right mouse button is the one you don't normally click. Point the mouse pointer at a "blank" part of the taskbar, where there aren't any buttons. Click the right mouse button once, and the taskbar shortcut menu pops up.

   ➠ See Figure 5-1 in Chapter 5 for a suggestion about how to click on the taskbar to see its shortcut menu.

3. Choose Cascade from the menu.

   This step arranges all the windows on the screen in a nice, overlapping fashion.

   You can also click on the Tile Horizontally or Tile Vertically buttons to arrange the windows in a tiled (not overlapping) fashion.

➠ Also see the section "The 'single window' approach to using My Computer," later in this chapter.

➠ See Chapter 7 for more information about using the taskbar.

➠ See Chapter 5 for the lowdown on the various shortcut menus that sprout up like weeds all over Windows, in the section "The Ubiquitous Pop-up Shortcut Menus."

Closing stuff

At some point, you may have several folders open, each of which displays a window full-o'-stuff. Those windows should eventually be closed.

To close a window, click on its Close button, the × button. This step closes that window and removes it from the screen. ✕

You can close any window you like and in any order; it doesn't matter which ones you opened first.

➡ Closing a window *does not* delete it or its contents. You can close the Programs folder window, and this doesn't affect what you have stored in that folder. If you do need to delete something, however, use the Recycle Bin. See Chapter 16, the section "Some Files Just Hafta Go, or Deleting Files," and also Chapter 5, the section "The Politically Correct Recycle Bin."

➡ Chapter 27 has more information about working with windows, if you need to brush up.

Closing My Computer, good-bye

When you're done using My Computer (and Your Computer), it's only polite to put it away, removing its window from the screen and giving up desktop real estate to other applications.

To close the My Computer window, click on its Close button, the × button. Yes, just like you'd close any window on the screen. No biggie. ✕

You cannot delete or otherwise remove the My Computer icon from your desktop. Don't even try.

⬅ If you want to open My Computer again, refer to the first section in this chapter, "Opening up My Computer and looking inside."

The Greeblies That Lurk Inside My Computer (Your Computer)

My Computer (the icon thing) contains three different things: disk drives, folders, and files. The bottom line here is the file. That's the basic information storage container on a computer. All computer programs are files — you put your stuff in files, and other files exist "just because." Everything is organized and represented by an appropriate icon inside My Computer. Altogether, I call them the *greeblies* that lurk inside My Computer.

Disk drives are the big, spinning, storage thingamabobs

Files and folders are stored on various disk drives inside your computer, which appear as icons inside the My Computer icon.

To see what files or folders lurk on your disk drives, double-click on one. This step opens a window that details the contents of the disk drive, which is a bunch of folders and files. Figure 2-2 shows the contents of drive C ("Behemoth," on my test computer).

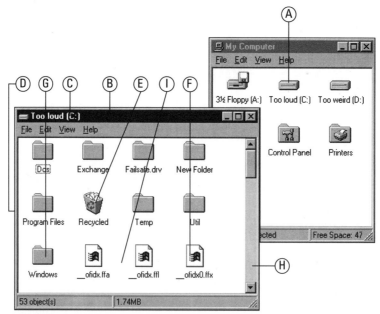

Figure 2-2
Drive C yields files and folders.
A. Double-click here . . . **B.** . . . to see this window. **C.** This is drive C's window. **D.** Files and folders located on drive C. **E.** See Chapter 5 for more information about this. **F.** File icons, the type where Windows doesn't know exactly what the file is. **G.** Folders; double-click to open them and see what's inside. **H.** See Chapter 27, the section "To Deal with Scrollbars." **I.** You can change the way My Computer displays this information; see the section "Different Ways to Look at the Stuff in My Computer," later in this chapter.

All the file and folder icons have names beneath them, giving everything a name. The file icons may also have pictures on them, which clues you in to what the file does or which program created it.

➡ Why is it called drive C and not Betty or something? See Chapter 14, the section "More than just a letter: Giving your disk a proper name."

➡ Floppy disk drives must have floppy disks inside in order for them to work. See Chapter 14, the section "Fun and Frivolity with Floppy Disks," for information about floppy disks.

➡ Some disk drives may be empty and not contain any files or folders. This is good news; it means that you can start putting stuff there. Chapter 3 discusses how you make stuff in Windows.

Just because they're called "folders" doesn't mean that anything is folded in them

Folders are used in your computer to store files. Actually, they're really used to help keep you organized. A disk drive may have tens of thousands of files. If all of them were in one place, it would be a mess. Imagine having to look through some massive window in My Computer for one teensy file. Instead, things are put into folders.

Fold Me

Folders contain files, usually files of a related type. For example, all the documents used to create this book live in a folder. That keeps them separate from other files and whatnot floating around my disk drive.

1. Open a disk drive icon.

   Double-click on a disk drive icon, such as your drive C icon. This step opens drive C and lets you see what files and folders live there.

(C:)

2. Look around.

   When you open a folder, you see another window full of files and maybe even more folders.

   To open another folder, double-click on its icon. This step displays another window, with even more greeblies inside.

➡ You may have to scroll the window about to see everything inside the folder. See Chapter 27, the section "Scrolling for dollars," for help with scrolling if you need it.

Fold Me

➠ Some folders may display their contents differently from others. See the section "Different Ways to Look at the Stuff in My Computer," later in this chapter, for more information.

   3. Close the folder when you're done snooping.

      Click on the folder window's × Close button to close it up. ☒

➠ To keep you from getting lost (and because a large number of windows on the desktop can drive one insane), the name of the current folder you're looking at appears at the top of the window. See Figure 2-3 for an example of the "Windows" folder, where Windows and its hoard of files and folders live.

➠ If you're getting lost with too many folder windows open, see the section "Oh, lordy, I have too many windows open!" earlier in this chapter, for help.

➠ Another way to help you negotiate your way through the depths of folders and their windows is to use a toolbar in any of the windows. See the section "Whip out the toolbar," later in this chapter.

➠ Folders are really all about organizing your stuff on a hard drive. Chapter 17 is also about organizing your stuff. Coincidence? What would Robert Stack say?

➠ Some folders appear with the "sharing hand" underneath them. This means that those folders are available to others on a network. See Chapter 22, the section "Surrendering Your Hardware to the Network."

Some folders may look different from others. A special case is the Start menu folders, which contain programs and files that appear on the Start Thing's menu. See Chapter 17, the section "Why some folders look strange or ugly," for more information.

Programs

Looks like a folder, is a folder. Maybe.

Folders contain files and maybe even other folders. This makes such perfect sense that I won't even bother with the tired cliché of the file-cabinet-is-your-disk-drive metaphor. Instead, you should know that folders used to be known as *directories,* or *subdirectories,* in DOS. They still are, and some programs may refer to them that way. Beware! Personally, I think that *folder* is a much better word. Check out the section "Crazy folder terminology" in Chapter 17, in any case.

File away the hours

The most basic element you find in any My Computer window is the file. It appears as an icon on the screen with a name floating beneath it. Hopefully, one or the other will clue you in to what the file is and does.

Figure 2-3
Files lurking inside the Windows folder window. **A.** You're looking at files in the Windows folder here. **B.** Folders in the Windows folder. **C.** Files in the Windows folder. **D.** Scroll to see all of them if you need to. **E.** There are 470 things in this folder. Golly. **F.** All the files displayed in this folder's window eat up 25.8MB of disk space. **G.** The Small Icons view, which you can change. **H.** Files are sorted alphabetically. Choose View⇨Arrange Icons, and then choose another way to sort the files in this window.

➠ You can actually "open" some files to either start a program or open a document, which is covered in Chapter 3. Other files cannot be opened, or if you try, you're greeted with an "Open With" dialog box. Press the Esc key to make that go away.

➠ If the name or the icon's picture doesn't help you identify the file's usefulness, you can peer into it and examine its contents. This subject is covered in the section "Who Knows What Evil Lurks in the Heart of Files?" in Chapter 15.

➠ Mostly you work with the files in My Computer by copying, renaming, moving, or deleting them. All that fun stuff is covered in Chapter 16.

Finding an icon in a window full of icons

Want to find a lone file icon in a full window? The easiest way is to start spelling its name. To find that MADMAC file, for example, press the M key. The first icon in the window that begins with *M* is then highlighted. Keep pressing M to see additional entries that begin with *M*.

Different Ways to Look at the Stuff in My Computer

What My Computer displays is only an interpretation of the stuff that actually lives on your hard drive. In reality, files and folders are a collection of bytes and electronic whatnot that would seriously bore you. Therefore, My Computer makes it all look fun by showing you everything with icons and pretty pictures. This is a big step up from the old text-only days of DOS and a huge leap from the bytes and bits that really live on disk.

Still, you can change the way My Computer shows you your stuff. There are big icons, little icons, filename lists, and other boring stuff. Though I personally favor the Big Icon approach, you may find yourself delighted with one of the other options, each of which is detailed in the following sections.

➡ All this information applies to the Explorer as well, which uses a toolbar similar to My Computer. See Chapter 17, the section "Let's go Explorering."

➡ As you discover new ways to look at information inside a window, you'll want to change the window's size on the screen. You can zoom it up big if you like, or you can grab the window's edges with the mouse pointer and drag the thing to the perfect size. See Chapter 27 for more information, in the section "Adjusting a Window's Position and Size."

Whip out the toolbar

All the windows in My Computer can have a toolbar attached to them. (The same toolbar also appears in the Explorer's window.) If you don't see it now, choose View➪Toolbar from the menu. The toolbar appears, as shown in Figure 2-4.

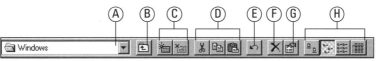

Figure 2-4

My Computer's toolbar.

A. Visit "parent" folders and other disk drives here (see the section "Working with folder trees in the Save As, Open, and Browse dialog boxes" in Chapter 17). **B.** The "Up one level" button for climbing the folder tree (also in Chapter 17). **C.** Boring network buttons you shouldn't bother with. **D.** Cut, Copy, and Paste buttons (see Chapter 16). **E.** Undo button (also covered in Chapter 16). **F.** Delete button (see Chapter 16). **G.** Display an icon's Properties dialog box (see the section "Gawking at a file's properties" in Chapter 15). **H.** Change the appearance of icons in the window.

Each of the buttons helps you work with the folders and files displayed in the window. For more information about how they work, see the chapters referenced in the figure. The last four buttons, which control the way My Computer displays information, are covered right here in this chapter.

Many of the buttons have similar menu commands, which you can use when you can't see the toolbar: The File menu has the Delete and Properties commands; the Edit menu has the Undo, Cut, Copy, and Paste commands; on the View menu, you find commands equivalent to the last four toolbar buttons: Large Icons, Small Icons, List, and Details.

If you forget what a toolbar icon represents, hover the mouse pointer over it for a few seconds (but don't click!). This displays a tiny bubble with the name of the toolbar button's command on it. The bubble is called a *tooltip*. See Chapter 4, the section "Hanging out at the toolbar," for more information.

Bar hopping, Part I: The status bar

In addition to the toolbar, windows in My Computer boast a status bar. This strip of information along the bottom of the window is used by most programs to display extra information or options (see Chapter 4, the section "Status bars: Your application's cheat sheet").

The status bar in My Computer tells you two things: how many files or folders are selected and their total size. If no files or folders are selected, the status bar tells you how many files and folders are in the current window and their total size. If you select one or more files or folders, that number and the total size are displayed in the status bar.

In My Computer, you can make the status bar visible by choosing View➪Status bar. Or you can choose that command again to remove the status bar, enabling you to see more of your stuff in the window.

The Big Icon view (most popular)

The most popular way to view information in My Computer is the Big Icon view, called *Large Icons* in the View menu. This is the way that My Computer initially shows you information (refer to Figures 2-1 and 2-2), and it can be quite handy because you can really see the icons.

To switch to Big Icon view, choose View⇨Large Icons. Or you can click on the Large Icon button on the toolbar.

The only time you may want to try the Small Icons view is when a folder contains way too many files (like the Windows folder in Figure 2-3) and you want to see more of them in a window at a time. If so, choose View⇨Small Icons or choose the Small Icons button from the toolbar.

In either view, Large Icons or Small Icons, you can move the icons around in the window and arrange them as you please. Just drag an icon to a new spot in the window, and it stays there. (This isn't possible with the List view, which always shows smaller icons in neat columns.)

The Details view (nerds love this)

Fans of DOS will appreciate the Details view of stuff in My Computer windows. Choose View⇨Details, or click on the Details button on the toolbar. This displays the files by icon, and then name, size in bytes, type of file, and, finally, the date it was created or last modified, each in a neat little column (see Figure 2-5).

A cool thing about the Details view is that you can easily sort the files and folders displayed in the window. To sort, just click the mouse on a column heading. To sort again but in reverse order, click on the same column heading again.

If you notice that the columns are a little too narrow, you can change their width. Follow these steps:

1. Position the mouse pointer between two column headings.

   To make the Name column wider, for example, point the mouse pointer between the Name and Size headings.

2. The mouse pointer changes shape.

   The change-width mouse pointer looks like a crosslet without arrows up or down. It means that you can drag the mouse left or right to change the width of a column.

C A   D E   B

Name	Size	Type	Modified	
4201.cpi	7KB	CPI File	4/9/91 5:00 AM	
4208.cpi	1KB	CPI File	4/9/91 5:00 AM	
5202.cpi	1KB	CPI File	4/9/91 5:00 AM	
Append	11KB	Application	5/31/94 6:22 AM	
Appnotes	10KB	Text Document	4/9/91 5:00 AM	
Assign	7KB	MS-DOS Application	4/9/91 5:00 AM	
Backup	36KB	Application	4/9/91 5:00 AM	
Chklist.ms	3KB	MS File	3/28/95 8:39 PM	
Chkstate.sys	41KB	System file	5/31/94 6:22 AM	
Command	54KB	MS-DOS Application	5/31/94 6:22 AM	
Command	1KB	Shortcut to MS-DOS...	1/7/92 11:25 AM	
Compdos	14KB	Application	4/9/91 5:00 AM	
Compress	21KB	Application	4/25/91 1:01 PM	

105 object(s)   3.79MB

Figure 2-5
The DOS folder, à la Details view with the toolbar hanging out.
A. The DOS folder is shown in this window. **B.** The Details view is active.
C. Click on one of these headings to sort the icons according to that column.
D. Point the mouse pointer between column headings, and drag left or right to
adjust the column width. **E.** Or you can double-click between column headings
to set the width equal to the widest item in that column.

3. Drag the mouse to change the column width.

Press the mouse's button, and drag left to make the column narrower or
drag right to make it wider. Release the mouse button when you're done
dragging.

Rather than drag the mouse in step 3, you can double-click on it when you
point it between two columns. This automatically adjusts the column size to
match the widest item in the column.

➠ Check out Chapter 29 if you need more help with the drag and double-click
mouse concepts.

Sorting it all out

You can sort the items in a window in a number of ways. First, you can use
the View menu. Choose View➪Arrange icons. A submenu appears, from which
you can choose from four ways to sort the icons in the window: by Name, by
Type, by Size, or by Date (the time the file was created or last modified).

If you're using the Details view (see the preceding section), you can instantly sort by clicking the mouse on a column heading. To see files sorted alphabetically, click on the Name heading. To see them sorted in reverse alphabetical order (from Z to A), click on the Name heading again.

To see files from smallest to largest, click on the Size heading. To see files from largest to smallest, click on the Size heading again.

To see files sorted by their type, click on the Type heading.

To see files sorted newest first, click on the Modified heading. To see the files oldest first, click on the Modified heading again.

If you want to see files sorted alphabetically by their type, click on the Type column first and then Name. This sorts them first by their type and then by their name. So all the program files are listed together alphabetically.

When you use the Large Icon or Small Icon view, the icons can become disorderly in the window — especially if you're dragging them around, copying, or pasting. To line things up, choose the View⇨Line Up Icons command. It instantly makes any sloppy window neat and tidy.

If you like order all the time, you can choose the View⇨Arrange Icons⇨Auto Arrange command. This automatically "snaps" all the icons to a grid all the time.

The "single window" approach to using My Computer

You don't have to see everything in My Computer by using a different window for each disk drive or folder. It's possible to use only one window for everything. That way, when you go to a new folder, its contents appear in the window rather than a new window appearing. You may find this a neater approach to working with files and folders in My Computer.

To use the single-window approach in My Computer, follow these steps:

1. Choose View⇨Options.

   This step displays the Options dialog box for My Computer.

2. Make sure that the Folder panel is up front.

   Click the mouse on the Folder tab if it's not in front.

3. Click the mouse on the text "Browse folders by using a single window that changes as you open each folder."

   A dot appears in the radio button by that text after you click on it.

4. Click on the OK button.

Now the essence of how My Computer works has changed. When you open a disk drive or folder, no new window appears. Instead, the contents of that disk drive or folder appear in the current window. Obviously, this means that some changes should take place to the way you use My Computer.

The best way to work things is to switch on the toolbar, as covered in the section "Whip out the toolbar," earlier in this chapter. Because you see only one folder in the window at a time, you need a way to view other folders.

To view the contents of any folder in the current window, just double-click on it. This opens that folder, and you see its goodies — but in the current window.

To see the contents of the preceding folder (the folder that contains the current folder), click on the up-one-level button on the toolbar.

Clicking on the up-one-level button closes the current folder — the one whose contents you see in the window. Then you see the next folder up. Keep clicking on this button, and eventually you're back at My Computer's main level, with all the disk drive, Control Panel, and Printers folders.

If your fingers are resting comfortably on the keyboard, you can go up one level without having to click on the up-one-level button. Instead, whack the Backspace key. That displays the preceding window just like the button, which is handy when you're typing or just too lazy to use the mouse. (By the way, this works regardless of whether you're using the one-window approach to My Computer.)

➠ To go quickly to any disk drive or folder, use the go-to-a-different-folder button on  the toolbar. It enables you to zoom to a folder you've previously opened or to another disk drive on the computer. See the section "Climbing the Folder Tree" in Chapter 17 for more information about this goodie.

To change My Computer back to where one folder equals one window, go through the steps in this section again but choose "Browse folders using a separate window for each folder" in step 3.

Starting Your Work

Windows tries its best to make you happy all by itself. Alas, it just doesn't cut it. Although you can dink with Windows all day — even make a lifetime hobby of it and, because it's so involving, no one else would think that you're doing anything other than work — you eventually do have to settle down and get something done. To make that happen, you have to start an application, run a program, or just get something going so that you and your computer can be happy and productive together.

"Where Should I Start?"

How you start something in Windows really depends on what you want to do. Although there are about a gazillion ways to start things, there is always the fastest and most convenient way, which isn't always the most obvious.

Before you start anything, ask yourself the following questions:

Am I starting a document I was working on recently?

⇒ If you're just returning to your computer and want to pick up where you left off yesterday, you have to start a document rather than a program. See the section "Finding your document lurking in the Documents menu," later in this chapter.

Am I starting a new document?

⇒ New documents can be created with the touch of a button in Windows. You don't have to start an application and then choose New from the menu. See the section "Taking advantage of the numerous New menu commands," later in this chapter.

Am I starting a new project (more than one document)?

⇒ If you're going to be starting a project that involves several documents, none of which may be created by the same application, you have to start a *project* rather than a document. See the section "Starting a New Project," later in this chapter.

Am I starting something that doesn't fit into either of those categories?

If so, just keep reading. This chapter has *all* the information you'll ever care to know about starting anything in Windows. The next few sections outline the more traditional ways to start something, especially when you don't really know what it is that you want to create.

Several Ways to Start Any Program, from the Obvious to the Obtuse

In its vain effort to make everything in Windows 95 simple and organized, Microsoft has created a veritable beef stew of contraptions you can use to start your programs. Prepare to be overwhelmed with options. Microsoft can't make up its mind! Just because the button on the screen reads Start doesn't necessarily mean that that's the place where everything begins. For the most part, however, it's true.

⇒ Before you can start any program, it must be installed on your computer. See Chapter 13 for information about installing programs.

⇒ If you want your Windows programs to start up automatically every time you start Windows, see Chapter 6, the section "Applications That Amazingly Start Automatically."

Marching through the Start button marsh

The way "they" want you to start new programs is by using the Start Thing button, located on one side of the taskbar. It says "Start," which means "to start a program," because your computer is already on and running at this point.

Activating the Start Thing button pops up a menu, which has even more menus hanging on. Buried somewhere in those menus is the name of a program you want to start. Here's how to get at it:

1. Activate the Start Thing.

   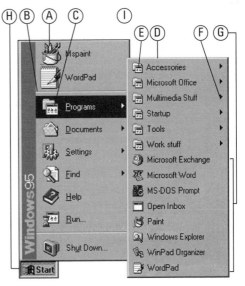

   Click on the Start Thing button by using your computer mouse. Click. This is the mousy way to activate the menu.

   If you like the keyboard, you can press Alt+S (the Alt and S keys together) to pop up the Start menu. This works only when you aren't using any other program (you're not in Word or Excel, for example, or painting a purty picture in Paint). This brings me to the most foolproof way to activate the Start button:

   Press Ctrl+Esc — the Ctrl (Control) and Esc (Escape) keys together. This always pops up the Start Thing menu, no matter what.

2. Choose Programs.

   Click on the Programs item. Click. The Programs menu appears (see Figure 3-1).

Figure 3-1
The Start Thing's menu and a submenu.
A. Programs added right on the menu! (See Chapter 6, the section "Sticking something on the main Start Thing menu.")
B. Dimple bar. **C.** Programs item. **D.** Programs submenu.
E. Little folders — more submenus. **F.** Submenu that-a-way. **G.** Programs on the Programs menu. **H.** Start Thing. **I.** Click out here somewhere to make the menus disappear.

The Programs submenu contains two things: programs and folders (refer to Figure 3-1).

Folders live near the top of the menu, and they lead to even more submenus off to the right.

Items in a submenu should pertain somewhat to the name of the menu: Accessories contains miscellaneous Windows programs; Microsoft Office contains its own programs; Work stuff contains your work stuff; and so on.

Programs on the menu have their own icon next to the name. The icon is just a cute little picture, often not representing at all what it is the program does. The name is more descriptive.

➠ Information about maintenance and upkeep of the Start Thing's menu system is offered in Chapter 6, in the section "All About the Start Thing."

➠ If one of your programs appears at the top of the Start Thing's menu, you're ready to start it now. Move on down to step 4.

3. If you don't see the program you want, click on a submenu folder to look for more programs.

This is called "marching through the Start menu marsh." There are lots of folders with lots of programs in them. After you get used to Windows, you know right where everything is.

➠ If you find this truly bothersome, alternative methods of starting a program are covered in the next few sections.

4. Click the mouse on your program.

When you find your program, click on it. You have to click only once, using the left (main) mouse button. This starts the program, "running" it on the screen.

➠ See Chapter 4 for helpful hints for using just about any Windows program.

➠ The section "Quitting Any Program," at the end of this chapter, discusses quitting a program, when you're ready for it.

Those submenus are slippery!

One reason to really, *really* hate the Start Thing's menus is that they're very sensitive about where you hover your mouse pointer. If you move the mouse pointer off a menu just slightly, it may disappear. And if the mouse pointer is hovering over another submenu item (the ones with the triangles by them), another menu pops right up. Annoying.

Alas, there is no way around this predicament. The only advice I can offer is just to "be careful." Or you can choose one of the alternative methods of starting a program that are covered in this chapter.

And those submenus can be tricky!

Another oddity with submenus is that they don't always pop up to the right. Popping up to the right is nice; because every submenu does it that way, you can always see the entire Start Thing menu marsh. However, some submenus have many, many files on them. To make room, Windows may pop one of them up to the *left.* The menu then covers up the other menus, making marching through the marsh much more muddling.

When you get one menu covering the others and you want that one menu to go away, just press the Esc key. This pops down the most recent menu and saves your sanity.

Starting an icon clinging to the desktop

Some programs live on the desktop, pictured there as little icons. This is very handy because you can always see the program there and because starting it is a snap.

1. To start an icon on the desktop, double-click on it.

   Hover the mouse pointer over the program's icon, and quickly press the mouse's main button twice; click, click. Try not to move the mouse between clicks.

➠ Double-clicking is tricky if you're just starting out. See Chapter 29, the section "The double-quick double-click," for helpful hints.

⟶ Anyone can place an icon on the desktop. It's an incredible shortcut and makes running popular programs a cinch. See Chapter 17, the section "Sticking stuff on the desktop," to see how it's done.

⟶ If you're using a program like Microsoft Office, it may already have its own icons living on the desktop, known as Microsoft Office Bar (where Bill Gates gets his grape Nehi). See Chapter 10 for more information about Microsoft Office.

Starting an icon in My Computer

My Computer shows you a graphical representation of the stuff in your computer. There are disk drives, folders, and files. And of course, some of those files are really programs you can double-click on to start. This technique needs to be used in only one instance: when the programs don't appear on the Start Thing's menu or anywhere else handy. If that's the case, follow these steps:

1. Open up the My Computer icon on the desktop.

   Double-click on the My Computer icon. It opens right up.

⟵ My Computer is the subject of Chapter 2, should you want to bone up on it.

2. Open a disk drive.

   Double-click the mouse on a disk drive, such as the drive C icon. This enables you to open that disk drive and see what lives there. Mostly that will be a collection of folders and files. Your goal is to find the folder that contains the files you're interested in.

⟶ You may have to scroll the window around to see the file or folder you're looking for. See Chapter 27 for information about scrolling a window.

3. Open the folder (or folders).

   Hunt for the folder that contains your programs, and open it. What you see should look similar to Figure 3-2. You may see the program you want to open (run), or you may see more folders.

   If you see more folders, repeat step 3.

   If you see your program, do step 4.

4. Open your program.

   Double-click on your program's icon to open it. Soon that application splashes itself all over the screen, and you can get down to work.

Figure 3-2
A mess of files and folders, courtesy
of My Computer.
A. The Accessories folder. **B.** More folders.
C. Backup program. **D.** Paint program.
E. WordPad program. **F.** This icon means
that Windows doesn't know what the file is;
best to leave it alone.

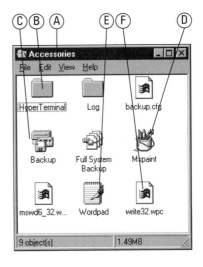

⬅▪▫ See Chapter 2 for additional hints and tips about using the My Computer thing.

▫▫➡ Lose your program? See Chapter 31, the section "I want to find my file now.
No messing around!"

Running to the Run command
to start a program

No one in their right mind runs to the Run command to start a program.
Most sane people run *from* it. Though it works, there are just easier, more
graphical methods for starting a program. The Run command exists only for
those situations in which you are asked to start a program that way, typically from some old crusty user manual.

If you're ever directed to use the Run command, follow these steps:

1. Activate the Start Thing's menu.

   Press Ctrl+Esc to pop that sucker up, or click on the Start
   Thing button if you can see it and a mouse is handy.

2. Choose the Run command.

   It should be the second one from the bottom, right above Shutdown.
   Click the mouse on Run, or press the R key if you're mouse-lazy. The
   Run dialog box appears, similar to the one shown in Figure 3-3.

Figure 3-3
The Run command's
dialog box.
A. Type the program name
here. **B.** Click here to reuse a
name you already typed.
C. See Chapter 4, the section
"Opening stuff," for
information about using the
Browse dialog box. **D.** Run
that program!

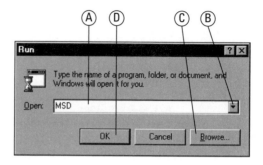

3. Type the name of the program you want to run.

    The name goes into the Open box. If you were told to run the MSD
    program, for example, you would type **MSD** in the box.

    If you're using the Run command to rerun a program, you can click
    the mouse on the down arrow next to the Open box. This displays a
    drop-down list of all the previous programs typed into the box. Click on
    one to run it again.

4. OK!

    Click on the OK button. Windows goes out, hunts down the program you
    typed, and, hopefully, runs it.

    If the program can't be found, an insulting dialog box is displayed.
    Check what you typed, because typing isn't graphical, and, well, mis-
    takes happen. Then try the command again.

➡ If you've done everything right and the program still hasn't been found, see
    Chapter 31, the section "File? File? Here, File! C'mon, Boy! Where'd You Go?"
    for help in tracking it down.

Starting a program you never did quite quit

One of the joys of Windows (and there are a few of them) is that you never really have
to quit a program when you're done with it. Instead, you can "put a program away," which
is covered in Chapter 4, in the section "Done for the Day? To Quit or Put Away," as well
as in Chapter 8. When a program is put away, it appears as a button on the taskbar,
just like the Start Thing's button. To start that program again (actually, it's more like
resurrection), just locate its button on the taskbar and click on that button with the mouse.
Ta-da! Instant program.

Starting a Document Instead of a Program

You use programs to create *documents.* In fact, documents are the whole reason for having a computer. They're the stuff you do. Your effort. Your work. Your soul.

The way most people use Windows is to start an application and then use the Open command to open up a document they've been working on. For other people, that's too many steps. Instead, why not start by opening a document? Windows then hunts down the application that created that document, starts that application, and then opens up the document automagically. This saves a step or two, but it involves some preparation beforehand.

Starting a document stuck to the desktop

Documents can stick to your desktop just like programs do, as shown in Figure 3-4. The icons even look similar, though that isn't really what's important. What's important is that you start the document just like you would start an application. It's a snap:

1. Point the mouse at the document's icon.

   Point the mouse pointer at the icon.

2. Open it up.

   Double-click on it. Click-click. (Try not to move the mouse between clicks.) The document opens, which starts the program that created it, and soon you're working on that document.

➡ See Chapter 29 for some tips for using a computer mouse. Stuff like pointing and double-clicking is covered there, along with some tutorials.

➡ Slapping a document icon down on the desktop is a snap. See Chapter 17, the section "Sticking stuff on the desktop," for information about how it's done.

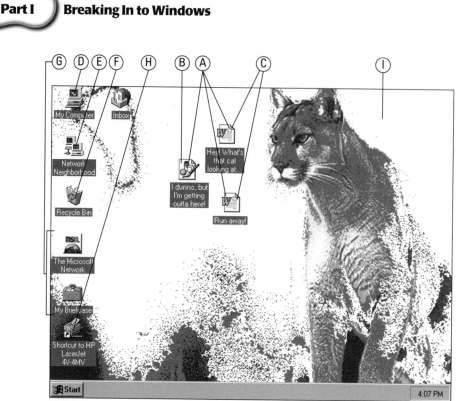

Figure 3-4
Starting a document on the desktop.
A. Documents stuck on the desktop, ready for action. **B.** A Paint document.
C. Two Word documents. **D.** My Computer (see Chapter 2). **E.** See Chapter 22, the section "It's a Beautiful Day in the Network Neighborhood." **F.** See Chapter 5, the section "The Politically Correct Recycle Bin." **G.** Other programs already stuck on the desktop. **H.** See Chapter 19, the section "I found a printer stuck on the desktop." **I.** See Chapter 24, the section "Wallpaper without the glue."

Finding a document nestled in My Computer

Just as you can use My Computer to open up a program, you can also hunt down files and such, opening them just as well. Here's how it's done:

1. Open up My Computer.

   Double-click on the My Computer icon to open it if it's not open already.

   My Computer is the subject of Chapter 2, should you want to bone up on it.

2. Open a disk drive.

   Double-click on a disk drive to open it. Try to open whichever drive holds your documents, which is probably drive C.

3. Open the folder (or folders).

   Open the folder that contains your document or the folder that contains your document's folder.

   For example, double-click on a Work folder to open it. Amaze yourself at its contents. Then hunt for a Travel Reports folder, and open it as well. Its window appears on your screen, along with graphical icons showing you the files that live there.

   ➡ Folders were once known as *directories* in computer lingo. See Chapter 17 for information about which is which and why you should bother.

4. Open the document you're looking for.

   Double-click on your document. It opens up on your screen, along with the program that created it.

⬅ See Chapter 2 for additional hints and tips for using the My Computer thing.

➡ If you can't find your program this way, see Chapter 31, the section "File? File? Here, File! C'mon, Boy! Where'd You Go?"

Finding your document lurking in the Documents menu

Lurking on the Start menu thing is a submenu called Documents. It doesn't contain a list of all the documents on your PC — just a few you've opened or peeked at. You can use this menu as a quick shortcut to documents you've been working on recently. Here's how:

1. Press Ctrl+Esc.

   This step instantly pops up the Start Thing's menu thing, no matter what.

2. Choose Documents.

   You can click on the word *Documents* by using the mouse or pressing the D key. This step slides out the Documents submenu, which contains a list of documents you've messed with recently (see Figure 3-5).

Sticking popular documents on your desktop

Most folks use the same documents over and over: travel reports, P&L spreadsheets, endless projects they'll probably never finish, and so on. To make getting at these documents much easier, you can slap them right down on your desktop. Or if you like, you can put them all in a folder and put that on your desktop. Either way, you get easy access to your most commonly used documents.

To put a document or folder on the desktop, first locate it by using the steps in this section. After you've found the folder or document, follow these steps:

1. **Click on the folder or document.** Click once to highlight the folder.

2. **Copy the folder or file.** Press Ctrl+C on the keyboard. This is the copy command, which you can also get by choosing Copy from the Edit menu, if you're in love with your mouse.

3. **Click the mouse once on the desktop.** Point anywhere on the desktop, and click on the mouse's main button.

4. **Paste the folder or file.** Press Ctrl+V on the keyboard, which is the Paste command. This puts a copy of your folder or file on the desktop for easy access.

   You should really consider pasting the folder or document as a *shortcut* rather than as a real file. See Chapter 16, the section "The second runner-up: Copy-and-paste as a shortcut."

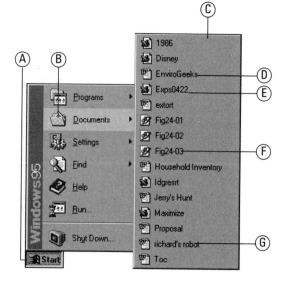

Figure 3-5
The Documents menu shows recently peeked-at files.
A. Click on the Start Thing.
B. Choose Documents. **C.** Recently opened or saved documents in alphabetical order. **D.** Microsoft Word document. **E.** Excel document. **F.** Paint bitmap graphic.
G. Click on one of these to open it.

If you see the hollow word *Empty* in the menu, it means that there are no documents to open there. (This happens because either

you haven't yet done anything or the Documents menu was cleaned up; see the nearby sidebar, "Clearing the Documents menu," for more information.)

➡ Documents in the Documents menu are all shortcuts. See Chapter 16, the section "Taking a Shortcut Instead of Copying Files," for information about shortcuts.

3. Pluck out a recent document.

   If you see your Household Inventory report looming there, for example, click on it. This step opens the document, which opens the application, which gets you off and running.

Clearing the Documents menu

The Documents menu continues to fill with the names of documents (shortcuts, actually), up to the last 15 items you've opened or saved. (Not all Windows applications stick documents there.) Eventually, this can get really junky. To clean up the Documents menu, follow these steps:

1. **Choose Settings⇨Taskbar from the Start Thing's menu.** Click on the Start Thing's button, and then choose the Settings menu's Taskbar item. The Taskbar Properties dialog box appears.

2. **Click on the Start Menu Programs panel.** This step brings that panel forward if it's not in front already.

3. **In the Documents menu area, click on the Clear button.** Clicking the button instantly clears the Documents menu; there is no warning here!

4. **Close the Taskbar Properties dialog box.** Click on its × Close button in the upper right corner.

More information about the Taskbar Properties dialog box can be found in Chapters 6 and 7.

Taking advantage of the numerous New menu commands

It's possible to start any old application by using a new document, one that you haven't worked on — a *new* one. To do that, you use the various New menu commands that lurk all over Windows:

1. Find a New menu command.

   These commands hide all over Windows. If you click the mouse's right button (right-click) on the desktop, you see the New command in the pop-up shortcut menu (see Figure 3-6). If you open any disk drive or folder in My Computer, a New command appears on the File menu. In either instance, the New submenu looks the same as in Figure 3-6.

Figure 3-6
The New submenu.
A. The pop-up shortcut menu from the desktop. **B.** New menu item. **C.** New submenu. **D.** New things you can start with the New menu. **E.** New documents you can open.

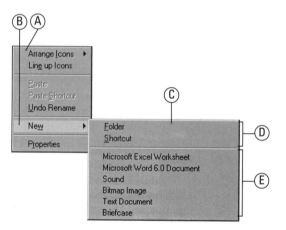

2. Choose the New command.

   A submenu appears. The top portion enables you to create a folder or shortcut. The bottom part lists types of documents you can create based on several Windows applications.

   ➠ Creating folders is done to help you stay organized. A tutorial for creating such an organizational folder appears later in this chapter; see the section "Making a home for your project." You can also check out Chapter 17 for more information about creating folders, naming them, and keeping them organized.

   ➠ A shortcut is a handy way to have several copies of a program scattered all over your hard drive without eating up a great deal of disk space. See Chapter 16, the section "Taking a Shortcut Instead of Copying Files," for more information about how you can put this tool to use.

3. Choose an application document to create.

For example, click on Microsoft Word 6.0 Document. Windows creates a new document with the name New [whatever] Document right there on the desktop.

4. Give the document a new name.

Type an appropriate name for the document. For example:

Nasty letter to the school board

You can use upper- or lowercase letters, spaces, punctuation — anything — in the name. It's best to keep the name short and sweet because short names fit better under icons and can be seen more easily in a scrolling list.

Press the Backspace key to back up and erase if you make a mistake.

See the sidebar "Basic file-naming rules and regulations" in Chapter 16 for more information about naming files.

5. Press Enter (the first time).

Pressing Enter the first time locks in the new name. The icon and its name remain highlighted on the desktop.

6. Press Enter (the second time).

This step opens the application that created the document, enabling you to start your work. You can always double-click on the icon, but because your fingers are on the keyboard already, it makes no big nevermind.

When the application starts, your document is presented in its window, ready for you to create stuff. See Chapter 4 for general information about creating stuff in a Windows application. Your program may be covered specifically in Part II of this book; see Chapters 9 and 10 specifically.

When you're done working, you may want to move the icon from the desktop to a folder on disk. See Chapter 17, which covers organizing files and folders, for suggestions about how to move around icons and store them in a proper place.

A tutorial that shows how to create a document by using the preceding steps — and move the icon to a proper folder on disk — is offered in Chapter 8 (see the section "A multitasking tutorial involving Paint and WordPad").

Starting a New Project

When your work involves using more than one application, it's best to start things off as a project, as opposed to doing one thing at a time. This is a radical departure from the normal way in which most people use computers, but it really helps keep things organized.

Making a home for your project

All the documents relating to one project should find their own special place on your hard drive. Suppose that you're planning to make a little money using the legal system to randomly sue various businesses around town. For that project, you're going to need a few documents, such as the following:

✘ A database listing businesses with positive cash flow and insurance (a.k.a. "deep pockets")

✘ A legal-looking form letter from a word processor

✘ A graphical image logo

Before you create any of these documents, you have to build a nice, comfy spot for them on the hard drive. That spot is a folder that will eventually contain all the necessary files relating to your endeavor. Follow these steps:

1. Start My Computer.

   Open the My Computer icon if it isn't open already.

   Chapter 2 discusses in depth the use of My Computer, including opening and closing folders and windows — knowledge that's required to complete the following few steps.

2. Open a disk drive.

   Double-click on drive C to open it. You create your project's folder there.

3. Open the Work folder.

   Double-click on the Work folder to open it up and see what's inside.

   You may have to scroll the window a little to help find the Work folder. A quicker way is to press the **W** key, which highlights the first icon starting with the letter *W* in the window. Keep pressing **W** until Work is highlighted.

   If you don't have a Work folder, you can create one. See the section "The useful Work folder organizational strategy" in Chapter 17 for more information.

➠ If you're using Microsoft Office, you can use the My Documents folder. See Chapter 10 for more information about Microsoft Office.

4. Bring up the shortcut menu for the Work folder window.

Point the mouse at a blank area in the My Documents window, and click the right button (a right-click). This step displays the shortcut menu for the folder, shown in Figure 3-7.

Figure 3-7
Making a new folder in the Work folder.
A. The Work folder.
B. Various other project folders. **C.** Right-click here to bring up the shortcut menu.
D. Choose New.
E. Choose Folder from here to make a new folder.

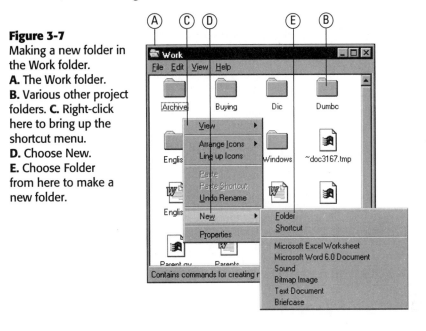

➠ Just about everything in Windows has a shortcut menu attached. You just right-click the mouse while pointing at that something, and a shortcut menu pops right up. See Chapter 5, the section "The Ubiquitous Pop-up Shortcut Menus," for more information about these handy tools.

5. Choose New⇨Folder.

From the shortcut menu, choose New. A submenu appears. Choose Folder from the submenu. This step creates a new folder inside the My Documents folder.

➠ The new folder may appear at the bottom of the window; use the scrollbar to scroll the window down to see all of the folder. Or you can resize the window, making it larger so that all the icons appear at one time. See Chapter 27, the section "Adjusting a Window's Position and Size," for more information about resizing a window.

6. Name the folder Tort Reform.

   The folder sits in the window with its original, stupid name ("New Folder") highlighted. To give it a new name, start typing. Type the following:

   Tort Reform

   Use a capital *T* in Tort, followed by a space, and then capital *R* in Reform. Press the Backspace key to back up and erase if you make a mistake. Press Enter when you're done. That locks in the new name.

⇒ Obviously, if you're creating a place for some other project, you give the folder its own unique and descriptive name. A folder can be named just about anything, and the name can contain just about anything you can type at the keyboard. Keeping the name short and descriptive is best. See Chapter 16, the sidebar "Basic file-naming rules and regulations," for more detailed information about folder-naming rules.

7. Open the Tort Reform folder.

   Double-click on the folder to open it and display its window.

The Tort Reform folder doesn't contain anything at this point. However, it's eager to accept new documents relating to your new project. In fact, all documents and files relating to your new project will be placed in this new folder. That way, all of them stay together, and you can easily find them when you need to.

Starting your project off rightly

In the preceding section, you created a home for your project's files. This is something you should do when you start each new project. The next step is to place some files there, to create new files for the project.

Starting a project in this way is a little backward from the way most projects start out: Rather than start your applications and then create documents, you first create the documents and then run the applications. There are three documents to create for the sample: a database, a word-processing document, and a graphics image.

 ⇐ For more detailed information about 1, 2, and 3 in the following steps, refer to the section "Taking advantage of the numerous New menu commands," earlier in this chapter. If you do, skip step 6 in that section (pressing Enter a second time) because you don't want to open these new documents after you create them. Not yet, at least.

1. Create a new database document.

   Right-click the mouse in the Tort Reform folder. From the shortcut menu, choose New⇨Database (or whatever the command is to start a new database document).

   Name the new document Local Suckers.

   This database will contain a list of local walk-in businesses you plan to visit and then later sue. They should each have lots of cash and be fully insured.

2. Create a new word-processing document.

   Right-click again in the Tort Reform folder window. Choose New⇨ Word Processing document (or whatever the command is to start one of those) from the shortcut menu.

   Name the new document Legal-sounding letter.

   This is the letter that will contain your complaint about how you were minding your own business in their store when you slipped and fell on your own shoelace, which is obviously their fault, and they must pay for such negligence.

3. Create a diagram of how you slipped and fell.

   Right-click in the Tort Reform window a third time to bring up the shortcut menu. From the menu, choose New⇨Bitmap Image. This is the command you use to create a new graphics file.

   Name the new document Illustration.

   You use the Paint program to work on the graphics file, illustrating how the shoelace incident happened, where you fell and injured your shoe-lace, and so on. Graphics files are very impressive this way.

4. Start your work.

   You can start by opening any one of the icons you just created. To work on the database, double-click on it. To work on the word-processing document, double-click on its icon. To start work on the graphics file, double-click on it as well.

   You can even select all three icons, choose File⇨Open from the menu, and open all three applications simultaneously, with all three documents ready for editing. See the section "Calf-ropin' files" in Chapter 16 for information about selecting a group of icons at one time.

The best bonus of all

The technique demonstrated in the preceding two sections, of creating a folder for a project and then creating document icons, can really be a boost to your productivity. For example, now you don't have to fuss over naming your documents and finding a proper place to save them on disk. All those steps are done because you purposefully created everything in its own, proper place to begin with.

➡ Alas, this trick doesn't work for spontaneous projects. But it can work for new ideas; simply create a folder called New Ideas and start individual documents there. If they grow into anything big, move them to a new folder and keep working from there. This is all covered in Chapter 17, in the section "Setting Up Folders Just So."

Quitting Any Program

After you start a program, you use it for a while and then you want to quit. (Sometimes you may want to quit sooner.) Not to be shy about it, Windows has lots of ways to quit a program. The most popular is the most polite, though there are other strange and often esoteric ways to wave bye-bye to your programs.

The common, polite, almost civilized way to quit

Quit any program by choosing the Exit command at the bottom of the File menu. Choose File⇨Exit, and you're out. The command may also be called Close, and in some rare instances you may even see the word Quit used. They're all the same.

➡ Using the Exit command is the best, but not the only, way to quit. The following sections illustrate other ways to quit, which you can try if you ever have the time.

➡ If you haven't yet saved your stuff before quitting, Windows tells you so and gives you a chance to save. See Chapter 4 for more information about saving your stuff.

Quitting by closing a window

In Windows, closing a window is often the same thing as quitting. (This is why some Quit commands are called Close.) You can close a window by clicking on the × in the window's upper right corner.

You can also press the utterly nonintuitive Alt+F4 key combination to close a window; press and hold the Alt key, press the F4 key, and then release both keys.

Use the taskbar to "Shut 'em down"

All programs you have running appear as a button on the taskbar. To shut down a program — even to be so rude as to not look at it directly — follow these steps:

1. Locate the program's button on the taskbar.

2. Click the mouse's right button on the program's button.

   A right-click on a taskbar button pops up a menu that controls that program's window. Now you can use the Close command to close the program's window and quit.

3. Choose the Close command.

   The program quits, just as though you chose the File⇨Exit command. You are asked to save any unsaved information, if necessary.

➡ More information about using the taskbar can be found in Chapter 7.

The drastic way to quit

Windows has a geeky way to kill off any program: Press Ctrl+Alt+Delete. This is the old DOS reset command, which used to restart the entire computer. You can do that too in Windows to shut down any program or "dead" programs. I recommend it only as a last resort.

When you first press Ctrl+Alt+Delete, you see the Close Program window (see Figure 3-8).

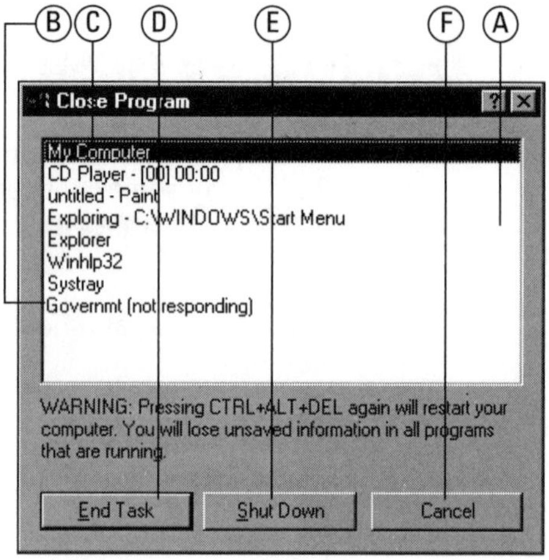

Figure 3-8
Press Ctrl+Alt+Delete to see
this window.
A. Programs currently running. **B.** A
"dead" program is identified as "not
responding." **C.** Click on a program
to highlight or select it. **D.** Quits the
selected program (shuts it down).
E. Quits Windows (drastic). **F.** Get
outta here!

The Close Program window lists all the programs currently humming away
in Windows. To close any program, highlight its name in the window and
then click on the End Task button. The program closes — just as though you
chose its Exit command — and you can continue working.

If the program doesn't close, a dialog box appears, announcing that the
program is "busy" or something. It's best to wait and try to shut down the
program in a more traditional way, as described in the preceding two sections.

When a program dies, it says "not responding" next to its name. You can
click on that program and then click on the End Task button to kill it off.
After doing this, however, I would quit Windows and start everything all
over again — just to be safe. (Dead programs may cause other programs to
come tumbling down as well.)

If you press Ctrl+Alt+Delete a second time, you reset your computer for sure.
This is a desperate thing. Don't do it unless you absolutely have to.

➠ Yes, Windows runs several programs at one time. Boggling, isn't it? To take
advantage of this feature, read Chapter 8.

Use One Program, You've Used Them All

There's something charming about consistency. Mankind just loves it when things can be expected: the car starts; checks come in the mail; it rains on your day off; and so on. These things assure us that everything's okay and allows the concept of "normal" to exist. Windows draws on this need, serving up its applications in a similar, predictable, and easy-to-get-used-to manner; almost all Windows programs work alike or have features so similar that you find yourself at home with any application.

➡ Part VII of this book discusses how Windows operates; Chapter 27 covers how the windows work; Chapter 28 discusses dialog boxes; Chapter 29 deals with the mouse; and Chapter 30 has information about working with text and graphics.

➡ The only oddity in the bunch is DOS and its hoary hoard of older applications, none of which worked like the others. These applications are covered in Chapter 12, which you can refer to . . . if you dare.

Scent of a Windows Application

All Windows applications share a common approach. The look of each is similar, and you can count on several items working the same way. The bonus here is that you'll find few surprises, even when you work with something new. This approach helps get your work done quickly.

Figure 4-1 shows a typical Windows program, WordPad, in this case. Everything common to most Windows applications is pointed out in the figure.

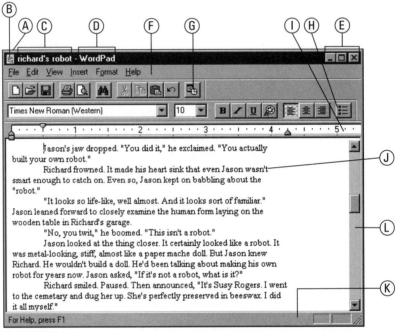

Figure 4-1
The WordPad program looks much like other applications.
A. The title bar. **B.** Document icon on the Control menu. **C.** Document name.
D. This is WordPad here. **E.** The window's control buttons. **F.** The menu bar.
G. Toolbar, common to many Windows applications. **H.** Formatting bar (specific to WordPad). **I.** Ruler (also specific to WordPad). **J.** WordPad document text. **K.** Status bar. **L.** Vertical scrollbar.

1. Start WordPad by using the Start Thing.

   Press Ctrl+Esc to pop up the menu.

2. Choose Programs⇨Accessories.

   WordPad should be listed in the Accessories submenu, probably toward the bottom.

3. Choose WordPad from the menu.

WordPad starts up in its own window on the desktop.

➡ Chapter 9, the section "Let WordPad Bring Out the Shakespeare in You," has more information about WordPad, if you're interested.

➡ See Chapter 27 for information about window pieces parts — the scrollbars, buttons, and parts you use to control a window on the screen. Also see the section "The Old Multi-Document Interface Gag" for information about how some applications can work with several documents at one time.

What's on the menu?

Computer programs work only when you give them commands. The commands are clustered in two places: the menu bar or a toolbar. Generally speaking, all the commands are attached to the menu bar. The toolbar contains only handy commands (covered in the next section).

The menu bar appears near the top of the program's window. It contains several key words, each of which supposedly describes a category of command: File, Edit, View, and so on. Each of these words is the name of a menu.

To activate a menu, click on its name by using the mouse. To see which commands are in the File menu, click on File with the mouse (see Figure 4-2). The menu contains commands plus their quick-key shortcuts. For example, you can pluck out the Save command by clicking on the word *Save* with the mouse or by pressing Ctrl+S on the keyboard.

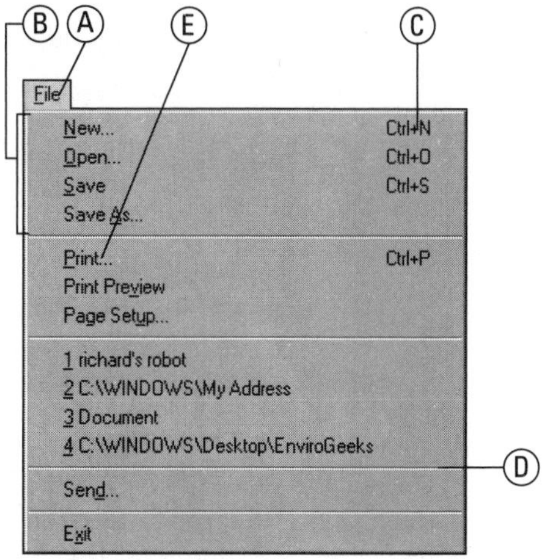

Figure 4-2
The File menu in WordPad.
A. Click on the menu's title to "drop it down." **B.** Menu commands. **C.** Keyboard shortcuts. **D.** Dimple bar separates commands into areas. **E.** Click on a command to activate it.

➡ You can also activate a menu by using the keyboard. The underlined letter in a menu title or command name is called a *hot key.* If you press the Alt key on your keyboard and then that hot key, it's the same as choosing a particular menu item with the mouse. Chapter 27, the section "Chasing Menus," discusses how it all works.

➡ Certain quick-key shortcuts are common to all Windows programs. See the sidebar "Common quick-key shortcuts," later in this chapter.

➡ Some menus have submenus attached to them. See Chapter 27 for a discussion of submenus; Chapter 3 shows you the Start Thing, which has way too many submenus on it.

⬅ Menus appear from left to right, with the most commonly used menu supposedly appearing on the left. Likewise, the most common menu commands appear on the top of a drop-down menu. The only exception here is the Exit command, which usually appears at the bottom of the first menu. Refer to Chapter 3, the section "Quitting Any Program," for more information about using that command.

➡ The first menu, typically the File menu, is the most important. It contains the saving, printing, opening, and other important commands. These commands are covered later in this chapter, in the section "Going About Your Business."

➡ The Help menu usually appears last in the menu bar (whether it's most important to you or not). See the section "Windows' Way of Offering Help," later in this chapter, for more information.

➡ At the bottom of most Help menus is the About command. This command displays a tiny box that tells you something about the program: its name or version or other information. Unfortunately, it doesn't tell you what the program actually does. Hopefully, you know that *before* you install the software (see Chapter 13 for information about installing new software).

Hanging out at the toolbar

Some programs offer quick shortcuts to common commands. These programs appear on a toolbar or strip-o'-buttons somewhere below the menu or occasionally on *floating palettes* (tiny windows that hover over your work). The idea here is simple: Click on a button with the mouse to quickly get at some command.

The only drawback to toolbars is that the wee li'l pictures on the buttons don't often fully explain what it is the button does. To make things easier, a bubble or balloon (like a cartoon balloon) appears over the icon, telling you what it does. The bubble is called a *tooltip,* as in "tiptoe through the tooltips."

To see the tooltip, point the mouse pointer at the button for a short while but don't press the mouse's button. The tooltip should appear, or text may appear at the bottom of the window, explaining what the button does. Figure 4-3 shows how the disk button in WordPad is really a shortcut to the Save command.

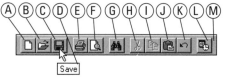

Figure 4-3
The bubble says that this button is really the Save command.
A. New document. **B.** Open. **C.** Save.
D. Hover the mouse pointer over a button to see its tooltip. **E.** Print. **F.** Print Preview command. **G.** Find. **H.** Cut. **I.** Copy. **J.** Paste. **K.** Undo. **L.** Inserts the date and time. **M.** Point here and drag to turn this into a floating palette.

➡ Some buttons you press once to activate some command. Other buttons are more like on-off switches. See Chapter 28, the section "On-off buttons," for more information about which is which. Also see the section "Drop-down lists" in that chapter for information about drop-down lists, which often appear on toolbars.

⬅ Chapter 2 covers My Computer's toolbar, in the section "Whip out the toolbar."

➡ The file commands on a toolbar (Open, Save, Print) are covered later in this chapter, in the section "Going About Your Business."

➡ More information about the Cut, Copy, Paste, and Undo commands is in Chapter 8, the section "The three amigos: Cut, Copy, and Paste."

Toolbars and floating tool palettes

By day, WordPad's toolbar sits there under the menu. By night, it's a wild floating palette, which you can drag anywhere in WordPad's window. How? Just point the mouse pointer at a blank part of the toolbar and drag it elsewhere. Depending on where you drag it, you have a toolbar (like Figure 4-1) or a floating palette. Personally, I prefer the toolbar because a floating palette tends to get in the way of my text.

This trick can be applied to just about any toolbar in Windows, by the way.

Status bars: Your application's cheat sheet

A *status bar* is nothing more than a strip of information across a window. In WordPad, the status bar may say "For Help, press F1" or tell you more about a command. Other applications use the status bar to tell you about the document you're working on or other information regarding the program. In a way, it's like a cheat sheet.

A few pointers from the mouse pointer

Aside from the keyboard, the thing you use to get work done in a program is the mouse. Use the mouse to point and click on menu commands, toolbar buttons, and other parts of the program.

➡ Please see Chapter 29 for more information about using a mouse, techniques, and other stuff. See the section "The Ever-Changing Mouse Pointer," which explains why the mouse pointer may change to something other than an arrow pointing north by northwest.

➡ See Chapter 25, the section "A More Lively Mouse Pointer," for some fun things you can do with the mouse pointer.

Going About Your Business

You use a Windows application to create something, what I call "stuff." For example, you use a word processor to write a nasty letter to your bank, you use a spreadsheet to figure out how you can afford a sports car to help you survive a midlife crisis, your kids use a Paint program for hours to create and then print a solid-black sheet of paper, and so on. No matter what it is you do, whatever stuff you create, there are common approaches you take to work with it in Windows. Basically, there are six things you do with stuff:

✗ Make new stuff

✗ Print stuff

✗ Save stuff to disk

✗ Open stuff already created

✗ Close stuff you're working on

✗ Start over again to make more stuff

These items are common to *all* Windows programs. The only programs that don't do these things are called utilities (which are used for dinking), which are covered in Part IV of this book.

Making stuff

What you create with your application depends on the application. So although everything works similarly and all programs have menus or toolbars and similar commands, the guts of what you do probably will differ from program to program. In all cases, you use the keyboard, mouse, and the various menu commands and tools in the application to get your work done. The end result? You've made stuff.

To begin making stuff in WordPad, just type. For example, type your name and address:

1. Start WordPad.

   See the instructions at the beginning of the section "Scent of a Windows Application," earlier in this chapter, if you haven't already started WordPad.

2. Type your name and address.

   Just use the keyboard like you would use a typewriter. Here's what I'd type:

   > Dan Gookin
   > 919 E. Hillsdale Blvd., Suite 400
   > Foster City, CA 94404

   Press the Enter key at the end of each line. Remember to press Enter after typing the last line.

➠ The stuff you create eventually is saved to disk for long-term storage and safekeeping. This subject is covered in the section "Saving your stuff," just a few inches from this spot.

➠ For some editing tips, see Chapter 30, the section "Basic Messing with Text Stuff."

➠ One of the best reasons for using Windows is that you can easily share information between two programs. See Chapter 8 for information about sharing information by using the Copy and Paste commands as well as object linking and embedding (called OLE).

➠ See Chapter 9 for examples of really creating stuff by using the small programs that come "free" with Windows.

Printing your stuff

Having your creation inside the computer just isn't enough. In most cases, you want a *hard copy,* or printout, of your stuff. The application takes your work and, hopefully, makes something beautiful of it, something that comes churning out of the printer in only a matter of seconds.

To print your stuff, you have several options. The most common is to use the Print command, which is usually found in the File menu.

1. Pull down the File menu.

   Click on the word *File* on the menu, or you can press Alt+F if your fingers are glued to the keyboard.

2. Choose the Print command.

   Click on the word Print or press the P key. This step brings up a dialog box with additional instructions, as shown in Figure 4-4.

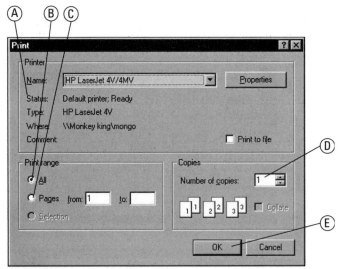

Figure 4-4
The standard Print dialog box.
A. Trivia about your printer; see Chapter 19. **B.** Prints your entire document.
C. Just prints a chosen range of pages. **D.** Enter a number here to print one or several copies of your document. **E.** Click here to print.

A quick way to skip the first two steps here is to press the Ctrl+P shortcut key. See the sidebar "Common quick-key shortcuts," later in this chapter.

3. Click on the OK button to start printing.

   You really don't need to mess with the rest of the dialog box (refer to Figure 4-4); just click on OK, and your stuff prints. You may see a tiny "I'm printing now" dialog box displayed. Whatever.

Your printer should be on and ready to print before you use the Print command. See Chapter 19 for more information about playing with your printer.

Actually, the stuff you print is sent to a special thing in Windows called the printing queue. Chapter 19, the section "Playing with the Queue," tells all.

Another quick way to print is to click on a Print button on the toolbar — if one is available. This button just prints your document instantly. It doesn't display the standard Print dialog box — it just prints.

The file should print right away. If not, you gotta problem! See Chapter 31 for information about troubleshooting printer problems. See the section "The All-Purpose, Amazing, Spectacular, Windows Troubleshooter."

Printing can be such a drag

One quick way to print is to set up your printer as an icon on the desktop. You can then drag your document to the printer icon to print it. This technique works fine, but I must criticize it for two reasons:

First, dragging a document to the printer icon works best only if you have a large amount of room on the desktop.

Second, although dragging a file to the printer icon sounds cool, it can really be a bother. Windows lets you drag okay, but then it starts the application that created the file, prints it, and then quits the application. This can be a rather roundabout and awfully busy way of doing things, which is why my advice is to stick with the Print command.

See Chapter 19, the section "I found a printer stuck on the desktop," for instructions for putting a printer icon on your desktop.

Printing the screen

A button on your keyboard is called Print Screen. This makes it sound like pressing that key sends a copy of the information on your screen to the printer. Alas, it just ain't so. Maybe under DOS, and then maybe not the way you like it; but the Print Screen key does have a function in Windows.

When you press the Print Screen key, Windows takes a "snapshot" of your screen. It then copies that graphical image into the Clipboard, which you can then paste into any paste-happy application. So you can press the Print Screen key, open up the Paint program and paste the image in there, and then print that document. It's a roundabout way of doing it, but that's basically a Print Screen.

By the way, if you press Alt+Print Screen, you copy only the top window on the screen as a graphical image. I used this technique to capture many of the screen images you see in this book.

See Chapter 8 for more information about copying and pasting in Windows.

Chapter 9 discusses the Paint program.

Saving your stuff

Sometimes you use an application to make something really quick, print it, and then be done with it. Most of the time, however, you want to save what you make. You save it for two reasons. First, it's nice to save things so that you don't have to do all that work all over again. Second, by saving your stuff to disk, you allow yourself the freedom to look at it later and then edit, modify, and otherwise change your stuff.

To save your stuff in just about any Windows program, follow these steps:

1. Choose File➪Save.

   Click on the word *File* on the menu bar, and the File menu drops down. Then click on the Word *Save.* You can also press Alt+F and then the S key, or you can press all three keys one at a time: Alt, F, S. Whatever, eventually a Save dialog box appears, similar to the one shown in Figure 4-5.

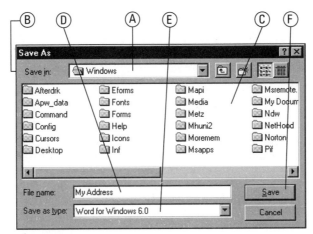

Figure 4-5
The Save dialog box.
A. Start here, choosing a folder for your document. **B.** See Chapter 17, the section "Working with folder trees in the Save As, Open, and Browse dialog boxes." **C.** Optionally choose a folder here as well. **D.** Type a filename here; see Chapter 16, the sidebar "Basic file-naming rules and regulations." **E.** See the section "Saving a file as a specific type" in Chapter 15. **F.** Click here to save.

If you don't see the Save dialog box, don't panic! Your stuff was saved to disk, no problem. The Save dialog box appears only the *first time* you save something to disk. After that, choosing the Save command just resaves the latest version of your stuff. See the sidebar "When to use the Save As command," later in this chapter, for more information.

The Save dialog box allows you to save your stuff to disk, putting in a specific folder and giving it a specific name.

2. Work the Save As dialog box from the top down.

You should save your stuff in three steps (use Figure 4-5 to help you find things):

First, choose a folder for your document.

Second, type a document name. Type something descriptive, short, and to the point. You can babble if you like, but saving something as "doodle" is much better than "something I just drew for the heck of it" (either name is okay, however). Press the Backspace key to back up and erase if you make a typing boo-boo.

Third, choose a document type.

⟶ See Chapter 17, the section "Climbing the Folder Tree," for more information about working with folders and picking a folder in which to save your document.

⟶ See Chapter 16 for more information about naming files. Look in the sidebar "Basic file-naming rules and regulations."

⟶ Finally, check out Chapter 15, the section "Saving a file as a specific type," for information about saving files as certain types.

Save your address in WordPad as My Address on disk. Type **My Address** in the File Name box, as shown in Figure 4-5.

3. Press the Enter key.

Or you can click on the Save button. Either way, your stuff is now saved to disk.

Your clue to whether a document has been saved is right on the main title bar of the application's window. Many applications change the window name after a document has been saved. If WordPad's window name is now My Address - WordPad, you can rest assured that your document was saved on disk.

⟶ The quickest way to save is to press the Ctrl+S shortcut key. This is mentioned in the sidebar "Common quick-key shortcuts," later in this chapter.

⟵ If your application has a toolbar, you can click on the Save button to quickly save or bring up the Save As dialog box. This button usually looks like a floppy disk, but if you can't find it, see the section "Hanging out at the toolbar," earlier in this chapter, for information about getting a tooltip to appear. The tooltip bubble should say Save.

When to use the Save As command

The first time you save your stuff to disk, you see the Save dialog box, as shown in Figure 4-5. After that, choosing the Save command merely saves your stuff to disk again, using that same filename. If you want to save your stuff to disk by using a different filename, you choose the Save As command. Another Save dialog box appears, and you are allowed to save your stuff to disk with a new name, in a different folder, or in a different format.

One reason for having a Save As command is that every time you use the Save command, Windows overwrites your older file on disk. That way, only the new version is saved (which is probably what you want), but the older version is gone forever. If you want to save that older version, you can choose the Save As command and save your newer stuff to disk using a new name. Another example is when you want to save a copy of your stuff to a floppy disk so that you can give it to a friend. If so, use the Save As command and choose drive A, your floppy drive, for saving the file.

Opening stuff

You never can finish all your work in a day, so all Windows programs enable you to open up files you've previously saved on disk. When you open them, they sit right there on the screen, ready for you to play with them, edit, print, and then save again when you're happy.

To open a file on disk for editing, obey the following rules:

1. Choose File⇨Open.

   You can go mousy: Click on the word *File,* and the File menu drops down. Then click on the word *Open.*

   You can go keyboardy: Press Alt+F and then O, or use the handy Ctrl+O shortcut.

   You can even use an Open button on the toolbar, if your program is so equipped.

2. Find the file you want by using the Open dialog box.

   The Open dialog box (see Figure 4-6) is a common part of every Windows program. You use it to scour your hard drive and folders, hunting down on disk a file you want to work with.

   You work this dialog box in three steps:

   First, locate the folder or disk drive in which the file is located.

   Second, choose a file type. Windows displays only files of that type in the Open dialog box's window.

   Third, when you've found your file listed in the window, double-click on it to open.

3. Open your file.

➠ If you see the "You haven't saved yet" dialog box, your document screen hasn't been saved. Save it! Refer to the section "Saving your stuff," earlier in this chapter, for more information.

➠ See Chapter 17, the section "Working with folder trees in the Save As, Open, and Browse dialog boxes," for more information about finding your file in another folder or on another disk drive.

➠ In Chapter 15, you want to read the section "Opening only files of specific types" for information about how to display only files of a specific type in the Open dialog box.

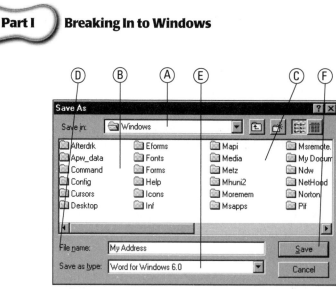

Figure 4-6
The Open dialog box.
A. Look here for your document in a folder or on another disk drive. **B.** Pick a folder from here (see Chapter 17). **C.** You can also double-click on a file listed here to open it. **D.** Optionally type the file's name (yechy). **E.** Sets which types of files Windows displays above (see Chapter 15). **F.** Click here to open.

Ideally, you see in the main window the file you want listed. Double-click the mouse on that file's name, and it's opened, thrust into your document for your fiddling pleasure.

➠ If you don't see your file lurking in the Open dialog box and it's ticking you off, you have to hunt for it. See Chapter 31, the section "'I want to find my file now. No messing around!'"

How to quickly open your most recent stuff

Some Windows applications keep track of the last few things you've been working on. These applications are kept in a list located in the File menu, usually numbered 1 through 4 (refer to Figure 4-2). You can quickly open these recently used files by choosing them from the File menu. For example, I usually press Alt, F, 1 after I start my word processor to open whatever document I was last working on. (Of course, you can also do this by choosing that document from the Start Thing's Documents submenu.)

Other nerdy terms for "open"

In Windows, the computer jargon for getting a file off a disk and into a program for fiddling is *open*. It wasn't always that way, and a few "legacy" programs from the DOS days use other terms rather than "open." Among them:

Load: This is a popular DOS command, actually cryptic compujargon. It was hard to tell whether you were loading something from disk or to disk, however. Oh, well.

Retrieve: Both WordPerfect and 1-2-3 used this term rather than "open." Some programs may use it to mean "open one document and insert it in another one." Strange.

Transfer: This turkey I've seen only once, in primitive versions of Microsoft's own Word program. The command to open a document was Transfer, Load. Kinda made you want to boogie.

Closing stuff

When you're done with your toys, you should put them away. Likewise, when you're done with your stuff, you should put it away. This is done with the Close command. However, unlike the preceding four commands, the Close command appears in just a few Windows applications (it's absent from WordPad, for example).

Close is not the same as Save. You save when you think that what you have is good. You close when you're done messing with it. As a side effect, closing something that hasn't been saved prompts Windows to save it for you. To wit:

1. Choose File⇨Close.

   With the mouse, click on the word *File* to drop down the File menu and then click on the word *Close.* With the keyboard, press Alt+F and then C.

   There is no universal shortcut key for the Close command, though many programs may use Ctrl+W (where the W means what? Window? Walk away? Whatever?). There also is no common toolbar shortcut, though I've seen many buttons with closed folders on them. Use the mouse-hover technique described in the "Whip out the toolbar" section of this chapter to confirm your suspicions.

2. If your document hasn't been saved, you're asked to save it.

   This is another handy thing about Windows: You can't walk away with unsaved work sitting around. Click on the Yes button to save your document.

➡ If you see the Save dialog box, refer to the section "Saving your stuff," earlier in this chapter, for more information.

Common quick-key shortcuts

Aside from sharing a common scent, many Windows programs use the same quick-key shortcuts. These are Control key (Ctrl) commands that are often easier to use than the various menus. Here's a smattering:

Key Combo	Command
Ctrl+A	Select All
Ctrl+C	Copy
Ctrl+F	Find
Ctrl+H	Replace
Ctrl+N	New
Ctrl+O	Open
Ctrl+P	Print
Ctrl+Q	Quit/Exit
Ctrl+S	Save
Ctrl+V	Paste
Ctrl+X	Cut
Ctrl+Z	Undo

The following shortcut keys don't use the Control key, but they're also popular in most Windows applications:

Key Combo	Command
Alt+Enter	Properties
Ctrl+Esc	Start Thing
F1	Help
Alt+F4	Close window

◄▥ The idea behind the Close command is that you don't have to quit your programs when you're done working on something. You can simply close your document and then work on something else. If you do want to quit, refer to Chapter 3, the section "Quitting Any Program."

▥➤ After you've closed your document, you see another document you're working on in the same application, a blank "new" document, or maybe even nothing. Refer to the next section to see what to do next.

Starting some new stuff

When the creative urge bubbles up, you'll want to start working on new stuff right away. This can be done in most Windows applications by choosing the New command.

1. Choose the New command from the File menu.

   Click on the word *File* with the mouse to expose the File menu. Click on the word *New*, which should be the first item in the list.

   With the keyboard, you can press Alt+F, N or use the handy Ctrl+N shortcut.

   The New command also lives as a button on most toolbars. It appears as a blank sheet of paper.

◄▥ Some applications may ask you to save your current work when you choose the New command. Click on the Yes button when asked, and then see the section "Saving your stuff," earlier in this chapter, for information about how to use the Save dialog box.

2. Your program starts over with a clean slate.

   Get to work!

The Windows Way of Offering Help

A common feature of nearly every Windows program is its extensive, on-line help. Of course, how you define "help" and what the program gives you are usually two entirely different things. Usually, in a Windows program, Help refers to an electronic version of the manual. In fact, Microsoft has made it a point to shift its manual text to a Help program and print only scant information in the traditional, bound manuals. (Although this may save a large number of trees, it doesn't do you any good when the power is out.)

The quick, desperate jab at the F1 key

The F1 key is the Help key. All Windows programs obey this law. Anywhere you are, at any time, you can stab the F1 key to get help. And not only that, the help you see is related to whatever you're doing; press the F1 key in a Save dialog box, and you'll see helpful information about saving files — that kind of stuff.

When you're done reviewing the helpful information, press the Esc key to return to your document.

When you first press F1, you may see a little window with a book and a magic pen. The magic pen writes something in the book — something about Microsoft stock being overinflated in value — and then you see the Help system on your screen. See the next section. (If you're lucky, you see the magic pen fill up several pages.)

➠ If you're not in a specific part of a program, you see the main Help screen, similar to the one shown in Figure 4-7, in the following section. This is the Help system, covered in the very next section.

Using the Help system

The Windows Help system is designed like a book. There are chapters, sections, and text. Figure 4-7 shows you the main Contents panel in the Help System. This is where you see an organized overview of information in the Help system — like chapters in a manual. That's what it is, in fact: an on-line version of the manual.

➠ If you don't see the Contents panel, click on the Contents tab in the upper part of the Help system window. See Chapter 28, the section "Panels, pages, and tabs," for more information about these tabs and panels if you need help.

To open a chapter, double-click on its name by using the mouse. This changes the icon by the chapter name from a closed book to an open book, and you see a list of topics in that chapter (refer to Figure 4-7).

To close a chapter and make the screen a little more readable, double-click on its name again: Click-click.

To open a topic, double-click on its name with the mouse. This opens a separate window that details information about the topic, often including step-by-step instructions (see Figure 4-8).

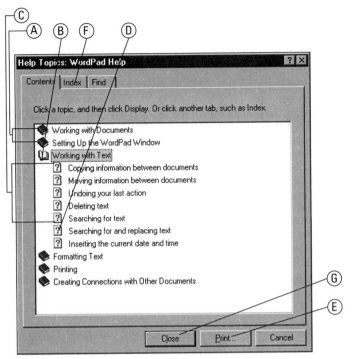

Figure 4-7
The Help system for WordPad, Contents panel.
A. Major "chapters." **B.** An open chapter. **C.** Contents inside the chapter. **D.** Double-click on this to read its information. **E.** Click here to print the topic's text. **F.** More panels with different ways to display the information. **G.** All done!

Figure 4-8
A sample topic window.
A. WordPad's Help system. **B.** Here is the question looked up. **C.** Step-by-step instructions on how to do it. **D.** Click here and choose Print Topic from the menu to print this topic. **E.** Click here to return to the Help system (refer to Figure 4-7). **F.** This button returns you to the preceding topic window (if any).

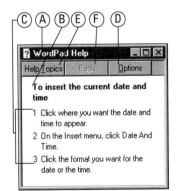

Some text in the Help window may appear with a dotted underline in the helpful description. Usually this text consists of terms or jargon that may baffle you. To see a definition of the text, hover the mouse pointer over it. The mouse pointer changes into a little hand with a pointy finger. Click the mouse once to see a pop-up definition. Click the mouse again to make the definition go away.

A square by some text indicates a *link* to that particular topic. If you move the mouse pointer over the square, it changes to a pointy finger hand. Click the mouse once and you're instantly zoomed to that topic for more information.

To return to the main Help system screen at any time, click the Contents button.

When you're done with the Help system, you must quit it — just like any other program. Click on the Cancel button in the bottom left corner of the Help system's window.

You can also quit the Help system by closing its window: Click on the tiny × in the window's upper right corner. Also refer to Chapter 3, the section "Quitting Any Program."

Please see Chapter 29, the section "The double-quick double-click," for more information about double-clicking, if you find the topic unusual.

Finding a specific topic by using the index

All information about a specific program or topic is organized into the Help system's index. You can use the index to find a topic if you know exactly what it is. For example, if you want information about formatting bold text in WordPad:

1. In your application (WordPad), press the F1 key to activate the Help system.

2. Click on the Index tab.

   This step brings that panel forward if it isn't forward already. You see a list of topics and subtopics displayed, just as you would find in any good index (see Figure 4-9).

3. Search for your topic.

   Begin typing a few letters of the topic in the #1 box at the top of the panel. For example, type **BO** for *bold text* and — behold! — the topic is displayed in the lower window.

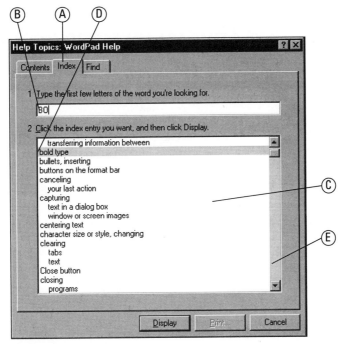

Figure 4-9

The Help system's Index panel.
A. Click on this tab to bring the Index panel forward. **B.** Type the first few letters of your topic here. **C.** Your topic is found here. **D.** Double-click the mouse on a topic to display its information. **E.** You can also use this scrollbar to search for a topic.

4. Open your topic.

   Double-click on your topic.

5. Read your help.

   Hopefully, it contains the information you requested. If not, you can try again or use the second method for finding information: the Find panel, covered in the next section.

Click on the Help Topics button (refer to Figure 4-8) in the Help window to return to the Help index.

The weird ? button on some windows

See the little question-mark button in the upper right corner of the window? This button activates a feature where you can point and click at anything in the window to get help on it.

After clicking on the ? button, the mouse pointer changes to an arrow with a question mark by it. At this point, you click on several items in the window to see a pop-up bubble explaining what the item is or how it works. Click the mouse again to make the bubble go away.

Finding a specific topic by using the Find panel

Another way to hunt down information is to use the Find panel in the Help system. It lists helpful information based on an alphabetically sorted list of words, commands, and meaningless jargon — which *does* mean something, if you heed the following steps:

1. In the Help system, bring the Find panel forward.

   Click on the Find panel by using the mouse. This step displays the first screen of the Find *wizard* — a common way of getting step-by-step things done in Windows.

   Don't bother with any of the settings.

   If the Find wizard doesn't appear, skip on down to step 4.

2. Click on the Next button.

   The final Find screen appears. Wow, that was difficult.

3. Click on the Finish button.

   Windows creates a word list, which assists you in finding the help you want.

4. The Find thing finally appears.

   The Find panel comes up, looking something like Figure 4-10.

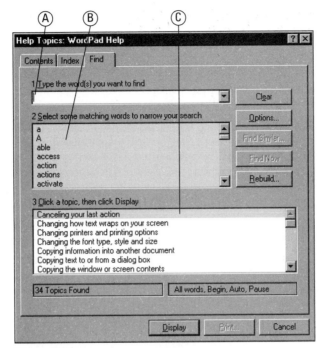

Figure 4-10
The Find panel for WordPad's help.
A. First type what you're looking for in here. **B.** Second, choose a topic from the short list here. **C.** Finally, double-click on the subject here.

5. In box 1, type the subject you want to find.

   For example, type the word **bold** to look up information about making text in WordPad bold.

   Normally, you have to type only the first few letters of your subject. This produces a "short list" of topics in box number 2.

6. Choose the topic from box number 2.

   If *bold* is listed there, for example, click on the word *bold.* This narrows the list of subjects in box number 3 to only a few, one of which is probably what you need.

7. Choose the help you need from box number 3.

   Highlight the Help topic with the mouse, and click on the Display button at the bottom of the dialog box. Hopefully, this displays the information you need.

Major help for Windows

One of the main items stuck to the Start Thing's menu is Help. When you choose this item, you are tossed into the Help system with all the chapters, topics, and subjects related to everything Windows does — a substantial amount of substance!

Everything in Windows' major Help works as described in this chapter. You have a Contents panel, Index, and the Find panel for looking up individual topics. The Contents panel even has subchapters and sub-sub-subtopics, which can be tiresome to wade through. For that reason, I recommend using either the index or the Find panels to look up something that interests you.

Like the Help system for any program, you should quit before you return to Windows to get your work done. Quit by pressing the Esc key, though you can also see Chapter 3 for information about quitting any program, which also applies to the Help system.

Printing, copying, or otherwise stealing the Help information

The information displayed in the various Help system windows is for your use. Although it would be illegal, for example, for you to print it, bind it, and sell it as your own book, Windows lets you manipulate the information in a variety of ways.

To print any window's information about your printer, click on the Print button associated with that Help system window. Make sure that your printer is on and ready to print before you use the Print command.

To copy any window's information, click on the Copy button associated with the window. You can also use the mouse to select bits of text in the window and then choose the Copy button or press Ctrl+C to copy it. Paste the text into WordPad or whatever application you're using (see Chapter 6 for more information about Copy and Paste; see Chapter 28 for information about selecting text).

If the Help window doesn't look like it has a Print or Copy button, look for a Menu button. That button drops down a menu with Copy and Print (or Print Topic) commands on it.

Done for the Day? To Quit or Put Away

It's not always necessary to quit your program when you're done working. In fact, you probably have two or three programs you use all the time, every day. Rather than quit them when you're done working on your stuff, I recommend that you put them aside instead.

Putting aside an application makes it easier for you to quickly use it again later. This is part of *multitasking,* which is covered in detail later in this book. For now, to put it aside, follow these steps:

1. Click on the *Minimize* button in the window's upper right corner.

    Thwoop! This button zooms the window down to a small button on the taskbar. The program isn't dead; it's just put away so that you can use it more easily later.

    To get the application back, just click on its button on the taskbar. This zooms the application back up to its previous size and location, ready for you to continue working.

◀ Also remember that you don't have to quit an application to finish working on a document or other stuff. See the section "Closing stuff," earlier in this chapter.

◀ If you really want to quit your application, see Chapter 3, "Quitting Any Program."

▶ If you think that this put away stuff sounds cool, check out Chapter 8, which goes into fine yet perky detail.

Places to Go, Things to See

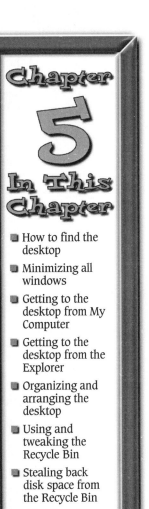

"**I**f you haven't been there, you just haven't lived. . . ."

Actually, most places you're urged to visit are overrated. It's those unexpected places that warrant excitement. For example, we don't get to the county fair for any other reason than to see people without teeth and tattooed. Often something that exciting is lurking just beneath the surface of what would otherwise be missed. That's what this chapter covers, a few additional items of interest when you're breaking into Windows. A bit of this and that. A quick tour of places to go and things to see.

Moseying Around the Desktop

The desktop can be your center of activity in Windows. You can put all your files and programs there, tacking them down like notes on a grocery-store bulletin board. It keeps them handy and means that you seldom have to mess with the Start Thing menu or My Computer. It can get junky, but there are ways to keep things tidy.

Although the desktop can be the center of activity, it shouldn't be the center of attention. It's only a way station, like an electronic Denver airport where thousands of people change planes between hither and thither. You have to stop and visit the desktop only from time to time. Hopefully, when you do, your stay will be a pleasant and productive one.

➠ Organizing the desktop, which means keeping it neat and tidy, is covered in Chapter 17, in the section "Bringing Order to the Desktop." Look there for tips on setting up your desktop "just so."

⬅ Of course, you don't have to use the desktop as your computer's way station. You can use the Start Thing (see Chapter 3) or even My Computer (see Chapter 2) or the Explorer as your center of activity.

A funny thing happened on the way to the desktop

Just as there are many paths to enlightenment, there are many paths to the desktop. Getting there isn't a problem, if you know where it is you're starting from.

Shoving it all aside to see the desktop

If you're like me and run your applications "full screen," you can't readily see the desktop. To get to it, you have to *minimize* any and all windows on the screen, shrinking them down to the taskbar so that you can see the desktop. Here's how to do that quickly:

1. Point the mouse pointer at the taskbar.

   If your taskbar is hidden, just move the mouse pointer to the edge of the screen, where the taskbar normally hangs out. It pops right back up.

2. Pop up the taskbar's shortcut menu (see Figure 5-1).

   Click the mouse's right button (a right-click) on the taskbar to pop up its shortcut menu. You have to be precise here. Don't click on any buttons or else you pop up that button's shortcut menu.

3. Choose Minimize All Windows.

   This step instantly minimizes every window on the screen, letting you see the entire desktop in a hurry.

➠ If the taskbar has too many buttons on it, see the section "Too Many Buttons on the Taskbar!" in Chapter 7.

➠ See Chapter 24, the section "Messing with the Taskbar," for additional information about changing the taskbar's look.

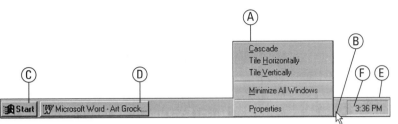

Figure 5-1
The taskbar's shortcut menu pops up.
A. Shortcut menu. **B.** Right-click here to see the shortcut menu. **C.** Start Thing.
D. Application window's button. **E.** The current time. **F.** See the sidebar "But I don't see the volume control!" in Chapter 7.

To *maximize,* or zoom out, any particular window when you're done with the desktop, click on its button. This is how the taskbar controls windows on the screen. See Chapter 4, the section "Done for the Day? To Quit or Put Away" for information about putting away a program instead of quitting; also check out Chapter 8 on multitasking.

To *maximize* all the windows, follow the preceding steps again but choose Undo Minimize All from the taskbar's shortcut menu.

You minimize a window by clicking on its Minimize button. More Windows mood-changing stuff is covered in Chapter 27, in the section "Adjusting a Window's Position and Size." To minimize all windows and see the desktop, however, you have to use the taskbar.

My Computer's view of the desktop

My Computer can display the contents of the desktop, similar to the way it displays the contents of a disk drive. Follow these steps:

1. Open My Computer.

   Double-click on the My Computer icon if you haven't started it already.

My Computer

2. Display My Computer's toolbar.

   Choose View➪Toolbar from the menu if the toolbar isn't already visible.

3. Use the list box menu to mosey up to the desktop.

   The drop-down menu, or *list box,* appears on the far left side of the toolbar (see Figure 5-2).

4. Click on the desktop item in the list.

   Click. The contents of the desktop appear in a window on the screen, similar to what you see in Figure 5-3.

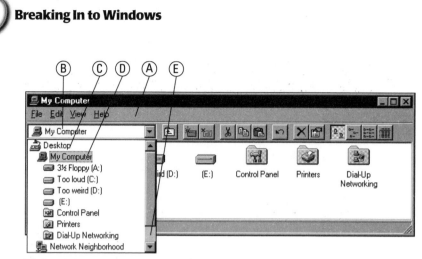

Figure 5-2
Getting to the desktop in My Computer.
A. Choose View⇨Toolbar to see this toolbar. **B.** The drop-down list box.
C. Here is the desktop. **D.** Here is what you're looking at already, the main
My Computer folder. **E.** Use the scrollbar to see the top of the list if you can't
find the desktop.

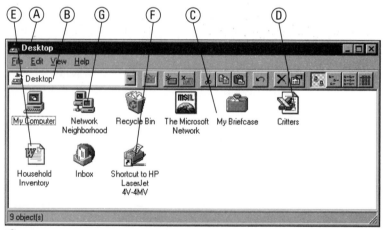

Figure 5-3
The desktop as seen by My Computer.
A. This tells you that you're looking at the desktop's contents. **B.** So does this.
C. Items located on the desktop. **D.** A Microsoft Excel document. **E.** A Microsoft
Word document. **F.** See Chapter 19, the section "I found a printer stuck on the
desktop." **G.** This appears only if your computer is attached to a network. See
Chapter 22.

←⊪ My Computer's toolbar can come in handy. See Chapter 2 for more information about My Computer, and pay attention to the section "Whip out the toolbar" for more information about what it can do for you.

⊪➡ The drop-down list box menu appears in a number of places throughout Windows. For example, it's also used in the Explorer, as covered in the next section. See Chapter 28, the section "Drop-down lists," for more instructions on how it works.

←⊪ The contents of the desktop can be viewed in several different ways: big icons, little icons, "details," and so on. See the section "Different Ways to Look at the Stuff in My Computer" in Chapter 2.

The desktop as depicted by the Explorer

If you grow fond of the Explorer for playing with files and folders on your computer, there's a quick way to get at the desktop and the items therein attached. Follow these steps:

1. Start the Explorer if you haven't already.

   Its icon lives in the Start Thing's menu. Choose Programs↪ Windows Explorer.

2. Scroll to the top of the left window.

   There are two windows in the Explorer. The one on the left shows the folder tree and is called All Folders. The other one shows files and folders and is called Contents of [whatever]. You may have to scroll to the top of the list in the window on the left (see Figure 5-4).

3. Click on the desktop item.

   Click. The Explorer displays the desktop's contents in its right window, which may look like Figure 5-4.

⊪➡ The Explorer is a rather nerdy way of looking at files and whatnot on your computer, preferred over My Computer because it lets you climb the folder tree without having to wade through a bunch of windows. See Chapter 17, the section "Climbing the Folder Tree," for more details.

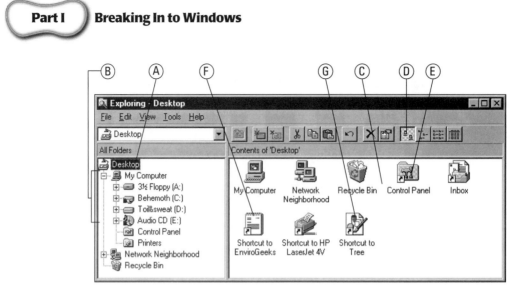

Figure 5-4

How the Explorer sees the desktop.

A. The desktop is up here (which you may have to scroll to). **B.** Other drives in your computer. **C.** Items on the desktop. **D.** This is the Big Icons view, which you can change here. **E.** A shortcut to the Control Panel is a handy thing to have on the desktop. **F.** Shortcut to a text document. **G.** Shortcut to a Paint graphics document.

Where the desktop really is, in case you're dying to know

The desktop, like so many things in Windows, is merely a graphical depiction of what's going on inside your computer. And I can tell you from personal experience that there is no desktop inside your computer. There are disk drives, files, folders, bits, and bytes, but no desktop. So what is the desktop, and how did it get there? Easy answer: Windows cheats.

The desktop is merely a handy place for you to put things. But inside your computer the desktop is really a secret folder located inside Windows' own folder. It can be used to help you get work done, like a shortcut. In fact, copying and pasting things on the desktop is the way many people prefer to use Windows. Please see Chapter 17, the section "Bringing Order to the Desktop," which goes into detail about organizing and using the desktop for this purpose.

Arranging the stuff that loiters on the desktop

Looking at the desktop in My Computer or the Explorer gives you a custom view of what's going on. You can arrange the icons in alphabetical order, see them as big or little icons, and even look at the geeky MS-DOS names of things. But the way those things are actually arranged on the desktop is totally different.

After an icon is on the desktop, you can move it anywhere and it will stay there. If you want My Computer in the lower left corner, for example, drag it there by using the mouse. If the Recycle Bin seems more familiar to you in the lower right corner, drag it there. Want to cluster your work documents and programs together? Drag them as well. And if you paste a printer on your desktop, stick it where you think it works best.

If the icons look sloppy, you can tighten them up by following these steps:

1. Bring up the desktop's shortcut menu.

   Point the mouse pointer at a "blank" spot on the desktop and click the mouse's right button. This step activates a pop-up shortcut menu.

2. Choose Line up Icons.

   This step doesn't move the icons on the desktop — it only brings them in line, organizing them in a "grid," more or less.

If you're after a little more organization, you can choose an item from the shortcut menu's Arrange Icons submenu. There, you can line up the desktop's icons by name, type of icon (what the icon represents), size in bytes, or the date it was last created or modified.

Be careful with the Arrange Icons commands. Selecting one of them lines up all your icons in columns starting at the left edge of the screen. This wrecks any organization you've made by dragging icons to special places on the screen.

By the way, if you like icons lined up in neat, orderly columns, choose Arrange Icons⇨Auto Arrange from the desktop's shortcut menu. That way, the icons always appear lined up in a grid, no matter what.

➡ Icons are placed on the desktop by using Copy and Paste — just like in kindergarten. You find an icon (file, program, folder) by using My Computer or the Explorer and then copy it and paste it on the desktop. See Chapter 16, which discusses several ways to copy and paste files and icons. Also see the section "Taking a Shortcut Instead of Copying Files" in that chapter for a discussion of what shortcut icons are and how they work.

⟶ You can combine your dragging and organizing of icons on the desktop with an interesting background pattern, as shown in Figure 5-4. See Chapter 24 for information about how to choose a background pattern in Windows. (The pattern in Figure 5-4 was designed using Windows' own Paint program, discussed in Chapter 8.)

The Politically Correct Recycle Bin

The Recycle Bin is where you throw things away. It's an icon that lives on the desktop but that is also used when you delete icons from My Computer, the Explorer, or any of a number of places where the urge to destroy becomes uncontrollable.

You use the Recycle Bin to throw away files, folders, and other stuff you don't need. The tossed-out stuff sits there, where you can "undelete" it, or, after a time, Windows eventually gets rid of whatever's in the Recycle Bin — most likely through decomposition.

How to find a Recycle Bin near you

The Recycle Bin lives as an icon on the desktop, but there are other ways to find it as well. For example, a copy of the Recycle Bin exists for each disk drive on your computer. It's in the topmost folder, called the *root* (the first window of files and folders on any disk drive).

Most of the time you toss away files and whatnot by dragging them to the Recycle Bin icon on the desktop. The details of this process are covered in Chapter 16, in the section "Some Files Just Hafta Go, or Deleting Files," in case you can't wait (though a small demo appears in the next section).

If you can't get to the Recycle Bin icon on the desktop, you can always dispose of unwanted files, folders, or icons by using a Delete menu command (see Figure 5-5). Both My Computer and the Explorer have a Delete command in their File menu, waiting to gobble up whatever you have selected and toss it in the Recycle Bin. Or if you like the keyboard, you can press the Del key to shuffle select files over to the Recycle Bin.

Why a Recycle Bin?

The Recycle Bin is basically a trash can, which is what it looks like. On the Macintosh, it's called the *Trash.* In OS/2 it's a paper shredder (which makes you wonder why OS/2 isn't more popular with the government). I have no clue about why Microsoft is being politically correct here. In one of its early operating systems, the command to delete a file was Kill! Whatever.

Figure 5-5
The Delete command in the File menu.
A. The File menu in My Computer or the Explorer. **B.** See Chapter 3, the section "Taking advantage of the numerous New menu commands." **C.** See Chapter 16, the section "Taking a Shortcut Instead of Copying Files." **D.** The Delete command. **E.** See Chapter 16, the section "Blessing a File with a New Name." **F.** See Chapter 15, the section "Gawking at a file's properties."

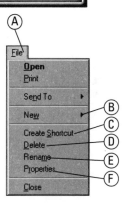

➠ You can delete a whole gaggle of files at one time by selecting a bunch of them as a group and then either dragging them to the Recycle Bin or choosing the Delete command. See Chapter 16, the section "Crowd Control, or Working with Groups of Files."

➠ The first folder on any disk drive is called the *root,* or often the *root directory* (as a throwback to primitive, MS-DOS times). Chapter 17 has more information about this concept, which you can find in the section "What's up with the root folder?"

"But the file *whatever* is a program!"

Whenever you delete a file, Windows confronts you with an appropriate dialog box that says, "Are you sure you want to move it to the Recycle Bin?" When you delete a program, Windows wants to make extra sure (see Figure 5-6). Are you sure?

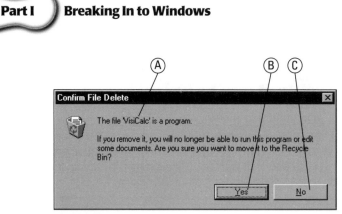

Figure 5-6
This dialog box pops up when you try to delete a program.
A. The program's name. **B.** Click here to delete the file, which is probably not a wise thing to do. **C.** Click here to be safe.

Well, you might or might not be sure. If you're deleting a *copy* of a program, go ahead. You can later *recover* things you accidentally delete from the Recycle Bin. However, this should not be an excuse for being cavalier about wantonly deleting anything.

A warning dialog box *does not* appear when you drag a group of icons or a folder to the Recycle Bin. Because you're dragging the stuff to the trash, Windows assumes that you must deliberately want to delete it and no warning is given. Beware!

A similar warning appears if you delete a folder that is *shared,* or being used by others on the network. Just as your parents told you, you can't share something you're about to destroy. Better think twice about it or just delete the folder's contents rather than the folder. Also check out Chapter 22, which goes into more detail about sharing and network stuff.

Using the Recycle Bin just once to see how it works

The idea behind the Recycle Bin is that you can toss things out without losing them. In the olden days, you would delete a file and it would be gone, gone, gone. But with the Recycle Bin — like any trash can — you can root through it after tossing something out and recover it. And the bonus here, of course, is that you don't have to worry about getting coffee grounds or a mushy banana peel on your arm while you do it.

To see how the Recycle Bin works, follow these steps. You won't actually delete anything important from your computer's hard drive because the final steps here recover the item you've deleted.

1. Open My Computer if you haven't opened it already.

   See Chapter 2 for a quick tour of My Computer if you haven't already.

2. Locate the Windows folder in My Computer.

   Open up drive C, and then look for the Windows folder. Open it.

   Again, you can refer to Chapter 2, the section "Opening up stuff inside My Computer," for more information about opening folders and windows in My Computer.

3. Locate the My Address document.

   My Address is a WordPad document, created in Chapter 4. Its icon should live in your Windows folder and look like the icon pictured nearby.

   My Address

   See Chapter 4, the sections "Making stuff" and "Saving stuff" for descriptions of how to create and save to disk the My Address document if you haven't done so.

   If you can't locate My Address and you really did create it in Chapter 4, turn to Chapter 31, the section "File? File? Here, File! C'mon, Boy! Where'd You Go?" for information about hunting down that lost file.

4. Choose the My Address document.

   Click on the document's icon by using the mouse. Click only once: Click. This step chooses the document, letting Windows know that you want to do something with it.

5. Toss the document into the Recycle Bin.

   If you can see the Recycle Bin on the desktop, drag the My Address document over to it by using the mouse: Click on My Address, keep the mouse button down, drag the icon over to the Recycle Bin, and then release the mouse button.

   If you can't see the Recycle Bin, choose File⇨Delete from the menu or just press the Del key. When you do this, you see a dialog box displayed, asking whether you really want to delete. Click on the Yes button with the mouse. (The dialog box doesn't appear when you drag an icon to the Recycle Bin on the desktop.)

This is a good argument for arranging your desktop, putting the Recycle Bin in a place where you can always see it so that you can always toss (drag) things into it. See the section "Arranging stuff that loiters on the desktop," earlier in this chapter, but also check out Chapter 17, the section "Bringing Order to the Desktop."

When you delete a file, a dialog box appears, showing that file being "tossed" into the Recycle Bin (see Figure 5-7). The more stuff you delete, the more papers fly into the Recycle Bin. You may not see this dialog box when you delete My Address, but it shows up when you delete large or multiple files. This just gives you something to watch while you twiddle your thumbs.

6. The file has been deleted.

Okay, so you tossed it out. Now it's gone. If you want it back, you have to keep reading in the next section.

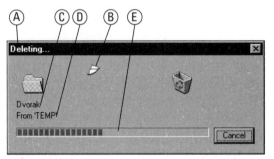

Figure 5-7
A file document is being deleted.
A. Something is being deleted. **B.** The paper flies from the folder to the Recycle Bin. **C.** File being deleted. **D.** Folder the file once inhabited. **E.** Progress thermometer.

A quick, odorless peek into the Recycle Bin to restore something

Deleting files is a fact of life, something you do a lot of. But there are those times when you delete something and want it back. That's why Microsoft made the Recycle Bin. Unlike a garbage disposal, it's easy to recover something tossed into a Recycle Bin.

1. Open the Recycle Bin on the desktop.

   Go to the Recycle Bin icon on the desktop. If you can't see it, minimize all the windows on the desktop, as described earlier in this chapter in the section "Shoving it all aside to see the desktop."

   Double-click on the Recycle Bin icon to open it. It may take some time to see all the stuff in there, especially if you haven't opened the Recycle Bin in a while.

   The Recycle Bin contains a list of all the files you've deleted (see Figure 5-8). They stay in the Recycle Bin for a given amount of time, allowing you to recover them if you eventually change your mind. (But after a time everything is deleted for good; see the section "Tweaking the Recycle Bin," later in this chapter, for more info.)

Name	Original Location	Date Deleted	Type	Size
My Address	C:\WINDOWS	6/11/95 4:48 PM	Microsoft Word Doc...	5KB
Document Scrap '...	C:\WINDOWS\Des...	6/11/95 11:30 AM	Scrap object	9KB
Scrap (2)	C:\WINDOWS\Des...	6/11/95 11:30 AM	Scrap object	22KB
Tree	C:\WINDOWS\Des...	6/11/95 11:30 AM	Bitmap Image	0KB
Scrap	C:\WINDOWS\Des...	6/11/95 11:30 AM	Scrap object	33KB
Document Scrap '...	C:\WINDOWS\Des...	6/11/95 11:30 AM	Scrap object	9KB
EnviroGeeks	C:\WINDOWS\Des...	6/11/95 11:30 AM	Microsoft Word Doc...	5KB
Document Scrap 't...	C:\WINDOWS\Des...	6/11/95 11:09 AM	Scrap object	8KB
Scrap	C:\WINDOWS\Des...	6/11/95 11:09 AM	Scrap object	22KB
New Text Document	C:\WINDOWS\Des...	6/10/95 9:44 PM	Text Document	0KB
Sounds like an Ele...	C:\WINDOWS\Des...	6/9/95 9:09 AM	Sound	7KB
Windows 95 Beta ...	C:\WINDOWS\Des...	6/2/95 12:09 PM	Shortcut	1KB
Microsoft WinNews	C:\WINDOWS\Des...	6/2/95 12:09 PM	Shortcut	1KB
Shortcut to Startsys	C:\TEMP	5/24/95 3:45 PM	Shortcut	1KB
UUCODE	C:\WINDOWS\Start...	5/24/95 12:01 PM	Shortcut	1KB

26 object(s)   120KB

Figure 5-8
The stuff in the Recycle Bin doesn't smell all that bad.
A. Dead-file list. **B.** You can choose View⇨Toolbar to see the toolbar.
C. You can also choose various views, such as Large Icons, from the View menu. **D.** Trivia about the files that are deleted. **E.** Date departed.

2. Look for a file to recover and restore, such as My Address.

   Look for the file My Address, which you deleted in the preceding section. If you have to, use the mouse to scroll through the list of files.

A quick way to find a file in a long, long list is to type the first letter in its name. So for My Address, you type an **M**. This tells Windows to display the part of the window with the M icons in it. From there, it's relatively easy to find the file you want.

To easily find files you just hacked off, choose View⇨Arrange Icons⇨by Delete Date. That shows you the most recently deleted files first.

You can also sort each of the columns by clicking on their titles. To sort the deleted files alphabetically, for example, click on the Name column head. Click on it again to sort them in reverse alphabetical order.

Oh, I'm just full of tips today.

Files are displayed in the Recycle Bin just as they are in My Computer or the Explorer. You can view them as Big Icons, details, whatever. See Chapter 2, the section "Different Ways to Look at the Stuff in My Computer," for information about changing the view. The instructions there also apply to the Recycle Bin.

3. Choose the file to restore.

    Click on the file you want to recover and restore by using the mouse. Find My Address. Click on it once with the mouse. Click. This highlights the file's icon, letting you know that it's selected.

    You can recover several files by selecting them all at once. See Chapter 16, the section "Crowd Control, or Working with Groups of Files," for information about selecting a whole boatload of files.

4. Choose File⇨Restore.

    Choose the Restore command from the File menu. The file is removed from the Recycle Bin and put back on disk in the exact folder from which it was deleted.

5. Close the Recycle Bin.

    Click on its little × Close button in the window's upper right corner.

    You should confirm that your file has been restored by checking the Windows folder window in My Computer and seeing whether the My Address file has been restored.

A restored file is no different from the way it was before it was deleted. There is only one warning here: After a given amount of time, Windows deletes files from the Recycle Bin and you can't restore them. So if you want to recover some accidentally deleted, fondly remembered, or long-gone files, do it as soon as you think about it or it may be too late.

"How long do I have before stuff in the Recycle Bin is *really* deleted?"

Windows keeps deleted files hanging around in the Recycle Bin for a long time. Usually they stay there until the Recycle Bin gets full. When that happens, Windows begins deleting older files in the Recycle Bin to make room for new stuff you drag in there. Because of this limitation, how long files stay there depends on how much stuff you throw away. The bottom line is to restore something from the Recycle Bin *immediately,* right when you think about it. Don't count on stuff lounging there forever.

Flushing the Recycle Bin empty

Normally, there's no need to venture into the Recycle Bin to utterly delete files; Windows takes care of that for you. There are times, however, when you may want to delete sensitive files, stuff you may not want anyone else snooping at or recovering. In those instances, you can permanently remove all or some of the files stored in the Recycle Bin.

To flush empty the entire Recycle Bin, choose the Empty Recycle Bin command, found in the Recycle Bin window's File menu and also on the Recycle Bin's shortcut menu. This is one command you shouldn't take lightly. After choosing Empty Recycle Bin, Windows whirls through the Recycle Bin like a tornado through a trailer park, smiting everything and laying all files to utter waste. Yes, it deletes it all. For good. Bye-bye.

If you don't want to be drastic about it, you can selectively delete files from the Recycle Bin. During a normal fit of organizational frenzy, for example, you may decide to purge some old and utterly useless files from the Recycle Bin. To do that, follow these steps:

1. Choose the file (or files) you want to delete permanently.

   Click the mouse on the file you want to delete. You can hold the Ctrl key down while clicking to select more than one file, or you can "drag-lasso" a group of files. (See Chapter 29 for more information about these concepts.)

2. Choose File⇨Delete.

   The Delete command in the Recycle Bin zaps files for good. A dialog box appears (see Figure 5-9), telling you that the files will really be gone if you click on Yes.

3. Click on the Yes button.

   The files are gone. A graphic dialog box may appear, showing the files as bits of paper flying from the Recycle Bin off into the electronic ether. Whoosh!

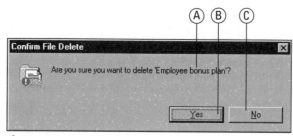

Figure 5-9
The files will be *seriously* deleted if you click on the Yes button.
A. The name of the file you're trying to zap utterly. **B.** Click here to do it.
C. Here not.

Tweaking the Recycle Bin

The Recycle Bin, like almost everything else in Windows, has a special Properties command that controls how it works. To see it, bring up the Recycle Bin shortcut menu and choose Properties: Right-click the mouse on the Recycle Bin icon or somewhere inside the Recycle Bin's window, and then choose Properties from the menu.

The Recycle Bin Properties dialog box (see Figure 5-10) helps you set up how the Recycle Bin works. Basically, you set the size of the Recycle Bin, telling Windows how much stuff you can throw away before it starts deleting anything.

Figure 5-10
The Recycle Bin Properties
dialog box.
A. Use this tab to set the Recycle
Bin for all hard drives at one
time. **B.** Other hard drives in your
system. **C.** A host drive to a
compressed DriveSpace drive
(see Chapter 18, the section
"Blowing Up Your Disk Drive with
DriveSpace"). **D.** Click here to set
each drive by itself. **E.** A ✔ check
mark here automatically zaps
every file with no possibility of
recovery from the Recycle Bin.
F. The slider to adjust the amount
of disk space the Recycle Bin
uses. **G.** The percentage of disk
space the Recycle Bin uses.
H. Always a good idea to keep
this item checked.

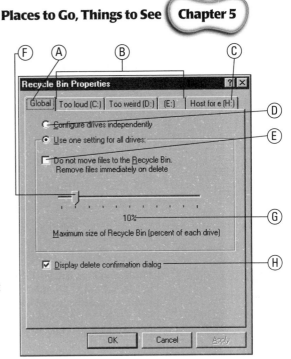

Reducing the amount of disk space the Recycle Bin hogs up

The way Windows comes out of the box, it sets aside 10 percent of your total hard disk drive space for throwaway stuff. This is a good number, though it may be a little big. On my 600MB disk drive, for example, Windows sets aside 60MB of space for throwaway stuff. That's way too much space, which I'd rather have available to store stuff I don't want to throw away.

It's possible to change the setting by using a "slider" in the Recycle Bin Properties dialog box. You can change the amount of disk space the Recycle Bin uses from 10 percent to something like 5 or maybe even 1 percent.

If you want to change the amount of space the Recycle Bin uses, follow these steps:

1. Bring up the Recycle Bin's shortcut menu.

   Click the right mouse button on the Recycle Bin's icon to bring up the shortcut menu.

   If you're inside the Recycle Bin, right-click the mouse inside the Recycle Bin's window.

2. Choose the Properties command.

3. If you have only one hard drive, skip to step 7.

4. Click on the Global panel to bring it up front if it's not in front already.

5. Click on the radio button by Configure drives independently.

   This step puts a black dot in the button, meaning that each of your hard drives can be adjusted separately, setting aside a different amount of space for the Recycle Bin for each drive.

6. Click on the panel associated with a particular drive.

   For example, use drive C: or D: to set the space for one of those drives.

7. Use the slider to set the amount of disk space the Recycle Bin uses.

   Point at the slider with the mouse, and drag it to a new percentage value. I set my drive to 1 percent, for example, meaning that the Recycle Bin takes up only 6MB of disk space, giving me back 54MB of space to use for storing programs, graphics files, games I play way too often, and other whatnot.

8. OK!

   Click on the OK button. Windows makes the proper adjustments to the Recycle Bin. This process may take some time (of course), especially if your Recycle Bin is already full. So have a little patience.

Displaying those warning boxes for the timid file-deleting person

If you prefer to be warned all the time whenever you throw anything into the Recycle Bin, whip out the Recycle Bin Properties dialog box (as described in the preceding section) and click the mouse in the box by Display delete confirmation dialog. This tells Windows to always ask whether you're sure before anything is put in the Recycle Bin.

Chomping down files without the possibility of recycling

If you'd rather not bother with the Recycle Bin, open up the Recycle Bin Properties dialog box, as described in the section "Reducing the amount of disk space the Recycle Bin hogs up" earlier in this chapter, and click the mouse in the box by the part that says "Do not move files to the Recycle Bin. Remove files immediately on delete." This means that the files are instantly munched up by Windows without any easy possibility of recovery. Do this only if you're very bold or just plain foolish.

Even Though It's Windows, There Is a DOS Prompt

It's a nice place to visit, but I wouldn't want to work there. That's the DOS prompt, of course. It's a holdover from earlier versions of Windows and DOS, when computers were used as text-only. Graphics? That was for games.

➡ The funny thing is that today most popular programs run under Windows, and the games, well, they actually all run under DOS. Chapter 12 goes into full-blown detail on running DOS programs in Windows, and Chapter 26, the section "Wrestling with DOS Games," discusses running DOS games. But for a quick look-see at the DOS prompt, follow these steps:

1. Activate the Start Thing's menu.

   Click on the Start Thing if you see it on your screen, or press Ctrl+Esc to pop it up immediately.

2. Choose Programs⇨MS-DOS Prompt.

   Select the MS-DOS Prompt icon from the Programs submenu. This step starts up a wee window on the screen that contains a copy of the old MS-DOS prompt, looking somewhat like Figure 5-11.

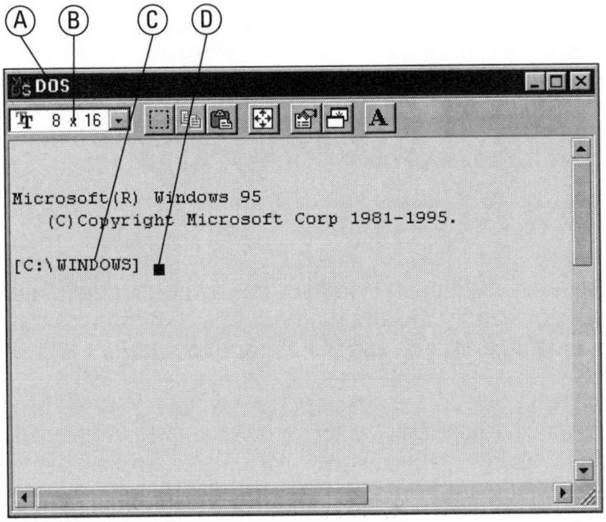

Figure 5-11
Back in the old days, all PCs used this interface.
A. DOS lives! **B.** Stuff you can read about in Chapter 12. **C.** The DOS prompt.
D. The text mode cursor.

You work DOS by typing commands at the prompt. For example:

C:\WINDOWS> **DIR**

Type **DIR** and press Enter. This displays a list of files on disk, yet another way of looking at the same information that My Computer or the
Explorer show you.

There is also a toolbar on the MS-DOS window, which lets you adjust
the way it operates and enables you to almost enjoy some of the times
you'll have there.

3. Close the MS-DOS Prompt window.

The best way to close the DOS window is to type the word **EXIT** at the
DOS prompt and then press the Enter key:

C:\WINDOWS> **EXIT**

This step closes the DOS window safely and returns you to Windows,
where you may frolic alive and free, without the burden of using DOS on
a daily basis.

➠ You can do anything with the DOS window that you can do with any other
window on the screen. You can minimize it, maximize it, shrink it down, and
so on. See Chapter 27 for a discussion of what can be done with a window.

➠ Using an older DOS application doesn't have to be a stick-in-the-mud thing.
There are lots of ways to make the DOS prompt in Windows useful and
interesting. See Chapter 12 for more information.

The Ubiquitous Pop-up Shortcut Menus

Just about everything in Windows has a shortcut menu attached to it. This
menu, activated by clicking the right mouse button, contains some handy or
popular commands you can use to control whatever it is you clicked on.

⬅ If you right-click on the desktop, for example, you see its shortcut menu,
which was discussed in the section "Arranging the stuff that loiters on the
desktop," earlier in this chapter. Also discussed was the taskbar's shortcut
menu, which you can see by right-clicking the mouse on a blank area in the
taskbar (see the section "Shoving it all aside to see the desktop").

Every icon on the desktop or in a window has a shortcut menu associated
with it. Figure 5-12 shows the shortcut menu for a file in a My Computer
window. It contains several common commands, most of which can be found
elsewhere, but having them on the shortcut menu keeps them handy.

Figure 5-12
The shortcut menu for some old icon in
a My Computer window.
A. Opens the icon, runs the program, etc. **B.** See Chapter 15,
the section "Carefully opening a file for a quick view." **C.** See
Chapter 16, the sections "Copying, or Doop-Doop-Duplicating,
Files" and "Deeply Moving Files." **D.** See Chapter 16, the section
"Taking a Shortcut Instead of Copying Files." **E.** See Chapter 15,
the section "Gawking at a file's properties."

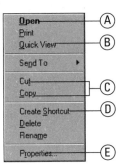

Inside applications, a shortcut menu usually contains a list of options or
commands for whatever it is you right-clicked on. If you right-click in the
main editing area in WordPad, for example, you see a menu of items to help
you edit your text (see Figure 5-13).

Figure 5-13
WordPad's shortcut menu.
A. Cut and Copy commands, available only when something
is selected. **B.** Other handy commands. **C.** Not-available
commands for some reason.

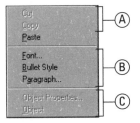

As a general bit of advice, I recommend right-clicking the mouse randomly
from time to time, just to see what sort of shortcut menu pops up. You may
find it easier to choose a command with a right-click than to use some of the
other, less obvious ways Windows has of doing things.

Using the shortcut menu is easy as cake

Unlike the menu bar, which is a traditional fixture of all Windows programs,
shortcut menus pop up anywhere you right-click the mouse. Other than that,
you choose commands from the menu in the same manner: Hover the
mouse pointer over the command name and click.

Some shortcut menus have submenus, identified with the right-pointing
arrows, just as they are on the normal menus. Click on the submenu
name to see the contents of the submenu.

Finally, if you don't choose a command from the shortcut menu, you can click (left-click) anywhere else on the screen to make the submenu go away. If you like the feel of the keyboard, whacking the Esc key also makes the shortcut menu vanish.

It's a monopoly of Properties commands

One command that lives comfortably at the bottom of nearly every shortcut menu is the Properties command. This is the dinking command, the one which brings up a dialog box that enables you to see more information about whatever it was you right-clicked on and optionally change some of that information.

← You can change certain aspects of the Recycle Bin, for example, by right-clicking on its icon and choosing the Properties command from the shortcut menu (see the section "Tweaking the Recycle Bin," earlier in this chapter).

On My Computer's toolbar (and in the Explorer), there is a shortcut button for Properties. Click on a file, and then click on that button to instantly see its Properties dialog box. Other applications may share this common toolbar button for the same purpose.

➡ Most of what you can change in the various Properties dialog boxes falls under the category of dinking. For example, refer to Chapter 24 for some major dinking with the desktop's properties.

➡ Dinking on other items in Windows, such as the Printer or disk drives, can be found throughout Part IV of this book.

Add/Remove
Programs

America
Online

Part
II

MSN

MSN

Getting
Work Done

PopUp

Winpopup

A

Cardfile

CompuServe

PRODIGY.

Prodigy

In this part

- All about the Start Thing

- Getting to know the taskbar

- Multitasking,
  sharing, loving

- Introducing the applets

- The quick and cheap
  look at Microsoft Office

- Wasting time with
  online communications

- Dealing with
  ancient DOS applications

- Installing new software

How do I . . . ?

Get right at my programs to start them?

Although you can use the Start Thing's menu to start stuff, using submenus is similar to climbing the proverbial slippery slope.

➠ The best way to access programs you use all the time is to put them right on the Start Thing's menu. See the section "Sticking something on the main Start Thing menu" in Chapter 6.

➠ If you want to start some programs automatically when your computer starts, put them in the special Startup submenu on the Start Thing. See the section "Applications that Amazingly Start Automatically" also in Chapter 6.

See those buttons on the taskbar?

Each button on the taskbar represents a window on the screen. You can click on a button to see the window, which comes in handy when windows are minimized or otherwise hidden from view.

➠ To learn more about buttons and windows, see the section "Buttons and Windows Galore" in Chapter 7.

➠ Too many buttons on the taskbar can be a headache, so see the section "Too Many Buttons on the Taskbar!" also in Chapter 7.

Set the time in Windows?

The current time is displayed in the lower right corner of the screen, on the taskbar, along with other information and some useful shortcuts.

➡ To set the time on your computer, see the section "Fooling with the time (or, setting the time on your PC)" in Chapter 7.

➡ Other items appear next to the time on the taskbar. See Chapter 7, the section "Having Fun with the Loud Time," for more information.

Copy more than one thing at a time?

The best way to copy and store multiple items is to paste them to the desktop for temporary storage. In that way, you can use the desktop as a scratch pad for interesting items you can paste into applications over and over.

➡ See Chapter 8, the section "Pasting to the desktop," for more information about how this trick works.

Quickly switch from one program to another?

You can use the buttons on the toolbar, but for true speed you should try using the Atl+Tab "cool switch" to switch quickly between two running programs.

➡ See the section "Using the 'cool switch' to switch applications" in Chapter 8 for more information.

Use those freebie programs?

Several programs come free with Windows. Some of them are bagatelles, but two of them are worth looking at: WordPad and Paint.

➠ See Chapter 9, the section "Making Purty Pictures with Paint," for information about using the Paint program.

➠ WordPad is mulled over briefly in the section "Let WordPad Bring Out the Shakespeare in You" also in Chapter 9.

➠ Another useful program discussed in Chapter 9 is the Phone Dialer. Check out the section "Making the call."

➠ Information about using Windows' Terminal program for online communications can be found in Chapter 11.

Run WordPerfect for DOS in Windows?

Windows is DOS-friendly, but that's almost like saying that orange juice tastes good after you brush your teeth, but only if you're thirsty.

➠ See Chapter 12 for everything to do with DOS in Windows.

➠ Having trouble with your DOS programs in Windows? See the section "Troubleshooting MS-DOS Program Problems" also in Chapter 12 for some quick solutions.

Install new programs?

There's a central place where all programs are installed in Windows; even Windows' own pieces parts are set up there. Not only that, but you also use the same place to remove programs (and pieces of Windows).

➠ See Chapter 13, the section "And Now for Something New," for information about installing new applications.

➠ The section "Adding the Rest of Windows" in Chapter 13 discusses how you can add bonus Windows components.

All About the Start Thing

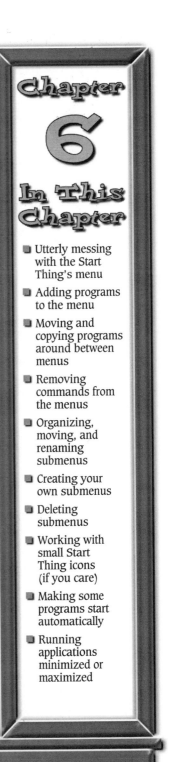

The Start Thing is where everything starts. Almost. Actually, the Start Thing looks like one of Microsoft's attempts to make things easier that turned out really bad. And then when it found out that it was bad, it tried to fix it up rather than kill it off, which just made it worse — like some massive but well-intentioned government project gone awry. But I digress.

The Start Thing isn't really that ugly to use. It's unwieldy, but the true point you have to remember is that the Start Thing can help you fire up your favorite programs — if you know how to tame it. That's the subject of this chapter — beating the Start Thing into shape.

To Gently Rule Programs on the Start Menu

There are so many ways to start an application in Windows that it's just best to forget all of them and concentrate instead on *using* the Start Thing's menu. Just click on the Start button or press Ctrl+Esc, and you see the pop-up menu, ready to help you work with Windows or start a new program.

- Utterly messing with the Start Thing's menu
- Adding programs to the menu
- Moving and copying programs around between menus
- Removing commands from the menus
- Organizing, moving, and renaming submenus
- Creating your own submenus
- Deleting submenus
- Working with small Start Thing icons (if you care)
- Making some programs start automatically
- Running applications minimized or maximized

Of course, what if your program isn't there? Or worse, what if your program is there but it's buried under submenu after submenu? That certainly isn't handy. To make your programs more accessible, you can modify the Start Thing's menu. In fact, you are the gentle ruler of the Start Menu, the benevolent dictator, the wizard deluxe. Messing with it really isn't a problem.

➡ The sections that follow deal with customizing the Start Thing's menu. Many of the programs there were set up automatically when Windows was installed on your computer. Even so, you may want to change the Start Thing's menu, making it more suitable to the way you work.

⬅➡ General information about starting a program by using the Start Thing's menu can be found in Chapter 3, in the section "Marching through the Start button marsh." Don't forget that you can also paste icons on the desktop, including document icons for the stuff you use frequently. See Chapter 17 for more information about pasting stuff on the desktop.

⬅➡ The Start Thing's menu is for your benefit. It's basically a control center that lists programs which live elsewhere on your computer's hard drive. To see where the programs really are, use My Computer or the Explorer. See Chapter 2 for information about My Computer; Chapter 17 covers the Explorer. Chapter 31, the section "File? File? Here, File! C'mon, Boy! Where'd You Go?," helps you hunt down lost programs, if you "swear" that they're on your computer somewhere.

Stuff that lives on the main Start Thing menu

Seven definite items are on the Start Thing's menu, divided into two groups. A thin dimple line separates the two groups (actually, it just separates the Shutdown command from the items above it). Table 6-1 lists everything.

In addition to the basics, you may also see a second dimple line and even more items on top of the Start Thing menu totem pole (such as in Figure 6-1, in the following section). These are quick-access programs and stuff you can stick on the menu yourself. It's a snap to do so, and it's covered in the very next section.

Table 6-1	Everything You May Normally See on the Start Thing's Menu	
Icon	*Text*	*What It Does*
	Programs	Lists a submenu of programs in your PC, along with even more submenus of programs. Using it is covered in Chapter 3, in the section "Marching through the Start button marsh." Changing it is covered in this chapter.
	Documents	Lists a submenu of recent documents you've opened and enables you to quickly access them again and start applications with them. See the section "Finding your document lurking in the Documents menu" in Chapter 3.
	Settings	Lists a submenu for quick access to three of Windows' dinking tools: the Control Panel (see Chapter 20), the Printers folder (see Chapter 19), and the Taskbar Properties dialog box (see Chapters 6 and 7).
	Find	A special command that helps you find files, folders, and programs on disk. Using this command is covered in Chapter 31.
	Help	Activates Windows' main Help system, where you can look up helpful information about any topic in Windows. See Chapter 4, the section "The Windows Way of Offering Help," for more information about what to do after you choose this option.
	Run	Boring. Brings up a dialog box in which you can *type* the name of a command to run. Yawn. See the section "Running to the Run command to start a program" in Chapter 3 if you can stay awake that long.
	Shutdown	Forces Windows into bankruptcy. Seriously, offers several options for quitting Windows or shutting down for the day. See the section "Quitting Windows and Turning Off Your PC" in Chapter 1.

Sticking something on the main Start Thing menu

You can easily avoid marching through the Start Thing's menu marsh by sticking your very most favorite and popular programs right there on the Start Thing's main menu. That way, you only have to pop up the menu, and you're just one mouse click away from your favorite program. Figure 6-1 shows an example of what I mean, with two popular programs used throughout this book: Paint and WordPad.

Figure 6-1
Popular programs can sit squat on top of the Start Thing's command totem pole.
A. Click here to start Paint. **B.** Click here to start WordPad.
C. Other, less popular programs are hanging on over here.

To place one of your favorite programs on the main menu, like I did in Figure 6-1, follow these steps:

1. Locate the program you want to put on the menu.

   Use My Computer or the Explorer to locate the folder containing the program you want to stick on the menu. Suppose that you want to put WordPad on the menu. Start by opening up My Computer, and then open the disk drive containing the program you want. Typically, this is drive C.

   Next, locate the folder containing your program or the folder containing the folder that contains your program. If you're hunting for WordPad, for example, look in the Program Files folder and then look inside the Accessories folder.

   Look for the program's icon. You may have to scroll the window around to find it.

2. Drag the program icon to the Start button on the taskbar.

   Figure 6-2 shows how it works. You click on the program icon and then keep the mouse button down as you drag it over the Start button. Release the mouse button to "drop" the icon there.

Figure 6-2
Dragging a program icon to the Start Thing's menu.
A. Pick a program's icon. **B.** Drag it with the mouse. **C.** Drag it to the Start Thing.

3. A shortcut copy of the program is now on the menu.

   To prove that you've done it, activate the Start Thing; click on the button or press Ctrl+Esc with the mouse. You see your program's icon living high and mighty on top of the pile.

➠ You haven't really moved the program or its icon. Instead, you've created a shortcut. That way, you can remove the icon later if you like, without worrying about deleting the original program. See Chapter 16 for a discussion of Windows' shortcuts and how they work.

See Chapter 2 for more information about using My Computer, opening folders, and finding program icons.

If you're totally lost and cannot find any programs, see Chapter 31, the section "File? File? Here, File! C'mon, Boy! Where'd You Go?," for some file-hunting help.

Adding a program to a Start Thing submenu

To add a program to a submenu in the Start Thing, you have to use a special corner of the Taskbar Properties dialog box that deals with the Start Thing's menu. You work one of Windows' many "wizards" to help you add the program, which supposedly makes this step as easy as cutting cold butter with a hot knife. Here are the steps:

1. Bring up the Taskbar Properties dialog box.

   Pop up the Start Thing's menu (press Ctrl+Esc), and then choose Settings⇨Taskbar. This step brings up the Taskbar Properties dialog box.

2. Click on the Start Menu Programs panel.

   This step brings it forward, looking much like Figure 6-3.

Figure 6-3
Here is where you add or remove programs from the Start menu.
A. Click here to add a program to the Start Thing's menu. **B.** Click here to remove a program from the Start Thing's menu.
C. Extra special Start Thing menu-tweaking.
D. Clears the contents of the Documents menu (see Chapter 3, the sidebar "Clearing the Documents menu"). **E.** "I'm done!"

Ⓐ   Ⓔ Ⓑ   Ⓒ   Ⓓ

Taskbar Properties   ? ☒

| Taskbar Options | Start Menu Programs |

┌─ Customize Start Menu ──────────────────────┐
│ [icon]   You may customize your Start Menu by │
│   adding or removing items from it.   │
│   │
│   [Add...]   [Remove...]   [Advanced...]│
└──┘

┌─ Documents Menu ────────────────────────────┐
│ [icon]   Click the Clear button to remove the │
│   contents of the Documents Menu.   │
│   │
│   [Clear]   │
└──┘

[OK]   [Cancel]   [Apply]

3. Click on Add.

   The Add button brings up another dialog box, Create Shortcut. What you're doing is creating a shortcut to a program elsewhere on your disk and placing that shortcut in the Start Thing's menu.

   → Shortcuts are a quick way of accessing a program, like making copies of the program but without using up all that extra disk space. Chapter 16 discusses shortcuts in more detail.

4. Click on the Browse button.

   This common button enables you to scour your disk drives and folders for the program you want to add to the Start Thing's menu. Clicking on the button brings up the common Browse dialog box, which is used like the Open dialog box to locate a specific file on disk.

   ← Your task is to locate the program you want to add to the Start Menu. Please turn to Chapter 4, the section "Opening stuff," for additional instructions for using the Browse dialog box, which works exactly the same as the Open dialog box.

5. Find your program.

   Suppose that you want to add the Welcome program to the Accessories⇨System Tools submenu. (Welcome is actually the silly little program that displays the Welcome dialog box when you first start Windows.) To do that, you hunt down the Welcome program.

   Welcome lives in the Windows folder on your C drive. In the Browse dialog box, you're already on drive C. If not, choose drive C from the Look in list box.

   Next, open the Windows folder: Point the mouse at it, and double-click.

   Finally, use the scrollbar at the bottom of the window to scroll right until you see the Welcome program's icon. You've found your program.

   → You don't always have to add programs to a submenu; you can also add documents and folders. To add a document, choose All Files from the Files of type drop-down list box near the bottom of the Browse dialog box. That way, Windows displays all the files on disk, allowing you to pluck out a document as well as a program. See Chapter 15, the section "Opening only files of specific types," for more information about the Files of type list box.

6. Select your program icon by clicking on it.

   Click once on the icon. This step highlights it, selecting the icon for more action.

7. Click on Open.

   This step closes the Browse dialog box and puts the program's geeky pathname into the Create Shortcut dialog box. Ugly, isn't it? For the Welcome program, it may look something like this:

   C:\WINDOWS\Welcome.exe

   ➡ See the nearby sidebar "Another, nerdy way to add a program" for more information about what the pathname really is.

8. Click on Next.

   Rolling right along . . . the next part of the wizard asks you to select a submenu for your program. All the submenus are shown in a list, each one of them represented by a little folder (see Figure 6-4). Just click on the folder you want your program shoved into.

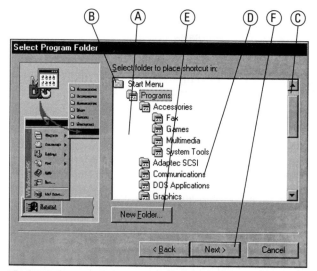

Figure 6-4
The Start Thing's Menu Setup wizard asks you where to stick your program.
A. Click on one of these folders. **B.** Click here to put your program right on the Start Thing's menu. **C.** Scroll up here to see the desktop for adding the program to the desktop. **D.** Logically, communications programs would go here. **E.** Click here to make a new folder (submenu). **F.** Rolling along. . . .

Click on the System Tools folder, for example, to stick the Welcome program there.

Another, nerdy way to add a program

If you're really smart and know exactly where a program lives on your computer, you can just type its name in the box. For example:

WELCOME

Typing this line in the box starts the process of adding the Welcome program.

For some programs, you have to type a full MS-DOS *pathname* in the box. This is for programs that live in out-of-the-way places. If WordPerfect is in the WP62 folder on drive D, for example, you type:

D:\WP62\WP

in the box. That is a pathname, which is covered in Chapter 17 in the section "Beating a pathname to a file's door." If the idea of using it drives you nuts, just stick with the steps for finding files as outlined in this section.

9. Click on the Next button again.

   If you like, you can type a nifty name for the shortcut or menu item you've created. Presently, Windows suggests a simple one, such as "Welcome" for the Welcome program. You can type something more descriptive if you like, such as:

   Welcome to the nightmare that is Windows

10. Click on Finish.

    This step closes the wizard dialog box and returns you to the Taskbar Properties dialog box.

11. Click on OK.

    All done. But check out the Start Thing's menu now. Click on the Start button, and then choose the various submenus to look for your program. It should be there, along with its icon and any rude description you managed to think of in step 9.

Moving things around between the menus

When you install new software, the setup program tends to put your new applications where it thinks they best belong. This usually isn't where *you* think the program should best belong. To make amends, you can cut and paste the program between various Start Thing submenus. This process works just like it did in kindergarten, though there's no eating the paste when you do it on a computer. Follow these steps:

1. Summon the Taskbar Properties dialog box.

   Here is the completely keyboardy way to do this:

   Ctrl+Esc, S, T.

   Press and hold the Ctrl key, and then tap the Esc key. Release both keys. Then press the S key and then the T key. The Taskbar Properties dialog box materializes on the screen.

2. Bring the Start Menu Programs panel to the front.

   Click on the Start Menu Programs panel to bring it forward if it isn't already. (Gaze at Figure 6-3 to see what it should look like.)

3. Click on Advanced.

   Advanced is a button that appears often in Windows dialog boxes. It's designed to scare you away from a feature so handy that only smart people should use it. To prove that you can use it, answer this simple question from the Mensa IQ test:

   What is your name?

   There. You passed, and you're now able to use a miniversion of the Explorer program to mess with the Start Thing's menu, which is shown in Figure 6-5.

   The dialog box you see essentially just concentrates on the Start Menu folder (which is in the Windows folder, if you're curious). Because it's the Explorer you're using, however, you can treat the submenu or folders just like "real" folders and the various menu items (or shortcut icons) just like icons in the Explorer (or even My Computer, for that matter).

   The only difference between this Explorer and the "real" one is that you can manage only those files in the Start menu here. For managing files with the real Explorer, see Chapter 17, the section "Let's go Explorering."

4. Find the file you want to move.

   The Exploring window works just like the Explorer does. You can use the left, All Folders window to climb up and down the folder tree — the *collapsible tree structure.* Or you can use it the My Computer way and stick to opening folders on only the right side of the window.

   Click on the plus sign (+) by a folder's name to open it up and see any folders inside. The plus sign changes to a minus sign (–).

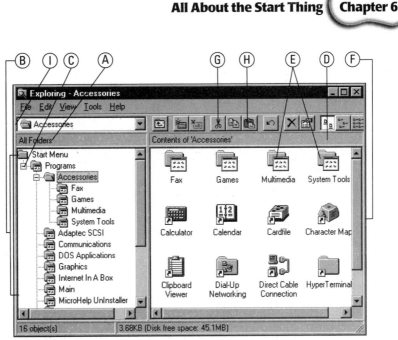

Figure 6-5
The Explorer lets you seriously mess with the Start Thing's menu.
A. The All Folders side of the window. **B.** The collapsible tree-structure thing.
C. Click on all the pluses to turn them into minuses. **D.** The Contents window.
E. These are folders (submenus) in the Accessories menu. **F.** Programs on the
Accessories menu. **G.** Click here to cut an icon. **H.** Click here to paste an icon.
I. See Chapter 2, the section "Whip out the toolbar."

I recommend opening all the folders at one time. Just find each of them
with a plus sign (+) by the name, and click on that plus sign once.
(Click.) Keep doing this from top to bottom until all the folders and
submenus are open. It makes working with them later a snap.

Click on the minus sign (–) by a folder's name to close it up and
"collapse" that part of the tree (if you feel it necessary).

Click on a folder to highlight it and see its contents in the right window.

Use the scrollbars to move the window around if its contents aren't
displayed all at one time.

You can choose a different view for the window. You can look at big
icons, for example, or you can see the files in a details-only view. See
Chapter 2, the section "Different Ways to Look at the Stuff in My
Computer," for more information about changing the way Windows
shows you information.

See Chapter 28, the section "The collapsible tree-structure thing," for
more information about using the collapsible tree-structure thing.

Suppose that you have stuck the Welcome program in the System Tools submenu and feel that it really should go in the Accessories submenu. If so, you have to move it.

Start by opening up the Programs and then Accessories and then System Tools folders and submenus. You'll find your icon, probably called "Welcome to the nightmare that is Windows," nestled there.

5. Select the file.

   Click the mouse once on the file's icon. This step highlights the file, letting you and anyone peeking over your shoulder know that it's selected.

6. Cut it.

   Choose Edit⇨Cut.

   If you love the keyboard, you can press the Ctrl+X key combination.

   Or you can click on the Cut command's button from the toolbar.

   After cutting the program, you'll notice that its icon appears dimmed. This means that it's been cut and hasn't yet been pasted. No biggie, but you should paste it as the very next step. Or two.

7. Locate the folder or submenu where you want to place the file.

   Find the folder where you want to paste the cut program. For example, find the Accessories submenu for pasting the Welcome program into. (This is yet another reason that it's a good idea to expand all the folders and submenus when you first begin.)

8. Highlight that folder or submenu.

   Click once on that folder to select it. The folder's name is highlighted, and you see its current contents in the right window.

9. Paste it.

   Choose Edit⇨Paste.

   Or you can press Ctrl+V or click on the Paste button from the toolbar.

   The icon has been pasted. Its original, faded one was moved up to the new folder, and it appears in the new folder or submenu on the Start Thing's menu. Oh, just you wait and see. . . .

10. Close the Explorer window.

    Click on the × in the window's upper right corner. Zoom! It goes away.

11. Click on OK.

    Finally, click on the OK button in the Taskbar Properties dialog box. Now you can check the Start Thing's menu to ensure that the icon or program name or shortcut was moved. (Don't worry — it was.)

⟹ Cut and copy is how you move files. See the section "Deeply Moving Files" in Chapter 16.

⟹ You can move groups of files by following the preceding steps, but in step 5 select a group of files to move at one time. See Chapter 16, the section "Crowd Control, or Working with Groups of Files."

⟸ You can move even more folders around by following these steps. The difference is that, in steps 4 and 5, you look for and highlight a folder to move. Also see the sections "Patiently organizing the submenus" and "Making your own, unique submenu," later in this very chapter.

Zapping a program from a Start Thing submenu

I believe that the best way to work the Start Thing is to fill its menus with those programs you use the most. As Windows comes out of the box, it puts several of its own programs on various submenus off the Start Thing. Okee-doke. If you're like me, however, you use only a few programs in Windows and rarely need to start any others. It makes sense, therefore, to clear out some of the dead wood.

Before following the steps for removing a program from a Start Thing submenu, you should keep two things bouncing around under your wig:

✗ Deleting a program from the Start Thing's menu doesn't delete the program from your disk. Instead, you're deleting only a shortcut.

✗ Rather than delete a program, you may just want to move it to another submenu. For example, move all the unknown programs to a Weird submenu — one you can create yourself. The following sections offer more details on how to do this.

1. Whip out the Taskbar Properties dialog box.

   You can choose Settings⇨Taskbar from the Start Thing's menu, or right-click the mouse on the taskbar and choose Properties from the menu. This step brings up the Taskbar Properties dialog box.

2. Click on the Start Menu Programs panel to bring it in front if it's not already.

   Refer to Figure 6-3, because I'm too lazy to reproduce it here.

3. Click on Remove.

Click. The Remove Shortcuts/Folders dialog box appears, looking eerily similar to Figure 6-6. It details a common Windows element: — the *collapsible tree structure* — which you can use to find the program you want to remove from the menu.

Figure 6-6

The Remove Shortcuts/Folders dialog box, in which you surgically alter the Start Thing's menu.
A. A minus means that the folder is already open. **B.** A plus means that you can open the folder to see what's inside.
C. Programs in the Accessories folder. **D.** See the section "To Deal with Scrollbars" in Chapter 27 for more information.

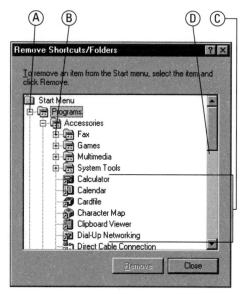

➠ See Chapter 28 for more information about the collapsible tree structure as well as other interesting gizmos and gadgets in Windows dialog boxes.

4. Find the program you want to remove.

Items on the tree structure are organized the same way the Start Thing's menu is organized. There are items and folders, with the folders representing submenus. Folders contain more items and maybe even more folders.

To open a folder or submenu, click on the little plus sign (+) by its name. This step displays the folder's contents and changes the plus sign (+) into a minus sign (–).

To close a folder and hide its contents, click on the minus sign (–) by its name. The minus sign changes back into a plus sign (+).

If you can't see the entire tree-structure thing, you can scroll the list to see items at the bottom.

Any items that are on the main Start menu appear at the bottom of the list by themselves. Yes, you can remove these things too.

5. Click on the program once to select it.

Click on the program's name with the mouse. This step selects it, and it appears highlighted on the screen.

6. Click on the Remove button.

Thwoop! The program's shortcut is gone — removed from the menu. Remember that the program itself hasn't been deleted, only its name.

If you're itching to remove more programs from the menu, repeat steps 4, 5, and 6.

7. Click on the Close button.

The Remove Shortcuts/Folders vanishes.

8. Click on the OK button.

It's Miller time.

You can check the Start Thing's menu to confirm your changes. Programs you've removed are no longer there.

Patiently organizing the submenus

If you don't like the way Windows set up the submenus on the Start Thing's menu, it's a snap to change them. This is all done from the Explorer window, brought up by clicking on the Advanced button in the Taskbar Properties dialog box. Here's how you get there:

1. Bring up the Taskbar Properties dialog box.

From the Start Thing's menu, choose Settings⇨Taskbar.

2. Click on the Start Menu Programs panel to put it in front.

3. Click on Advanced.

◀▥ Refer to the section "Moving things around between the menus," earlier in this chapter, if you need more details about these steps.

◀▥ The Advanced button brings up a miniversion of the Explorer, where you work specifically with folders and files that represent submenus and commands on the Start Thing's own menu. Refer to Figure 6-5 for an illustration.

Open up all the folders on the left side of the Explorer window; click on any plus sign (+) you see by a folder's name or submenu's name. Keep clicking, from top to bottom, until you've opened them all. That makes working with them much easier.

Moving a folder or submenu to a better neighborhood

To move a folder or submenu, follow these steps:

1. Select the folder you want to move.

   Look for the folder in the list on the left side of the window. You may have to use the scrollbar to see those on the very top or bottom.

   When you find the folder you want to move, click on it once using the mouse. This step highlights the folder on the screen, which means that it's selected and ready for play.

2. Choose Edit⇨Cut.

   Use the Cut command in the Edit menu to cut the folder. The folder appears dimmed on the screen, which means that it's about to be cut and pasted elsewhere.

   You could use the Edit⇨Copy command in this step if you want only to copy a menu. However, I can't think of any legitimate reason that anyone would want to do so.

3. Look for the "elsewhere" to paste the folder.

   Climb up and down the Start Thing's menu tree in the left window to find a spot to paste the folder or submenu. If you want the submenu to be a new submenu off the Accessories submenu, for example, click on and highlight the Accessories folder.

   If you click on the main Start menu folder, the submenu hangs right off the Start Thing's menu.

4. Choose Edit⇨Paste.

   The Paste command in the Edit menu completes the Cut operation, moving the folder or submenu over to its new location.

5. Quit the operation, and examine the submenu.

   Close the Explorer window by clicking in its × box. Then click on OK to close the Taskbar Properties dialog box. Now you can examine the Start Thing's menu to see what kind of damage you've done, good or evil (see Figure 6-7).

Renaming a submenu is also possible

To rename a submenu, locate it on the left side of the mini-Explorer's window. (Again, this is a cinch if you expand all the folder or submenus when you start.)

Figure 6-7
A folder pasted right on the Start Thing's menu for quick, handy access.
A. Start Thing. **B.** The regular Programs submenu.
C. A new submenu pasted to the top of the Start Thing.

Right-click the mouse on the submenu's name. A pop-up shortcut menu appears.

Choose Rename.

The folder or submenu's name appears on-screen highlighted and in a box, meaning that you can type a new name.

Type a new name. Make it brief and descriptive. You can use upper- or lowercase letters, spaces, whatever. Shorter is better, though you can stick a massive run-on sentence in there if you like. (Don't.)

Press the Enter key when you're done typing.

Windows may move the folder or submenu in the window after you're done. That's because it alphabetizes the folders. Don't let the pause freak you out.

Close the mini-Explorer window by clicking in its Close (×) box, and then click on the OK button in the Taskbar Properties dialog box. You can now check the Start Thing's menu to justify and gloat over your modifications.

➡ See Chapter 16, the section "Blessing a File with a New Name," for more information about naming a file, including the all-important file-naming rules.

Making your own, unique submenu

To create your own, custom submenu, in which you can place your own, favorite programs, follow these steps:

1. Activate the mini-Explorer, where you can mess with the Start Thing's menu in an "advanced" manner.

   Choose Settings⇔Taskbar from the Start Thing's menu. This step brings up the Taskbar Properties dialog box. Click on the Start Menu Programs tab to bring that panel in front. Then click on the Advanced button. This brings up the mini-Explorer, where you can do the most damage to the Start Thing's menu, all in once place.

2. Choose where you want your new submenu to appear.

   Find the folder or submenu where you want to add on your submenu.

   If you want to add a submenu to the Accessories menu, for example, click on that folder in the left window. This step highlights that folder or submenu and displays its contents in the window to the right.

3. Bring up the shortcut menu for the window on the right.

   Right-click the mouse in the window on the right. Click in a blank part of the window, not on an icon. The shortcut menu for the window (actually for the folder whose contents you're viewing) appears.

4. Choose New⇔Folder.

   Pick Folder from the New submenu on the shortcut menu.

   The new folder's icon appears in the window. It's given the name New Folder, which you should change in the very next step.

5. Type a new name for the folder.

   Make the name brief and descriptive. You can use spaces, capital letters, lowercase, whatever. Press Enter when you're done.

   Remember to keep the programs in the submenu related to its name or topic. For example, a Weird submenu should contain truly weird stuff. Put graphics programs and such into any Graphics submenu you create. Follow this pattern to help keep the Start Thing's menu — and yourself — organized and sane.

6. You witness a menu being created.

   You can view your new baby in the window to the left (though you may have to click on the plus sign (+) by the current folder's name to see it).

7. Close up shop.

   Click on the × button to close the mini-Explorer window. Then click on OK in the Taskbar Properties dialog box.

   The menu you created is empty. In fact, if you were to choose it from the Start Thing's menu, you'd see the word *Empty* displayed in hollow-looking text rather than any program names.

← Your job now is to add programs and commands to the new menu. See the section "Adding a program to a Start Thing submenu," earlier in this chapter, for information about how that's done. Or look at the section "Moving things around between the menus" for information about cutting and pasting programs from other menus into your new menu.

Cruelly deleting a submenu

Making a submenu go away for good is a drastic but sometimes necessary step. Most of the time this happens when you feel comfortable tweaking the Start Thing's menu and, lo, discover that there are some submenus you really could do without. When that happens, feel free to delete them.

→ When you delete a submenu, you also delete all the commands inside it. Keep in mind that these are only shortcuts, not the real programs themselves. So it's not anything important you're deleting, it's just a nifty way to start a program from the Start Thing's menu. If it's a program you want to delete rather than a submenu or menu command, see Chapter 13, which covers uninstalling programs (as well as installing them).

1. Bring up the Taskbar Properties dialog box.

   From the Start Thing's menu, choose Settings⇨Taskbar. This step displays the Taskbar Properties dialog box.

2. Bring the Start Menu Programs panel forward by clicking the mouse on its tab.

3. Click on the Advanced button.

   A copy of the Explorer appears, one that enables you to tweak and modify programs and submenus on the Start Thing's menu.

   Programs and menu commands appear as icons in the right window.

   Menus and submenus appear as folders in a collapsible tree structure in the left window and as folder icons in the right window.

4. Find the folder or submenu you want to utterly zap.

Search through the collapsible tree structure in the left window. Click on the plus sign (+) by a folder or submenu to see its submenus. Keep doing this if you don't find the submenu you want to blow to smithereens.

5. Select that submenu.

Click on it once with the mouse. This step highlights the folder or submenu on the screen, ready for action.

6. Choose File⇨Delete.

A warning dialog box may appear, questioning whether you want to remove the submenu. Click on Yes.

The submenu is gone. Or rather the submenu has been evicted to live in the Recycle Bin with the rest of Windows' refuse.

Just because the submenu was deleted doesn't mean that it's gone for good. You can always recover it from the Recycle Bin later. See Chapter 5, the section "A quick, odorless peek into the Recycle Bin to restore something," for all the gory details.

7. Close the mini-Explorer window.

Click on its × Close button.

8. Close the Taskbar Properties dialog box.

Click on OK.

You will notice that the submenu is missing the next time you use the Start Thing's menu.

Radically Altering the Appearance of the Start Thing

Unfortunately, you can't radically alter the Start Thing. Instead, there is only one tiny modification you can make: The icons can be either small or large. That's it. And here's how:

1. Conjure up the Taskbar Properties dialog box.

Bring up the Start Thing's menu by clicking on the Start button. Then choose Settings⇨Taskbar. This step displays the Taskbar Properties dialog box.

2. Find the check-box option that reads "Show small icons in Start menu."

3. Click in that box.

   This step puts a ✔ check mark in the box, meaning that the option is switched on. You see the little icons previewed in the window near the top of the dialog box.

   Do you like the preview? If so, move on to step 4. Otherwise, click in the box again to remove the ✔ and restore the Start Thing to how you liked it before.

4. Click on OK.

   You're done.

◄■■■ Any other modifications to the Start Thing's menu involve changing the submenus or programs. This subject is beaten down in the first part of this chapter.

■■■► You can also move the taskbar to various other positions on the screen. I believe that this subject is covered in Chapter 24, along with information about the other check-box items in the Taskbar Options panel of the Taskbar Properties dialog box.

Applications that Amazingly Start Automatically

Why bother with the Start Thing at all? Aren't computers supposed to make your life easier? Well, what's so easy about having a computer go through all that startup hoopla, and then you have to mess with the Start Thing the same way, every day, to start the same program? Doesn't sound time-saving, does it? And does every sentence in this paragraph end in a question mark?

Windows has the capability to automatically start a given program — or a set of programs — every time you turn on your computer. Ideally, these should be either programs you start yourself every day (the manual approach) or programs you just like to have handy, humming along and ready when you need them.

Adding programs to the Startup submenu

A special submenu in the Start Thing is named Startup. It contains a list of programs, just like any other menu. The difference is that Windows goes through this menu and starts every program in it, all automatically, all every time you start Windows.

Obviously, this is a handy thing to have. In fact, you may already have a few programs there, such as the Microsoft Office toolbar or button bar, maybe some networking programs, or a screen saver like After Dark.

← To add a program to the Startup menu, follow the steps for adding a program to any menu, as outlined earlier in this chapter, in the section "Adding a program to a Start Thing submenu."

➡ For suggestions on what to add, see the next section.

← Obviously, if you have a program that starts up every time you start Windows and you don't like that fact, you can remove it from the Startup menu (or just move it elsewhere). To remove it, see the section "Zapping a program from a Start Thing submenu." If you just want to move it to another menu, see the section "Moving things around between the menus."

Some cool programs to add to the Startup submenu

It makes sense to add to the Startup submenu any program you first start up when you run Windows.

If you always start the day by dialing up Prodigy, for example, just stick a copy of its icon in the Startup submenu. That way, your computer always starts and Prodigy is up there, waiting for you to make your first call.

Prodigy

Cardfile is a handy little Rolodex of sorts, one you can use to store names, phone numbers — even graphical images. I use it as a Rolodex myself, shunning those other sophisticated programs that take too long to use.

Cardfile

➡ Read all sorts of cool tips about Cardfile in Chapter 9, in the section "Your Own Li'l Rolodex (the Cardfile)."

← Another cool networking tool to use is the WinPopup program. That program can be found in your Windows folder. Use the steps detailed in the section "Adding a program to a Start Thing submenu," earlier in this chapter, for information about adding that program to the Startup submenu.

Winpopup

➠ See Chapter 22, the section "The joys of WinPopup," for more information.

Other ideas for handy things to add to the Startup menu include: a day planner; a contact or "tickler" program (so that you can have your names, dates, and contacts ready every time Windows starts); the Explorer (some folks like starting the Explorer every time Windows starts); and if you always plan on starting some other, major application, consider copying that program from its submenu in the Start Thing over to the Startup menu.

Running a program "minimized" when it starts

When you start a program in Windows, it normally appears full-blown, big on the screen, massive to deal with. This may not be the case with the programs you want started automatically in the Startup menu. You may want to start your Rolodex, for example, but because you don't need it right away, it would be nice to run it minimized, out of sight.

To make a program start *minimized,* or as a button on the taskbar and not as a full-screen program, follow these steps:

1. Locate the Startup menu in the mini-Explorer.

   From the Start Thing's menu, choose Settings⇨Taskbar. This step displays the Taskbar Properties dialog box. From there, click on the Start Menu Programs tab to bring that panel forward. Then click on the Advanced button. This displays the mini-Explorer you can use to work with the programs and submenus on the Start Thing.

   From the left side of the dialog box, choose the Startup folder. Click on it once with the mouse. This step displays the items on the Startup menu in the window on the right.

2. Right-click on the program's shortcut icon.

   Suppose that you're modifying the WinPopup program to run minimized. Find that program's icon in the window, point the mouse at it, and then right-click. This displays the program's shortcut menu.

3. Choose Properties from the shortcut menu.

   The program's Properties dialog box appears.

4. Click on the Shortcut tab.

   This step brings the Shortcut panel up front (see Figure 6-8).

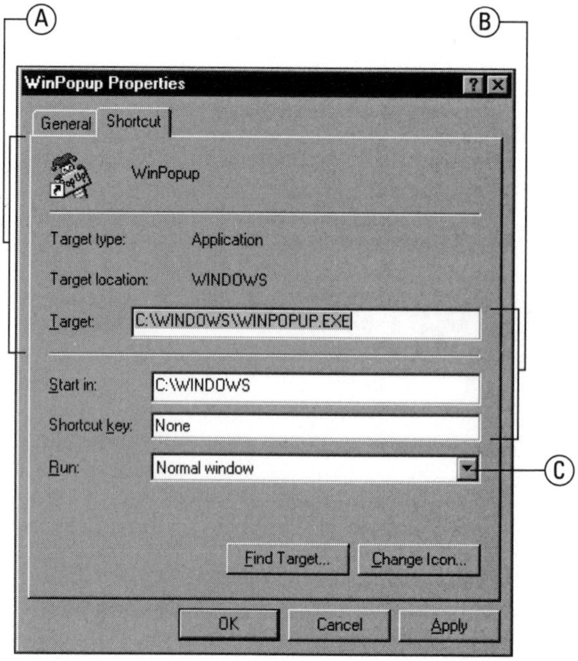

Figure 6-8
Here, you can choose how a program is initially run.
A. Yeah, yeah. **B.** Whatever. **C.** From here, choose how you want the program to run.

5. Choose Minimized from the Run drop-down list box.

   Near the bottom of the dialog box is a list box with the word *Run* by it. Click on the down arrow by that list box. This displays three options for the program's window when it starts. Click the mouse on the word *Minimized.*

6. Click on OK.

   This step closes the Properties dialog box.

   If you want to reset more programs to run minimized, repeat steps 2 through 5 for each of those programs. Choose Minimized in their Properties dialog box, and those programs will start unobtrusively as buttons on the taskbar rather than as full-blown programs.

7. Close the mini-Explorer.

   Click on the × in the upper right corner of the window. This makes that window go away.

8. Click on OK in the Taskbar Properties dialog box.

   It goes away as well.

Now your Startup programs will run minimized — at least those you've set to do so. Personally, I find this neater than cluttering the desktop with big windows when Windows starts.

Maximizing your programs is also possible

Just as you may want to run some of your Startup applications minimized, you'll probably want to run most of your other programs maximized, to fill the screen. You can do this when the program starts by clicking on its Maximize button, or you can preset the program to always do that by altering the steps in this section.

Start in step 1 by locating the program you want to always start maximized. Look in its own folder or submenu. (It probably won't live in the Startup menu, which is what step 1 helps you find.)

Change step 5 so that you choose Maximized from the list, not Minimized. This ensures that Windows will start the program full screen, which is the way I recommend running most of your major applications.

Continue with the rest of the steps as necessary. This saves you a few mouse clicks when you start a program, because Windows will automatically start it full-screen.

Part II Getting Work Done

Getting to Know the Taskbar

The taskbar is Windows' home base. It's the place where the Start Thing lives, the spot you return to time and again to do something new or to revive something old. (Boy, would that make great copy for a travel brochure or what?) The taskbar ties in to much of what Windows does. In addition to starting new tasks with the Start Thing, the taskbar is the main tool you use to switch between tasks in the fun game that is multitasking. Plus, the taskbar has controls for setting the PC's speaker volume and time. It's just chock full o' excitement.

➡ This chapter assumes that the taskbar is on the bottom of your screen. Yes, it's true: The taskbar can be moved. It can even be removed. For more information, see Chapter 24.

➡ Multitasking is the art of running more than one program at a time, which can really be a boost to your productivity. See Chapter 8 for all the details and plenty o' demos.

Chapter 7

In This Chapter

- Taskbar buttons and the windows they love
- Dealing with too many buttons on the taskbar
- Playing with the things in the Loud Time area on the taskbar
- Setting your PC's speaker volume
- Introducing the printer dude, modem guy, and fax/modem things
- Setting the current time in Windows
- Messing with the taskbar's shortcut menu

Buttons and Windows Galore

For every window that is open on the desktop, there is a corresponding button on the taskbar. Open a window, grow a button. Open lots of windows, grow lots of buttons. And when you close the windows, the buttons go away.

The main reason for connecting a window on the screen with a button is that the taskbar helps you to find that window in a hurry. Figure 7-1 shows several buttons on the taskbar. Each button represents a window, either somewhere on the desktop or a window that's been minimized.

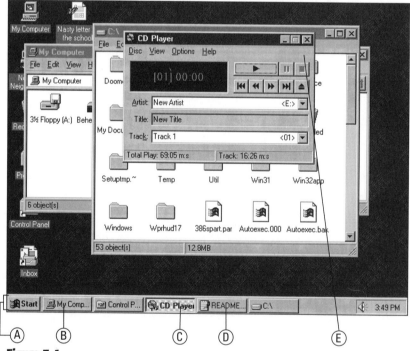

Figure 7-1
Quickly find a window in this mess by using the taskbar.
A. Each of these buttons (except for Start) represents a window. **B.** To switch to the My Computer window, click on this button. **C.** The CD Player button is "down" because that window is on top. **D.** You can't see this window on the desktop because it's minimized. Click on this button to see the window. **E.** For more information about the CD Player, see the section "Playing a musical CD" in Chapter 14.

➥ Clicking on a taskbar button to display a window comes in especially handy when all windows are "zoomed," or *maximized,* to fill the entire screen. In that case, you can't see any other windows on the desktop, and clicking on a button on the taskbar is one of your only other options. See Chapter 27, the section "The Wonder of Maximize and Restore," for more information about maximizing a window.

➥ Windows and their buttons also represent programs you're running. Yes, you can run more than one program at a time in Windows. Yes, you can click on their buttons on the taskbar to switch instantly between two or more running programs. See the section "An Episode in Multitasking," in Chapter 8, for a taste of how that works.

Too Many Buttons on the Taskbar!

Figure 7-2 shows what a normal button looks like on the taskbar. Ahhh. Figure 7-3 shows the nightmare of what happens when too many buttons are on the taskbar. The icons go away. The names get truncated. Pretty soon, it gets so ugly that, well, you might as well be using DOS.

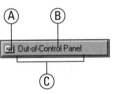

Figure 7-2
A nice, fat, healthy button on the taskbar.
A. The program or window's icon. **B.** The program or window's name. **C.** A nice, fat, easy-to-read, wide-screen button.

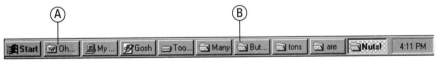

Figure 7-3
A messy, overbuttoned taskbar.
A. A mere fragment of text to "describe" the button. **B.** Buttons closer together than houses in a San Diego housing tract.

A taskbar with too many buttons on it doesn't do you any good. It doesn't make any fashion sense. Put too many buttons on a cotton shirt and it looks gaudy. If you put a lot of buttons on a rubber shirt, however, and then stretch the shirt out to a larger size, it becomes more aesthetically pleasing. For those times when the taskbar has too many buttons, your only solution is to stretch out the taskbar and make it fatter. Here's how:

1. Hover the mouse pointer over the top edge of the taskbar.

   The mouse pointer changes to an up-down pointing-arrow thing. That means that the mouse is set to drag and move something. ↕

2. Press and hold the mouse's button.

   Press and hold down the main button, the one on the left. You notice that a fuzzy line appears around the taskbar.

3. Drag the mouse up, making the taskbar fatter.

   The line drags up in given increments, each time making the taskbar's outline appear fatter on the screen. If you don't notice the taskbar's outline getting fatter, keep dragging the mouse upward.

4. Release the mouse button when the taskbar is twice as large.

   Or maybe even release the button when the taskbar is three times as large. What you see looks something like Figure 7-4 — a fat taskbar, where the buttons are legible.

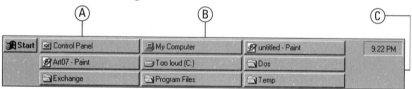

Figure 7-4
With a fatter taskbar, you can see all the buttons.
A. Grab the taskbar on this edge and drag up. **B.** Buttons you can read! **C.** To give you more desktop space, drag back down after closing some windows.

These steps essentially just stretch out the taskbar, the way you'd stretch out a rubber shirt. You can use the same steps to restore the taskbar down to normal size: Just drag the taskbar's top edge down rather than up.

➡ A fat taskbar shows buttons with *both* their icons and text. It makes using the buttons easier, but the trade-off is that the taskbar eats up more screen space. If you like the fatter taskbar, you can get by with a smaller screen area, by changing the screen's resolution, a subject found in Chapter 24, in the section "The Screen-Resolution Revolution."

➡ If you drag the mouse too far left or right, you actually flip the taskbar over to another side of the screen. This action changes the look of Windows and is one of many things you can do to make Windows look different, a subject also covered in Chapter 24, in the section "Messing with the taskbar" specifically.

Having Fun with the Loud Time

Off to one end of the taskbar, playing teeter-totter with the Start Thing, is what I call the *Loud Time*. It's a graphic of a megaphone apparently shouting out the current time of day (see Figure 7-5).

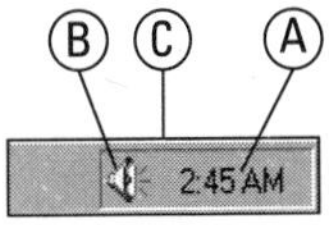

Figure 7-5
The Loud Time shouts out that it's 2:45 A.M., way past the author's bedtime.
A. The time of day. Click here to see the full date. **B.** Click on the volume button to set the PC's speaker volume. **C.** Other things appear in here from time to time.

The Loud Time can show you several things, depending on how your computer is set up and what it's doing:

This is the volume button, which enables you to adjust the PC's speaker volume (if you have a sound system installed).

The printer dude appears whenever you're printing something and then immediately goes away.

The modem guy appears when you're connected to an online service, such as the Microsoft Network. Speaking of which. . .

When you're connected to the Microsoft Network, its little icon appears on the taskbar.

See Chapter 11 for more information about the Microsoft Network (as well as other online services that may or may not have figured out how to put their logo next to the modem guy).

You have mail! When you're connected to a network and mail awaits you or when mail is available on CompuServe or the Microsoft Network, you see the little, happy mail guy.

See Chapter 22 for more information about reading your mail.

Whenever you send a fax or your computer is set up to receive one, the fax guy appears in the loud-time area. There are variations on a theme here; for example, a sheet of paper appears next to the fax when you're sending something.

The current time, A.M. or P.M.

To find out more information about any of these items — and even more that may appear from time to time — hover the mouse pointer over it. A pop-up bubble appears, telling you more than you need to know about what your computer is doing.

If you click the mouse on one of the little taskbar guys, something interesting happens: Either you get more information about what the little guy does, or you see a dialog box in which settings can be adjusted.

Setting the PC's speaker volume

If you click the mouse on the taskbar's volume button, a volume slider pops up (see Figure 7-6). This is where you can adjust the PC's speaker volume, making the noise your computer squawks louder or softer or turning it off altogether.

Figure 7-6
The volume button helps adjust the PC's speaker volume.
A. Use this slider to adjust the PC's speaker volume. **B.** LOUDER.
C. Softer. **D.** Put a ✔ here to mute the volume. **E.** Click out here anywhere to make the volume adjuster go away.

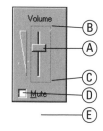

➡ Obviously, this little sucker doesn't appear if you don't have a volume guy on your taskbar. See the nearby sidebar "But I don't see the volume control!" for more information.

Hanging out with printer dude

The little printer icon comes and goes as quickly as you print. When printing stops, he goes away. Sometimes, if you have a fast printer, you never see him. Nope, not ever.

If you hover the mouse pointer over printer dude, you see information about which printer is printing and who's printing what. For example, it may say something like this:

    1 document(s) pending for Mary Munchkin

➡ You can always get information about what's printing by checking out the printer icon associated with your PC's printer. Chapter 19 discusses how that stuff works.

"But I can't see the clock!"

The clock isn't a fixed part of the taskbar, and, in fact, nothing on the right side of the taskbar is there permanently. To see the clock if you can't presently (or to hide it), follow these steps:

1. **Activate the Start Thing.** Click on the Start button, or press Ctrl+Esc. Either way, the Start Thing's menu pops up.

2. **Choose Settings⇨Taskbar.** The Taskbar Properties dialog box appears.

3. **Click in the box by Show Clock.** If a ✔ appears in the box, the current time appears on the taskbar. If the box is empty, the clock doesn't show up. Click on the mouse once in the box to change from the ✔ to nothing or back again.

4. **Click on OK.** The Taskbar Properties dialog box is retired, and you now have a clock (or not) on the taskbar.

"But I don't see the volume control!"

If you don't see the volume control, you either don't have a PC that can bleep or, somehow, your computer wasn't set up properly. To see the volume control, follow these steps:

1. **Open My Computer.** See Chapter 2 if you need help with this step.

2. **From My Computer's main window, open the Control Panel.** It's a folder with a hammer and some other tool on it.

3. **In the Control Panel's window, locate the Multimedia icon.**

4. **Double-click on the Multimedia icon to open it.** This step displays the Multimedia Properties dialog box.

5. **Click on the Audio panel to bring it in front.**

6. **Click on the mouse in the box by Show volume control on the taskbar.** This step puts an × in the box, which causes Windows to display the volume button.

7. **Click on OK in the Multimedia Properties dialog box to close it.** The volume button appears on the taskbar when the window disappears.

8. **Close the Control Panel window and My Computer's window if you want.** Get back to work.

Messing with the modem guy

The modem guy on the taskbar tells you when you're online and sending or receiving information. When you click on him, a dialog box appears, telling you what the modem is doing (see Figure 7-7).

Figure 7-7
The dialog box you see when you click on the taskbar's modem guy.
A. An external modem. **B.** Bytes sent. **C.** Bytes received. **D.** A modem happily communicating at 14400 BPS. **E.** Click here after being totally thrilled.

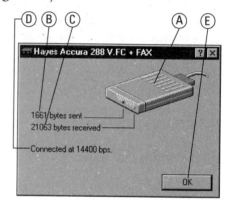

If you just hover the mouse pointer over the modem guy when you're connected to another computer (or "online"), you see the bytes sent and received appear in a little bubble. Major whoop-de-doo factor there.

➠ The modem guy on the taskbar lets you know that your modem is on and working, which can be beneficial if you have an internal modem. On external modems, you can see the reassuring blinking lights. For more information about the fun world of computer communications, flip the pages up to Chapter 11.

"But I don't see the modem guy, fax thing, et cetera!"

Relax. He shows up only when your computer is talking to another computer with the modem. Same deal with the fax/modem things, unless your computer is configured to answer incoming faxes, in which case you see the tiny fax-machine guy all the time.

The envelope, please

Seeing the wee, little envelope guy on the taskbar means that you have mail waiting somewhere, either from your computer network or an online service, such as CompuServe or the Internet or the Microsoft Network.

Hover the mouse pointer over the envelope guy, and he says, "You have new mail."

To read your mail, double-click on the little "you have mail" envelope guy. This starts the Microsoft Exchange program, which enables you to read and compose mail.

➠ See Chapter 22 for more information about Microsoft Exchange, in the section "Stop! Oh, Yes, Wait a Minute, Mr. Postman!"

➠ Obviously, you have to connect to an online service before you can get mail; see Chapter 11.

The fax/modem things

The fax/modem thing, or rather, *things,* appear only when you're messing with faxes, either sending or receiving.

➠ Sending a fax is much like printing, which is why all that information has been conveniently located in that same place, Chapter 19.

Fooling with the time (or, setting the time on your PC)

Forget the date? Point your mouse pointer at the time in the taskbar, and a bubble pops up, displaying the current date and time in its full format. That way, you can find out whether it's Saturday so that you can stop working on the computer.

If you double-click on the time, a dialog box appears (see Figure 7-8), enabling you to set the current date and time for your computer. This feature comes in handy for those times, which is probably most of the time, when your computer has lost track of the time.

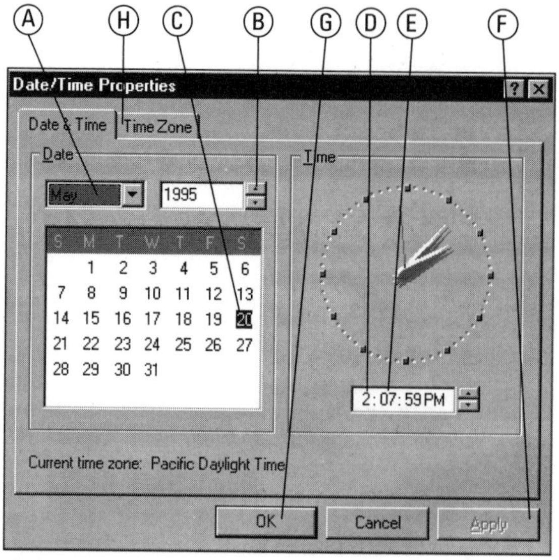

Ⓐ   Ⓗ Ⓒ   Ⓑ   Ⓖ Ⓓ Ⓔ   Ⓕ

Date/Time Properties   ? ✕

Date & Time | Time Zone

┌─ Date ──────────────────┐ ┌─ Time ──────────────┐
│ May ▼   1995   ▲▼   │
│   │
│ S M T W T F S   │
│   1 2 3 4 5 6 │
│   7 8 9 10 11 12 13 │
│   14 15 16 17 18 19 **20** │
│   21 22 23 24 25 26 27 │
│   28 29 30 31   │
│   │
│   │   2:07:59 PM ▲▼
│   │
│ Current time zone: Pacific Daylight Time │

        OK   Cancel   Apply

Figure 7-8

Set your PC's date and time in this dialog box.
A. Set the month from the drop-down list here. **B.** Use this spinner to set the current year. **C.** Click the mouse on the current date. **D.** Double-click the mouse here, and then use the spinner to set the hour. **E.** Set the minutes the same as the hour. **F.** Click on this button to set the time. **G.** Click here when you're done with this dialog box. **H.** Click on this tab to set your time zone.

➠ "Drop-down list?" "Spinner?" Crazy gadgets like these infest many Windows dialog boxes. Take a tour of Chapter 28 to get more information about how each of them works.

Set the time in the Date/Time Properties dialog box to about a minute from now. Set the seconds to zero-zero. Then dial up the time on your phone. When the nice lady says that it's blah-blah o'clock and blah minutes *exactly*, click on the Apply button. This step sets the PC's time to whatever time you've entered.

The Time Zone panel in the Date/Time Properties dialog box enables you to set which time zone your computer lives in. Click on that tab with the mouse to bring that panel forward in the dialog box. It shows a global map with the current time zone highlighted (see Figure 7-9). To set a new time zone, click the mouse on the part of the map where your computer lives.

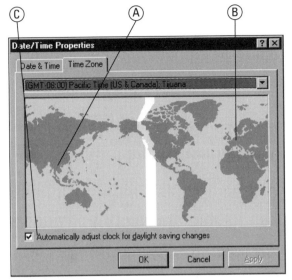

Figure 7-9
Windows must know the time zone or else it zones.
A. Know your geography? Click on your house on this map. **B.** Si vous habitez à Paris, cliquez ici. **C.** Click here if your part of the country obeys daylight savings time. A ✔ appears in the box when this option is set (optional in some parts of Indiana).

Click on the OK button in the Date/Time Properties dialog box when you're done messing with it.

Other Taskbar Stuff

Like everything else in the Windows universe (or almost everything else), the taskbar has its own pop-up shortcut menu. Figure 7-10 shows what it looks like.

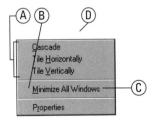

Figure 7-10
The taskbar's shortcut menu.
A. These three commands arrange any open windows on the desktop. For an example of why this would be necessary, see Chapter 2, the section "Oh, lordy, I have too many windows open!" **B.** To see how to use this command, visit the section "Shoving it all aside to see the desktop" in Chapter 5. **C.** Activates the Taskbar Properties dialog box. **D.** Click out here somewhere to make this pop-up menu go away.

You have to right-click the mouse on a blank area of the taskbar to see the shortcut menu. This can be tricky. Finding a blank area on a taskbar full o' buttons is similar to finding a parking space at the mall during Christmas. If you can't find a blank spot, however, click on the current time on the far right side of the taskbar. That displays the time thing's shortcut menu, which is identical to the taskbar's, with the addition of one time-specific item on top.

◄─ One technique guaranteed to get you a blank space on the taskbar is to make the taskbar fatter. See the section "Too Many Buttons on the Taskbar!," earlier in this chapter, for more information.

◄─ To arrange icons on the desktop, you have to use the desktop's own short-cut menu. See Chapter 5, the section "Arranging the stuff that loiters on the desktop."

──► The Taskbar Properties dialog box contains four items, only two of which
◄─ control the way the taskbar looks or behaves. Those two items, Always on top and Auto hide, are covered in Chapter 24, in the section "Messing with the Taskbar." The other two items there, Show small icons in Start menu and Show Clock, are covered in Chapter 6, in the section "Radically Altering the Appearance of the Start Thing," and in this chapter, in the sidebar "But I can't see the clock!," respectively.

──► Each of the other little guys on the taskbar has its own shortcut menu and items. Sometimes these items are just the same as those on the taskbar's shortcut menu, plus a few specific ones. Most of the time, the shortcut menus enable you to adjust the properties for whatever it was you clicked on or to see special dialog boxes pertaining to whatever it is the little guy does. As an example, see Chapter 19 for information about the shortcut menus for the printer and fax/modem things.

Multitasking, Sharing, Loving

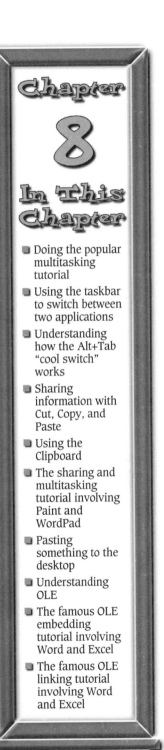
Multitasking is a scary computer term. Honestly, it really means "can do more than one thing at a time." I remember watching a home movie where I was fishing and chewing gum. My mother jibed, "See, you can do two things at once!" Ever since then, I've remembered that as *multitasking*. Fishing and chewing gum at the same time is multitasking.

Windows can multitask quite well. It can run dozens of programs at one time. You never really have to quit one to start another. Aside from that, Windows also ensures that each program remains friendly to any others that are running at the same time. It does this by allowing you to copy or cut and then paste information between two programs, even two programs of different natures. It's all part of sharing and loving, which plays in well with Windows' multitasking motif.

An Episode in Multitasking

Multitasking is one of those "How did you do that?" tricks. It's something a seasoned

Windows user casually does in front of you, and it just pops your eyeballs out. "I didn't know you could do that!" Yet it really isn't that big of a deal to do and can save you hours of time and dozens of steps after you know how it works.

◄▬ The only part of multitasking madness you have to remember is that you don't really have to quit one program to start another. Try minimizing once in a while. See Chapter 4, the section "Done for the Day? To Quit or Put Away," for more information.

Switching applications with the taskbar

Each button on the taskbar represents a window on the screen. Most of the time, windows on the screen represent programs. One window equals one program. In Figure 8-1, which shows only the taskbar, you can see that two programs are running in Windows: Paint and WordPad.

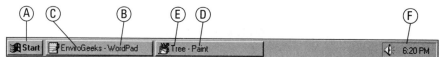

Figure 8-1
The taskbar shows you that both Paint and WordPad are running.
A. The Start Thing. **B.** This button represents WordPad. **C.** The EnviroGeeks document is loaded. **D.** This button represents Paint. **E.** The Tree document is being worked on. **F.** See Chapter 7, the section "Having Fun with the Loud Time."

To switch from one program to the other, simply click the mouse on its button on the taskbar. Click on Paint, go to Paint. Click on WordPad, go to WordPad. You never really have to quit one program and start another.

◄▬ If the program has been minimized, or shrunk down to a button on the taskbar, clicking that button automatically unminimizes the program's window and zooms it back up to the size it was. If the program is full-window, or maximized (see Chapter 1, the section "Working in Windows"), clicking the button is just about the only way to get to other windows or programs on the desktop.

◄▬ Remember that you don't really have to quit any program in Windows. Instead, you can merely put something aside, by shrinking it down to a button on the taskbar, which you can then use later. See the section "Done for the Day? To Quit or Put Away" in Chapter 4.

▬► Switching between two running programs is called *multitasking*. It can really come in handy, especially when you're creating something that requires the tools offered by more than one program. For a good example of this type of application using both Paint and WordPad, see the next section.

← Most programs have only one window and, therefore, have only one button on the taskbar. Some programs have more than one window, in which case they hog up the taskbar with lots of buttons. An example is My Computer (covered in Chapter 2). My Computer may have several windows open at one time, yet all of them belong to the same program. Check out the section "Too Many Buttons on the Taskbar!" in Chapter 7 for help in dealing with an overbuttoned taskbar.

A multitasking tutorial involving Paint and WordPad

Figure 8-2 shows a WordPad document that contains graphics. This is something very simple that you can slap together in only a matter of moments. What makes it so easy is Windows' capability to switch documents.

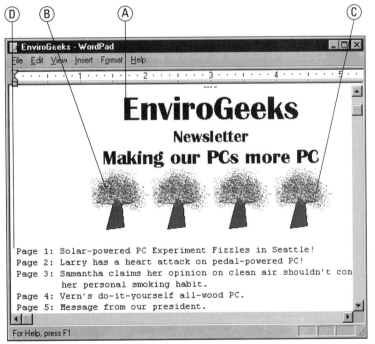

Figure 8-2
You too can create this nifty WordPad document with a Paint picture in the middle.
A. Text created in WordPad. **B.** A picture created in Paint. **C.** The picture was pasted in several times and then centered. **D.** More text from WordPad.

To create the document shown in Figure 8-2 (or at least one similar to it), you need two tools: the Paint program and WordPad. Paint helps you create art; WordPad, text. Because working with text is the main purpose of the document, you mix the art with the text in WordPad. (Conversely, if there is less text than art, you mix in the text in Paint.) Here are the steps to take:

1. Start a new Paint document.

   Don't rush ahead! It's tempting to start the Paint application by trudging through the Start Thing's menu. But don't! This is Windows 95. Instead, do this:

2. Bring up the desktop's shortcut menu.

   Right-click the mouse on a blank part of the desktop.

   Minimize some windows if you can't see any desktop. You can always right-click the mouse on the taskbar and choose Minimize All Windows from the shortcut menu. That guarantees you a blank screen with lots of acres for clicking.

3. Choose New⇨Bitmap Image.

   A new icon is created and placed on the desktop. It's a bitmap image icon, the type of document that belongs to the Paint application that came with Windows.

   There is an off, off chance that you may not see Bitmap Image on the menu. This means that Windows' Paint program was not installed when Windows was set up on your computer. Boo-hoo. This situation can be remedied, however. All you need are Windows' original installation disks (or the CD) and the information found in the section "Adding the Rest of Windows" in Chapter 13.

4. Give the file a name.

   The document icon you created is given the boring name New Bitmap Image.

   Yawn. Give it a better name. It's going to be a picture of a tree, so name it Tree. Type **Tree**.

   Notice that Tree replaces the other, boring name the file was given.

   Press the Backspace key to erase if you make a mistake.

   Press the Enter key when you're done.

5. Press the Enter key to open the document.

   Because the Tree document is already highlighted on the desktop, press the Enter key to open it. This step starts the Paint application, loaded with your Tree document ready for editing.

It's possible to start any application by starting the documents it creates. This subject was hashed over in Chapter 3, specifically in the section "Starting a document stuck to the desktop."

6. Maximize Paint.

It's best to work with an application full-screen, so click on the Paint application window's Maximize button. This step zooms the window out to full-size, which makes anything on the desktop or in the background less distracting.

If you find the taskbar distracting, you can temporarily get rid of it as well. See Chapter 24, the section "Messing with the Taskbar."

7. Create art.

Draw a picture that looks sort of like the one in Figure 8-2 (see Figure 9-5, in Chapter 9, for a close-up). Basically, it's a tree. This is something that just about anyone can draw; you'd be surprised how easy it is on a computer.

Would you believe me if I told you that expert tree-drawing instructions can be found in Chapter 9? See the section appropriately titled "Expert tree-drawing instructions."

8. Save your work.

Choose File⇨Save. This step saves your work in the Tree file on the desktop.

9. Put the Paint program aside.

This is the point where you normally quit the Paint program, but here you're just setting it aside while you work on something else. To put the Paint program aside, click on its Minimize button. This step shrinks it down to a button on the taskbar. The Paint program is still "on," but you've just set it aside while you work on something else.

10. Start a new WordPad document.

Unfortunately, you can't start a WordPad document on the desktop like you can start a Paint (Bitmap) document. (If you choose New⇨Text Document from the desktop's shortcut, you get a Notepad document, not WordPad.) Therefore, you have to resort to the old-fashioned way of doing things:

From the Start Thing's menu, choose Programs⇨Accessories⇨WordPad. This step starts WordPad with a fresh document for you to edit.

11. Save the Document on the desktop.

Inside WordPad, choose File⇨Save As. You see the Save As dialog box displayed.

In the list of folders, look for one named Desktop. (It's in the Windows folder, in case you don't see Windows in the Save in drop-down list.) Double-click on Desktop to open it.

Press the Tab key until the File name input box is highlighted; the text that reads "Document" should appear in inverse highlight. Then type the following line:

EnviroGeeks

Type EnviroGeeks as shown here, with capital *E* and capital *G.* Press the Backspace key to back up and erase if you make a mistake.

Click on the Save button. You've just saved your new document on the desktop. (To prove it, minimize WordPad and you'll see "EnviroGeeks" right there next to your Tree document.)

See Chapter 4, the section "Saving your stuff," for more information about using the Save As dialog box.

12. Maximize WordPad.

    Zoom WordPad out to fill the entire screen, which makes working with it much easier. Click on the window's Maximize button to do so. Thwoop! The window fills the screen.

13. Compose your text.

    Write away.

    The text you want to enter is found in Chapter 9, in the section titled "Let WordPad Bring Out the Shakespeare in You." Enter the text as described in that chapter to create a document similar to the one in Figure 8-2.

14. Save your work.

    Choose File⇨Save, or click on the wee Save button on the toolbar. This step saves your work in the Tree file on the desktop.

15. Minimize WordPad.

    Put WordPad away. Don't quit. There's no need to quit.

16. Switch to Paint.

    Click the mouse on the Paint button on the taskbar.

    The Paint program's window zooms out to fill the screen. Everything is as you left it.

17. Switch back to WordPad.

    Don't bother minimizing Paint this time. Just click on the WordPad button on the taskbar. Voom! WordPad fills the screen, just as you left it.

18. Keep both programs open for the next tutorial in this chapter.

▸ As you work between two programs, you also share information. This is done by using Windows' popular Cut, Copy, and Paste commands. A demo using both WordPad and Paint is offered later in this chapter, in the section "Sharing between Paint and WordPad."

▸ Eventually you will want to quit programs you don't plan to use. Start up too many programs at one time, and Windows eventually slows to a sluggish crawl. In addition to quitting, you'll also want to perform a little file maintenance to keep your disk drives from filling with clutter. This subject is touched on later in this chapter, in the section "Ending the tutorial with a bit of cleanup."

Using the "cool switch" to switch applications

Another option for switching windows is to use the *cool switch,* the Alt+Tab key combination. This switch enables you to change quickly from one application to another and also see which applications are running without being boggled by buttons on the taskbar.

To use the cool switch, press and hold either Alt key on your keyboard. (Most people use the left Alt key because it's close to the Tab key.) Press the Tab key once. You see a pop-up window, displaying all the programs Windows is running, similar to what's shown in Figure 8-3.

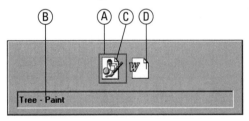

Figure 8-3
The Alt+Tab cool switch displays a list of running programs.
A. The highlight box tells you which program you'll switch to when you release the Alt key.
B. The name of the highlighted program, document name first. **C.** Paint. **D.** WordPad.

Keep your finger on the Alt key! Press the Tab key again. The highlight box moves from left to right every time you press the Tab key. This highlights a different program.

To switch to a program, release both keys. Windows instantly brings up whichever program you've highlighted.

The highlight box moves from left to right one icon for each time you press the Tab key. If the list of icons is very long and moving from right to left would seem quicker, press Alt+Shift+Tab.

The best way to use the Alt+Tab cool switch is quickly. If you're working with both Paint and WordPad, for example, switch between the two by pressing Alt+Tab. Just press the key combination quickly, and Windows switches you to whichever program you were using previously. To switch back, press Alt+Tab again.

➡ Pressing Alt+Tab comes in especially handy when you're auto-hiding the taskbar. Auto-hiding gives you more screen room to see your programs, but it also makes getting at the taskbar tougher. See Chapter 24, the section "Messing with the Taskbar," for more information about auto-hiding the taskbar.

Sharing Information

In addition to sharing a common look and feel, all Windows programs can also share information. This is done with the Cut, Copy, and Paste commands, which appear in almost every Windows application in the Edit menu.

In an application, you use the Cut, Copy, and Paste commands to move around bits and pieces of the stuff you're working on. For example, you can copy your name and address from the bottom of one letter to another in a word processor. You can cut a graphic of the sun and move it to the other side of a picture to change from a morning to an evening mood. This is all cinchy Cut, Copy, and Paste stuff.

Beyond using Cut, Copy, and Paste in one program, you can cut, copy, and paste information *between* programs. Copy a picture and paste it in your word processor, for example. This works because all Windows programs can share information without getting overly fussy about it. It makes creating interesting and complex-looking documents a snap.

⬅ Even if they don't appear, you can use Cut, Copy, and Paste commands just about anywhere in Windows, especially if you're working with text. For example, you can copy and paste information inside fields in a dialog box. This is done by selecting the text and using the Ctrl+X, Ctrl+C, and Ctrl+V key-command shortcuts for the Cut, Copy, and Paste commands, respectively. (See the sidebar "Common quick-key shortcuts" in Chapter 4.)

The three amigos: Cut, Copy, Paste

Three commands common to all Windows programs helps you share information. They are shown in Table 8-1.

Table 8-1	Cut, Copy, and Paste Commands		
Command	*Menu*	*Keyboard Shortcut*	*Toolbar Button*
Cut	Edit⇨Cut	Ctrl+X	
Copy	Edit⇨Copy	Ctrl+C	
Paste	Edit⇨Paste	Ctrl+V	

The Cut, Copy, and Paste commands are also found on shortcut menus when you right-click the mouse on something that can be cut, copied, or pasted into. Right-click on an icon in My Computer, for example, and you'll see the Cut and Copy commands in a shortcut menu.

Notice that these three keys are clustered together on your keyboard. Ctrl+X for Cut is okay because cutting something is like deleting it or crossing (X'ing) it out. Ctrl+C for Copy is obvious, which leaves only Ctrl+V for Paste. Maybe it means *vomit?*

To copy something, or make a duplicate, you copy and then paste. First, the original material is selected, and then it's copied and pasted.

To move something, you cut and then paste. Cutting seems to delete, but in fact it merely copies the information to a special storage place in Windows called the Clipboard (see the next section). From there you can paste the information elsewhere in the same application or in another application.

You can paste and paste and paste the same image over and over. Whatever you last cut or copied can be repasted until you cut or copy something else or shut off your computer.

Undo it!

Another common editing command is Undo, which is also found on the Edit menu and is assigned the shortcut key Ctrl+Z (right next to the Cut key, Ctrl+X). The Undo command undoes whatever it was you just did in Windows. If you deleted a file and want it back, use the Undo command. Undo recovers from just about any other Windows command, restoring things to the way they just were. You have to use the Undo command quickly, however; the more you work, the less likely Windows will remember what to undo.

Everything goes to the Clipboard

Whenever you cut or copy something, it's placed in the Clipboard. What the Clipboard is isn't important. What is important is that your cut or copied whatever stays in the Clipboard until you cut or copy something else. The reason is that the Clipboard can hold only one thing at a time.

The Paste command automatically inserts whatever is in the Clipboard into whichever application you're using. This works for text and graphics objects as well as for programs, sounds, and other whatnot you can cut or copy in Windows.

If you like to, you can see what's in the Clipboard by using the Clipboard Viewer program:

1. Activate the Start Thing's menu.

   Click on the Start button with the mouse, or press Ctrl+Esc.

2. Choose Programs⇔Accessories⇔Clipboard Viewer.

The Clipboard Viewer program appears on the screen, looking similar to the one shown in Figure 8-4. Whatever is "in" the Clipboard, having been cut or copied there, appears in the Clipboard Viewer's window just as it would appear in the program that created it.

Most of the time you don't have to use the Clipboard Viewer. It's easy enough to see what's in there by using the Paste command and then examining what's pasted down. If you don't like it, you can choose the Edit⇔Undo command to get rid of it.

➡ The Clipboard Viewer may occasionally contain a filename or a list of filenames, shown in the cryptic MS-DOS pathname format. This means that a file or group of files has been cut or copied in My Computer or the Explorer, probably to be pasted elsewhere. See Chapter 16 for more information about this type of file management.

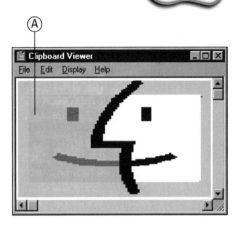

Figure 8-4
The Clipboard Viewer program
shows you the Clipboard's contents.
A. The last thing cut or copied.

Sharing between Paint and WordPad

Using the three amigos Cut, Copy, and Paste in any program is old hat.
Cutting and pasting a block of text in a word processor is called a *block
move.* Copying and pasting is a *block copy.* You can do the same thing in a
graphics program with images, making one tree into a forest or removing
Uncle Ed's head and pasting it into Aunt Bessie's purse. Easy stuff.

What is new is using Cut, Copy, and Paste between documents. This can be
done and comes in quite handy when you create complex-looking documents:

1. Start the tutorial earlier in this chapter if you haven't already.

   Do the tutorial in the section "A multitasking tutorial involving Paint
   and WordPad."

2. Switch to Paint.

   Click on the Paint program's button on the taskbar to bring its window
   up front and center.

3. Select the tree.

   Click the mouse on the rectangular selection tool.

   See Chapter 9, the section "Whirlwind tool tour," for more
   information about using the selection tool.

   Select the entire tree by dragging a rectangle around it. Click on a spot
   somewhere to the northwest of the tree, and then drag the mouse down
   to the southeast. Release the mouse button. The area within the "line of
   ants" is selected (see Figure 8-5).

Figure 8-5
A graphical tree has been selected.
A. Start dragging here. **B.** The "line of ants."
C. Release the mouse button here. **D.** The selection mouse pointer.

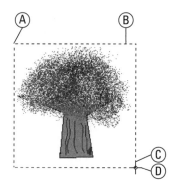

If you can't quite get all of the tree, try the operation again with a new starting point. Drag the mouse farther down or to the right to lasso more of the tree.

4. Copy the tree.

   Choose Edit⇨Copy. This step places a copy of the image inside the line of ants in Windows' Clipboard.

5. Switch over to WordPad.

   Click on WordPad's button on the taskbar. This step zooms that application back out to its full-screen glory.

6. Click the mouse in the blank line between the first and third lines.

   Clicking the mouse in a text document moves the flashing toothpick cursor to that spot. That's where any new text you type will appear, but also where anything you paste will appear.

7. Paste the tree.

   Choose Edit⇨Paste. There is a tree in your document!

Keep in mind that you don't have to run two programs at one time to cut and paste between them. You can just quit one program, play a game of Solitaire, and then start another program and paste. Windows lets you do that, because the cut or copied image stays in the Clipboard until you cut or copy something else or turn off the computer.

➡ The tree appears as a graphics object inside WordPad, like a big letter of the alphabet. You can select it for cutting or copying again, or you can resize the tree by using the wee little thumb tabs located on the corners and edges. This subject is covered in Chapter 30, in the section "Basic Messing with Graphics Stuff (Stretching)."

➡ You're not done with the tutorial yet. To finish up, see the section "Ending the tutorial with a bit of cleanup," later in this chapter.

Pasting to the desktop

One of the main drawbacks to cutting, copying, and pasting is that you can cut or copy only one thing at a time. Cut or copy anything new, and it replaces the old contents of the Clipboard. What a gyp!

To make things easier, you can cut or paste something to the desktop rather than to the Clipboard. That way, your pasted stuff sticks to the desktop like any other icon, which can then be pasted into any other document. This can come in incredibly handy for pasting common items you use over and over, such as your name and address, company logos, and common phone numbers.

➡ Only applications that are OLE-friendly can paste to the desktop. If your application doesn't let you do it, it's not OLE-friendly. See the section "An Episode with OLE," later in this chapter, for more OLE information.

To copy or cut something to the desktop, follow these steps:

1. Select whatever it is you want to copy or cut.

➡ Follow the instructions in Chapter 30 for selecting text. Select graphics by dragging around the graphics with a selection tool, as described in Chapter 9, in the section "Making Purty Pictures with Paint."

2. Choose Edit⇨Copy or Edit⇨Cut.

   Cut or copy the stuff, whichever you need.

   If the program's window doesn't fill the screen, you can point the mouse at the selected text or graphic and drag it from your document out onto the desktop. This is cut-and-paste in one fell swoop. If you press and hold the Ctrl (Control) key before you start dragging, the information is copied and pasted.

3. Bring up the desktop's shortcut menu.

   Right-click the mouse on a blank part of the desktop.

4. Choose Paste from the menu.

   The object is pasted on the desktop as a Scrap icon.

   If you have more than one Scrap icon, they'll be named Scrap (2), Scrap (3), and so on.

Scrap

If you paste a text item to the desktop, it will be named Document Scrap, followed by the first few words of the copied text in quotes. That really helps you identify what's pasted on the desktop.

➠ If your pasted stuff is named only Scrap or Scrap (10), it makes it harder to recognize what's in the file, so I heartily recommend renaming these icons right after you paste them. You can rename the icon by selecting it and then pressing the F2 key. Type a new name, and press Enter. More detailed instructions for renaming icons can be found in Chapter 16, in the section "Blessing a File with a New Name."

To paste the icon back into any document, follow these steps:

1. Bring up the scrap icon's shortcut menu.

   Right-click on the icon. This step brings up its shortcut menu.

2. Choose Copy or Cut.

   Select the command you want, depending on whether you want to copy the information in the icon or cut it.

3. Activate the program you want to paste into.

   Click the mouse in that program's window, or click on the program's button on the taskbar. This step brings the program into the foreground, ready for action.

4. Choose Edit⇨Paste.

   The information is pasted into the application.

For a text document, you should position the toothpick cursor first. The information is inserted into your document at that location.

It's also possible to drag the icon from the desktop into your document, if the application's window doesn't fill the screen. This works as a combined cut-and-paste. If you press and hold the Ctrl (Control) key before you drag the icon, you do a copy-and-paste.

Ending the tutorial with a bit of cleanup

Suppose that all your work is done on the EnviroGeeks newsletter. If so, it's time to print it, save it one last time, and get on with things. And you have to put the files you created in a memorable spot so that you can easily find them later; keeping things stuck to the desktop leads to clutter, and that's a no-no.

Normally, when you finish a project, you go through two steps:

1. Quit all applications, and save your work to disk.

2. Do file cleanup, by putting files away in their proper folders.

Because the files for this tutorial were created on the desktop, they have to be put elsewhere for long-term storage. Keeping them on the desktop is fine, especially when you're working on them. But when you're done, you should put them in a better spot.

Here are the steps you should take to wrap things up:

1. Bring up WordPad one last time.

   Click on WordPad's button on the taskbar to move it up front on your screen. (This is technically referred to as "moving an application into the foreground," if you care to know.)

2. Print the EnviroGeeks document (optional).

   As an optional step, you can print your document now. Choose File⇨Print or click on the Print button on the toolbar.

   If you choose File⇨Print, you see WordPad's Print dialog box. Click on the OK button to begin printing. When you click on the Print button on the toolbar, WordPad goes ahead and prints without bothering you with a dialog box.

   Cherish that hard copy.

3. Save the EnviroGeeks document.

   This step is much more involved than you would think. The reason is that you pasted a picture into your document and added a little formatting. WordPad normally deals with text documents. By pasting, however, you have *more* than a plain text document. Therefore, you must save the document in a special format to retain that extra information.

   Choose File⇨Save As. You need the Save As command here, as opposed to the normal Save command, because you want to save the EnviroGeeks document in a special format that keeps the picture and formatting. In the special "you're about to lose your formatting" dialog box (see Figure 8-6), choose a format for your document. When in doubt, click on Rich Text Document.

   After clicking on the proper button in the "you're about to lose your formatting" dialog box, the Save As dialog box appears. This is where you really save the document to disk. Click on the Save button here, or just press the Enter key.

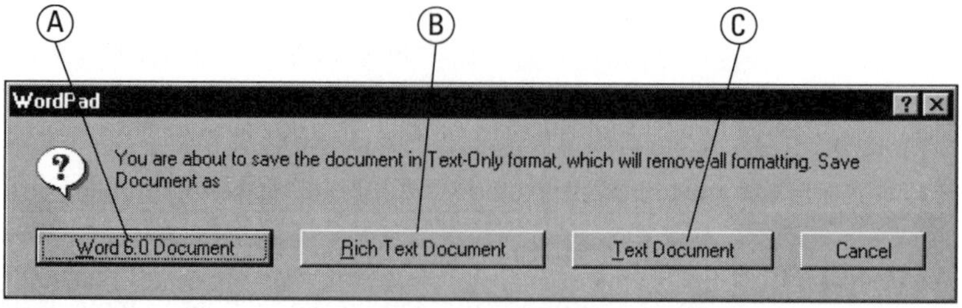

Ⓐ Ⓑ Ⓒ

WordPad	? X

⚲ You are about to save the document in Text-Only format, which will remove all formatting. Save
Document as

Word 6.0 Document	Rich Text Document	Text Document	Cancel

Figure 8-6
The WordPad "you're about to lose your formatting" dialog box.
A. If you have Microsoft Word on your computer, click here. **B.** If you don't
have Microsoft Word, click here. **C.** Ignore the Text Only Document option
because that won't save the picture or your formatting.

For more information about the Save As dialog box, see Chapter 4, the
section "Saving your stuff."

Finally, when you're asked to "Replace existing file?" in yet another
dialog box, click on Yes.

Wow. The document is finally saved to disk. Done. Finished. Kaput.

If all this drives you insane, read more about different file types in
Chapter 15, in the section "Who Knows What Evil Lurks in the Heart
of Files?"

4. Quit WordPad.

Choose File⇔Exit.

Quick-as-a-wink, WordPad is gone. No struggle. No fuss. If only saving
in an alien format were that quick and sweet. . . .

See Chapter 3, the section "Quitting Any Program," for more information
about quitting any Windows application in a variety of interesting and
often useful ways. Personally, I prefer clicking on the × Close button in
the upper right corner of the window. Some people double-click the
mouse on the program's mini-icon Control menu in the upper left corner
of the window. It takes all types in this world.

5. Bring up Paint one last time.

Click on the Paint program's button on the taskbar. This step brings it
up front and center, ready for action.

6. Quit Paint.

Choose File⇔Exit. This step quits the Paint program and also saves your
art to disk one last time if you haven't done so recently. Click on the Yes
button if you're asked to save the document.

Paint is gone!

7. Clean up the desktop.

   The EnviroGeeks and Tree documents are still plastered to the desktop. Unless you plan to use them again, you should put them away in a special folder on disk.

8. Click on both the EnviroGeeks and Tree document icons.

   Ctrl+click on both of them; first hold the Ctrl key and click on EnviroGeeks, and then, keeping the Ctrl key held down, click on the Tree document's icon. Release the Ctrl key.

   ➠ You can also drag a lasso around both icons with the mouse, selecting them both together. See Chapter 16, the section "Calf-ropin' files," for more information if you want to try this selection trick.

9. Choose the Cut command from the icon's shortcut menu.

   Right-click on either one of the icons to bring up its shortcut menu.

   Choose Cut from the menu.

   Both icons appear "hazy" on the desktop. They've been cut and are waiting to be pasted elsewhere.

10. Open the My Documents folder in My Computer.

    Open My Computer. Then open the Drive C icon. Then open the folder in which you want to save the documents (a Work or Projects folder if you have one).

    ⬅ Mosey off to Chapter 2 if you need more help working with My Computer.

    ➠ If you don't have a Work or Projects folder on drive C, you can create one. See Chapter 17, the section "The useful Work folder organizational strategy," for more information about creating your own Work folder on drive C.

11. Paste dem files.

    Inside the My Documents folder window, right-click the mouse to bring up the shortcut menu. Choose the Paste command.

    The two documents are cut from the desktop and then copied into the My Documents folder window.

12. Close any of My Computer's windows to clean up the desktop.

    You're now ready to move on to your next project.

➠ I can't emphasize enough how important it is to keep files neat and organized. Every document, file, icon — whatever — on your computer should live in its own, proper folder somewhere on disk. Chapter 17 goes into great detail about how to make this possible — how to create an organized and sane PC.

An Episode with OLE

There are two things you have to know about OLE. First is that it stands for Object Linking and Embedding, which is a much fancier way of copying and pasting information. Second, it's pronounced "oh-lay," as in what you would say at a bullfight if you were politically opposed to the way bulls treat human beings.

The main difference between OLE and regular cut-and-paste is that, with OLE, what you paste has more brains. If you *link* that pasted object, then changing the original also changes the pasted link. If you *embed* that pasted object, you can change it at any time by using the original program that created it. Obviously, demos are in order to truly drive home these points.

The OLE tutorial involving Word and Excel

Unlike with Cut, Copy, and Paste, not every Windows application is receptive to OLE. Only those programs that are OLE-serious can accomplish it. The way to tell is to check two of the programs' menus. This is usually the dead giveaway, though it's not a guaranteed way of finding out whether an application is OLE-serious.

First, check the Edit menu. If it has a Paste Special command, you have an application that can OLE-link.

Second, check the Insert menu for an Insert Object command. The command may be named something different, and it may be on a menu other than Insert. This is the OLE embedding command, the one that lets you embed or forcibly insert part of another program into the one you're using.

Two programs that are OLE-serious are Microsoft's Word and Excel. This may or may not be due to the fact that they're made by Microsoft and that — what the heck! — the OLE people work in a building just across campus. Other applications may use OLE and use similar commands, but for this tutorial I'm using Word and Excel.

➡ Microsoft Word and Excel are two of the popular packages included with Microsoft Office. These subjects really deserve a book unto themselves, but I've taken most of the good information and stuffed it into Chapter 10 for a quick and dirty look. Look there for more information.

The OLE embedding tutorial

Embedding an object works much like pasting does, but with two subtle and useful differences.

First, you don't have to run two different programs at one time in order to embed. You simply insert an object into the current application. For example, you insert an Excel spreadsheet object into a Word document. A special menu lists a number of applications and the types of documents they create that can be inserted.

Second, after you embed the object, you can easily edit its contents. Unlike pasting, which just slaps down a picture, for example, an embedded object is smart. If you don't like what you've embedded, you can quickly edit it and make changes. With a pasted object, you're stuck with what you pasted and will have to repaste if you don't like it.

1. Start Microsoft Word.

   The easiest way to start Word is to click on the Word button on the Microsoft Office toolbar. If you don't have Microsoft Office but you have Word, use the Start Thing to locate Microsoft Word. It may be on its own submenu, it may be on the main menu. You have to hunt.

   Winword

   Word takes a moment to start. It always does.

2. Write the following text:

   May 18, 1997

   Dear JB:

   Here are the figures you wanted me to fudge. The IRS will never figure this out:

   Type each line. Press Enter at the end of each line: after the date and then after the colons that end the two following lines. Press Enter at the beginning of a line to keep it blank. Press the Backspace key to back up and erase if you make a mistake.

   Be sure to press Enter after the colon on the last line.

3. Choose Insert⇨Object.

   This is Word's OLE command. It summons a dialog box (similar to Figure 8-7) that lists all the different types of objects you can embed in your document. Oh, you could waste a whole serious day here, but keep moving on to the next step.

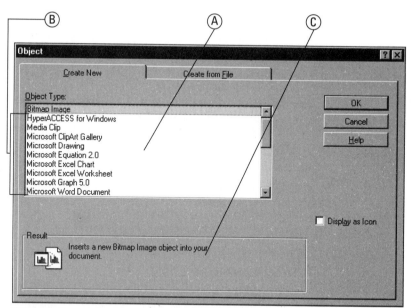

Figure 8-7
Word's OLE Object embedding dialog box.
A. A list of OLE-friendly applications on your computer. **B.** Double-click on one of these to insert a new document inside Word. **C.** A better explanation of what's what.

4. Scroll through the list to find Microsoft Excel Worksheet.

   You may have to scroll a little, or it may be staring you in the face. If you don't find it, you probably don't have Excel installed on your computer. Oh, well. Keep reading anyway.

5. Double-click on Microsoft Excel Worksheet.

   This step selects a new Excel worksheet to insert right smack-dab into your Word document. Just like that.

   An easier way to insert the spreadsheet is to click on the Insert-Microsoft-Excel-Worksheet button on Word's standard toolbar. This step does the same thing as both steps 4 and 5, if the button is on the toolbar.

   Eventually you see the new Excel worksheet living in the middle of your Word document (see Figure 8-8). Congratulations — that's an embedded object. Odd-looking, isn't it?

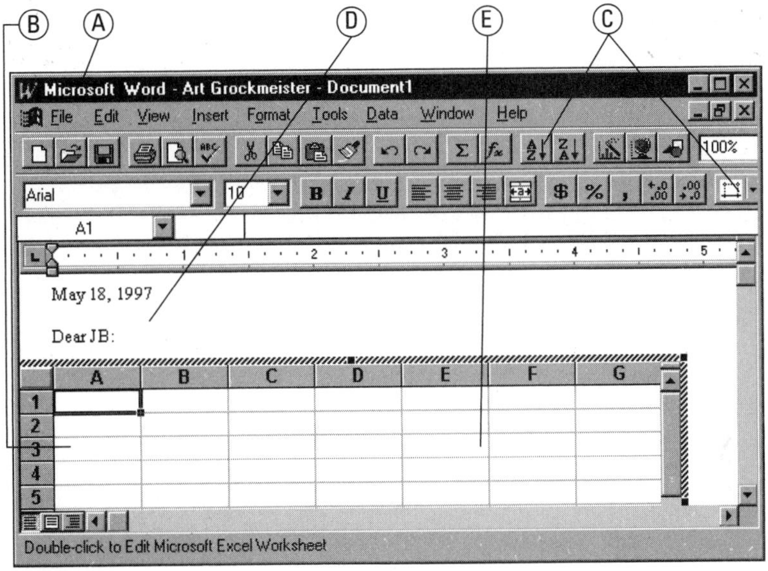

Figure 8-8
The Excel worksheet squat-dab in the middle of a Word document.
A. This is Microsoft Word. **B.** An Excel spreadsheet stuck in a Word document.
C. These are actually Excel commands, available while you're working on the
spreadsheet. **D.** Click out here to return to Word and work on your document.
E. Double-click in here to work on the Excel-embedded object.

6. Work the worksheet.

   Do whatever has to be done. For this example, you can fill in the
   worksheet with the values shown in Figure 8-9.

   Notice that the Word document actually appears in Excel (refer to
   Figure 8-8). Those aren't Word's menus or toolbars on the screen; that's
   Excel. Essentially, and even though the window's title bar tells you
   otherwise, you're working in Excel right now.

   Finish the embedded worksheet.

7. Return to the Word document.

   When you're done working the worksheet, click the mouse somewhere
   outside the worksheet's hash-mark corral. Just click on whatever you
   recognize as part of the Word document: the words "Dear JB," for example. This step returns you to Word, where you can continue to work
   on your document.

Ⓐ   Ⓑ

W Microsoft Word - Art Grockmeister - extort	_ □ ✕
File Edit View Insert Format Tools Table Window Help	_ ∂ ✕

Normal ▼ Times New Roman ▼ 10 ▼ **B** *I* U ≣ ≣ ≣ ≣ ≔

Dear JB:

Here are the figures you wanted me to fudge. The IRS will never figure this out:

Money in off-shore accounts	$	654,328.00
Stolen from little old ladies	$	564,287.04
"Borrowed" from the Bank	$	266,551.00
Extorted lunch money	$	5.63
Total	$	**1,485,171.67**

Please note that I'm sending this on the Internet. I really hope no one else has your ID.

Art

| Page 1 | Sec 1 | 1/1 | At 3.6" | Ln 11 | Col 4 | REC | MRK | EXT | OVR | WPH |

Figure 8-9
The finished result.
A. This is actually an Excel object. **B.** Double-click anywhere in here to edit the Excel object.

When you're back in Word, the embedded Excel worksheet looks and acts like a picture you pasted into Word. It is treated as one large object (like a big letter) and usually sits on a line by itself.

➠ If you click on the Excel object, you notice little handles that appear on the edges and corners. You can use these handles to resize the image, changing its shape to better fit your document. See Chapter 30, the section "Basic Messing with Graphics Stuff (Stretching)," for more information.

8. Brush up the worksheet object thing.

Unlike a pasted piece of an Excel worksheet, the one you've created doesn't sit still. If you have to adjust the figures, you can instantly edit the worksheet in Excel.

To reactivate the Excel worksheet, double-click on it with the mouse. Click, click.

Windows whines. Windows whirs. Eventually, your old pal Excel is back in charge, complete with menus on the screen, and you can work with your worksheet, buffing it out to perfection or whatever.

To return to Word, just click on the Word document outside the worksheet's holding pen.

All day you can switch back and forth between Word and Excel — or any two programs — when you've embedded one inside the other. The secret is to use the Insert⇨Object command rather than Paste and then double-click on the embedded object to edit it.

9. Quit Word.

Choose File⇨Exit.

A dialog box appears, asking whether you want to save your document. If you don't, click on the No button. Word quits. All is safe in the universe.

Other objects you can embed

The Object dialog box contains a whole list of programs that are OLE-friendly and that enable you to embed their objects into other applications.

One of the most common for a word processor is the Bitmap Image — a graphics file created by the Paint program. In the cut-and-paste tutorial earlier in this chapter, it would have been much easier just to OLE-embed a Paint picture into WordPad; choose Insert⇨New Object, and then pick Bitmap Image from the list. Unfortunately, that wouldn't have shown you the ease of cut-and-paste, which was the purpose of that tutorial.

My list of favorite and most interesting things to embed includes the ones in this list:

Microsoft WordArt: A program that enables you to make creative text for logos and whatnot.

A MIDI song or sound clip: These appear in the document as an icon or button. Double-click on the icon, and the music or sound plays over the PC's speakers.

An animation file: Click on this embedded icon, and a little movie or computer-animation clip plays.

Of course, none of this may be very practical, but it can be fun. (Most of the time you embed a Paint picture, Excel worksheet, or a piece from some other OLE-friendly program.)

If you want to save the document, click on Yes. You see the standard Save As dialog box, enabling you to give the sample document a name and save it in a proper place on your hard disk. The art of using this dialog box is covered in Chapter 4, in the section "Saving your stuff." The document you save is a plain Word document. The embedded information is saved (and printed) just as it appears on the screen, and the file can even be read on other computers that may not have the embedded object's application.

The OLE linking tutorial

OLE linking is closer to a simple copy-and-paste operation than OLE embedding is. In fact, OLE linking is really Super Paste because changes in the original are instantly reflected in the pasted copy. This can be very impressive to see:

1. Create a new Excel worksheet.

   Right-click the mouse on the desktop to bring up its shortcut menu.

   From the menu, choose New⇨Microsoft Excel Worksheet.

   A worksheet icon is created and slapped down on the desktop. It's given the name New Microsoft Excel Worksheet. Before doing anything else, type a new name for the worksheet; call it Critters. Type the following line:

   Critters

   Press the Enter key to lock in the name change.

   This step automatically replaces the old, stolid name automatically given by Windows.

   Detailed steps for creating documents in this manner can be found in Chapter 3, in the section "Taking advantage of the numerous New menu commands." You should get used to these steps because they are the handiest way to create a new document, to start new work.

   It doesn't matter where you create the document. Just create it on the desktop for now. You can move the icons to a proper folder when the tutorial has been completed, if you like. See Chapter 17, the section "Setting Up Folders Just So," for more information.

2. Open the Excel worksheet.

   Double-click on its icon to open it. Excel splashes itself all over the screen.

3. Fill in the worksheet.

   Place the following text and numbers into the first few cells in the worksheet:

Babies	3
Cats	2
Dogs	0
Bugs	5000
Total	

   Use the arrow keys to move from one cell to another.

   For the final cell, the one by Total (cell B5), you calculate the sum of all the critters. To do this, locate the Sum button on Excel's standard toolbar (the one right under the menu bar). Click on the Sum button. This places the following formula in cell B5:

   =SUM(B1:B4)

   That's Excelspeil for "Add the amounts in the cells just above here." Press the Enter key, and you'll see the total.

   The total is 5,005, by the way.

   ➠ A worksheet is a grid you can fill with numbers or text. The numbers can be related to each other, calculated, totaled, and so on, all of which is gone into in mediocre detail in Chapter 10, which discusses the use of Excel in the Microsoft Office.

4. Save the worksheet.

   Click on the Save button on the standard toolbar. This step saves the Critters file to disk.

5. Shove Excel aside for a moment.

   Minimize Excel; click on its Minimize button to shrink it down to a button on the taskbar.

   Now you're going to create a new Word document, one you'll use for an OLE link with the Excel spreadsheet you've just made.

6. Fire up a new Word document.

   Go back to the desktop and right-click the mouse, bringing up the desktop's shortcut menu.

   Choose New⇨Microsoft Word Document.

A brand-new Word document icon is created and lovingly placed on the desktop. Change the boring name New Microsoft Word Document to Household Inventory. Type the following line:

Household Inventory

Press the Enter key. This step changes the document's name to something more descriptive.

➡ See the section "Blessing a File with a New Name" in Chapter 16 for more information about renaming icons on the desktop.

7. Open the document.

Double-click on the Household Inventory icon to open it. After a time, Word appears on the screen with the document up and ready for editing.

8. Write some text.

Scribble the following as the first line of text in the document:

Here is an inventory of all the living creatures in our house:

Double-check your typing. Press the Backspace key to back up and erase if you make a mistake. Be sure to press the Enter key at the end of the line.

9. Split the screen.

This is for demo purposes only: You can display any windows on the screen tiled — like in your bathroom — if they're open on the screen. Because Word is already on the screen, you have to make Excel a window again: Click on the Excel button on the taskbar to make it big again. Now you have two windows open: Excel and Word (any other windows should be minimized).

Right-click the mouse on the taskbar to bring up its shortcut menu. You have to find a blank spot on the taskbar; don't click on a button or you'll bring up its shortcut menu.

If you can't find a blank spot to click on the taskbar, right-click on the time. That brings up the Date & Time's shortcut menu, but all the menu items (save for the top one) are the taskbar's.

Choose Tile Vertically from the menu.

The screen splits, with Excel on one side and Word on the other (see Figure 8-10). You don't have to do this in practice. In fact, I still recommend keeping your applications at full-screen size for the best viewing. But this way you can dramatically see the results of OLE linking.

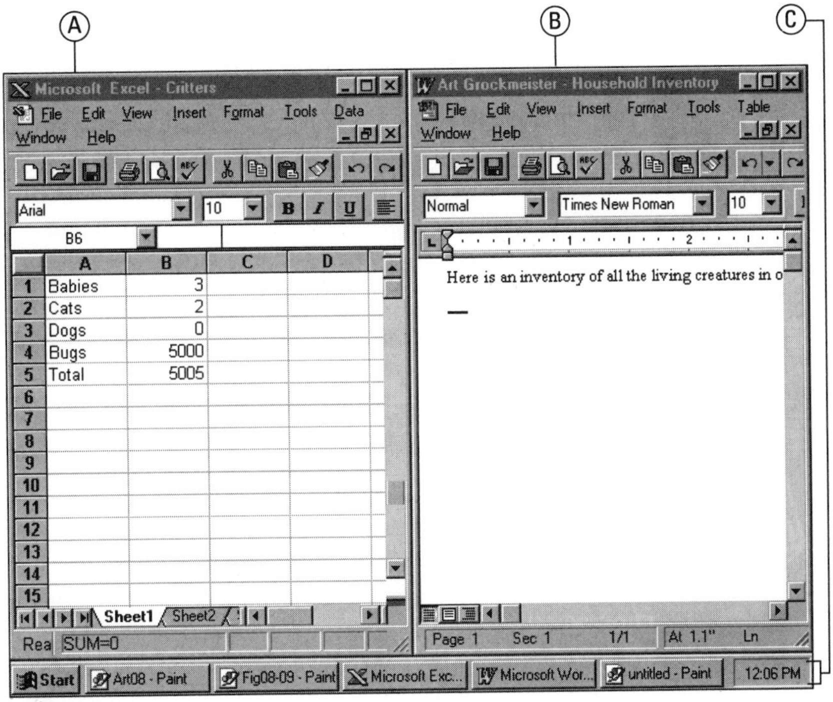

Figure 8-10
The split-screen way of viewing OLE.
A. Excel is tiled over here. **B.** Word is tiled over here. **C.** Other buttons on the taskbar represent minimized windows that aren't tiled.

10. In Excel, select cells for copying.

    Drag the mouse from cell A1 down and to the right, ending up at cell B5. This step highlights all the cells, except for A1, where you began dragging.

    Choose Edit⇨Copy.

    A tiny row of graphical ants starts marching around the selected area of the spreadsheet. Pay no attention to them!

11. In Word, paste the cells.

    Mosey on back over to Word, and choose Edit⇨Paste Special. The Paste Special dialog box appears (see Figure 8-11), showing you some very special ways to paste.

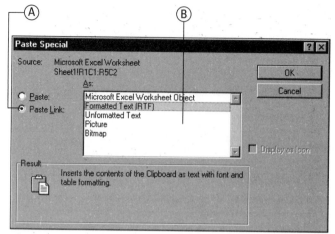

Figure 8-11

The Paste Special dialog box.
A. Click on the Paste Link radio button because you want this to be an OLE-link operation. **B.** Leave this part of the dialog box alone. If you select Microsoft Excel Worksheet Object, however, you're combining both OLE linking and OLE embedding in a rolled-up knot of a nightmare I don't bother explaining here.

Click on the OK button.

The information from the worksheet is pasted into your Word document in a special table. But don't spell *neat-o* just yet.

12. Go back to Excel, and change the number of bugs.

Suppose that wee little Jonah is found eating bugs again in his crib. Oops! The total number of bugs has dropped down to 4,567.

Use your mouse to click on cell B4 in the Excel worksheet. Type the new number of bugs. Type this number:

    4567

Press the Enter key.

Notice that two things change. First, the total number of critters has changed to 4,572, which accurately reflects the total in your worksheet. Second, and more surprisingly, the pasted copy of the worksheet in the Word document has changed, reflecting the exact results (see Figure 8-12).

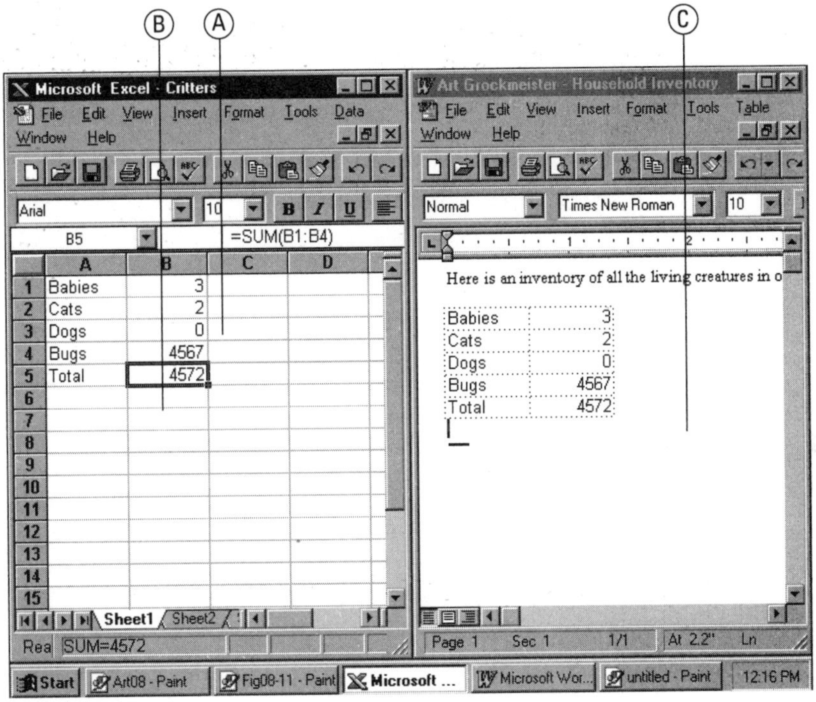

Figure 8-12
The final result.
A. A number changed right here . . . **B.** Changed this total here. **C.** And it changed over here as well.

Welcome to the miracle that is OLE linking! It works whether one document or the other is open. It works almost instantaneously. But it works only when you choose Paste Special or Paste Link rather than a regular Paste.

13. Clean up!

Close both Excel and Word by clicking on their × Close buttons. You can save the files if you like. Otherwise, click on No when you're prompted to save.

When you're back at the desktop, select both icons and drag them to the Recycle Bin. See Chapter 16, the section "Calf-ropin' files," for information about dragging a lasso around both icons to select them together; see Chapter 5 for information about the Recycle Bin.

➠ If you elect to save the documents, click on Yes when you're prompted to save. Then, when you're back at the desktop, move the icons to a proper folder on disk for long-term storage. Try to avoid the trap of keeping them on the desktop, where they only clutter things up (unless, of course, you plan to use the files frequently). See Chapter 16 for more information about organizing your stuff in this manner.

Introducing the Applets

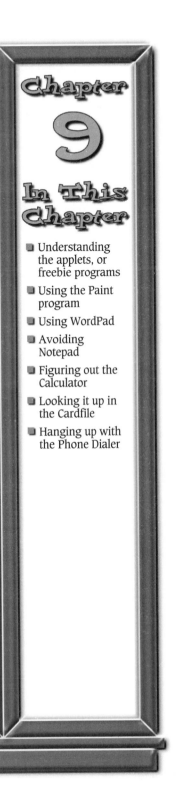

Chapter 9

In This Chapter

- Understanding the applets, or freebie programs
- Using the Paint program
- Using WordPad
- Avoiding Notepad
- Figuring out the Calculator
- Looking it up in the Cardfile
- Hanging up with the Phone Dialer

No, the Applets weren't a '50s rock band. *Applet* is Windowspeak for a mini-application, a little program, something handy that comes "free" with Windows. It's basically a feeble version of something much better you could get if you paid real money for it. But for handling basic tasks, such as painting or writing, an applet is more than adequate. In fact, you may never need anything more than these little programs Windows comes with.

Secret Background Information on the Applets

Windows comes with a dozen or so Applets, or mini-applications. Nearly all of them can be found in the Start Thing's menu: Choose Programs⇨Accessories, and you'll see them all nestled there.

◀▥ If you want to find them by using My Computer, they're located on drive C, in either the Program Files folder, the Accessories subfolder, or the Windows main folder itself. See Chapter 2 for more information about My Computer.

➠ This chapter covers only a few of the applets, mainly Paint and WordPad. Chapter 11 has more information about the Terminal applet — the Windows modem program.

➠ By the way, you may notice that your copy of Windows doesn't have all the applets. Pity, but there is a way to install them all. Chapter 13 tells you how, in the section "Adding the Rest of Windows."

Making Purty Pictures with Paint

Windows comes with its own drawing program, officially called *MSPaint*, though you can call it *Paint.* You can use it to create graphical images, doodle, make artwork for your documents, design new desktop wallpaper patterns, and edit any bitmap graphics images. It's actually quite handy and will suit most of your needs most of the time. (I created most of this book's artwork by using Paint.)

Expert tree-drawing instructions

I think that I shall never see, something as beautiful as a tree drawn by using the Windows Paint program, as shown in the following demo:

1. Find a place for your new Paint document.

   Open your Work folder by using My Computer, or open a Temporary or Misc folder if you just want to goof around. Find the place where you want to create your new Paint document.

   ➠ See Chapter 17 for more information about finding a place for your work. See specifically the section "Random folders for random stuff."

   ⬅ Refer to the tutorial that runs throughout Chapter 8, "A Multitasking tutorial involving Paint and WordPad," if you want to make this tutorial here part of a larger deal.

2. Create a new Paint document.

   In the proper folder, choose File⇨New⇨Bitmap Image from the menu. This step slaps down a new Paint document in the window.

3. Rename the New Bitmap Image document.

   Give it the name Tree; type **Tree** over the old, cruddy name, New Bitmap Image.

   Press the Enter key to lock in the new name.

➡ See Chapter 16 for more information about renaming an icon if you're having trouble. See the section "Blessing a File with a New Name."

4. Open the document.

Double-click on the document's icon, or just press the Enter key if it's still highlighted on the screen. This step starts the Paint program with your new document ready for editing (which looks like Figure 9-1, but with a blank canvas).

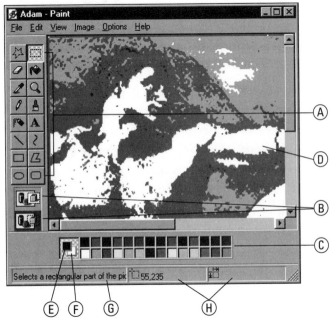

Figure 9-1
The Windows Paint program, ready for action.
A. Tool palette. **B.** Tool options, line size, and so on. **C.** Color palette. **D.** Canvas (just something I whipped up). **E.** The foreground, or line, color. **F.** The background, or fill, color. **G.** Describes the current tool. **H.** Needless trivia.

5. Set the image size.

Your first job is to set the size of the image.

6. Choose Image➪Attributes.

The Attributes dialog box appears (see Figure 9-2), in which you can set the image size (the dimensions of the electronic canvas you're about to draw on). Normally, Paint gives you an area about half a sheet of paper in size. But this tree should appear on a canvas maybe two inches square.

Figure 9-2
The Attributes dialog box.
A. Type 2 here, for a canvas two inches wide. **B.** Type 2 here, for a canvas two inches tall. **C.** Click here to set the canvas measurement in inches. **D.** Everyone wants to draw in color. **E.** Click here to do something nasty to your mortgage. **F.** Click here when you're done.

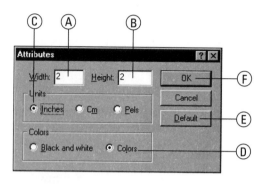

Enter a value of 2 for both the Width and Height of the canvas. Be sure to click on the Inches radio button so that you're creating a 2-inch-by-2-inch canvas and not some silly 2-centimeter-by-2-centimeter canvas or a 2-pixel-by-2-pixel canvas (which would be really teensy).

See Chapter 28 for more information about text-input boxes, radio buttons, and other gizmos that appear in a Windows dialog box.

7. Click on OK.

This step closes the Attributes dialog box and returns you to the Paint program, but with a smaller canvas. That's okay; you're making a tiny tree.

How big is my screen?

Setting the canvas size depends on what you're creating. If you're creating desktop wallpaper, for example, you want the canvas to be the same size as your desktop. That's typically 640 × 480 *pels,* or pixels. You have to be sure to enter 640 and 480 in the Width and Height input boxes, respectively, and click on the Pels radio button. That way, you create an image that fits right on your screen.

Make sure that you pick the proper resolution for your screen. To see what the resolution is currently, follow the instructions in the section "The Screen-Resolution Revolution" in Chapter 24. Just don't change the resolution (skip over steps 4 and 5), and make a mental note of the numbers.

General painting instructions

Whenever you paint an image, you have to choose three things in this order:

The tool: This is one of the 16 different tools that appear on the left side of the screen (refer to Figure 9-1).

The tool's options: Choose the line style, width, and other options from the options area.

The colors: Set the line and fill colors, which determine how your object will be colored when it's drawn.

8. Choose the Polygon tool.

   Click the mouse on the Polygon tool button. This step selects that tool for drawing.

9. Choose the filled and outlined polygon style.

   Click the mouse on the filled and outlined style, which means that the polygon will be drawn as both an outline and a filled middle. (It's the one in the middle.)

10. Pick the colors.

    Click the mouse's left button (the main button) on black. That's the outline color.

    Click the mouse's right button on a brown, treelike color. That's the fill color, the one that fills the inside of the polygon.

11. Draw the tree.

    Start by dragging a line from point A to B (see Figure 9-3). This must be a drag; everything else is a click.

    Then click the mouse at the remaining points, from C to J, in order. Here, you're creating the "branches" of the tree.

    Yes, this is much like connect-the-dots when you were a kid.

    Finally, double-click the mouse on point K. This finishes the polygon, which looks something like Figure 9-4.

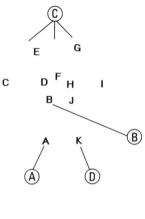

Figure 9-3
Points to drag to when you're creating the tree.
A. Start here. **B.** Drag to point B. **C.** Click the mouse once on all remaining points, in order. **D.** Finally, double-click the mouse here, on point K.

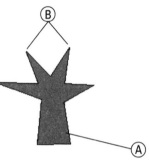

Figure 9-4
The finished polygon.
A. This is brown. **B.** Supposedly, these are branches. Must be winter.

12. Time to spray-paint the leaves.

    For leaves, you use the spray-paint can tool and just dapple the leaves down in an assortment of colors.

13. Choose the spray-paint can tool.

    It's actually called the *Airbrush* tool, but it really looks like a spray can to me.

14. Choose the widest possible pattern of spew.

    Click on the biggest spew pattern.

15. Pick a color for the leaves.

    Click the left mouse button on a color. Be creative: Use a green for spring, a yellow-brown for fall, and purple for the apocalypse.

16. Click and drag the mouse a few times around the tree's branches.

Click the mouse to put down a light smattering of leaves. Drag the mouse around to make a more fuller, leafier look. Lay down a layer of leaves on the branches, and fill out the tree.

17. Repeat steps 15 and 16 a few times to build up a layer of leaves.

Choose a subtly different color each time. Then one time choose a bizarre color, such as red or blue. Use that color sparingly.

18. The tree is done; save it to disk.

Choose File⇨Save to save your Tree document to disk.

Figure 9-5 shows what my tree looks like after following these directions. It's really quite lovely, as you can see.

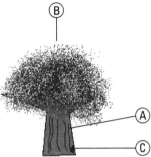

Figure 9-5
A fine, proud tree.
A. You might also consider drawing some lines in the trunk. Use the Pencil tool.
B. White spray-paint can highlights the outer leaves. **C.** Damn dog.

⬅ You can now quit the Paint tutorial and, if necessary, return to Chapter 8 to finish that tutorial there.

Whirlwind tool tour

The following are some highlights and suggestions for using the various tools in Paint. I don't have the space to go into everything. The most fun you can have in Paint, in fact, is just goofing around to see how the tools work. Remember to tell the boss that this isn't exactly "goofing around"; it's scientific experimentation, of course.

Use the selection tools to select graphics on the screen for dragging, copying, or cutting. Use the star-shaped selection tool to drag around unusual shapes and select them; the rectangle selection tool selects only rectangular shapes (duh).

You can drag the selected graphics to another part of the screen or cut or copy them. Several of the commands in the Image menu affect the selected graphics. And you can stretch the selected graphics by grabbing one of the "handles" on the rope of ants and dragging the mouse (see Figure 9-6).

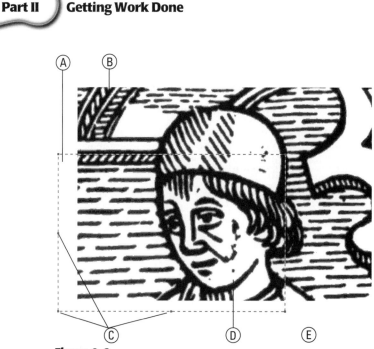

Figure 9-6
A selected graphic.
A. This part of the image is selected. **B.** This part is not. **C.** Drag one of these handles to resize the graphics image. **D.** You can choose Cut or Copy from the Edit menu to duplicate or move this graphic. **E.** You can also drag the selected image around by using the mouse.

Use the eraser to erase part of the screen; drag the mouse over the graphics you want erased. You select a size for the eraser in the options palette. Note that the eraser uses the background color to erase. If you choose a color other than white, it erases in that color.

If you click the right mouse button while erasing, you're actually using the *color eraser.* In that mode, only the selected foreground color is erased, replaced by the current background color. This tool is handy for erasing only certain parts of your image without the need to be precise.

The Paint bucket fills an area on the screen with a specific color. Click with the left mouse button to fill with the foreground color; click the right mouse button to fill with the background color.

The Eyedropper tool is used to choose a color from the canvas' image. Click on a weird-looking puce with the Eyedropper tool, for example, and that color is selected as the current foreground color.

The pencil is used to draw a thin line. It's best used when you zoom in to a graphic for tight or tiny work. Press Ctrl+Page Down to zoom in; press Ctrl+Page Up to zoom out.

The brush draws a thicker line than the Pencil does and in one of the shapes chosen from the tool options palette.

The Text tool enables you to type graphical text. Choose View⇨Text Toolbar so that you can choose the font, size, and style for the text. Note that the text is drawn in the current foreground color; if you don't see the text, it's probably because you've chosen white as the foreground color.

The Line Draw tool enables you to draw a straight line from one point to another. You do this by dragging the mouse. If you press the Shift key while you drag, the line is drawn at a right, or 45-degree, angle from its origin. Choose a line width from the tool options palette.

The shape tools draw their respective shapes. The width of the line is chosen by clicking on the Line Draw tool and setting a width. Then you can choose how the shape is filled by clicking in the tool option palette (see the preceding tutorial).

If you press and hold the Shift key while drawing an oval or rectangle, you actually draw a perfect circle or square, respectively.

Let WordPad Bring Out the Shakespeare in You

WordPad is Windows' freebie text editor, though it's more than just a program for jotting down text. With WordPad, you can format your text, add some fancy effects, and generally fool the neighbors. Although it lacks such features as a spell-checker, page numbering, and footnotes, it does have features that make it a handy, if somewhat limited, writing tool.

Figures 9-7 through 9-10 describe various aspects of WordPad and its toolbars and ruler. The main purpose of WordPad is to write, which is demonstrated in the following tutorial to prepare the EnviroGeeks newsletter (or at least part of it), which is also used in the multitasking tutorial in Chapter 8.

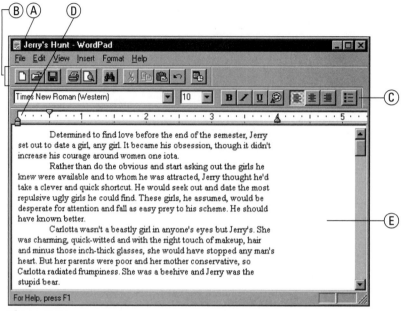

Figure 9-7
WordPad in its (limited) glory.
A. WordPad edits the document saved as Jerry's Hunt. **B.** Choose View⇨Toolbar to see this handy toolbar. **C.** Choose View⇨Format Bar to see this toolbar. **D.** Choose View⇨Ruler to see Queen Elizabeth, er, this thing here. **E.** Here is where you write, la-de-da.

Figure 9-8
WordPad's handy shortcut toolbar.
A. Standard New, Open, and Save shortcut buttons. **B.** Standard Print

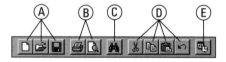

and Print Preview shortcut buttons. **C.** A shortcut to the Find command. **D.** Standard Cut, Copy, Paste, and Undo buttons. **E.** Something different! This button inserts the date and time into the document in a number of different formats.

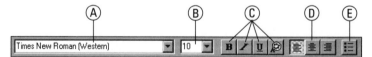

Figure 9-9
WordPad's handy formatting toolbar.
A. Pick a font here. **B.** Choose a size here. **C.** Standard Bold, Italic, Underline, and text-color buttons. **D.** Left, Center, and Right justify buttons. **E.** Cool trick — slaps bullets on a selected group of paragraphs.

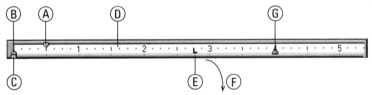

Figure 9-10
WordPad's ruler.
A. Drag this to set the indent for the first line of a paragraph. **B.** Drag this to set the left margin for a paragraph. **C.** Drag this to set both the indent and left margin together. **D.** Click anywhere in here to set a tab stop. **E.** A tab stop. **F.** Drag the tab stop off the ruler to remove it. **G.** Right margin-dragging doojobbie.

1. Start WordPad.

   Summon the Start Thing's menu by pressing Ctrl+Esc. Then choose Programs⇨Accessories⇨WordPad.

   WordPad explodes on the screen. (Well, maybe "explodes" is an improper adjective here.)

   If WordPad becomes one of your favorite word processors, consider slapping it down right atop the Start Thing's menu. See Chapter 6, the section "Sticking something on the main Start Thing menu."

2. Choose New from the File menu.

   Or click on the New icon on the handy toolbar. Either way, you see the New dialog box (see Figure 9-11), which enables you to pick which type of document you want to create.

Figure 9-11
Choose which type of document you want to create.
A. Use this one most of the time.
B. Good for exchanging files with alien word processors (formatting remains intact). **C.** Choose this only when directed to do so by a user manual or someone bigger and meaner than yourself.

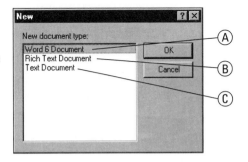

3. Choose Word 6 Document, and click on OK.

   This is WordPad's standard *modus operandi.*

4. Type the newsletter's title.

   Without regard to formatting anything, type the following four lines and press the Enter key after each one:

   the

   EnviroGeeks

   Newsletter

   Making our PCs more PC

   If you make a mistake, press the Backspace key to back up and erase.

   ➠ You can also use all the standard Windows text-editing commands, as discussed in the section "Basic text-editing stuff" in Chapter 30.

5. Select the first line of text.

   Move the mouse pointer to the document's left margin, just before the word *the.* When it's positioned correctly, the mouse pointer points to the NE rather than the NW.

   Click the mouse. This step highlights the entire line.

   You can also click the mouse three times on the text to select the entire line, though a triple-click requires warmer fingers than I can manage most of the time.

6. Format the text.

   Change the font to Arial MT Black (Turkish). Choose that option from the drop-down list on the formatting toolbar. (If you don't have that font, choose another Arial-type font.)

   Change the text size to 12; choose 12 from the size drop-down list.

   ➠ Check out Chapter 21 for more information about font names, types, and sizes.

   Center the line by clicking on the Center formatting button.

7. Select the second line and format it.

   Follow the instructions in Step 5 for selecting the second line of text.

   Change the font to Arial MT Black (Turkish) or whatever.

   Change the text size to 36.

   Center the line.

8. Select the third line and format it.

   Heed the instructions in step 5 to select the third line of text.

   Change the font to Arial MT Black (Turkish).

Change the text size to 18.

Center.

9. Select and format the fourth line.

   Arial MT Black (Turkish) at 22 points, centered.

10. Press the End key and then the Enter key twice to add a blank line.

    This goes after the last line in the title and before the table of contents. (It's where you paste the trees in the other tutorial.)

11. Set the formatting for the table of contents.

    Since you're formatting before any text is written, there's no need to select anything.

    Choose the Courier font from the drop-down font list on the formatting toolbar. The font may also be called Courier New or Courier New (Western).

    Choose 10 as the size.

    Click on the Align Left justification button to slam the text up against the left side of the page.

    Adjust the left margin for a "hanging indent"; drag the lower pointer on the ruler to a position 3/4 inches from the left margin. Use Figure 9-12 for help.

Figure 9-12
Creating a hanging indent in WordPad.
A. Drag the lower pointer to about this position. **B.** A line of ants shows you how text will line up in the window.

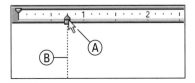

12. Type the first table of contents entry.

    Type the following text, but don't press Enter just yet:

    Page 1:

    After the colon, press the Tab key. This tabs you over to the hanging-indent thing. Continue by typing the rest of the line:

    Solar-powered PC Experiment Fizzles in Seattle!

    Press Enter to end the line.

    The reason for pressing the Tab key after the colon — and the weird hanging-indent format — will become apparent in a moment.

13. Type the second line.

    Enter the text as follows. Press the Tab key after the colon; press Enter to end the line of text:

    Page 2: Larry has a heart attack on pedal-powered PC!

14. Type the third line.

    Enter the following line, and then press Tab after the colon and the Enter key to end the line:

    Page 3: Samantha claims her opinion on clean air shouldn't conflict with her personal smoking habit.

    Note that this text is longer than a single line. Watch what happens as you type the line. Nifty, eh?

15. Type the final two lines.

    Enter the last two lines, and press the Tab key after the colon in each line and Enter at the end of each line:

    Page 4: Vern's do-it-yourself all-wood PC.

    Page 5: Message from our president.

    Figure 9-13 shows how the final letter should look, providing you've used the same fonts I did.

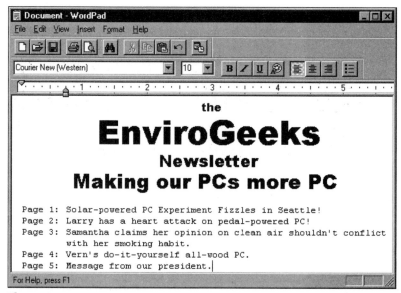

Figure 9-13
The finished EnviroGeeks newsletter (so far).

16. Save to disk.

    You can continue writing if you like, but in any case you should save your work to disk first.

    Choose File⇨Save As.

    Find a proper folder for your work.

    Give the file a name: EnviroGeeks.

    Click on the Save button.

    ⬅️ See Chapter 4 for information about saving stuff to disk, in the section "Saving your stuff."

17. Quit WordPad and move on.

    If you're done, quit WordPad by clicking on its × Close button, or keep working. There's massive potential in that EnviroGeeks newsletter.

Notepad: Windows' Feeble Text Editor

Lesser than WordPad is the Notepad, which is Windows' text editor. It's not a word processor at all, even lacking some of the features WordPad has. No, with Notepad you can work on and create only plain, boring text documents. No formatting, nothing fancy. In fact, few people even use it as a *notepad;* personally, I keep a green steno pad by my computer for taking notes. It's just handier.

Notepad is ideally suited for working on short, text-only documents. This is actually an anachronism because few of the things you do in Windows require a plain text file. Anyway, Notepad hangs around for whenever you need it.

To start Notepad, press Ctrl+Esc to fire up the Start Thing's menu, choose Programs⇨Accessories⇨Notepad. Figure 9-14 shows what it may look like. Kinda boring, really.

Figure 9-14
The Notepad sits alone and waiting.
A. Feeble menu commands. **B.** Text would appear here.

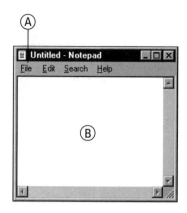

⟹ The Notepad automatically opens any text-type file. See Chapter 15 for more information about file types.

⟹ The Notepad is summoned to edit the old CONFIG.SYS file in Chapter 14. See the section "RAM Drives Belong in the Past."

Figure It Out Yourself (the Calculator)

Windows has a calculator, but don't throw away that solar-powered one you got as a freebie from your title company. Windows' Calculator lets you make all sorts of calculations, and you can even copy and paste the results between Calculator and other applications.

To start the Calculator, press Ctrl+Esc to pop up the Start Thing's menu, and then choose Programs⟹Accessories⟹Calculator. The Calculator splashes all over the screen, which may look like Figure 9-15.

A smaller version of the Calculator is available. Choose View⟹Standard from the menu, and the left side of the dialog box goes away, which is okay for us nonscientific folk.

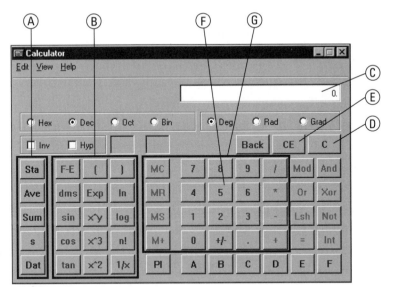

Figure 9-15
A calculator to make Einstein happy.
A. Incredibly ugly scientific stuff. **B.** Boggle, boggle, boggle. **C.** Answers and input appear here. **D.** The "Clear" button. **E.** Clear Entry — erase just the last number. **F.** Numbers you can click on like on a real calculator. **G.** Only the essential stuff stays on the Standard calculator.

Your Own Li'l Rolodex (the Cardfile)

The Cardfile program is an attempt to give you an electronic rolodex, a list of names and numbers but without any database muscle behind it. You can look up names and numbers, for example, but you can't tell the Cardfile to print mailing labels to everyone you know in Arizona over 75 years old (which is just about all of them).

To start the Cardfile, choose its command from the Start Thing's menu:

1. Press Ctrl+Esc to pop up the Start Thing.

2. Choose Programs⇨Accessories⇨Cardfile.

   Don't be shocked if you can't find it there. Cardfile exists only if you updated from an older version of Windows. Alas, Microsoft just didn't see fit to include it with the current go-round.

   If you have Cardfile, you see it on the screen, looking something like Figure 9-16. Of course, that's part of my personal Cardfile, which I've already filled in with names and addresses.

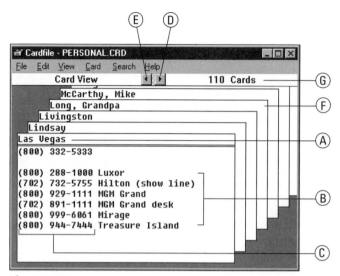

Figure 9-16
The fabulous Las Vegas card from the author's personal Cardfile.
A. The card title, or "index." **B.** Contents of the card, which can be anything, really.
C. If you highlight a phone number and press the F5 key, Windows dials it for you
(sort of). **D.** Click here to see the next card in the stack. **E.** Click here to see the
preceding card in the stack. **F.** More cards in the stack. **G.** This Cardfile database
contains 110 cards, more than two decks!

You add cards to the Cardfile by pressing the F7 key or by choosing
Card➪Add. This displays a chintzy little dialog box in which you enter the
card's title, or *index*. Be clever here; the Cardfile sorts the cards alphabetically
by their index name. So if it's a person's name, you probably want to type it
last name first.

You can change a card's title by using the Edit➪Index command or by just
pressing the F6 key.

After adding the new card, just type anything in the card contents area.
There is no form, no field, no pattern or anything, other than you can't type
more than a certain amount of text or else the computer starts beeping at
you; each card holds only about 11 lines of text. That's all.

You can also paste graphical images into the Cardfile. I suppose that if you
really want to toss your desktop rolodex, you can use a scanner to read in all
those business cards and then graphically paste them into the Cardfile — but
that seems like it would create work on a device that's supposed to make
things easier. I digress.

To paste a graphical image into the Cardfile, first choose Edit⇨Picture. That puts you in picture mode. Then you can use the Edit⇨Paste command to slap down a previously copied graphical image. You can drag the image around inside the card, right over any text, until it's positioned just right.

Other commands are available for searching through the cards and deleting. Nothing major, nothing worth wasting more than 600-odd words here.

◀▥ The Cardfile is one of those programs you might consider putting in your Startup group. That way, every time Windows starts, your Cardfile is on the screen, ready for you to dial someone up. See Chapter 6, the section "Applications that Amazingly Start Automatically."

Is This the Party to Whom I'm Speaking? (the Phone Dialer)

The Windows phone dialer enables you to make phone calls using the convenience of your computer, modem, and mouse — which comes in especially handy when you feel that it's too much effort to dial the phone using your fingers. *A-hem!*

To display the phone dialer, press Ctrl+Esc to pop up the Start Thing's menu, and then choose Programs⇨Accessories⇨Phone Dialer. The Phone Dialer appears in Figure 9-17. It's not visually impressive, nor is it threatened with any type of creativity; that is, it could have looked like a phone or had some clever elements, but it's hard to be creative on a deadline.

Figure 9-17
The Phone Dialer is ready to ring up some killer phone bills.
A. The number to dial, which you can type. **B.** Click here to dial. **C.** Click numbers here to enter a phone number. **D.** Click on one of these to speed-dial. **E.** If one of these is blank, click on it to add an entry. **F.** Sometimes the names can get too long. **G.** Click here to see previously dialed numbers.

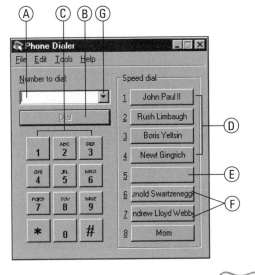

Obviously, to make use of the Phone Dialer, you need a modem. Your modem must be on, ready and connected, before you can dial out.

◄▥ As with the Cardfile, the Phone Dialer may be one of those toys you always want to have handy every time you start Windows. See the section "Applications that Amazingly Start Automatically" in Chapter 6 for more information.

Making the call

To use the Phone Dialer, type a number or click it in using the mouse and the phone keypad. Click on the big Dial button to dial.

When the other party answers, click on the Talk button in the Call Status dialog box.

You should type the person's name in the Active Call dialog box for the phone log (providing the name isn't entered automatically, such as when you use the Speed dialer).

Click the Hang Up button in the Active call dialog box when the phone call is over. That way, the call's duration is kept in the handy Call Log. Hmmm, that deserves its own little section.

Keeping track of who you call

One interesting feature of the Phone Dialer is that it keeps a log of your phone calls. This feature can be incredibly handy if you work in one of those busybody offices where they insist that you keep phone logs. To see the log, choose Tools⇨Show Log.

The log shows who you called (providing you typed their name), the number called, and the date and time. It also shows the call's duration.

Hold on for speed dialing

The Speed dial entries enable you to press and click to immediately dial up someone. To create a Speed dial entry, click on a blank button and then type the name and number in the dialog box provided.

You can edit, change, or delete speed-dial entries later by choosing Edit⇨Speed Dial from the menu. To delete an entry, just erase its name and number.

The Quick and Cheap Look at Microsoft Office

When Windows can't do it all, you buy more software. I'm not partial to any particular program or another (in fact, all my favorite stuff runs under DOS; Windows . . . eh?). Even so, the most popular applications available are provided by Microsoft, *the* most popular being the bundle of software known collectively as Microsoft Office.

With Microsoft Office, you get: Word, a word processor; Excel, a spreadsheet; PowerPoint, a presentation program; Schedule+, some type of scheduler, planner, and calendar; and the Binder, which enables you to combine various documents. Of all these, Word and Excel are the most popular, which is why I chose to cover them in this chapter.

The Wonderful Office Toolbar

If you've installed Microsoft Office, you see the handy Microsoft Office toolbar (also known as "MOM") hanging out somewhere on your screen. This is the handy device you can use to instantly start your Office applications. Figure 10-1 shows what's where.

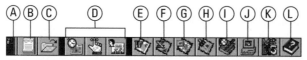

Figure 10-1
Which buttons mean what on MOM.
A. Right-click here to bring up MOM's control menu. **B.** New document. **C.** Open document. **D.** Stuff you do in the Schedule+ program. **E.** Start Word. **F.** Start Excel. **G.** Start PowerPoint. **H.** Start the Binder. **I.** Schedule+. **J.** Run the Explorer. **K.** Whip out a DOS prompt window. **L.** The Answer Wizard thing.

➡ Your toolbar may not have all the buttons shown in Figure 10-1. Indeed, the toolbar is customizable. Chapter 24 discusses how, in the section "Tweaking Your MOM."

➡ You can also move your MOM to a different spot on the screen. This technique is also covered in Chapter 24.

Starting up an application by using the toolbar

To start any program in the Office suite, simply click on one of MOM's proper buttons. Wanna start Word, click on the Word button. Same thing goes for Excel, PowerPoint, or whatever else is on the toolbar. Cinchy.

◀ If you're working on a document in Word and that document is on Windows' Documents menu (hanging right off the Start Thing), it's quicker to start that way; see Chapter 3, the section "Finding your document lurking in the Documents menu," for more information.

Starting up a new document by using the MOM toolbar

If you don't really know what you want to do, you can always choose to start a new document rather than just start an application. Using the New Document button on the MOM toolbar lets you do this, and it has the advantage of letting you fire up a template or wizard to help you get your document started. Here's how:

1. Click on the Start a New Document button.

   Click.

   The New dialog box appears (see Figure 10-2), along with its numerous tabs and panels. Each tab contains a topic or category that describes the type of new document you may want to create.

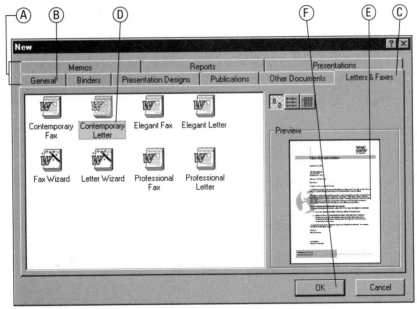

Figure 10-2
The New document dialog box.
A. Click on one of these tabs to choose a new type of document to create.
B. The General tab contains "blank" documents that don't fit any other category. **C.** The Letters & Faxes tab contains wizards and templates for starting your own letter or fax. **D.** Click on a document to see it previewed. **E.** The document preview window. **F.** Click on OK to open or start your new document.

3. Choose a tab.

Find a tab that best represents what you want to do. Click on that tab. For example, click on the Letters & Faxes tab to see some sample letter and fax documents you can open or start with.

The General tab has icons for "plain" documents. So if you don't find what you like, go to the General tab.

4. Choose a new document icon.

Click once on the document icon. You see a preview of coming attractions in the Preview window. If you don't like what you see, choose another document.

5. It's OK.

Office starts your application with the document template or wizard you selected.

If you chose a wizard, you see a wizard dialog box displayed, asking you step-by-step questions that help fill in the document.

If you chose a document template, you see a blank "new document" screen displayed. Some items may already appear on the screen; type over them with new information. You can also take advantage of the fonts and styles prepared for you in the document (more on what that means in the section on Word, later in this chapter).

You always start a new Excel worksheet or Word document by using any of the various New menu items scattered throughout Windows. See the section "Taking advantage of the numerous New menu commands" in Chapter 3 for more information about this technique.

A Quick Look at Those New Save and Open Dialog Boxes

About the biggest improvement with Office 95 over the older version of Office is that the new programs accept Windows' long filenames. (If you're using the older versions of Office programs, you're still bound to the crummy eight-letter filenames. Egads!)

The dialog boxes used by Office's applications for saving and opening documents are a little more enhanced (or you could say "junkier") than their standard Windows counterparts.

← See Chapter 4 for more information about the standard dialog boxes for saving, printing, opening, and so on. Look in the section "Going About Your Business."

The My Documents folder idea

When Office 95 was installed, it created on your hard drive a folder named My Documents. This folder is used to store various Office documents; it's what you first see when you choose the Open or Save As command.

My Documents

Obviously, you shouldn't really stuff everything into this folder. Instead, I recommend creating various subfolders and sub-subfolders for your projects. That keeps you truly organized, but in the meantime it's nice to know that Office has a special place for you to store stuff, which is (at least) a step in the right direction.

Another interesting folder is the Favorites folder. This folder is full of shortcuts, which also helps keep you organized. Even though your files may be in different folders and on different hard drives, you can easily create a shortcut to those files and store the shortcut in Office's Favorites folder. Information about how this is done is covered in the following section.

Favorites

→ See Chapter 17 for more information about storing stuff in folders and generally keeping organized. See the section "Setting Up Folders Just So."

The brand-new Open dialog box

When you open a document by using Word or Excel, you see a fancy new Open dialog box, one with many handy new features in it. Figure 10-3 points out some of my favorites.

The basic parts of the dialog box work the same as other Open dialog boxes do: You find a folder, choose a file, and then click on the Open button. No problem.

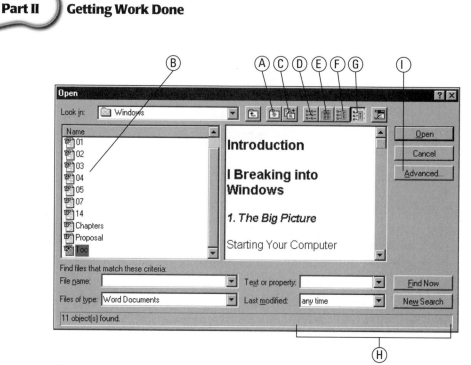

Figure 10-3
The fancy new Open dialog box.
A. Click here to see the contents of the Favorites folder. **B.** Choose a file over here. **C.** Puts a shortcut to the highlighted file into the Favorites folder. **D.** Displays files by using the List view. **E.** Displays files by using the Details view. **F.** Displays files and their properties. **G.** Displays a file preview window (currently on). **H.** Commands to help you find specific files. **I.** Advanced file-search button.

Extra features in the Office Open dialog box enable you to direct Windows to display only files containing a certain bit of text or created on or around a certain date. There's also the Advanced button, which helps you search for files anywhere on your computer.

About the most interesting things are the Favorites buttons:

Click on the Add to Favorites button to add the selected file (or files) to your Favorites folder. Windows makes shortcuts to whichever files you have selected and copies those shortcuts over to the Favorites folder.

You click on the Favorites button to see your Favorites folder. That way, you can pluck out common files while still keeping their original copies neatly organized in their own folders.

For more information about working the standard Open dialog box, see Chapter 4, the section "Opening stuff."

The brand-new Save As dialog box

Office's Save As folder has only a few extra goodies on it beyond what the standard Save dialog box offers. Figure 10-4 gives you a quick rundown.

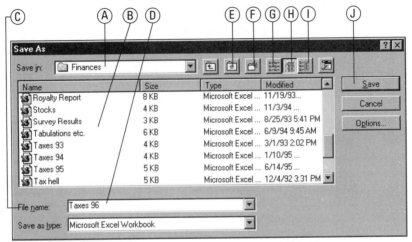

Figure 10-4
The Save As dialog box in Excel.
A. Pick a folder here. **B.** Choose a folder here as well. **C.** Type a filename here.
D. Windows may suggest the first few words of your document as a filename.
E. The Favorites folder shortcut. **F.** Create a new folder here. **G.** List view. **H.** Details view. **I.** Properties view. **J.** Click here to save.

The only remarkable things here are the Properties button, which lets you check out information about any files displayed in the Save As dialog box's window, plus the Favorites button.

Actually, I wouldn't click on the Favorites button in the Save As dialog box. Keep that folder reserved for shortcuts you create in the Open dialog box. Always remember to save a file in a special folder on your hard drive. Don't just randomly save the file anywhere.

◄═ For details about how the standard Save dialog box works, see the section "Saving your stuff" in Chapter 4.

New Help for Everything

Office 95's Help system works just like Windows' Help system, so there's really nothing to get used to. However, there is an extra tab in the Help

System's dialog box: the Answer Wizard (see Figure 10-5). This intelligent dialog box panel enables you to type a question, and then — shockingly — a list of possible topics that answer that question appears. Amazing.

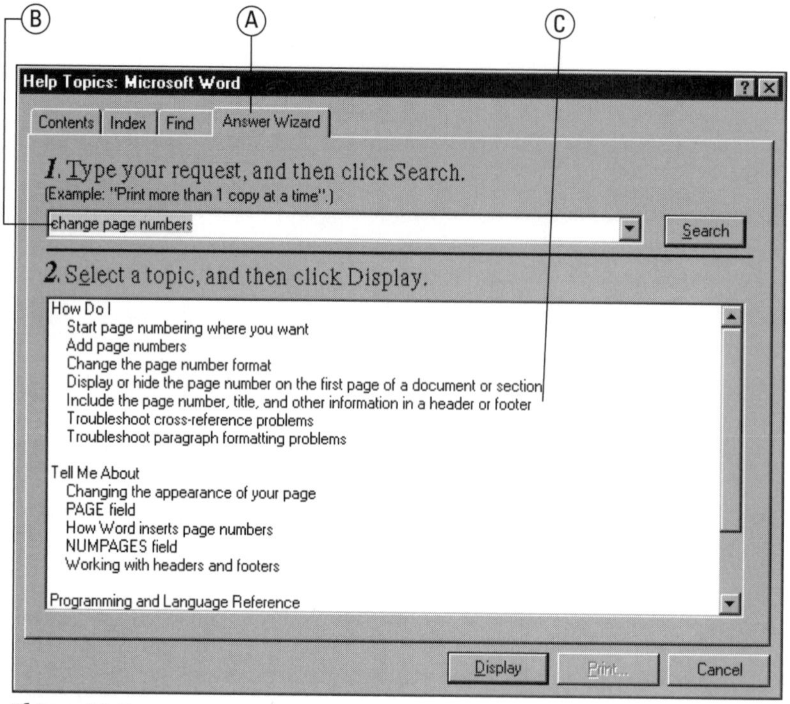

Figure 10-5
The Answer Wizard for Microsoft Word.
A. The Answer Wizard tab. **B.** I typed this in. **C.** And these are the topics Windows displayed.

In Figure 10-5, for example, I typed **change page numbers**, and the dialog box listed a slew of topics relating to that one question.

← You should also check out the section "The Windows way of offering Help" in Chapter 4 for more information about getting help in Windows.

"Tell Me All the Good Stuff About Word 95"

Microsoft Word is a word processor dee-lux. It has *all* the bells and whistles. As a writer, I'm the first to admit that there's nothing I do that can't be done in WordPad — or even the limited Notepad text editor. (This is primarily because the formatting for my books is done by the publisher, and spelling is done there too.) Still, many of Word's more prominent features are very slick and can make writing fun. Even so, keep in mind that a word processor won't make you a great writer.

The following sections highlight a few special things you can do with Word 95. This is not a complete list. If you're really into Word, I advise buying a good book on the subject. *Word For Windows 95 For Dummies,* written by me and published by IDG Books Worldwide, is an excellent reference for both the befuddled and experts alike.

New stuff on the screen

Word 95 looks much like Word 6.0. Okay, it really should be Word 6.1. And even Word 6 should be Word 3 (they skipped from Word 2.0 to Word 6.0, probably because WordPerfect did it too). Some of the new items you notice on Word's screen are pinpointed in Figure 10-6.

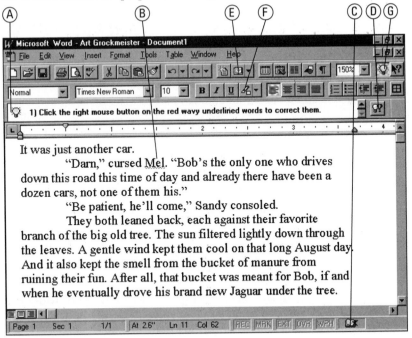

Figure 10-6
A few new things with Word.
A. The TipWizard box (offers suggestions, annoys you). **B.** Word underlines mis-spelled words "on the fly." **C.** Spell-check button. **D.** The "Show me" button (tells you how to do things). **E.** Inserts an address from your e-mail address book. **F.** A highlight marker (works like a highlight marker). **G.** Turns on the TipWizard box.

Annoying on-the-fly spell checking

Who wants to be constantly reminded that they're a horrid speller? Well, Word thinks that *everyone* does. All you have to do is type a word that Word doesn't recognize, and it's flagged on the screen as *Wrong! Wrong! Wrong!* for everyone to see. Anyway . . .

Here is how you turn on on-the-fly spell-checking:

1. Choose Tools⇨Options.

   The Options dialog box appears. Lotsa tabs. Lotsa panels.

2. Click on the Spelling tab to bring that panel forward.

3. Put a ✔ check mark in the Automatic Spell Checking box.

4. Click on OK.

   It's okay! Now Word flags any unknown word you type. The words appear with a squiggly underline beneath them, like this:

Right-click the mouse on the word to get a suggestion in a pop-up menu. 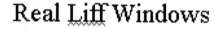 Real Liff Windows
Even though this is "cool," it can really slow you down, which is why most good writers will probably turn this ugly, new feature off.

Turn off on-the-fly spell-checking by repeating the preceding steps but ensuring that the ✔ check mark is removed from the Automatic Spell Checking box.

Personally, I'd rather write than spell-check. My brain works better when the thoughts fly right down my arm, into my fingers, and on the computer screen. When some robotic, spell-checking, moronic software is interrupting my thoughts with a jagged, red underline, I tend to loze, uh, er, I mean . . . I can't . . . I mean, I *lose* concentration.

Automatic formatting tips

Some cool abbreviated formatting tricks are included with the new version of Word. These are really shortcuts more than any new features, but they're stuff you'll probably quickly get in the habit of using.

To draw a line across the screen, type three hyphens, and then press the Enter key. This creates an automatic border.

If you type three equal signs, you get a double border.

Want to draw an arrow? Type **==>** (two equal signs and a greater-than sign). Press Enter or the spacebar, and you see your arrow.

Happy faces? Type a colon and a paren, like this **:)**. That changes into a smiling happy face when you press Enter or type a space.

Certain fractions are created automatically in Word 95. If you type **1/2** for one-half, for example, Word automatically changes it to a proper fraction: $^1/_2$.

Ordinal numbers also work the same way: Type **1st**, and Word changes it to 1st.

These tricks have much to do with the AutoCorrect feature, which is also available in Word 6. So if you really like typing 1/2 and then getting $^1/_2$, you can make it so in Word 6 (if you're still using it). See your favorite Word book (hint, hint) for more information about AutoCorrect.

"So what else is new with Word?"

Nothing much, really. There are a few other goodies, but primarily it's the on-the-fly spell-checking, Answer Wizard (common to all Office applications), and the new features of AutoCorrect, as described in the preceding section.

"Tell Me Some Good Stuff About Excel 95"

I'll admit that I'm more of a spreadsheet *nut* than a true expert. I find spreadsheets invaluable for many things I do plus many nontraditional things. For example, I use Excel to print invoices. Its graphical capabilities enable me to pull a few tricks that make the invoices look like they came from some "professional" program rather than something I slapped together by using Excel.

As with Word, if you truly want to learn the program, I advise buying a good book on the subject. The following sections highlight some tricks I'm fond of plus some new stuff available with Excel 95.

The old fill-in-the-cells trick

One Excel shortcut that I use all the time, but that I always seem to amaze everyone with, is the old fill-in-the-cells trick. This Excel feature makes it really cinchy to create days-and-month rows or columns. Figure 10-7 illustrates the concept, but follow along with these steps just in case:

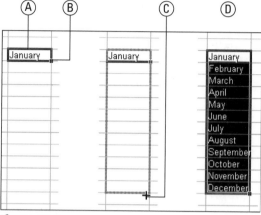

Figure 10-7
Slapping down a column of months in Excel.
A. Start by typing the first month. **B.** Point the mouse pointer here to drag.
C. Drag from that month down 12 cells in a row or column. **D.** Release the
mouse button, and the cells are filled.

1. Click the mouse on your starting cell.

   Click.

2. Type a day of the week or a month.

   This trick works with only days of the week (Monday, Tuesday, and so
   on) or months (January, February, and so on).

   For the sample in Figure 10-7, I typed **January** and pressed the Enter key.

3. Click the mouse on the starting cell again.

   This step is necessary because pressing Enter sometimes moves the cell
   selector down to the next cell.

4. Point the mouse pointer at the dot on the selected cell.

   The dot is in the lower right corner of the highlight rectangle surrounding the cell.

5. Drag the mouse down or to the right.

   This step creates your row or column headings. In Figure 10-7, I
   dragged down to create row headings. As you drag down, the cells you
   drag over become selected, surrounded by that fuzzy-line thing.

6. Release the mouse button.

   As shown in Figure 10-7, you see your days of the week or months
   filled in.

Unfortunately, this trick doesn't work with anything else in Excel. If you want to create headings based on years or some other progression of numbers, you have to drag-copy a cell formula. For example:

1. Type the first number into a cell.

   The current year is 1995, "The Year of Windows." I typed **1995** in the cell at the top of Figure 10-8.

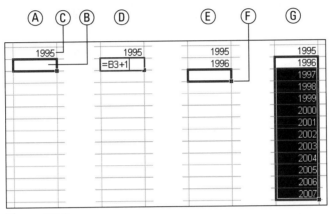

Figure 10-8
Creating a series of numbers.
A. Type your starting number here. **B.** Click the mouse here to create a column of numbers. **C.** Click the mouse over there to create a row of numbers. **D.** Enter the formula into the proper cell. **E.** Press the Enter key to see the calculation. **F.** Point the mouse pointer at this thing to drag. **G.** Drag down or to the right to fill in the numbers.

   Press Enter after typing your number.

2. Position the cell selector.

   If you're making a column of numbers, the cell selector is already positioned underneath the starting number. Great.

   If you're making a row of numbers, click the mouse in the cell just to the right of the cell containing the starting number.

3. Type the formula.

   Just type the following:

   =

   Now click the mouse back on the original number (1995, in my example). This step sticks that cell's number into the formula, looking something like this:

   =B3

Now type **+1** (plus one), the formula to increase that number by one:

=B3+1

That's your formula, though the cell number B3 may be different on your computer.

4. Press Enter.

This step directs Excel to make the calculation, putting the proper number in that cell. Now you only have to drag and fill to create the rest of your row or column.

5. Click the mouse on the formula cell again.

This step is required to reselect it (refer to Figure 10-8).

6. Point the mouse pointer at the dot on the selected cell.

That's the dot in the lower right corner.

7. Drag the mouse down or to the right.

Depending on whether you're creating a row or column, drag down or right. Figure 10-8 shows a drag down.

8. Release the mouse button.

The numbers are filled in, each one being one notch larger than the one before it.

If it's your desire to create jumps of 5, in step 3 change the number you type after the plus sign to 5:

=B3+5

You can specify any value there to make each number in the series jump by that much.

Let Excel do the work for you

If you're using Excel to create lists of things (because a spreadsheet can be used as a sort of database), you'll appreciate the new AutoComplete feature. It enables you to type only the first few letters of an item in a column. Excel automatically types the rest for you.

In Figure 10-9, I started a column of various places my kids demand that we go for nourishment. I had to enter only the original items. For the rest, just typing an M, P, W, or K filled in the rest; as you can see in cell B10, I had to type only a P, and AutoComplete filled in the *izza Hut* part.

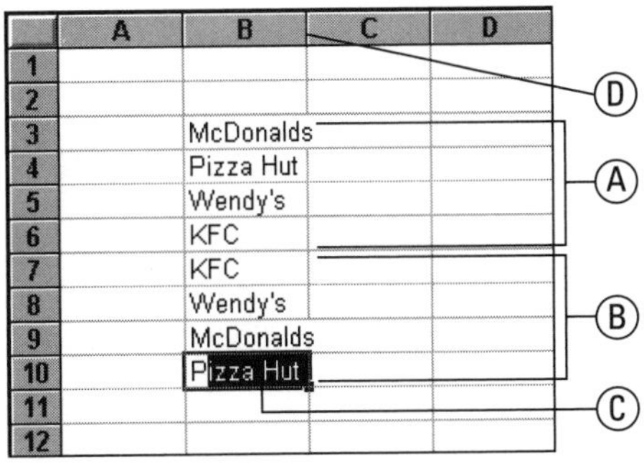

Figure 10-9
An example of AutoComplete in action.
A. Original items in the list. **B.** These items are typed automatically. **C.** AutoComplete fills in the rest after you type P. **D.** Double-click here to automatically adjust the column width.

Another shortcut blessing (though not necessarily new) is that you can double-click the mouse between two columns to automatically adjust the column width. For example, the width of column B in Figure 10-9 is a bit narrow. By clicking on the crack between B and C, the column width adjusts to the widest item in column B.

Different things you can do with a spreadsheet that you probably didn't think of

A spreadsheet is a grid, and just about anything you can fit into a grid can be put into a spreadsheet. For example, Figure 10-10 shows a game grid I designed using Excel.

To make this type of grid, I first adjusted the column widths to match the row heights (a column width of 1.71 was selected). Choose Format⇨Column⇨Width to precisely set the column width in Excel.

Then, to fill each cell with a pattern or outline it with a border, click the mouse at that cell (or drag to select a group of cells) and press the Ctrl+1 key combination. This step displays the Format Cells dialog box (see Figure 10-11). Use the Border and Patterns tab to design the cells in your grid.

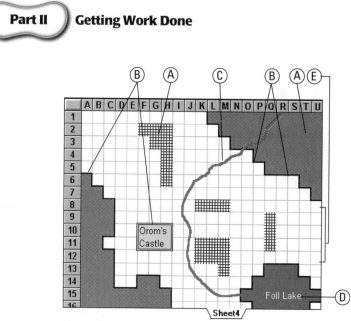

Figure 10-10

A sort of game grid designed in Excel.
A. Cells filled with patterns. **B.** Borders around cells. **C.** An object drawn freehand.
D. Plain text. **E.** The Goongas will probably attack from this direction.

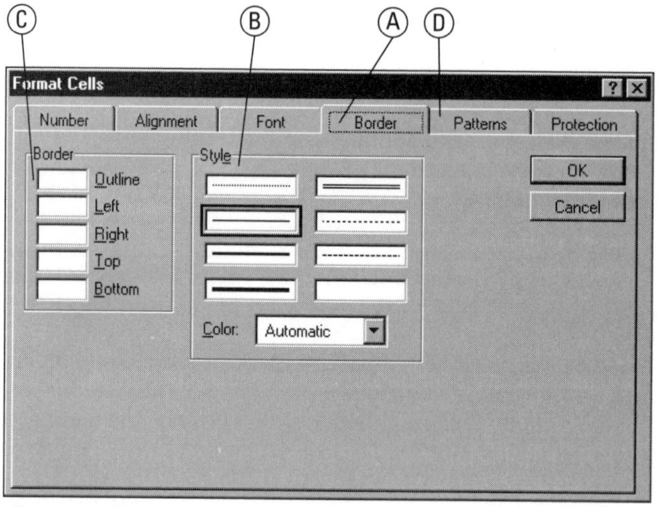

Figure 10-11

The Format Cells dialog box.
A. Use this tab to set a cell's border. **B.** First choose a line style. **C.** Second, click on which sides of the cell you want to have a border. **D.** Use the Patterns panel to set color and texture for a cell's innards.

This kind of manipulation doesn't have to apply only to weird stuff in Excel. You can shade and draw borders around your regular Excel projects to make them, er, *excel*.

Wasting Time with Online Communications

To end your computer's loneliness and despair, you can buy a modem and hook it up. This gives your computer access to the phone lines and all sorts of other computers. It's the Information Age! With a modem, you can waste hours of time, chatting on America Online, surfing the Web, dialing up local systems and BBSs, playing online games, and all sorts of technologically advanced things. You'll never have to leave your house again!

Modem Mayhem

Obviously your computer can't dial up another computer unless you have two vital pieces of hardware: a modem and a phone line. The modem is your computer's phone — what it uses to dial up and talk ("sing," actually) to other computers. You also need a phone line to make that possible.

My advice is to get a separate phone line for your computer. Although you can use your main line, a dedicated line for the modem makes a great deal of sense. The most important reason is that you don't have to worry about someone else picking up an extension and disconnecting you. Also, you can't receive any calls while your computer is using the phone, so having a second line means that people can still call your house while you're off modeming.

You don't pay any extra for using a computer on your phone lines. There is no toll or extra tax involved (at least not yet). You still pay for long distance, and if you pay per call, each call the computer makes gets racked up like any other call.

Modems must also be connected to a COM or serial port. If you have an external modem, it hooks up to one of the ports located on your computer's rump. Internal modems plug inside of your computer, though they still use a COM port.

⟶ The COM port your modem uses was configured by Windows when you installed your modem. If not, see Chapter 23. Everything should be set and ready to go after you've fully informed Windows about your modem.

The Joys of HyperTerminal

A modem just doesn't do it by itself. I learned this the hard way when I bought my first modem. You need *software,* a special program to control your modem, before you can even so much as dial the phone. This software is called *communications software.* One such program is included "free" with Windows: HyperTerminal, which, as communications software goes, really isn't that bad.

Then again, coffee isn't that bad, but it does take time to get used to it.

⟵ HyperTerminal is one of Windows' many free programs, or applets. See Chapter 9 for more information about Windows' other free programs.

Scaring up HyperTerminal

To start HyperTerminal, follow these steps:

1. Pop up the Start Thing's menu.

   Click on the Start button, or — the guaranteed way — press Ctrl+Esc.

2. Choose Programs⇨Accessories⇨HyperTerminal.

The HyperTerminal menu item appears as a folder, not as an icon. Click on it to open the folder window (see Figure 11-1).

Figure 11-1
A typical HyperTerminal window.
A. Open the HyperTerminal program to start a new session.
B. Open a session icon to dial up that system. **C.** Companion program files. To hide these, choose View⇨Options, click on the View tab, and put a dot by Hide files of these types.

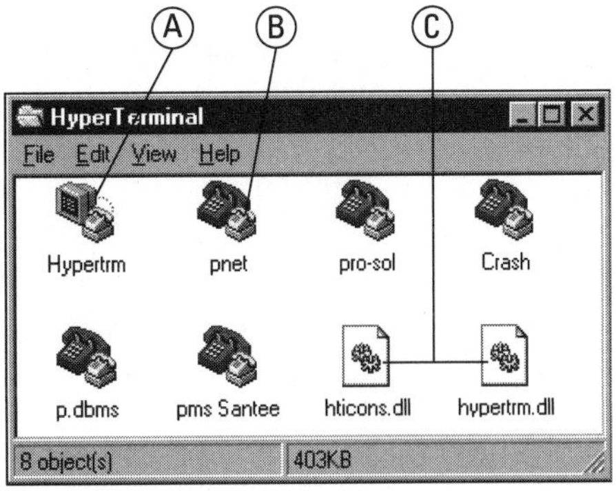

➠ Having a folder/window is a different approach from other Windows programs. The reason has to do with the way you use HyperTerminal, which is discussed in the following section.

⬅ Yes, you can stick folders on the Start Thing's menu. See Chapter 6, the section "Adding a program to a Start Thing submenu," and just add a folder rather than a program.

Gazing through the HyperTerminal window

Unlike other applications, HyperTerminal struts its stuff in a window, such as the one in Figure 11-1. You have two choices:

Open up a session icon, which dials up a specific computer.

Create a new session by opening the HyperTerminal program itself. The session is then saved in the window so that you can run it again to access that same computer.

Hypertrm

The details of how you do these things are covered in the following two sections.

"Who you gonna call?" (Creating a new session in HyperTerminal)

A *session* is something you dial up by using your modem. The session contains all the information for calling up that system, its phone number, technical communications junk, and other information. After it's assembled, you can then click on that session's icon in the HyperTerminal folder to connect with that system at any time in the future.

The following steps show you how to create a session for the Microsoft Downloads computer, a massive system at Microsoft corporate headquarters that contains all sorts of freebie files and updates. This is a handy system to have in your group of sessions.

1. Open up the HyperTerminal program.

   Hypertrm

   Double-click on its icon in the HyperTerminal folder. This is how you create a new session.

   The Connection Description dialog box is displayed (see Figure 11-2), which is sort of a wizard for telling HyperTerminal about the other computer you plan to dial up.

Figure 11-2
The Connection Description dialog box.
A. Type the system name here. **B.** Pick an icon from this scrolling list. **C.** Click here to move on.

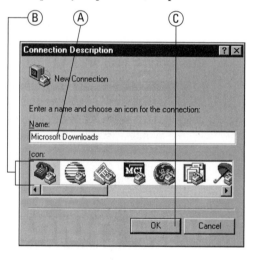

2. Name that system.

   Type a name for the system you're calling. For this tutorial, it's the Microsoft Download system, so type **Microsoft Download** in the box (refer to Figure 11-2).

3. Chooza icon for the system.

   Pluck out a handy icon for the session. Me, I always pick the first icon because I lead a boring life. But you can choose any of the icons listed, including some that are predestined for such systems as AT&T Mail, MCI Mail, GEnie, and the Radioactive Yellow Phone.

4. Click on the OK button.

   The Phone Number dialog box appears, in which you type the number you're dialing. For the Microsoft Download system, enter the number listed in Figure 11-3.

   In case you can't see the number clearly enough in the figure, it's (206) 637-9009.

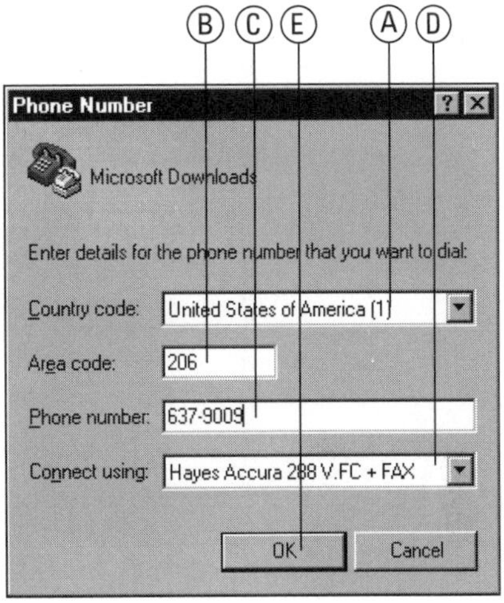

Figure 11-3
The fill-in-the-phone number dialog box.
A. Choose the country you're calling. **B.** Type the area code (if it's not your area code). **C.** The phone number goes here. **D.** This is your modem. Do not change. **E.** Moving right along . . . .

5. Click on the OK button.

   The Connect dialog box is displayed. Don't bother with anything in the dialog box, just . . .

6. . . . Click on the Dial button.

   This step directs Windows to dial your modem and connect to the Microsoft Download computer, located somewhere near Seattle.

   You hear your modem dial the number.

   You hear the other computer answer the phone.

   You hear them sing to each other in glorious harmony as a connection is made.

   If a human answers the modem's call by mistake, click on the Cancel button.

If the other phone doesn't answer or it's busy, click on the Dial Now button to try dialing again.

7. You're connected!

When you're online and connected, you see the terminal screen displayed (see Figure 11-4). It shows you text sent from the other computer as well as text you type yourself.

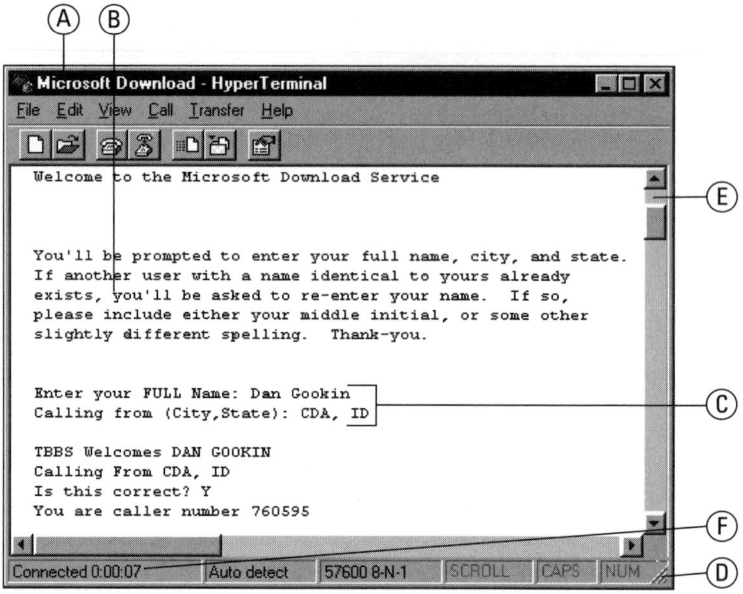

Figure 11-4
The terminal screen.
A. Connected to Microsoft Download. **B.** Text sent by the other computer, the "host." **C.** Text I typed. **D.** You can adjust the size of the window. **E.** Use this scrollbar to see text that has wandered past. **F.** This tells you how long you've been online, great for gauging long-distance charges.

Your first task is to log in, just as you logged in to Windows. Type your name or ID for that system. Then you're usually asked for a password.

Some systems, such as Microsoft Download, merely want your name and location.

Some systems don't let you in until you've officially registered. Messages displayed on the screen give you more information, or you may have to search for a menu of options to register yourself as a member.

If you don't see anything after you've connected, try pressing the Enter key once.

What you can do when you're online is usually up to whatever computer you've called. A menu of options is usually available. Figure 11-5 shows the menu for the Microsoft Download system. Type a number at the prompt to see more choices or a list of files to retrieve.

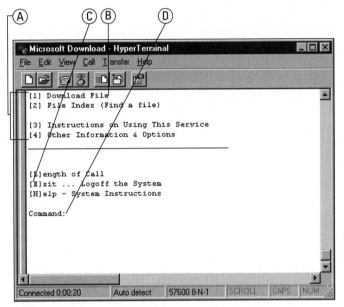

Figure 11-5
The menu on the Microsoft Download system.
A. Menu choices. **B.** This gets you to the files available for downloading.
C. Type E to hang up when you're done. **D.** The prompt, where you type your commands.

Also check out the section "Doing the Online Thing," later in this chapter for more suggestions about what to do, downloading, reading mail, and so on.

8. Hang up properly.

Just as you wouldn't just slam down the phone when you're done talking to a human, you don't randomly hang up on another computer. Don't turn off your external modem. Don't choose Call⇨Disconnect. You should first tell the other system that you want to go bye-bye.

In Figure 11-5, you see the Exit command listed in the Microsoft Download system's menu. Type **E** and press Enter at the prompt to hang up. Use similar commands on other systems. The idea is simple: Let the other computer hang up the phone.

9. Quit HyperTerminal.

Eventually, after hanging up, you'll want to quit HyperTerminal and go off and do something else.

When you quit, you're asked whether you want to save the new session you've created. Click on the Yes button. This saves the session for future use and reuse whenever you want to dial up that system again.

← Remember that you don't always have to quit. You can put HyperTerminal away temporarily by minimizing its window. See the section "Done for the Day? To Quit or Put Away" at the end of Chapter 4.

What about the speed, data word format, and all that?

In Windows 95, you no longer have to mess with the trivial aspects of setting up your modem in a communications program. That is done instead by using the modem's Properties dialog box.

In HyperTerminal, click on the Properties button on the toolbar to see the session's Properties dialog box. Click on the Configure button located near the bottom of the dialog box. That brings up your modem's Properties dialog box.

In the modem's Properties dialog box, in the Maximum speed drop-down list box, set the maximum speed your modem can handle. For a 28.8 modem, choose 57600; for a 14.4 modem, choose 19200; all other modems choose their top speed as rated.

In the Connection panel, you can set the *data word format,* but I wouldn't bother. Keep everything set at 8, None, and 1.

Click on OK to exit the various dialog boxes, and then don't bother with this stuff ever again.

Dialing up a something you already created

After you create a session, you can dial it up again simply by opening its session icon in the HyperTerminal window. After saving the Microsoft Download session to disk, for example, you only have to double-click on its icon to instantly redial that computer.

This point is important to remember because it works differently from most other communications programs: Open HyperTerminal itself to create a new session, and open up session icons to dial that system. It's all part of the "getting used to the way Windows does things" state of mind.

Doing the Online Thing

When you're connected to another computer, there are several things you can do. The most popular thing is to download software, which means that you copy it from the other computer to your own computer. Also popular is uploading (downloading in reverse), chatting, and reading mail and news.

➡ The big online services have their own ways of doing things: reading mail, downloading files, and so on. Read through the following sections to get a rough idea of what's going on, though. The major online services are covered near the end of this chapter, in the section "Other Modem Programs You May Have."

Reading your mail

Most people read their mail first when they log in to another computer. Even though downloading is more popular, it's just nicer to read your mail. After all, seeing that "You have mail" message appear on the screen reassures you that someone out there loves you (or at least is mad enough by something you did or said to send you an e-mail letter).

Of course, reading your mail is different on every system. Refer to the menu that appears at a prompt for information about accessing your mail.

Sometimes the mail command is Mail, so try typing that at the prompt.

Another tip: The best way to get mail is to send it. Or you can participate in the online discussions going on. It also helps to be a jerk, because online jerks and obnoxious people tend to get a great deal of mail. (Hey, you didn't say that you wanted a bunch of *nice* mail.)

Downloading (taking files from the other computer)

Downloading is about the most frustrating thing anyone ever tries to do with a communications program. It's the art of directing the other computer to send you a file and having your computer receive the file and having you get the file okay and not lose your sanity in the process.

Here are the steps to downloading:

1. Connect to the other computer and all that.

2. Go to the place where you download files.

    Use the menu to find the area where files are available for the taking. In the Microsoft Download system, you press 2 from the main menu and then choose other menu options to get to the specific software section you're looking for.

3. Browse through the file listings for something you want to download.

    Suppose that you spy the file RACERX.EXE. It's a cool game you just can't live without.

4. Tell the other computer which file you want to take.

    (Sometimes this step and step 5 are reversed.)

    Type the download command. In the Microsoft Download, it's D:

    > <D>ownload, <P>rotocol, <N>ew, <L>ist, or <H>elp

    > Selection or <CR> to exit:

    Type **D** to pick Download.

    (The CR to exit means to press the Enter key; CR equals *c*arriage *r*eturn, which is nerdspeak for the Enter key.)

    Then you're asked for a filename:

    > File Name?

    Type the name of the file you want the other computer to send you. For example:

    > **RACERX.EXE**

    Type the entire filename, including the dot-EXE part. This is not Windows you're dealing with, and you must be specific.

    Press the Enter key.

5. Choose the Zmodem protocol.

   A *protocol* is the way the other computer sends you the file. It's a special way of sending information to ensure that what your computer gets is what the other computer sent.

   The other computer displays a list of available protocols. You have to choose the one called Zmodem (pronounced "ZEE-mo-dem," like a French spy in a bad movie would say "Tell me where you hid zee modem!").

   After you pick Zmodem, the other computer should fall right into its file-sending mode (unless this step and step 4 are reversed). If it doesn't, you may have to press a key or something, but in most instances the transfer begins immediately.

6. The transfer takes place.

   The computer is really doing the work now. You see a busy dialog box that details the transfer (see Figure 11-6). There's really nothing you can do here but sit and watch.

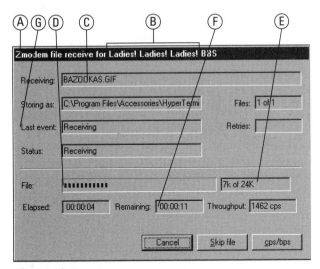

Figure 11-6
A file is being received via Zmodem.
A. A Zmodem file receive (other protocols may display a different dialog box). **B.** The name of the system you're calling. **C.** The file you're downloading. **D.** Progress thermometer. **E.** The size of the file and how much of it has been sent already. **F.** Guestimate of how much longer it will take to send. **G.** Other junk.

You don't really have to sit there and watch the entire thing. If you're downloading a major chunk of file and the dialog box (refer to Figure 11-6) says that you have a few hours to go, feel free to minimize HyperTerminal's window and go off to do something else. Keep an eye on the time, and check the program when you think that the download will be done. (The tiny modem lights on the loud time stop blinking after a while when downloading is done.)

7. I'm done!

After the file has been sent and successfully received, the receiving dialog box goes away. You can now dig it up and do whatever with it by using My Computer or the Explorer.

What next?

You can stay online, download another file, chitty-chat, do whatever. Just remember to properly hang up when you're done; choose the Exit, Hang up, or Good-bye command from the other computer. Let it be the one who hangs up the modem.

➡ Most files you download are stored right in HyperTerminal's window. You might want to move them elsewhere; see Chapter 16, the section "Deeply Moving Files," for more information.

After a hard day of downloading, it's time to unzip

Some files you download are stored in a special format called a *ZIP archive*. It means that the files were compressed and packed into one single, lite file for easy transportation. When you get the file over on your computer, you have to decompress or unZIP it to use it.

Alas, Windows doesn't have anything to help you unZIP. You need a special program called a *utility* to decompress the files. This program is usually available for downloading on the same system on which you found the ZIP files. Look for a file called PKUNZIP or PKZIP or some variation.

By the way, the PKZIP and PKUNZIP files are not freebies. They're shareware. If you use them, you're expected to pay for them (I have). Information included with the files tells you where to send your cash.

Uploading (sending files to another computer)

If you haven't yet downloaded anything, my best advice is to do that first, before you attempt to upload. Because uploading works exactly like downloading — but in reverse — it's better if you're already familiar with how that works:

1. Dial up the other computer.

2. Go to the place where you send it (upload) files.

   The menu on the screen should tell you where this happens. (You can't do it on the Microsoft Download system.)

3. Enter whichever option you need to for uploading files.

   For example, the menu may say:

   > <D>ownload, <U>pload, <L>ist files, <M>enu:

   Press U to upload, and press the Enter key.

4. Choose the protocol.

   The other computer lists a host of protocols for receiving files. Choose the Zmodem option if it's available. Otherwise, choose Ymodem, and then Xmodem.

   If you choose something other than Zmodem, you have to tell the other computer which files you're sending. The other system asks you to type the filenames. Do so, by typing the complete filename.

   Keep in mind that some systems do not accept Windows filenames. You should limit your filenames to eight characters or less. Use only numbers or letters. If you know the filename's three-letter extension, type it as well.

   At this point, the other computer is waiting to receive the file. It's your turn now.

5. Send the file.

   Click on the Send button on the toolbar, or choose Transfer⇨Send File. This step displays the Send File dialog box, shown in Figure 11-7. Fill in the dialog box with the name of the file you're going to send, and, optionally, choose the protocol.

Figure 11-7
The Send File dialog box.
A. Type the name of the file you're sending. **B.** You can use the Browse button to locate a file. **C.** Zmodem is the best protocol to use. **D.** Choose other protocols if the other computer doesn't support Zmodem. **E.** Click on this button to send the file.

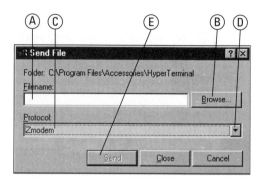

6. Click on the Send button.

   The file is sent. The two computers happily exchange the file, and you sit there and wait. As with uploading, you see a busy dialog box displayed during the transfer (it looks similar to Figure 11-6).

7. All done!

   After the file is sent, you can send more files, download files, or just hang around and do the online thing.

Don't forget to inform the other computer when you want to hang up. Use its Exit, Logoff, Good-bye, or whatever command, and let the other computer hang up the phone line. Never just unplug your modem or disconnect on your end.

Reading the news

What passes for "news" on an online system usually refers to public messages left by others for everyone to read. These are more along the lines of discussions as opposed to "Live from Beirut" type of news.

News discussions usually center on some sort of topic. Basically, find a topic that interests you, and read the news. Use whatever menu commands enable you to do this on whichever system you call.

There are generally two types of discussions: serious and wholly worthless. The serious discussions usually center on some topic of concern or research. For example, I posed a question on a discussion topic dealing with an ancient computer I owned. Several qualified people responded, and my problem was fixed. The other type of discussions are usually dominated by adolescent males (of all ages) who would rather insult people and be crude than do anything constructive.

Don't feel compelled to contribute to the public conversations. Most people don't "post" public messages.

Other Modem Programs You May Have

Most sophisticated online systems have their own software. This makes it a heck of a lot easier to get around than having to deal with a text-based communications program such as HyperTerminal. This section presents a quick rundown of what you may encounter.

The Microsoft Network is Microsoft's foray into the world of online communications. What makes this one unique is that it's instantly integrated into Windows, actually a part of the operating system. Unfortunately, because it's so new, there's really little to do there. This should change — indeed, the whole Microsoft Network will evolve and become something completely different — in a few years. When it does, the information offered in this book will be much more beefy.

MSN

If you don't have the Microsoft Network on your computer — even if you don't have a modem — don't fret. You paid for it, and it's in there somewhere. An icon stuck on the desktop when Windows was installed helps you set up MSN, get an account, and arrange for endless monthly payments. Yippee!

CompuServe is the granddaddy of online networks. Heck, I bought my CompuServe account back in 1982! It's gotten much better since then, with a Windows-based program that makes sending mail and reading news messages a snap. Of all the online services, this is the one you can get the most from. It can also be the most frustrating.

CompuServe

Prodigy, often viewed as the dumb person's online network (which is how they used to advertise it), has come a long way. It's much more fun and family oriented than any other service, but its graphics and splashy looks make it appear slow. Also, its mail system is probably one of the worst out there. Still, it's much easier to find stuff in that slow graphical interface than it is on other systems.

Prodigy

America Online is very popular, especially among Macintosh users. It has a graphical interface and lacks Prodigy's stodginess. My main complaint with it is the proliferation of the chat rooms. Now, you may like chatting with different people and having fun with your modem. If so, AOL is your cup-o-tea. For me, it always feels like I'm walking in on some 22-year-old's birthday party instead of visiting the library.

America Online

Finally, there's the Internet. That isn't an online service as much as it's a ganglia of online things, UNIX computers, major corporations, and millions of people who think that being "on the Net" is just the coolest thing. Granted, there are many fun and interesting things on the Internet. But the Internet is anarchy. No one is in charge. As a result, things are often nonprofessional and clumsy. Still, there are a few jewels out there.

Windows 95 has direct connections to the Internet, some of which are included with the Plus! package. However, until I can figure out how it all works and tell you how to set it up in a simple manner, my advice is to stick with one of the commercial Internet packages. Get something like Internet in a Box, and then go out and buy a good book about setting things up (until space allows and this book sports its own Internet chapter).

Dealing with Ancient DOS Applications

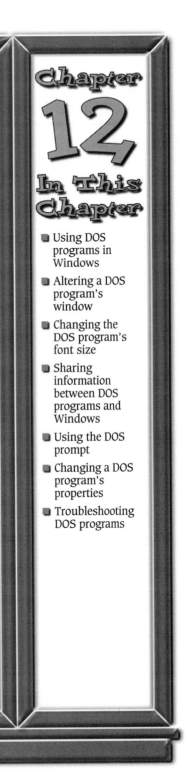

Chapter 12

In This Chapter

- Using DOS programs in Windows
- Altering a DOS program's window
- Changing the DOS program's font size
- Sharing information between DOS programs and Windows
- Using the DOS prompt
- Changing a DOS program's properties
- Troubleshooting DOS programs

DOS isn't dead; only the smart people are using it now. Why? Because, though it may be ugly, it's simple. There's nothing to get frustrated over. DOS doesn't claim to multitask or offer a common look and feel for all its programs. And DOS is fast. Very fast. DOS smokes on a Pentium computer. But I digress. . . .

Like myself, you may be hanging on to some old, fond DOS applications, stuff from the last decade, jewels like WordPerfect 5.1, Magellan, dBASE, the diehard 1-2-3, or a host of other programs — solid software — good applications that you still need to use, still enjoy. If so, you can use them under Windows. Maybe not as fast as they'd run if you were still running DOS by itself, but you can use them nonetheless.

If you really need to, you can start your computer in MS-DOS mode. It comes up with the DOS prompt — CONFIG.SYS, AUTOEXEC.BAT, all that — just like it did before. The secret is divulged in Chapter 26, in the section "DOS games? Forget Windows!"

Tolerating DOS Programs in Windows

Windows is DOS-impaired. There's this heated jealousy going on. In the old days, Windows actually — and I'm not making this up — was a DOS program. You typed WIN at the DOS prompt to run Windows. With Windows 95, the computer starts right up, loads DOS, and then loads Windows right away. You no longer have to type WIN, but DOS is in there nonetheless. So Windows tries its best to pretend that DOS is just another program. And it does this quite well.

Starting your old, favorite DOS program

When you upgraded to Windows 95, it kept any memory of your older DOS programs you used with your previous version of Windows. They should all be there, sitting as menu items off the Start Thing's menu.

To start your program, simply pluck it from the Start Thing's menu:

1. Pop up the Start Thing's menu.

   Press Ctrl+Esc, or click on the Start Thing if you see it loitering on one end of the taskbar.

2. Choose Programs . . .

   . . . and then choose any submenus where your DOS program is located.

3. Click on your DOS program to start it.

   It starts in its own graphical window on the screen, which is covered in the next section. You can also make the DOS program run full-screen — just like it used to in the old days — which is covered later in this chapter (but I'm too lazy to look up the exact spot right now).

◀ On my computer, I've moved all my old favorite DOS programs to one submenu right off the Programs menu (see Figure 12-1). It's called DOS Applications. See Chapter 6, the section "Making your own, unique submenu," for more information about creating your own submenu.

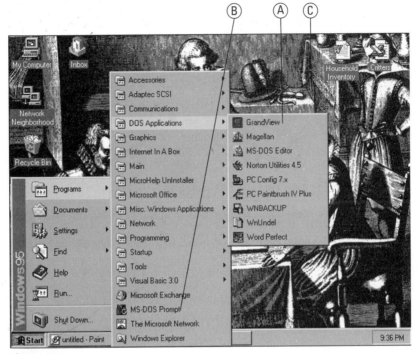

Figure 12-1
All DOS programs nestled into their own Start Thing menu.
A. Here they are (most of them, anyway). **B.** The DOS prompt is right here on everyone's computer. You can always start any DOS program from here.
C. See Chapter 24 for information about adding an interesting desktop background to Windows.

➡ You can also create shortcuts to your DOS programs and stick them right on the desktop. See the section "Sticking stuff on the desktop" in Chapter 17.

⬅ If your programs aren't on the Start Thing's menu, you have to add them manually. Alas, there is no cute or clever way to do this. Instead, you have to hunt down the programs and add them to the Start Thing's menu manually. This process is detailed in Chapter 6, in the section "Adding a program to a Start Thing submenu."

⬅ If you're installing a new DOS program, such as a game (which is about all the DOS software there is left), see the section "Installing DOS software (is a pain)," later in this chapter.

➠ You notice that the DOS prompt, MS-DOS Prompt, is right on the Programs main submenu (refer to Figure 12-1). See the section "Running a DOS Prompt for the Heck of it," later in this chapter.

Messing with a DOS window

DOS programs run inside a graphical window on the screen, which is shown in Figure 12-2. This is how all your DOS programs look in Windows, but you're not stuck with *exactly* what you see on the screen.

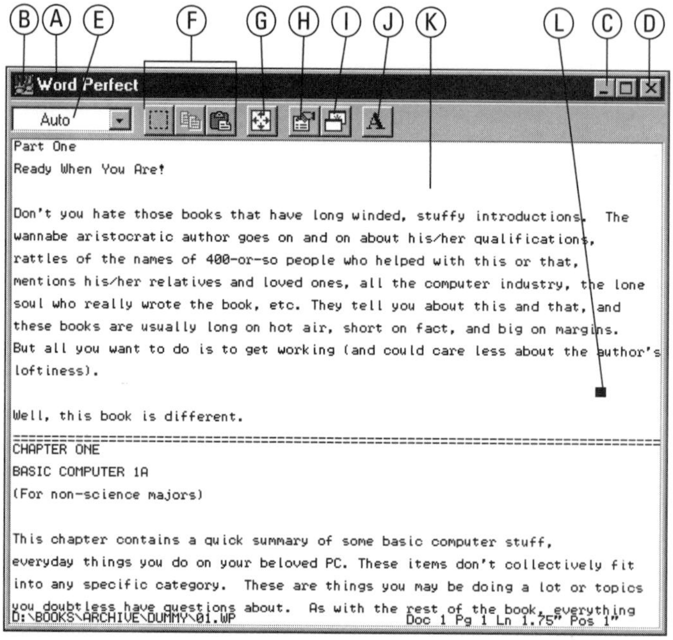

Figure 12-2
WordPerfect 5.1 looking sad and bored in a Windows window.
A. It's WordPerfect! **B.** The DOS control menu. **C.** You can minimize and maximize this window like any other. **D.** Don't click here (see the section "Quitting a DOS program," elsewhere in this chapter). **E.** Avoid using this thing. **F.** Buttons for selecting, copying, and pasting text. **G.** Switch to full-screen mode. **H.** Display the Properties dialog box. **I.** I have no idea. **J.** Use this to change the window size and font. **K.** Text is displayed here. **L.** This is the "simulated" mouse for WordPerfect.

You can change the DOS program's window size in a number of ways:

As with any window, you can minimize it to a button on the taskbar.

Or you can maximize the window. When you do, it may not fill the screen; Windows tries to keep the DOS text proportional, so the window may not be "full size."

Perhaps the best way to resize the window is to click on the Font button — the A button — on the toolbar. In addition to setting a new font size, the dialog box that's displayed helps you gauge the DOS window's size on the screen.

Figure 12-3 shows what you see when you click on the Font button. It's really the DOS program's Properties dialog box, Font panel forward. In addition to choosing a font (see the figure), you get to preview how the DOS window will size up on your screen.

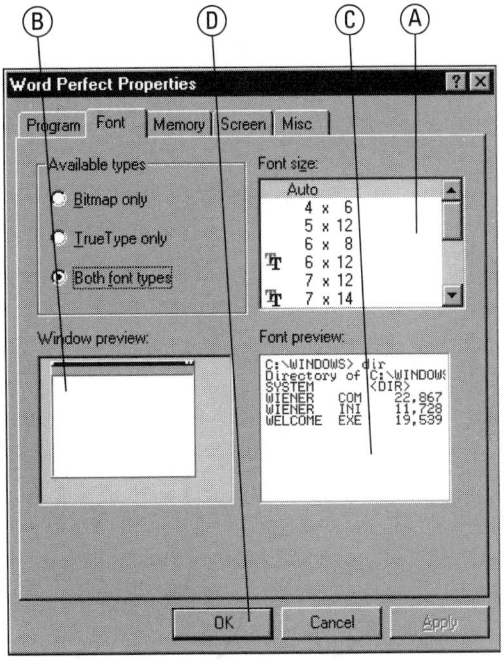

Figure 12-3
A DOS program's Properties dialog box, Font panel forward.
A. Chooza font size from here — anything but Auto.
B. A preview of your DOS application's window size and position. **C.** A preview of the font size. **D.** Click here to save and exit.

After toying around with the Font panel in the program's Properties dialog box, click on the OK button. This returns you to the DOS application, where you can keep on working.

A final DOS window trick you can employ is to see your DOS program the way it oughtta be: text only, no graphics. To do that, you can click on the Way It Oughtta Be button or press the Alt+Esc key combination (which normally brings up a Properties dialog box, but not here).

TIP

To return from full-screen to Windows mode, press Alt+Enter again. Keep that in mind! You don't want to forget and think that you're using only DOS again. The joy would kill you.

For more information about tweaking a DOS application's window, see the section "Messing with a DOS Program's Properties," later in this chapter.

Copying and pasting between DOS programs

DOS isn't as friendly as Windows is when it comes to sharing and loving between programs. But under Windows, you can get your DOS programs to share text with each other and with Windows programs when text has been copied. You can select and copy text in a DOS program's window, and then you can paste that text into another DOS program's window or into a Windows program. The key is the Selection tool.

When you click on the Selection tool, your DOS application changes modes. What you see on the screen freezes, and the title bar changes to tell you that you're in text-selection mode (see Figure 12-4). You can use the mouse to block out a large chunk of text for copying, as shown in the figure nearby.

After roping off a section of text, click on the Copy button. This returns you to normal mode, where you can use your DOS application again. But the text you selected is now stored in Windows' Clipboard. You can paste it into any Windows program that can accept text, you can paste it into any DOS program, and you can even paste it into the DOS program you're working on right now.

To paste, first position the cursor in your DOS program and then click on the Paste tool. The text flows into your DOS program just as though you typed it at the keyboard.

Granted, you cannot cut and paste graphics this way; Windows doesn't understand DOS graphics, and severe beatings won't help it any. Also, the pasting is rather inelegant because the text seems to spew everywhere — but at least you can do it. Sort of.

Also, you can't pull this trick when you run your DOS program full-screen (as God intended). You have to press the Alt+Enter key combination to switch back to the graphical window mode to play with copy and paste.

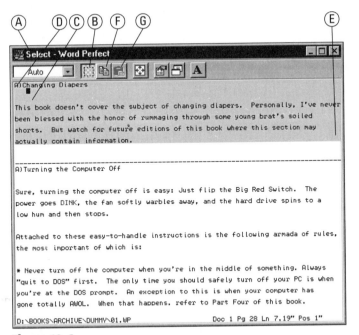

Figure 12-4
A chunk of text in WordPerfect is selected.
A. This tells you that you're in selection mode. **B.** The on-off select button is down, meaning that you're in selection mode. **C.** Use the mouse to drag and select a chunk of text on the screen. **D.** Start here. **E.** Drag to here. **F.** Use this button to copy the text. **G.** Paste button (not working in this mode).

You can run several DOS programs at a time in Windows — multitasking them just like Windows' own applications. See Chapter 8 for more information about multitasking programs and switching between them. Everything there applies to DOS programs that are run in Windows as well.

Quitting a DOS program

This is very special: You should quit your DOS programs the same way as you did under DOS. Use whatever command you used to use to quit to the DOS prompt. In WordPerfect, for example, it's the F7 key. Use this command *first*.

If you absolutely have to, you can close a DOS program by clicking on its × Close button. When you do, you probably will see a warning dialog box (see Figure 12-5). Click on No, and go back to close the program properly.

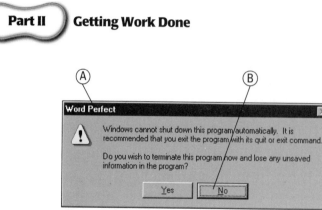

Figure 12-5
Oops! Can't close a DOS window that way.
A. The program you tried to sneak out of. **B.** Click here.

→ One exception to this rule is the DOS prompt. When you're at the DOS prompt, you can click on the × Close button to close the window. But this happens only at the DOS prompt, not when you run a program. See the section "Running a DOS Prompt for the Heck of it," later in this chapter, for more information about the DOS prompt in Windows.

← Never, ever, quit a DOS application by pressing Ctrl+Alt+Delete. This may have worked under DOS, but it's taboo under Windows. See the section "The drastic way to quit" in Chapter 3 for an explanation of why you should avoid this.

Installing DOS software (is a pain)

Oh, if you have Windows software, it can just be so beautifully installed by using the Add/Remove Programs icon in the Control Panel. Alas, that probably won't help you install your DOS software.

To install DOS software, run a DOS prompt window, as described in the next section. Then follow the instructions for installing the software according to the installation manual. That gets things running.

Beware DOS programs that insist on resetting the computer after they're installed. In all cases, answer No to the question "Do you want to reset?" If your program does go ahead and try to reset the computer without asking, only your DOS window closes. Shut down Windows properly, and then reset if you need to.

→ See Chapter 13 for more information about installing new Windows programs — which is such a breeze that it will make you insanely jealous.

Running a DOS Prompt for the Heck of It

If you find yourself swelling with nostalgia, consider running a DOS prompt for the heck of it. To do so:

1. Pop up the Start Thing's menu.

   Click on the Start button, or press Ctrl+Esc.

2. Choose Programs⇨MS-DOS Prompt.

   A DOS prompt window starts, like any other window on the screen and looking something like Figure 12-6.

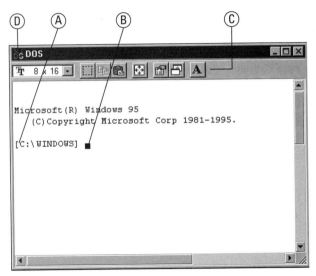

Figure 12-6
The lonely DOS prompt window.
A. The DOS prompt itself. **B.** The cursor, which marks where you type things.
C. See the section "Messing with a DOS window," earlier in this chapter, for more information about this toolbar. **D.** Click here and choose Toolbar from the menu to hide or show the toolbar.

The DOS prompt works by your typing commands and pressing the Enter key. The commands are either the names of DOS programs you want to run or DOS commands, which do certain things to the files on disk or the computer system. It's all really crude and primitive stuff compared with the way Windows handles things. But in that primitiveness is some simplicity that Windows lacks.

I won't bore you here with details of DOS commands. Buy *DOS For Dummies* (published by IDG Books) if you really care. (I mean *really* care.)

There are some subtle differences from your old version of DOS, because what you're looking at is essentially DOS Version 7. Here's a brief list:

In addition to running DOS programs, you can also start Windows programs. For example:

> C:\WINDOWS> CLIPBD

This command starts the Clipboard Viewer program — right from a DOS prompt. Just type **CLIPBD**, and press the Enter key.

◄▪ See Chapter 8, the section "Everything goes to the Clipboard," for more information about the Clipboard Viewer.

Another new deal surrounds long filenames. In a typical DIR command, you see the long filenames listed last in their full format. The first filename is the truncated DOS version. Here's a partial DIR command listing:

> CASTLE~1.BMP   778 03-02-95 12:00p Castle Walls.bmp

The first name contains the first six letters of the long filename (minus any spaces) and then a tilde and a number. Then comes the rest of the standard DIR command's output and then the really long filename.

You can use longer filenames at the DOS prompt, but you must enclose them in double quotes. To wit:

> C:\WINDOWS> DIR "CASTLE WALLS"

You must also use the double quotes when you're manipulating the file. For example:

> C:\WINDOWS> COPY "CASTLE WALLS.BMP" C:\TEMP

In a way, this makes DOS easier and harder. It's easier because the filenames are more descriptive. It's harder because it requires more typing.

Messing with a DOS Program's Properties

Just like witches have warts, everything in Windows has a Properties dialog box attached. DOS programs are no exception. Of course, what passes as a Properties dialog box for a DOS program is really the universal DOS Properties dialog box (see Figure 12-7); it isn't specific to whichever program you're running, just to DOS.

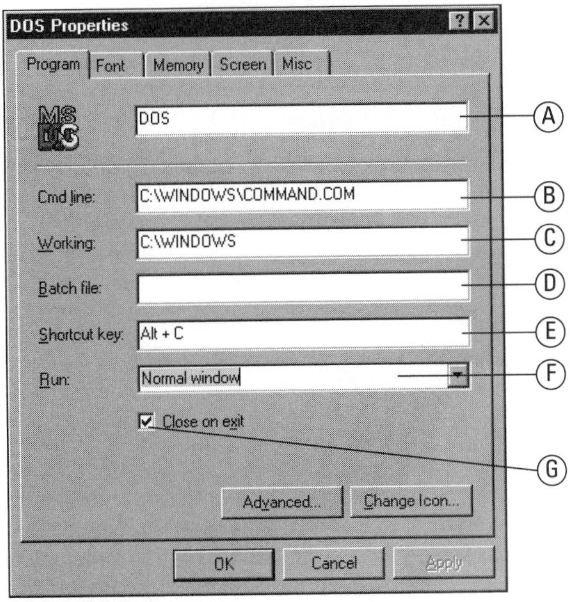

Figure 12-7
A DOS program's Properties dialog box.
A. The program name. **B.** The actual program being run. **C.** The starting folder.
D. Whatever. **E.** Press this key combination to start this DOS program instantly.
F. How to run the program at first: Normal, Maximized, or Minimized.
G. Keep this checked.

To see a DOS program's Properties dialog box, click on the Properties button on the toolbar. If you can't see the toolbar, click on the window's Control menu and choose Properties (the last item). Figure 12-7 shows the Properties dialog box for a DOS program.

Several different panels are in the dialog box, but nothing worth wasting any time over. Highlights for the Program panel are shown in Figure 12-7. The Font panel was discussed in the section "Messing with a DOS window," earlier in this chapter.

The Screen panel has a few interesting items in it. Click on the Screen tab to bring that panel forward. What you see looks similar to Figure 12-8.

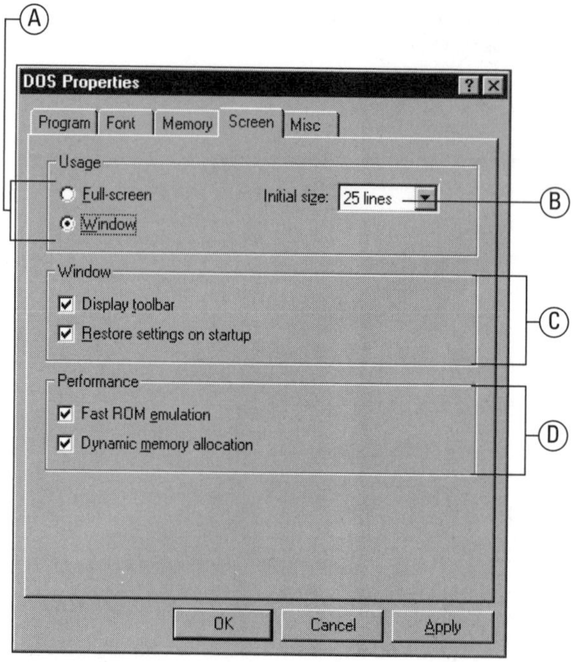

Figure 12-8
The Screen panel.
A. Click here to start the DOS program full-screen (text mode). **B.** Set the number of text lines here: 25, 43, or 50. **C.** Other startup options. **D.** Who really knows?

If you prefer to run your DOS program full-screen, click on the Full Screen item. That way, everything starts up just like it did in the old days. Of course, when you quit, or if you switch away from the full-screen DOS program, everything switches back to graphical Windows.

The Initial size drop-down list enables you to set the number of lines that appear on the screen. Pick 25 for a traditional DOS screen, though many programs (including WordPerfect) adjust themselves nicely to 43 or even 50 lines.

All these settings are remembered by Windows so that next time you start your DOS program, things look similar to when you last used it. Of course, you can still dink with things later, which is one of the things Windows is passionate about.

Troubleshooting MS-DOS Program Problems

Trouble looms for some DOS programs, especially those stubborn ones that refuse to behave or some programs that are, honestly, startled to find themselves running under Windows. When the cloud of doom rolls in for your DOS programs, you can try your hand at the MS-DOS Troubleshooter, which is part of the Windows Help system. Here's how:

1. Start Help.

    Choose Help from the Start Thing's menu. Press Ctrl+Esc, H.

2. Bring the Index panel forward.

    Click on the Index tab if that panel isn't forward already.

3. Type Installing . . .

    Type the word **INSTALLING** in the number-one box on the Index panel. This step scrolls the index list to the word *Installing.* You see various items listed under that heading, one of which is MS-DOS programs.

4. Click on MS-DOS programs.

    Click once with your mouse to highlight that item.

5. Click on the Display button.

    You see the MS-DOS Program Troubleshooter on the screen (see Figure 12-9). It lists several situations that might go wrong when you run a DOS program under Windows.

6. Choose the item that bugs you.

    For example, choose "The program doesn't run correctly." That covers a wealth of problems. Click on the little button by that item, and you see another dialog box either explaining a solution or asking more questions.

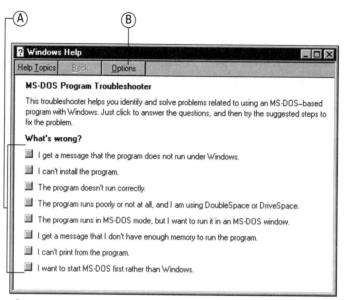

Figure 12-9
The MS-DOS Troubleshooter thing.
A. Pick one of these. **B.** Click here and choose Print Topic from the menu to get a hard copy of these instructions.

Keep answering questions and trying solutions as you work through the Troubleshooter. Eventually, and hopefully, the problem will be solved.

Sometimes it pays to get a hard copy of the detailed instructions offered by the Troubleshooter. Click on the Options button, and a special menu appears. Choose the Print Topic item to print the instructions. That way, you have them for reference as you dig through the bowels of your DOS program to fix something.

Installing New Software

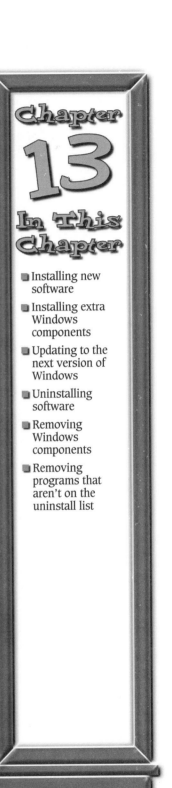

Buying a computer is only half the cost of owning one. The other half is software, the programs you buy for your computer. That's an ongoing purchase. Even if you already have an all-encompassing program such as Microsoft Office, you still have to buy other software to make your PC go. And then there's the whole ordeal of updates and upgrades. Fortunately, it's all handled in a sane, central place in Windows, which is at the core of this chapter.

And Now for Something New

Computer software comes on disks, either floppy disks or compact discs (CDs). To get that software off those disks and on your computer's hard drive, it must be installed. That process involves not only copying the programs, but also customizing the new software to work with your computer, letting Windows know about the software, and setting other options along the way. To make this process as painless as possible, follow these steps:

1. Open a friendly Control Panel near you.

   You can find the Control Panel lurking right inside My Computer's main window, or a copy of it is nestled in the Settings menu right off the Start Thing's main menu.

   Control Panel

   Double-click on the Control Panel icon to open it.

2. Open the Add/Remove Programs icon.

   The Add/Remove Programs icon is the computer software equivalent of Chicago's O'Hare airport: It's where your computer software arrives or departs, depending on your schedule.

   Add/Remove Programs

   Double-click on the Add/Remove Programs icon to open it up. The Add/Remove Programs Properties dialog box is displayed (see Figure 13-1).

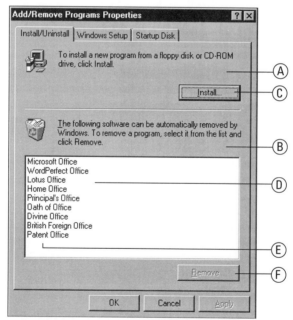

Figure 13-1
New arrivals and departing software start here.
A. Installation happens up here. **B.** Uninstalling happens here. **C.** Click here to begin installing new software. **D.** A list of installed Windows 95 software: the "uninstall list." **E.** Not everything you have on your computer appears here.
F. The software-removal button.

3. Make sure that the Install/Uninstall panel is forward.

   Click on the Install/Uninstall tab if that panel isn't up front already. What you see looks something like Figure 13-1.

4. Click on the Install button.

   Click.

5. Stick the installation disks into the drive.

   If it's a CD, put it in your CD-ROM drive.

   If you're installing from floppy disks, put the first floppy disk (#1) in your computer's drive A.

6. Click on Next.

   Windows ferrets out your installation disks.

   Eventually, it locates your software's installation or setup program and displays technical information, such as you see in Figure 13-2.

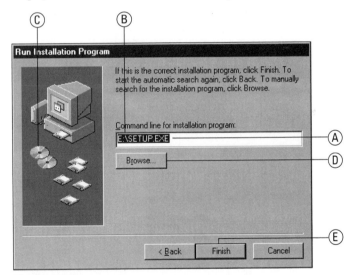

Figure 13-2
Windows has found your installation program.
A. The setup program's pathname goes here (see Chapter 17, the section "Beating a pathname to a file's door," for more about pathnames). **B.** Drive E is probably a CD-ROM drive. **C.** Never let your CDs lie around like this. **D.** The Browse button you can use if Windows picks the wrong installation program (rarely). **E.** Click here to continue.

7. Click on Finish.

   You're not really done; only the Windows setup part is finished. At this point, your new application's setup or installation program takes over, completing the task of copying and configuring the new software.

What happens next? Generally, every application sets itself up differently. You may be given several options for installation: Custom or Advanced; Minimum; and Express or Typical.

Express or Typical installation. Choose this option first. It's not the "stupid" option; you are allowed to make some decisions here. Many of the nerdier details are just left out, that's all.

Custom installation. Only fussy users should bother with the Custom setup options. These options usually include every minute detail and pages and pages of setup options. Most of this stuff is standard for all PCs, so there's no need to bother (I don't).

Minimum setup options. Use the Minimum setup for laptops or other computers on which disk space can be tight. A working version of the application will be installed, but no options, bells, whistles, and so on get in your way. And you usually can add them later, if you like, by rerunning the installation program.

Adding the Rest of Windows

Windows comes with tons of stuff, most of which wasn't installed when you first got Windows. This may come as a shock, but keep in mind that there was probably a reason for it; some stuff isn't installed because your computer lacks the proper hardware. For example, sound files don't work well on a computer without sound capabilities; networking programs can't help you on a nonnetworked computer; no modem means no communications software; and so on.

Sometimes programs may not have been installed because there wasn't enough room on your hard drive. Windows tries its best not to be disk-piggy, but if you're swimming in spinning megabytes, you can later install some of the programs Windows forgot. Or you can install the rest of Windows right now by following these steps:

1. Wrassle up the Add/Remove Programs Properties dialog box.

   Follow along with steps 1 through 3 in the section "And Now for Something New," earlier in this chapter.

2. Bring the Windows Setup panel forward.

Click on the Windows Setup tab. You see the Windows Setup part of the dialog box, as shown in Figure 13-3. It displays a scrolling list of Windows components and options. Those items without a ✔ check mark or with a ✔ in a gray box are only partially installed; you can add the other components at this time.

Some items have a gray check mark in their box. The check mark means that only one of several options has been selected. You can click on the Details button to choose from among the options available (covered in the next step).

Figure 13-3
Here is where you add or remove bits and pieces of Windows.
A. A list of Windows' options installed or not.
B. Not installed at all.
C. Fully installed.
D. Partially installed.
E. Amount of memory taken up by the options.
F. Memory required for the new options you've chosen.
G. Free space on your hard drive. **H.** Click here to select additional options.
I. Click here if you have a disk from Microsoft with other, additional items on it. **J.** The clue that there are additional options. **K.** Click here to install.

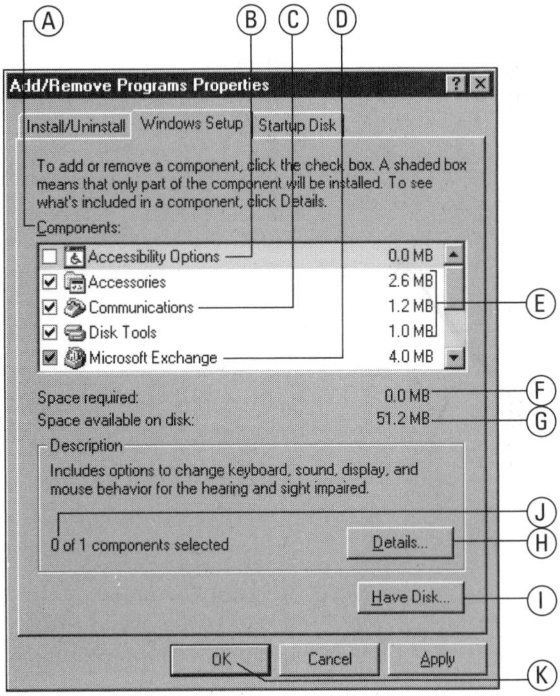

3. Choose the items you want to install.

Put a ✔ check mark in the box by those items you want to add to Windows. If you want to install the WinPopup program (for networking), for example, look for that item in the list and put a ✔ check mark in its box.

If the item has more than one option, click on the Details button. You see another, similar dialog box that lists individual components (see Figure 13-4). Click in the box next to the items you want to add. (There is yet another Details button, just in case even more options are available. This can get hairy.)

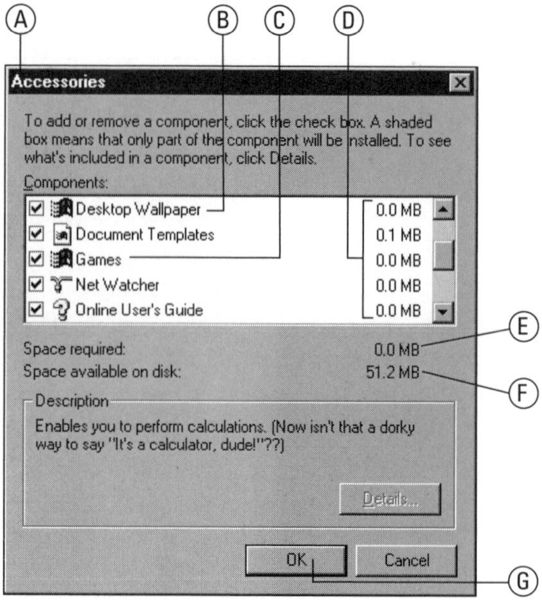

Figure 13-4

Adding individual components.

A. These are all various Accessories. **B.** Here are some wallpaper assortments (see Chapter 24). **C.** Games! (See Chapter 26). **D.** Disk space eaten by each item. **E.** Total disk space everything will need when installed. **F.** Total disk space you have available on your hard drive. **G.** Returns you to the other dialog box.

Ⓐ   Ⓑ Ⓒ   Ⓓ

Accessories   ✕

To add or remove a component, click the check box. A shaded box means that only part of the component will be installed. To see what's included in a component, click Details.

Components:

☑ 🖼 Desktop Wallpaper —	0.0 MB ▲
☑ 📄 Document Templates	0.1 MB
☑ 🖼 Games ———	0.0 MB
☑ 🎾 Net Watcher	0.0 MB
☑ 🔮 Online User's Guide	0.0 MB ▼

Space required: 0.0 MB — Ⓔ

Space available on disk: 51.2 MB — Ⓕ

Description

Enables you to perform calculations. (Now isn't that a dorky way to say "It's a calculator, dude!"??)

Details...

OK   Cancel — Ⓖ

4. OK!

   Click on the OK button when you're ready to add your stuff.

   ⬅ You may be asked here to quit any other programs you're running. See the sidebar "How to carefully exit any other programs while you're installing," on the next page.

5. Stick the Windows setup disk in your disk drive.

   Windows asks for its setup disk, so either put the CD into your CD-ROM drive or put whichever disk it begs you for in your floppy drive A.

   If you're using floppy disks (and I really feel for you), you'll probably be asked to remove one disk and insert another. These things take time (an argument for upgrading your PC with a CD-ROM drive, in my opinion).

6. You're done.

   Eventually the changes are made. Windows may inform you that it needs to reset. If so, do it right now; don't put it off.

Enjoy your new toys!

How to carefully exit any other programs while you're installing

You may see an alert dialog box appear when you're setting up new software on your computer, asking you to shut down, or "carefully exit," any other programs you may have running. This is a wise idea because some unruly program may barge in and spoil your installation. To quit any other running program, follow these steps:

1. **Press Alt+Tab.** This step switches you to the next running program if you're running more than one program.

   See the section "Using the 'cool switch' to switch applications" in Chapter 8 for more information about how Alt+Tab works.

2. **Are you back at the setup program?** If you've switched back to the setup program, you're done. It's okay to install now. If not, keep working the next two steps.

3. **Close the application.** Click on the × Close button in the upper right corner of the window.

4. **Go back to step 1.** Continue looking for and closing programs.

The idea here is to keep switching programs by using the Alt+Tab key combination. When there are no more programs to switch to, you've closed everything down, and the setup program can proceed safely.

Updating Windows

Every so often an update to Windows appears. These updates may be called "maintenance releases" or "updates" or even "patches." Whatever, they're some additions and improvements to Windows that are made available every so often. As long as you registered your copy of Windows with Microsoft, you should be alerted to when these updates are available and where to get them.

Updating Windows works like adding any new software: You just stick the CD into your CD-ROM drive or the first disk into your floppy drive A. Then run the Add/Remove Programs tool, as described earlier in this chapter. Windows updates itself to the latest, most improved version, and you're off and running in a few minutes.

As a general rule of advice, I usually wait a few months before updating my software. I apply this rule to any software, not just to Windows. After a few months you can get feedback from other users and the major computer magazines. That way, you can judge whether the update is worth the risk and expense. For most minor Windows maintenance releases, this shouldn't be a problem. But keep an ear to the ground anyway.

The Subtle Art of Uninstalling

Sometimes it happens. You set up some program on your computer, and then you don't like it. Or it could be that you really need the space and suddenly notice that the 14-megabyte spreadsheet you installed eight months ago doesn't get any use. In that case, you can uninstall the software, safely peeling it off your hard drive.

Uninstalling is better than just dragging something off to the Recycle Bin. When you uninstall, you also remove secret pockets of programs hiding in various unobvious places. Not removing those hidden bits can lead to trouble later, so it's always best to officially uninstall stuff.

Officially uninstalling stuff

Some Windows 95 programs can be uninstalled the same way they were installed. Here's how:

1. Incant the spell that summons the Add/Remove Programs Properties dialog box.

   Work through steps 1 through 3 in the section "And Now for Something New," earlier in this chapter.

2. Highlight in the uninstall list the application you want to remove.

   Look through the list for your application (refer to Figure 13-1). Click the mouse on its name once to highlight it.

3. Click on Remove.

   You see a Confirm File Deletion dialog box, asking whether you're really sure that you want to utterly remove the program from your hard drive.

4. Click on Yes.

   Chugga-chugga. You hear the hard drive chipmunks chirping away as your program is removed from memory.

   What actually happens is that the program's special uninstall or anti-setup program is run. It's this program that removes your application from disk; just as the Add/Remove Programs Properties dialog box only starts the setup program from an installation disk, here it only runs the uninstall program. (I hope that that doesn't disappoint you.)

"But my programs don't appear in the uninstall list!"

Only certain Windows 95-approved software appears in the ready-to-uninstall list. In Figure 13-2, the only real program that appears there is Microsoft Office — the 95 version. The other programs, I just made up (in case it isn't obvious). Older software you already had on your computer and any and all DOS programs don't appear on the list.

See the section "Unofficially uninstalling stuff," later in this chapter, for some suggestions on how to uninstall software that doesn't appear on the list.

5. Resume your de-installation.

   Continue with the un-setup program that appears on your screen. If you're removing the Microsoft Office, for example, click on the Remove All button to uninstall all its components.

There is an off chance that Windows will want to reset after uninstalling. If so, do it right then.

Uninstalling bits and pieces of Windows

Just as you can "add the rest of Windows," you can also remove bits and pieces of Windows — stuff you don't use — to free up disk space. To do so, work through steps 1 through 3 in the section "Adding the Rest of Windows," earlier in this chapter.

When you get to the Windows Setup panel in the Add/Remove Programs Properties dialog box, simply remove a ✔ check mark by an item. When you click on the OK button, Windows carefully deletes whatever it was from your computer, freeing up that much disk space.

Unofficially uninstalling stuff

Not every application on your computer is listed in the uninstall list in the Add/Remove Programs Properties dialog box. Even so, those programs may sport their own uninstall program.

The first way to find out whether your program has an uninstall feature is to browse through its Help file. Use the Index to look up Setup or Install. Then check under that heading to see whether there is an uninstall procedure.

Sometimes the uninstall program is located on the disk from which you installed the program. In those cases, it may be necessary to rerun the application's setup program and then choose an uninstall option.

Always remember to try these options first. Never just wantonly delete a program from your hard drive.

See Chapter 4 for more information about using Help in Windows, in the section "Finding a specific topic by using the index."

Part III

Disks, Folders, Files, Whatnot

In this part

- What drives your disk drives

- The secrets of documents, files, and icons

- Manipulate those files

- Organizing files, folders, and the desktop

whatami

Printers

Dial-Up Networking

Shortcut to Recycle Bin

Fonts

How do I...?

Format a floppy disk?

All floppy disks must be formatted before you can use them. So you either format new disks you buy or reformat old disks to use over again.

➡ See Chapter 14, the section "The thrill of formatting a floppy disk," for all the details.

Make an emergency boot disk?

You need some type of boot disk to start your computer and Windows "just in case." This type of disk contains special software to assist in the recovery of anything missing on your hard drive.

➡ See Chapter 14, the section "Creating a disk to start your computer: The fun yet useful Emergency Boot Disk."

Use my CD-ROM drive?

CD-ROM drives are used to read special CDs that can hold as much as 600 megabytes of interesting stuff. You can also slip in a music CD to hear it over your PC's speakers.

➡ See the section "The Joy of CD-ROMs" in Chapter 14 for all the CD-ROM info.

➡ To play a musical CD in your computer, see the section "Playing a musical CD" in Chapter 14.

Take a sneak peek inside an icon?

"Who knows what evil lurks in the heart of files?" Windows does, for one. In addition to using the file's name and icon, there are several ways you can sneak a look inside a file to see what it contains.

➡ See the section "Wantonly opening a file to see what's inside" in Chapter 15.

Save a document as a "plain text file"?

Saving a file in a plain text, or ASCII, format is a common command given by obscure user manuals.

➡ To see how it's done, see the section "Saving a file as a specific type" in Chapter 15.

Make a shortcut?

Shortcuts are handy little copies of a program, document, or folder. They enable you to reference the original without wasting as much disk space as a real copy would chew up.

➡ See Chapter 16, the section "Taking a Shortcut Instead of Copying Files."

Copy, move, or rename a file?

These are the file-manipulation commands — things you need to know about when you work with a program, document, or folder in Windows.

➡ To copy a program, document, or folder, see the section "Copying, or Doop-Doop-Duplicating, Files" in Chapter 16.

➡ To move a program, document, or folder, see the section "Deeply Moving Files" in Chapter 16.

➡ Renaming programs, documents, or folders is covered in Chapter 16, in the section "Blessing a File with a New Name."

Find the root folder?

The root folder is essentially the first window you see when you open a disk drive. Its icon isn't a folder, but is the disk drive icon itself. All other folders are "children" of the root. (Sounds earthy, eh?)

➡ See the section "What's up with the root folder?" in Chapter 17.

➡ Also look into the section "Crazy folder terminology" in Chapter 17.

Use the Explorer?

The Explorer is a file-finding alternative to My Computer, though you can't see more than one window full of files at a time.

➡ Discover the explorer in the section "Let's go Explorering" in Chapter 17.

Organize the junk on my hard drive?

This is vitally important to keeping yourself sane. Too many people neglect to organize their stuff, and it takes only a wee bit of effort.

➡ Learn how to organize your hard drive in Chapter 17, in the section "Setting Up Folders Just So."

➡ You'll also need the file-manipulation commands found throughout Chapter 16.

➡ And you should organize your desktop as well. See the section "Bringing Order to the Desktop" also in Chapter 17.

What Drives Your Disk Drives

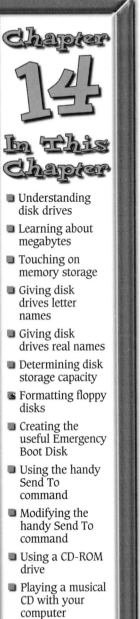

The typical PC hardware tour starts off with the disk drives. Oh, some may start with the keyboard and monitor. But they're boring. Disk drives, they offer 'round-the-clock excitement. This is because they spin wildly, with some hard drives reaching dizzying speeds of 3,600 RPM or even faster. That's enough centrifugal force to more than flatten Silly Putty. It's more centrifugal force than you get when Grandma's driving and she thinks that the "Slow to 25 MPH" sign on the off ramp is merely a suggestion. It's fast.

Many types of disk drives can be in your computer. Primarily, you have two: a floppy disk and a hard drive. You may have more of those, and you may have a CD-ROM drive or even a RAM drive lurking in your computer. Understanding and dealing with each of them is covered here, though please consider this a general introduction to this part of the book, which also includes information about files, folders, and organizing everything, as covered in the following chapters.

➠ This chapter offers only a get-acquainted session with your disk drives. Chapter 18, on the other hand, deals with maintaining and tuning your disk drives. Go there for regular maintenance chores.

The Big Spinnin' Deal with Disk Drives

Your computer has two types of storage: permanent and temporary. The disk drives, with their massive storage capabilities, give you permanent storage. Computer memory, or RAM, gives you temporary storage. Both types are important.

Permanent storage is important because that's where you store your stuff — not only the stuff you create but also all the programs you run on your computer, Windows itself, plus any new programs you buy or new stuff you create. It all stays there, humbly waiting for you when you need it.

Temporary storage is also important because your PC's microprocessor can deal only with information stored in memory. Programs run only in memory. You can create new stuff or edit old stuff only in memory. When you're done, you save the stuff to disk for long-term storage. When you do, that memory is made available by Windows for use with other programs.

✗ The only major drawback to disk storage is that it's up to you to keep it organized. Unfortunately, Windows only gives you the tools to keep it organized. It's up to you to find a proper place for your files and keep a handle on managing what is in reality a great deal of information. Chapter 16 offers some suggestions about how to handle enormous tasks with a minimum of headaches.

✗ A 340MB hard drive can store a great deal of information. That's enough space to store all the information you read last year in your newspaper, magazine subscriptions, books you read, and probably from all the scripts of any TV shows you watched. To get a better idea of what a MB, or megabyte, is, read the nearby sidebar, "A megabyte is a big bite."

✗ Although it's up to you to manage the information stored on your hard drive, Windows itself manages temporary storage, or RAM. All I can say about that is "Thank God."

✗ By the way, a *disk* is the flat, round media on which computer information is stored, like a cassette tape but smashed flat like a pancake. The *drive* is the device that writes information to and reads information from the disk, like a cassette recorder/player.

A megabyte is a big bite

The bottom-line basic storage unit in a computer is the byte. Essentially, a *byte* is one character of information. That means that it takes four bytes to store the word *PORB* in a computer.

To store as much information as fits on a single-spaced sheet of paper, it takes about 1,000 bytes. This is abbreviated KB, for a *kilobyte*. That's a modest-size chunk of storage. Most files are measured in KB, with the typical computer file being anywhere from 12KB to 24KB in size, or roughly 12,000 to 24,000 bytes.

The *megabyte,* or MB, is about 1 million bytes. That's enough space to store the Sunday *New York Times* or a good-size novel. Hard drives and computer memory storage are measured in MB, with the typical computer having a 200MB hard drive and anywhere from 4MB to 32MB of memory.

Beyond the megabyte is the *gigabyte,* GB, which equals 1,000 million bytes, or 1 billion bytes. A few high-end hard drives can hold this much information.

By the way, these figures are approximations. Everything in a computer is based on the binary counting system, base 2. Because of that, and for strange mathematical reasons I need not bore you with here, a kilobyte is really 1,024 bytes. A megabyte is really 1,048,576 bytes. A gigabyte is seriously 1,073,741,824 bytes. And finally, not to scare you or anything, but the national debt of the United States is $4,700,000,000,000, or $4.7 trillion.

So how much memory does this beast hold?

Memory is the other type of computer storage, the temporary storage. It's temporary because, after the power is turned off, poof! goes memory. That's not a problem, really, because all the good stuff is saved on disk before that can happen.

The only really burning memory question you're often faced with is "How much of that stuff do I have in my PC?" To find out, follow these steps:

1. **Bring up My Computer's shortcut menu.** Right-click on the My Computer icon. A shortcut menu appears right then and there.

2. **Choose Properties from the menu.** This step displays the System Properties dialog box, which tells you much of the mundane and a bit of the technical stuff about your computer system.

(continued)

267

Disks, Folders, Files, Whatnot

(continued)

3. **Click on the General tab to bring that panel forward (if it isn't already).** The General panel contains some basic information about your computer. Among the information listed, at the bottom, is how much memory is in your PC.

   Wow! My PC has _____ MB of RAM. Cool.

4. **Click on OK.** The System Properties dialog box sulks off.

The three basic types of disk drives

There are three basic types of disk drives:

✗ Floppy drives, with removable disks

✗ Hard drives, without removable disks

✗ CD-ROM drives, with removable discs

Almost every computer has one floppy drive, and some have two.

Almost every computer has one hard drive, and some have two.

Most computers also have one CD-ROM drive.

You can have more than one CD-ROM drive, but it's uncommon. Other uncommon things include having removable hard drives, magneto-optical hard drives, and high-capacity floppy drives that act like hard drives but really aren't hard drives. It's enough to make your head spin at 3,600 RPM.

All disk drives store information. However, you can only read information from a CD-ROM; the RO in ROM means "read only." So CD-ROMs are used only for information storage, not for saving files. Other than that, you have to know how the disk drives are recognized by your computer, which means understanding their uncreative letter names.

Disk drive A:, B:, C:s

Every disk drive living in your computer has two names. First comes the letter name and then a more creative name. The letter name you can't change. The other name is yours to play with. This whimsy is granted probably because the letter names are so boring.

Disk drives are given letter names, one for each letter in the English alphabet. The first disk drive is A; the next one, B; and then C on up until you hit drive Z.

The letter name ends in a colon (see Table 14-1). Furthermore, in My Computer and the Explorer, the letter and colon are put in parentheses. After all, the more characters you have in addition to the letter, the more cryptic and scary it looks.

Traditionally, drives A and B are floppy drives. Drive A is your computer's first floppy drive. If you have a second floppy drive, it's drive B.

Your first hard drive is given the letter C. This is true whether you have one or two floppy drives. So if you're missing your second floppy drive, B, your first hard drive is still named drive C.

Any additional hard drives in your computer are named D, E, and on up for every hard drive.

Table 14-1	Drive Letters, Drives, Icons, and Fun			
Drive	*Type*	*Letter*	*Comments*	*As Seen in My Computer*
First	Floppy	A:	First floppy drive	
Second	Floppy	B:	(Second floppy, maybe a 5¼-inch disk)	
Third	Hard disk	C:	First hard drive	
Fourth	Hard disk	D:	(Additional hard drive)	
Next	CD-ROM	One letter after the last hard drive	The CD-ROM drive	
Next	RAM drive	One after preceding drive	Fast memory drive	
Next	Network drives	Assigned their own letter, not in order	Drives on someone else's computer	

If you have any other types of disk drives in your computer, such as a CD-ROM or RAM drive, they're given the next letters right after your last hard drive.

The typical PC has the disk drive arrangement shown in Figure 14-1: one floppy drive and one hard drive. The floppy is drive A, and the hard drive is drive C. Figure 14-2 shows a PC with one floppy drive, two hard drives, and a CD-ROM drive.

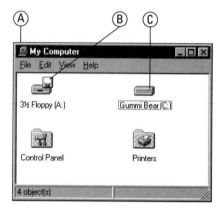

Figure 14-1
Drives A and C as seen by My Computer. **A.** My Computer shows you the disk drives that live in your computer. **B.** Here is drive A, a 3½-inch floppy disk. **C.** Here is drive C, a hard drive given the name Gummi Bear. You can change the name to anything you want; see the section "More than just a letter: Giving your disk a proper name," later in this chapter.

➠ When you stick a musical CD into your CD-ROM drive, Windows changes the CD-ROM icon to a disc with a pair of eighth notes by it. See the section "Playing a musical CD," later in this chapter, for more info.

➠ Network drives are those that represent other computers' hard drives elsewhere on the network. Visit Chapter 23 for more information about pulling those drives into your system for use and abuse.

➠ RAM drives. Bah! Ignore them. Remove them. *Get rid of them now!* RAM drives gulp precious memory in a Windows 95 computer. See the section "RAM Drives Belong in the Past," later in this chapter, for information about their disposal.

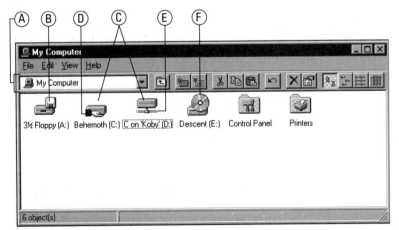

Figure 14-2
Drives A, C, D, and E as seen by My Computer.
A. The toolbar can really help you navigate through folders in My Computer, especially when you choose the "one window" approach. See Chapter 2, the sections "Whip out the toolbar" and "The 'single window' approach to using My Computer," for more information. **B.** Drive A, a floppy drive. **C.** Drives C and D are hard drives. **D.** This little "sharing hand" under drive C means that this drive is available for use by other computers on the network — like offering an hors d'oeuvre to the network gods. (See Chapter 22 for information about sharing your disk drives.) **E.** The pipe structure under drive D means that it's a network drive; someone else's disk drive is located elsewhere on the network. (Again, see Chapter 22 for information about hooking one up.) **F.** Drive E is a CD-ROM drive. That round thing is supposed to be a CD-ROM; the drive is not playing doctor.

More than just a letter: Giving your disk a proper name

In addition to assigning the letter, you can give each disk drive in your computer a clever name, one you can use your imagination in creating. That name appears before the boring drive letter when it's listed by My Computer or the Explorer.

To give your disk drives a clever name or to change a name they might currently have that's not too clever, follow these steps:

1. Locate the disk drive you want to give a new name.

   Use My Computer for this. See Chapter 2 for more information about opening My Computer and looking at the disk drives.

2. Right-click on the disk drive to bring up its shortcut menu.

   Point the mouse pointer at the disk drive's icon in My Computer, and then click the right mouse button. This step displays a shortcut menu.

   Alas, you cannot rename a disk drive icon as you can rename other icons in My Computer or on the desktop. Instead, you must dive down deep into the disk drive's Properties sheets.

   If you're checking the label on a floppy disk, make sure that the disk is in the drive and that the drive-door latch (if any) is closed. You cannot read from a disk that isn't in the drive.

   You cannot change the label on a CD-ROM drive. It's the RO in ROM again — read only — that prevents you from writing to the disc. This is too bad because most CD-ROMs have lousy names.

3. Choose Properties from the shortcut menu.

   Click the mouse on Properties. The disk drive's Properties dialog box appears.

4. Click the mouse on the General tab to bring that panel forward if it isn't forward already.

   Click. Figure 14-3 shows you what you should see on your screen.

Figure 14-3

The Properties dialog box for drive C, with the General panel forward. **A.** Here is where you type a new disk drive label. The current label appears highlighted, meaning that it's ready to be sacrificed for a newer label. **B.** This number tells you how many bytes of junk you have stored on your hard drive. The actual amount in bytes is listed first, followed by a shorter number, which is just megabytes. **C.** This figure shows you how many bytes are available, or waiting to be filled up. **D.** The Capacity number tells you how many bytes of total storage the disk drive has. Here it shows a 324MB disk drive, a moderate size. **E.** The pie chart provides a visual summary of how your disk drive is making use of its storage space. **F.** Grape.

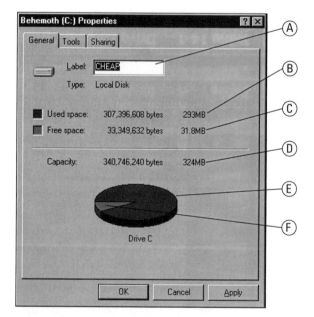

5. Look for the Label input box.

   The Label input box is the top thing in the dialog box. It contains the name currently given to the disk drive, all highlighted and ready for editing.

➠   If the label name isn't highlighted, double-click the mouse in that box, click-click. This step selects the old name for editing, enabling you to replace it easily with a new name. You can also refer to Chapter 28 for more hints about how all those doodads work; see the section "Input boxes."

6. Make your naming choice.

   Now you can do one of the following:

   If you like the current name, skip up to the next step. That way, it won't be changed.

   If you don't want any name for your disk drive, press the Del key to erase the current name and then skip up to the next step. That erases the name, cruelly leaving the disk drive nameless. Nothing wrong with that.

   If you want to type a new name, do so. However, you can use only letters, numbers, and spaces when you name the disk. You cannot use any other special symbols or be creative in any way. Also, the name can be no more than 11 characters long. (Truly, this is the only time you're limited in naming something inside Windows.)

7. Click on OK.

   This step closes the disk drive's Properties dialog box, adjusting the name as you saw fit in step 6. You see the new name appear in My Computer, in the Explorer, and in any of the number of collapsible tree-structure things that infest Windows.

Checking on disk usage, or "Fills up fast, doesn't it?"

Disk drives literally bloat with information. You may have megabytes of space on your disk drive, thinking that it could never fill up, not in your wildest dreams. Then one day you get an ugly error message telling you that your disk is full. Nothing can be more frustrating.

To help you keep an eye on disk usage, Windows has a special pie chart you can view, showing you, for every disk drive in your computer, how much disk space is used and how much remains (refer to Figure 14-3). You can use the chart, maybe not to prevent a disk from filling up, but to prepare you for when it does.

To see the chart, follow steps 1 through 4 in the preceding section (even if it's a CD-ROM you're looking at, though I can promise you that the disc will be "full").

➡️ The first thing you can do when a disk gets full is to begin removing files. Files, like junk in your closet or garage, tend to accumulate. Many of them you can really do without. See Chapter 16 for information about deleting excess files. Also see Chapter 5, the section "Reducing the amount of disk space the Recycle Bin hogs up," for information about adjusting the size of the Recycle Bin to reclaim some disk space.

➡️ Another step you can take to ease the storage burden is to run the Drive Space program to double your disk storage capacity. Personally, I recommend against this step (you can read me drone on and on about it in Chapter 18) because buying a second or larger hard drive is always the best solution.

Nothing Much to Say About Hard Drives

Hard drives are your main storage device, where Windows and all your applications live and where you save all the stuff you work on. There's nothing much you can do to your hard drive after it's set up and running fine. However, you can keep the following points in mind:

✗ Never format a hard drive. It should be installed and initially formatted according to the instructions that came with the drive. After that, you should never, never, format a hard drive — even though the hard drive's shortcut menu has a Format command on it. You can format only floppy disks, which is covered in the next section.

➡️ ✗ Keep the information on your hard drive organized. Put files in folders, and ensure that the folder's name accurately describes what's in it. Don't be afraid of creating more folders to help continue the organization process. See Chapter 17 for more information.

➡️ ✗ Perform routine disk maintenance on your hard drive. Back up your files. Check the disk for errors, and beware of the curse of disk fragmentation. Check out Chapter 18 for the how-tos on each of these subjects.

Fun and Frivolity with Floppy Disks

Floppy disks seem rather useless; they don't store enough information to be used regularly, they tend to wear out over a period of time, they cause clutter, and carrying one around earmarks you as a nerd. Even so, floppies do come in handy for a few things.

First, most new software you get comes on one or more floppy disks. Second, floppy disks are ideal for file transfer. You can copy your work to a floppy disk and then take that disk home and show your spouse, who will then ridicule and belittle you because he or she could do a much better job. Finally, floppy disks are used for *backups,* which are safety copies of information on the hard drive in case anything deleterious happens to it there.

Floppy disks also make excellent mini-Frisbees, though I don't have room here to provide a tutorial.

A refreshing view

You switch one floppy disk with another by removing the first disk and replacing it with another disk. But if you have a window open (in My Computer, for example), displaying the floppy disk's contents, it doesn't reflect your disk-swapping. This isn't Windows being dumb here; it's a limitation of your computer's hardware; it just doesn't know when you've changed floppy disks.

To view the new disk's contents in a window on the screen, choose View↔Refresh. Or you can whack the F5 key. This updates the information on the screen to match the files and whatnot on the floppy disk.

The View↔Refresh command can actually be used in any window to update any part of any disk. However, hard drives are updated by Windows whenever you tweak files around, so the command is truly best used on floppy disks.

The thrill of formatting a floppy disk

All floppy disks must be formatted before you can use them. It's the law. Some disks come formatted out of the box. Hallelujah! But you may one day have to erase all their data and start over with a fresh disk. If so, you can reformat. Whatever the case, the following steps must be taken:

1. Place a floppy disk in drive A.

   Drive A is your computer's first floppy drive.

   If you want to format a disk for drive B, put a disk in there instead.

   Make sure that the disk you use matches the size of the floppy drive. Put only a 5¹/₄-inch disk into a 5¹/₄-inch drive, and the same thing for 3¹/₂-inch disks. Also make sure that you're using high-density disks, unless you have an older computer that can use only the lower-density disks.

   For 5¹/₄-inch disks, make sure that you close the drive-door latch before proceeding.

    Format only an old floppy disk — one you want to completely erase — or a new disk straight from the box. Formatting erases any information already on a disk. To see what's on the disk, use My Computer as described in Chapter 2: Open the disk by double-clicking on it to view its contents.

2. Open My Computer.

   Open the My Computer icon on the desktop by double-clicking on it with the mouse.

3. Right-click the mouse on drive A to display its shortcut menu.

   Or right-click on drive B if you're formatting a disk in that drive.

4. Choose Format.

   The Format dialog box appears, looking similar to the one shown in Figure 14-4. This is where you can set various options for formatting your disks. All of them are probably preset the way you want them, however, so it's safe to move to step 5.

5. Click on Start.

   The formatting operation starts a-hummin'. Graphics in the bottom of the Formatting dialog box keep you occupied while you wait.

   When the operation is done, a summary dialog box appears (see Figure 14-5). It tells you all sorts of interesting and barely useful information about the disk that was just formatted and blah, blah, blah. Click on Close to make that information go away.

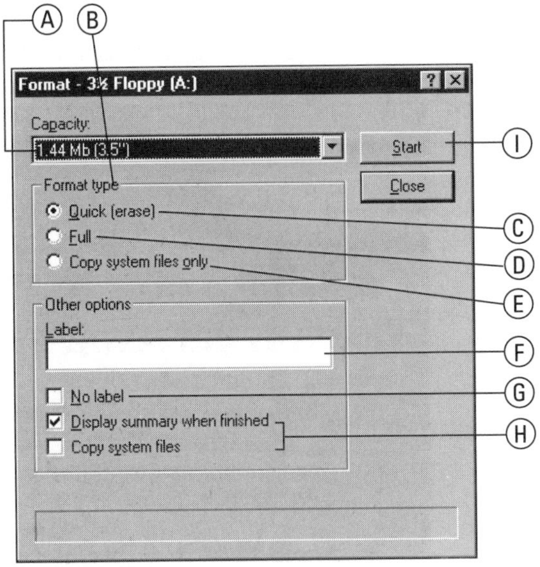

Figure 14-4

The Format dialog box, in all its glory. **A.** Windows automatically sets the capacity of the disk you're about to format. Don't mess with this drop-down list unless you must deal with another computer that can eat only lower-capacity disks. **B.** Three ways to format, please. **C.** The Quick way quickly reformats used disks. **D.** Choose the Full method for new disks, straight out of the box, or for older disks whose quality may be in doubt. **E.** Don't bother. **F.** You can pretype a disk label here if you like. By the way, if you want, do this now 'cause you won't be asked for a label later. **G.** Click here so that you can't pretype any label. **H.** Ignore. **I.** Click here to Start.

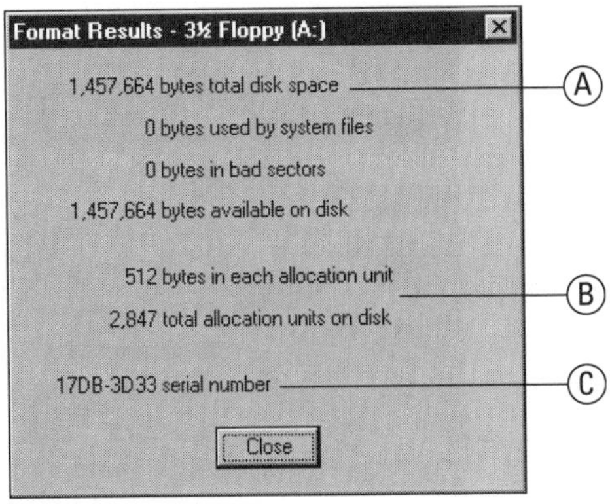

Figure 14-5

The boring results. **A.** Big deal. **B.** So what. **C.** Who cares?

6. Click on Close in the Formatting dialog box.

   You're done.

7. Remove the formatted disk from the drive.

Label the disk right now! Write the disk's name or contents (or both) on a sticky label, and then peel and stick that label to the disk. Don't use a PostIt note because those flit off and sometimes do so right inside your disk drive. Make the label right now! Unlabeled disks are a pain.

If you want to format another disk, start over again with step 1.

Creating a disk to start your computer: The fun yet useful Emergency Boot Disk

One of the options in the Format dialog box (refer to Figure 14-4) is to Copy system files to the new disk. What this does is to create a DOS boot disk, one you can use to start your computer and run MS-DOS Version 7 as opposed to Windows. Whoop-de-do. That probably won't come in handy anytime soon.

Boot disks can be useful, however, especially when you have hard drive trouble and need some way to start your computer. When that happens, you should create a *system disk,* or a special boot disk you can use to start and troubleshoot Windows.

To make a special Windows Emergency Boot disk, follow these steps:

1. Open My Computer.

   See Chapter 2 for more information about My Computer and the greeblies that live within it.

2. Open the Control Panel.

3. Open the Add/Remove Programs tool inside the Control Panel.

   The Add/Remove Programs icon is used to install new software on your computer, to add or remove Windows components, and to make a special Windows startup disk. Double-click on that icon to open its exciting dialog box.

Add/Remove Programs

   The Add/Remove Programs Properties dialog box appears.

4. Click on the Startup Disk tab to bring that panel forward (see Figure 14-6).

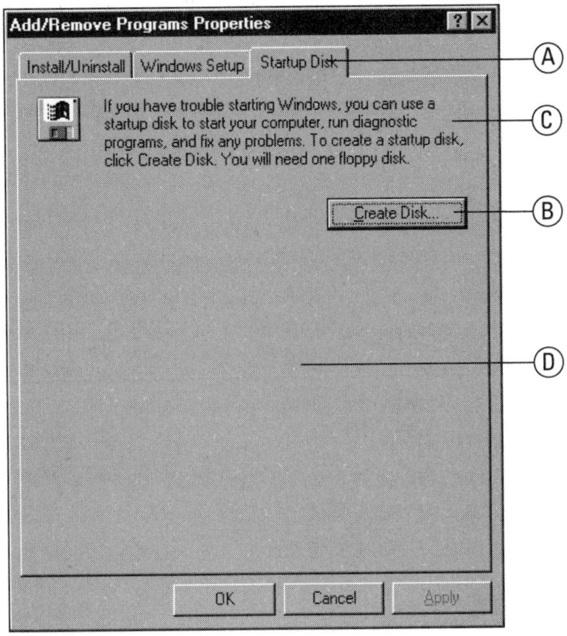

Figure 14-6
The Startup Disk panel in the Add/Remove Programs dialog box.
A. This is the tab. **B.** This is the button. **C.** This says it all, though it could be edited to say it better.
D. By the way, these are all the nice things Newt Gingrich has recently said about the Clinton Administration.

➧ The special Startup Disk contains special Windows startup files plus tools you can use to recover a damaged or flaky hard drive. One of those tools is ScanDisk, a disk-recovery utility. See Chapter 18 for more information about how ScanDisk works.

5. Click the Create Disk button.

Windows hums and whirs.

At this point, you may be asked to insert a few of your original Windows distribution disks, or the CD-ROM if you installed Windows that way. Obey! Windows needs special files.

While Windows hums and whirs, you see some fancy graphics and the message "Preparing startup disk files."

6. Read the Insert Disk dialog box.

It basically tells you to stick a sacrificial disk into drive A. It must be drive A, by the way, so get a disk that fits into drive A.

7. Click on OK.

More whirring.

Doh-dee-doh.

Takes a while, don't it?

8. Whoops! All of a sudden, you're done.

   The disk is created. Not much fanfare. It's now ready for use.

9. Click on the OK button.

   This step closes the Add/Remove Programs dialog box.

10. Close the Control Panel's window.

    Click on its × Close button in the upper right corner.

Remove the disk from the drive and properly label it. Give it a name, such as Windows Emergency Boot Disk. If you have more than one computer, label the disk for whichever computer created it, and keep that disk close to its computer. Also, date the disk. You'll want to make a new disk every year because disks get old and can wear out.

Sending information to a floppy disk

The subject of moving icons and files around on a disk drive is reserved for Chapter 15. For now, you should be aware of a quick shortcut for copying information to a floppy drive. It's the ubiquitous Send To submenu.

Suppose that you used the scanner at the office to scan in a picture of your kids. You now want to take that picture home and use it for wallpaper on your home computer. Here's what you need to do:

1. Locate the file or icon you want to copy.

   Use My Computer for this step. Open My Computer if it isn't open already (see Chapter 2). Then hunt for your file on a specific disk drive, in a specific folder. For example, hunt down the My Address file you created in Chapter 4, in the tutorial in the section "Going About Your Business." It should be found in your Windows folder on drive C.

2. Make sure that there is a disk in drive A.

   Find a floppy disk you can use for drive A. If this is a disk you'll be taking home, find your "home" disk or whichever disk you use when you're sneaking stuff off to the house.

   Make sure that the disk is formatted. See the section "The thrill of formatting a floppy disk," earlier in this chapter, if you need to format a disk.

   Place the disk in the drive all the way. A 3½-inch disk eventually is snatched up by the floppy drive, meaning that the disk is all the way in. For a 5¼-inch disk, slide it in all the way, label side up, and then close the drive-door latch.

3. Bring up the icon's shortcut menu.

   Right-click the mouse on the icon you want to copy. This step brings up the icon's shortcut menu (see Figure 14-7).

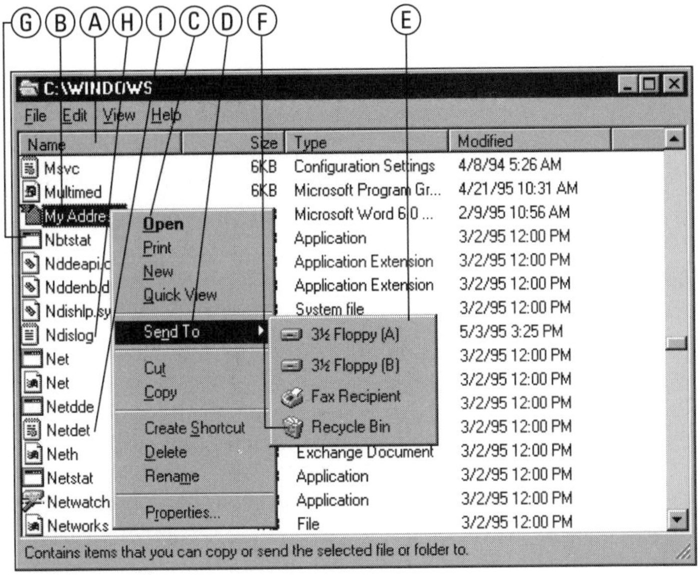

Figure 14-7
The shortcut menu attached to the My Address icon.
A. The Details view in a My Computer window is ideal for looking at long lists of files in bursting-at-the-seams folders, such as Windows. **B.** To quickly find any filename in the list, begin typing its name. I typed M and then Y, and the My Computer file was instantly highlighted. **C.** Right-click on a file or icon to bring up its shortcut menu. **D.** The Send To submenu offers several choices for different places to which to send a copy of a file. **E.** Other things you might see here include the Microsoft Exchange, the My Briefcase application, and other special folders or devices. **F.** What ho! Read the following section, "The secret method of messing with the Send To submenu," to find out how you can put the Recycle Bin on the Send To submenu. Choosing this item automatically sends the file to the Recycle Bin, sort of deleting it. (See Chapter 5 for more info about the Recycle Bin.) **G.** This icon is given to DOS programs or applications that lack a specific icon. **H.** This icon represents a text file, editable by the Notepad program. **I.** This icon represents a configuration file (it's a tiny gear in the middle).

4. Choose Send To⊃3½ Floppy (A).

   If the file is large enough, you see the Copying dialog box, where the file moves one "page" at a time between two folders. This is to prevent you from going catatonic during large file transfers.

➠ If a copy of the file already exists on drive A, you see a Confirm File Replace dialog box. Whoops! Read the information in the box to determine whether you want to replace the existing file with the one you're copying. (Generally, it's okay if the other file is older.) You have to refer to Chapter 16, the section "Copying, or Doop-Doop-Duplicating, Files," for more information about dealing with this phenomenon.

5. You're done.

   After copying the file, the Copying dialog box disappears, and you're back in My Computer, staring at a file you just copied.

You can check drive A to ensure that you did copy the file. It will be sitting right there, in drive A's window, providing that you open it up and take a peek in My Computer.

Oh, and you can send the file to drive B, providing that you have a drive B, and then, obviously, it would appear as a menu item.

➠ The Send To command is like a quick Copy-Paste shortcut. Normally, when you copy a file from one place to another, you select the file (or a group of files), choose Edit➪Copy, find the destination (the place you want to copy to), and choose Paste. This copies the file (or files) to that location. However, the Send To command is a quick shortcut for copying a file to a floppy drive. See Chapter 15 for more information about copying files.

➠ If you want to move the file (cut and paste as opposed to copy and paste), you have to use the Cut command rather than Send To. See Chapter 16 for more details.

➠ You can select a group of files and then use Send To to copy them to a floppy drive. See Chapter 16, the section "Crowd Control, or Working with Groups of Files," for information about selecting a group of files in My Computer.

➠ By the way, *wallpaper* is the background you see on the desktop. It can be changed to just about anything, even a scanned-in picture of your kids. See Chapter 24 for more information.

The secret method of messing with the Send To submenu

By the way, if you want to, you can change the Send To's submenu. You can add items to or remove them from the Send To submenu, whatever you like. This is because items in the submenu are really icons located in a secret folder on disk.

Suppose that your B drive is the 5¼-inch kind. You never plan to use that drive or buy any disks for it, so you can remove it from the menu if you like. Here's how:

1. Open My Computer.

   Double-click on My Computer to open it.

2. Open drive C.

   Double-click on the drive C icon to open it.

3. Open the Windows folder.

   Double-click on the Windows folder to open it.

4. Open the SendTo folder.

   A-ha! Double-click on the SendTo folder. It opens and you see, right there inside its window, a list of the items found in the Send To submenu (see Figure 14-8). Cool.

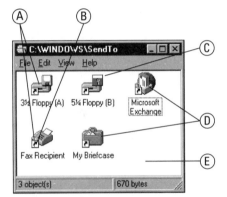

Figure 14-8
Things found in the SendTo folder appear in a Send To submenu.
A. These are shortcuts, abbreviations representing the real somethings — disk drives and a fax machine — that exist elsewhere. **B.** Shortcuts are marked by this little doojobbie. See Chapter 16, the section "Taking a Shortcut Instead of Copying Files," if you want to know more about shortcuts. **C.** You can delete one of these icons if you like (for example, floppy drive B if you don't ever want to send anything there). **D.** Some of this stuff may not appear in here; it all depends on how your computer is set up. **E.** You can also paste new things into the Send To submenu, which enables you to easily copy icons there. Windows is open to having just about anything pasted in here, from the Recycle Bin to a folder to whatever. Be sure that you paste a shortcut, however (see the main text).

5. Select the drive B icon.

   Click on the icon once with the mouse.

5¼ Floppy (B)

6. Choose File⇨Delete.

   You may be asked whether you want to send the file to the Recycle Bin. Click on Yes.

   The icon is deleted, and that menu item is removed from the Send To menu.

You can also paste a shortcut into the SendTo folder, in which case that item appears in the Send To submenu. To do so, follow these steps:

1. Follow steps 1 through 4 in the preceding steps to open the SendTo folder's window.

2. Find whatever you want to appear in the Send To menu.

   For example, you can select the Recycle Bin, your printer, a special folder, or whatever. It can be just about anything, but it should be something you can drag an icon to, something you can copy information into.

3. Bring up that icon's shortcut menu.

   Right-click on the icon to make its shortcut menu appear.

4. Choose Create Shortcut from the menu.

   A duplicate of the icon appears, renamed Shortcut to [whatever] with the tiny shortcut arrow appearing on the icon.

   Shortcut to
   Recycle Bin

   If there is no Create Shortcut menu item, choose the Copy command.

5. Drag the shortcut to the SendTo folder.

   If you can't drag the shortcut, bring up its shortcut menu and choose the Cut command. Right-click on the shortcut icon, and then choose Cut from the menu. Click the mouse again in the SendTo folder's window to select that window. Then choose Edit⇨Paste from the menu.

6. Rename the shortcut in the SendTo folder's window.

   Whatever name you give the icon is the name that appears in the Send To submenu. For example, the Recycle Bin shortcut is named Shortcut to Recycle Bin. To change that name, click on the icon once and then choose File⇨Rename. Type a new name, or press the Home key and then use the Delete key to erase the Shortcut to part of the name.

   Press the Enter key when you're done renaming.

By the way, if you copy the Recycle Bin into the SendTo folder, selecting it from a shortcut menu actually deletes the file, not a copy of it. For everything else you select, a disk drive or folder, the file is copied there.

Figure 14-9 shows what the SendTo folder looks like with a gallimaufry of things pasted into it.

Figure 14-9

The results of placing the Recycle Bin, Printer, and a folder shortcut in the SendTo folder.

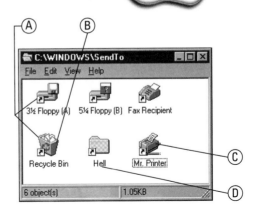

A. These commands are merely shortcuts pasted into the SendTo folder. Clicking on an icon and selecting one of these items sends a copy of that icon to the appropriate location. **B.** Shortcut to the Recycle Bin. **C.** Shortcut to the Printer, renamed Printer here because the original name, Shortcut to HP LaserJet 4V, is a tad cumbersome for a submenu item. See step 5 in the text for information about how to rename an icon. **D.** The folder shortcut was renamed Hell, so there is a Send To⇨Hell command. This just means that Windows sends a copy of the icons to the special Hell folder. Nothing blasphemous is implied here.

The Joy of CD-ROMs

CD-ROMs are part of that multimedia thing, the other part being a sound card to let your computer squawk. This is because the big stuff usually comes on a CD-ROM; it's much easier than fussing with a stack of floppies. For example, I prefer to install Windows from one CD-ROM as opposed to messing with the 15-odd floppy disks. (What a nightmare!)

Everyone should have a CD-ROM disc in his computer. You can have two or more or even a whole Wurlitzer jukebox-style CD-ROM disc changer, but most people have just one.

The essence of CD-ROMs and drives

A CD-ROM is a cross between a floppy disk and a hard drive. Like a floppy disk, the CD-ROM is removable. Like a hard drive, a CD-ROM holds megabytes of information — as much as 600MB on a single disc. This is why you find large programs stored there, graphical images, multimedia games, sounds, and other stuff that can be too massive for a stupid stack of floppy disks.

Unlike either a floppy or hard drive, you cannot write to a CD-ROM drive; the information stored there is "etched in silicon." This explains why the CD-ROM always appears full; see the section "Checking on disk usage," earlier in this chapter. And if you attempt to change anything on a CD-ROM (rename or delete a file) or copy anything to the disc, you get a message telling you "Access denied."

➡ See Chapter 32 for more information about the "Access denied" error message.

Take care of your CDs. Although they are advertised as indestructible, they still should be cleaned if they get smudged or scratched; buy a cleaning kit at a record store. To keep your discs in good shape and prevent smudges and scratches, put them back in their "jewel boxes" when you're not using them. You can buy extra jewel boxes for stray discs. And never stack CDs. If you have to give one a rest, set it label-side down.

Auto-ejecting CD-ROMs – Ptooey!

This is nothing big, though it is something Windows can do automatically on some computers. It's auto-eject! Like how James Bond got rid of the goon in the passenger seat. Though with this auto-eject, it's a command on a short-cut menu and not a button in the stick shift, and the disks don't go flying out the roof.

To eject a disc, follow these steps:

1. Bring up the CD-ROM's shortcut menu.

   Right-click the mouse on a CD-ROM drive in My Computer.

2. Choose Eject.

   Click on the Eject command. If your CD-ROM drive understands the command, it ejects the disc from the drive. If it doesn't, the Eject command doesn't work and, in some situations, may not even appear on the menu.

In all cases, you can always eject a disc manually by pushing your CD-ROM's eject button, switch, or knob.

There is no corresponding Insert command that automatically closes the CD-ROM drive caddie.

Playing a musical CD

Windows is very smart when it comes to knowing the difference between a CD-ROM with computer information and a music CD. If you stick a music CD into your CD-ROM drive, Windows recognizes it and — in an amazing feat of intelligence for a computer — begins playing the music.

When you insert a musical CD disc, you see the music-is-playing CD icon in My Computer and the CD Player program runs (see Figure 14-10). If on the off chance that doesn't happen, you can manually start the CD Player program; press Ctrl+Esc to bring up the Start Thing's menu, and then choose Programs⇨Accessories⇨ Multimedia⇨CD Player. (Whew!)

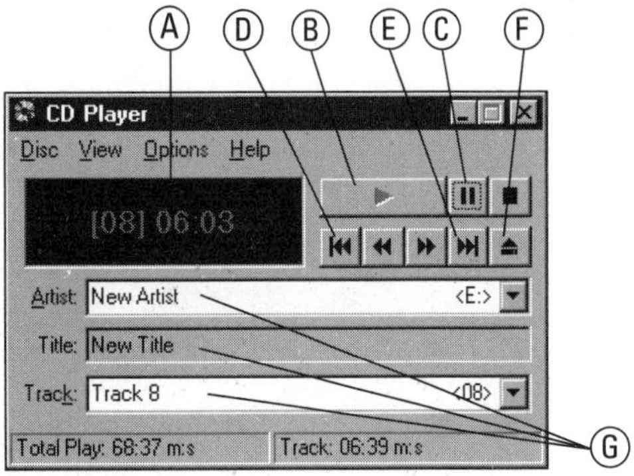

Figure 14-10
The CD Player program starts whenever you shove a musical CD into your CD-ROM drive.
A. Tells you which track is playing and how long it's been playing, similar to the information you cheerfully ignore on the front of your musical CD player.
B. The Play button. **C.** The Pause button, which you click on when the phone rings so that you don't let on that you're listening to music while you're working. **D.** Skip to the preceding track. **E.** Skip to the next track. **F.** The Play button. **G.** If you have serious time to waste, you can fill in this information about the disc and the music on various tracks.

If you can't hear the CD or the neighbors are pounding broomsticks on the ceiling, adjust the volume. Use the Volume thing, as described in Chapter 7, in the section "Setting the PC's speaker volume."

RAM Drives Belong in the Past

No one needs a RAM drive with Windows 95. It's a waste of memory that would be better put to use by Windows itself.

If you have a RAM drive, it's probably left over from the operating system you were using before you upgraded to Windows 95. If so, you can and should remove the RAM drive, making more memory available to Windows, which not only needs it but also occasionally breaks down sobbing without it.

To see whether you already have a RAM drive in your computer, look for a RAM drive icon in My Computer. If you find one there, you have a RAM drive, and it would be a good idea to remove it. Follow these steps:

1. Choose the Run command from the Start Thing's menu.

   The Run dialog box appears. (Refer to Figure 3-3 for rude comments.)

   The Run command is the most obtuse way to start a program in Windows, according to Chapter 3, in the section "Running to the Run command to start a program." Much more obvious ways are available; for this exercise, however, it's the most direct and brief way to tackle a complex situation.

2. Type the following line exactly:

   notepad c:\config.sys

   Type the word *notepad* and a space. Then type the letter *C,* a colon, and a backslash. It's the backward slash, not the slash you get by pressing Shift+?. Then type *config,* a period, and *sys.*

3. Double-check what you typed.

   Does it look like the text shown in step 2? If so, continue. Otherwise, press the Backspace key to back up and erase your mistakes.

4. Press the Enter key.

   This step tells Windows to run the Notepad program, which is a tiny text editor, kind of like a feeble version of WordPad. The Notepad program loads CONFIG.SYS, a special startup file, from disk (see Figure 14-11).

5. Look for the line of text in the CONFIG.SYS file that starts the RAM drive.

   Look for a line that looks somewhat like the following:

   device=c:\dos\ramdrive.sys 1024 /e

   or maybe:

   device=c:\windows\ramdrive.sys

or possibly:

> device=c:\dos\vdisk.sys

It might also say "devicehigh" rather than "device." Whatever, the key word is RAMDRIVE.SYS (or maybe VDISK.SYS, if you have an older Compaq or IBM computer).

Figure 14-11
The CONFIG.SYS file, ready for editing in the Notepad.
A. CONFIG.SYS is a special startup file used by Windows, but mostly by DOS. The file you see on your screen will probably look similar, but not identical, to the one illustrated here. **B.** These lines contain commands used to configure

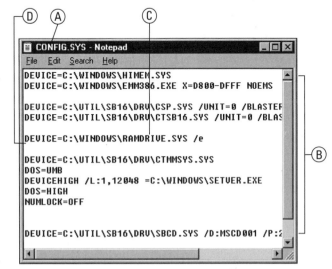

your computer and start special programs called device drivers. Major yawner material. **C.** The RAMDRIVE.SYS device driver creates a RAM drive on your system. This is the type of line you should remove. **D.** Click the mouse pointer here to insert the word REM, which disables the RAM drive. You want to type **REM** and then a space.

6. Edit the line by sticking the word REM at the beginning.

   Move the cursor to the beginning of the line that loads the RAMDrive device driver program. Click the mouse pointer just in front of the D on that line. The toothpick cursor should blink right in front of the D.

   Type the word **REM**. Then type a space. The line should look something like this when you're done:

   > REM device=c:\windows\ramdrive.sys

   Double-check to make sure that there is a space after the word REM.

7. If your computer has more than one RAM drive, disable it as well.

   If you have in the CONFIG.SYS file more than one line that starts a RAM drive, repeat steps 4 and 5 for it; insert the word **REM** at the beginning of each line. Sometimes this happens if your PC was configured to have several RAM drives. No big deal; disable them all.

8. Choose File⇨Save.

   This step saves the CONFIG.SYS file back to disk.

9. Close the Notepad.

   Click on its × Close button in the upper right corner. Notepad goes away.

   You're done, except for one step you can take at a later time:

10. Eventually, reset your computer.

   For some reason, Windows doesn't obey the instructions in CONFIG.SYS until *after* you start or restart your computer. If you're able to do that now, go ahead. Otherwise, the RAM drives are not removed until you reset.

   See Chapter 1, the section "Quitting Windows and Turning Off Your PC," for more information about restarting Windows. In step 3 in that section, you click on the radio button by the Restart the computer option — not the Shut down the computer option. When the computer restarts, the RAM drives are gone. Bye-bye.

The Secrets of Documents, Files, and Icons

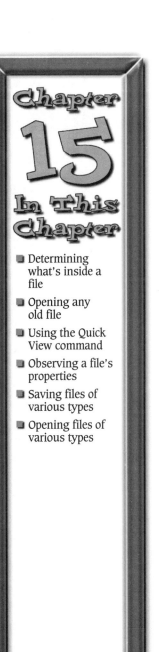

Chapter 15

In This Chapter

- Determining what's inside a file
- Opening any old file
- Using the Quick View command
- Observing a file's properties
- Saving files of various types
- Opening files of various types

Documents, files, and icons are all really the same thing: ways of representing the stuff on your computer. Icons are how the files appear in My Computer, the Explorer, and on the desktop. If you ever dare to tread on the DOS prompt, files appear name-only on an ugly text screen. (Ugh!) Documents are merely a type of file, specifically one you created by using an application. Other types of files include programs, data files, support files, and numerous other files, each of which holds some special Easter egg required to make your computer run the way you like.

➡ This chapter discusses files, what's in them, and how to work with them. One thing that's not covered here is how files can get lost. How that happens is anyone's guess. Finding the lost files is a subject covered in Chapter 31.

⬅ Also check out Chapter 2 for more information about using My Computer.

Who Knows What Evil Lurks in the Heart of Files?

Ideally, a file's name and its icon should tell you a lot. The name should describe the file's contents. The icon should tell you which type of file it is, whether it's a program, a document created by a specific program, or what.

For example, all of Microsoft Word's document icons look alike. You can instantly spot one, which tells you which type of file it is and which application created it. Furthermore, if it's well-named and placed in a proper folder, you know just about everything about the file without having to peer into its soul.

Property Tax Hike

That's the ideal circumstance. In practice, however, you find many files that don't tell you much about what the file does or where it fits in. In these cases, it's safe to leave the icon alone. It's always best not to mess with something you don't know anything about.

whatami

A lesson to learn here is that you should properly name your files: short, sweet, to the point.

➠ File-naming rules are found in Chapter 16, in the sidebar "Basic file-naming rules and regulations."

Wantonly opening a file to see what's inside

When you're in doubt about a file's nature, you can always open the file to see what's inside. Here's how:

1. Find a file you want to peer into.

⬅ You can use My Computer, as described in Chapter 2, or use the Explorer. Both of these are file-finding fun tools.

2. Open it.

Double-click on the file's icon. This step does one of three things:

✘ If the file represents a program on your hard disk, that program runs.

✘ If the file represents a document created by some program, that program runs and the document is opened for editing.

✘ Finally, if the file generates a big "Huh?" from Windows, the Open With dialog box is displayed, as shown in Figure 15-1.

Figure 15-1

You see the Open With dialog box when Windows doesn't recognize a file you tried to open. **A.** The name of the file you tried to open. **B.** Sometimes a box appears here, asking you to describe what type of document you've opened. **C.** Here is a list of programs Windows recognizes. You can choose one with which to open your file; because Windows couldn't figure it out, however, there's no point in your guessing here. **D.** Clicking on Cancel is the best option in this dialog box.

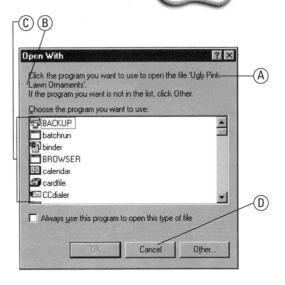

Most of the time, you're met with option 3 because the majority of the files on your hard drive are used by Windows or other programs, and they get really confused if you attempt to open them spontaneously. Therefore, do this only when you have a burning desire to know what's inside a file. Of course, you can try a few other tricks, which are mentioned in the following few sections.

Not everything that claims to be a program really is.

Be careful when you open unknown packages! Suppose that during your file-finding travels in My Computer or the Explorer, you find a program named IDUNO.EXE; *don't start it!* When you don't know what the program is or what it does, it's best to keep out. Otherwise, the program may do something unexpected or cause your computer to react in an unpredictable (though predictably bad) manner.

Carefully opening a file for a quick view

A safer way to test a file's murky waters is to use the Quick View command, which displays a Quick View dialog box for a quick view of certain files' contents.

The Quick View command is most easily found on an icon's shortcut menu, though you can also choose File⇨Quick View from My Computer's menu bar.

1. Whip out an icon's shortcut menu.

   Right-click the mouse on the file to see the shortcut menu pop up.

   You see a few items in the menu that can be used to open the file; Table 15-1 shows some of the menu items you may see; Figure 15-2 shows the shortcut menu for a text file.

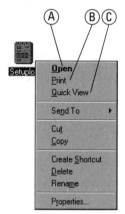

Figure 15-2
A text file's shortcut menu.
A. The Open command enables you to open the file by using a text editor, such as the Notepad or WordPad. This command is the same one you get when you double-click on the icon. **B.** The Print command appears for those icons you can drag to a printer and instantly print. **C.** The Quick View command appears for certain files you can take a quick peek at, such as text files, graphics files, program files, and others I probably don't know about.

Table 15-1	Some Shortcut Menu Commands to Help You Find What's in a File
Command	*What It Does*
Open	Opens the file by using the program that created it
Play	Plays a multimedia file or a sound or video clip or directs the computer to go outside and play
Open With	Opens the Open With dialog box (refer to Figure 15-1) because Windows is baffled about what created the file
New	Opens the application that created the document and also starts a new document
Print	Prints the file
Quick View	Displays the file's contents in a special viewer

2. Choose Quick View.

   The file's contents are displayed in the Quick View dialog box — a sneak preview. Figures 15-3 through 15-5 show how Quick View displays various types of files. Click on the × Close button when you're done ogling.

   You may not have Quick View installed with Windows. If so, you have to add it. Follow the instructions in Chapter 13, in the section "Adding the Rest of Windows," and look for Quick View in the Accessories section of Windows goodies.

The Open, Play, and Open With commands appear in boldface in the shortcut menu. That just means that double-clicking on the icon is the same as choosing the command. Not all shortcut menus have these items; if all you see is Open With, Windows is pretty much clueless about what type of file it is.

Figure 15-3
A Quick View look at a text file.
A. Click here to open the text file for editing. **B.** Click here to "zoom in," or make the text bigger.
C. Click here to "zoom out," or get a bird's-eye view of the text.

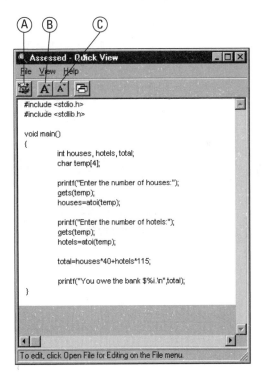

Figure 15-4
A Quick View look at a graphics image.
A. Click on this thing to open the graphic in the Paint program. **B.** Choose View⇨Toolbar to see this toolbar

Figure 15-5
A Quick View look at a program file.
A. Click here if you dare to run the program (not recommended). **B.** Zoom in to see the meaningless text larger. **C.** Zoom out to see the meaningless text teensy.

Gawking at a file's properties

What the heck is that file all about? An interesting way to find out is to check its properties, kind of like X-raying the file but without the need to wear a lead apron. To see a file's properties, do this:

whatami

1. Click on a file's icon by using the mouse.

2. Press the Alt+Enter key combination.

   Press and hold the Alt key, and then press the Enter key. Release both keys. This step displays the file's Properties dialog box, which may help you discover what the file's up to, as shown in Figure 15-6.

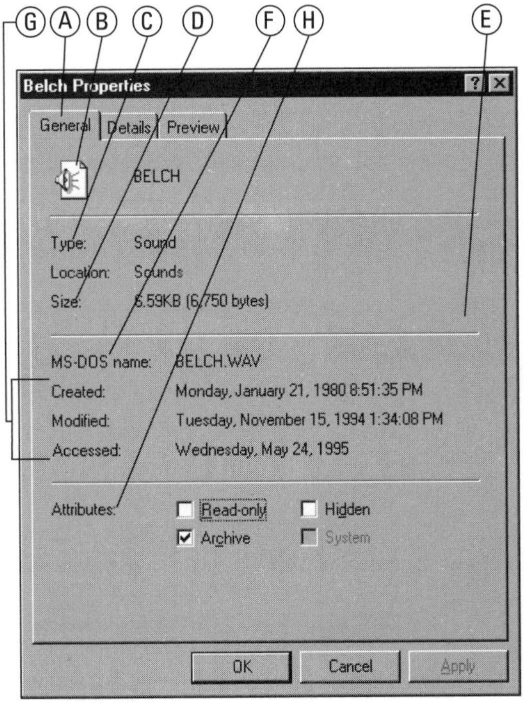

Figure 15-6
A typical file's Properties dialog box.
A. The General tab is the most informative. Other tabs appear for other types of files. **B.** The file's name and icon come first. **C.** This is the key. The Type tells you which type of file you're looking at. In this case, it's a sound file, one that contains an audio clip. Of course, it may occasionally say something obscure, in which case this trick still doesn't tell you much about a file — except that you should leave it alone. **D.** File size information. **E.** If this were a folder's Properties dialog box, you would see information about how many files and folders were located inside the current folder, but because this is a file's Properties dialog box, you don't see that information here. **F.** Here is the file's ugly MS-DOS name, which may be shorter and more cryptic than the name shown below the icon. Ignore this. **G.** Trivial history information.
H. Don't bother.

G A B C D F H E

Belch Properties   ? X

General | Details | Preview

BELCH

Type: Sound
Location: Sounds
Size: 6.59KB (6,750 bytes)

MS-DOS name: BELCH.WAV
Created: Monday, January 21, 1980 8:51:35 PM
Modified: Tuesday, November 15, 1994 1:34:08 PM
Accessed: Wednesday, May 24, 1995

Attributes: ☐ Read-only   ☐ Hidden
              ☑ Archive   ☐ System

                    OK   Cancel   Apply

Other ways to bring up a file's Properties dialog box include the ones in this list:

✗ Choosing the Properties command from the icon's shortcut menu

✗ Pressing and holding the Alt key and then double-clicking on the file's icon

✗ Choosing the Properties button from My Computer's toolbar

Personally, I feel that Alt+Enter is easier to remember, and it's also pretty universal throughout Windows for seeing various Properties dialog boxes.

A Preview tab appears on sound files, midi music files, and video clips. It enables you to view the file's contents. Of course, you can just double-click on the icon to play the file.

Summary and Statistics tabs appear on certain documents, such as Microsoft Word documents. They offer more information about the document, such as who wrote it, how long it is, and whether it's a good read.

If you check the properties of a shortcut icon, a special shortcut tab appears. In that panel, you can find out about the original file and change the file's icon if you like.

In addition to General, other tabs appear on other files, including the whole half-dozen that appear on a DOS program's Properties dialog box.

◄ⁿ If you dare to check out the properties of a DOS program, you will see many panels with lots of technical stuff. Refer to Chapter 12 for any pertinent information.

ⁿ► If you look at the properties of an animated cursor file, the icon image in the dialog box is animated, just as the cursor will be. For more information about animated cursors, see Chapter 25.

Messing with File Types in an Application

Files are given their icons by the programs that create them. This all keeps in line with the harmonic nature of the Windows universe: Documents created by certain applications remain married to each other. It's what enables you to double-click on an icon and have the program that created it start up all ready for editing.

Of course, it's entirely possible to mess up that scheme. Not accidentally, of course. But you can, on purpose, direct a Windows application to save a file as a different type or even open a file created by another application. This isn't the miracle of every computer program finally being able to share its data with every other program. But it does make working with other applications tolerable.

Saving a file as a specific type (such as a text-only file)

Whenever an application saves a file to disk, it saves it as a certain type. This is how Windows knows which files belong to which programs and can then start them automatically.

Most applications save their files as one type. But in a few applications, you have a choice of which type of file you want to save. Suppose that you're directed to save a file as a text-only, or ASCII-formatted, file. Who knows why? This is how you do it:

1. Start WordPad, and write something brilliant.

   See the tutorial in Chapter 4, in the section "Scent of a Windows Application," for more information about starting WordPad and creating something interesting.

   Don't save anything until the next step.

2. Choose File⇨Save As.

   You should always choose the Save As command when you save a file to disk as a different type (see Figure 15-7). If you choose Save, the application saves the document in its regular format, nothing special. But if you are directed to save the file to disk as a plain text file, for example, you have to use the Save As command.

3. Pick Text Document from the Save as type drop-down list.

   This step directs WordPad to save the file in the plain text format, as opposed to its regular document format. (The Text Only format is the same thing as the ASCII format, in case you were wondering.)

Other applications have different items in their Save as type drop-down list. In Microsoft Word, for example, you have about 20 different types to choose from. Gads!

It's a good idea to save the file first in the application's "native" format. Then save the file again by using the Save As command and choosing the different file type from the Save as type drop-down list.

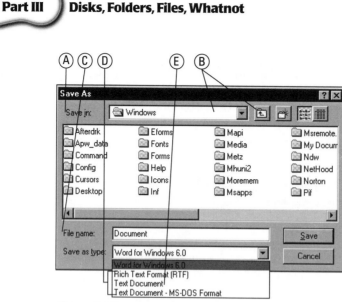

Figure 15-7

The Save As dialog box for WordPad.

A. These controls help you save the file to a specific spot on disk. Read about how the details work in Chapter 28, in the section "All Them Gizmos." The procedural part of saving something to disk is covered in Chapter 4, in the section "Saving your stuff." **B.** Use these controls to first set a folder location for the file. **C.** Here is where you type the file's name. **D.** Use this drop-down list's various different formats for saving the file. **E.** Pick Text Document here to save the file in a plain text format.

When you save a file by using a different type, its icon reflects that. You see two different icon types for a WordPad document saved first as a WordPad document and second as a text document.

WordPad native doc   WordPad text doc

By the way, when you save a WordPad document as a text file, that file then becomes associated with the Notepad application; double-clicking on a plain text file opens Notepad, not WordPad. Don't fret over this; that's just what happens when you have text files (for whatever reason you were asked to save the file as a text type).

Opening only files of specific types

When you use an application's Open command, it displays an assortment of files you can pluck from disk for editing. Normally, the Open dialog box lists only those documents the application created itself, the application's native type. For example, WordPad shows only WordPad-created documents in its Open dialog box, Paint shows only Paint-created documents, and so on. However, you can use the Files of type drop-down list to let the application open files of another type (see Figure 15-8).

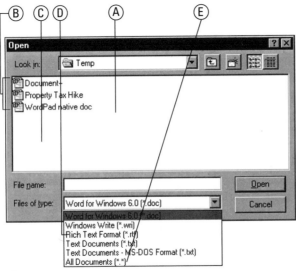

Figure 15-8
The Open dialog box for WordPad.
A. Listed here are documents the application can open. **B.** These are Word for Windows documents, which WordPad creates automatically. **C.** Folders may also appear here, which you can open to look for more documents. **D.** This drop-down list directs Windows to display files of one type or another. Only those files matching the type listed here are displayed above. **E.** The All Documents option displays all the files in a folder above, regardless of their file type. Although this is good for seeing all the files in a folder, the application cannot successfully open every file.

Not all applications can swallow files created by another program. Most do. For example, Microsoft Word can read documents created by several other popular word processors. But to see them, you must choose that file type from the Files of type drop-down list.

Rather than mess with selecting each file type separately, you can choose the All Documents (which may also be called All Files) option. This option displays all the files in the current folder. Although you cannot open everything, it helps you quickly locate a file of a type that might be open-able by the application.

For example, I use the All Documents option in Word to open ancient WordPerfect documents I once created. The WordPerfect documents are so old that they aren't recognized as a WordPerfect file type by Windows; choosing the All Documents type is the only way I can see them in the Open dialog box.

◀ You might also want to check out the section "Opening stuff" in Chapter 4 for general information about using the Open command. Chapter 28 discusses in general terms using the gizmos you find in the Open dialog box.

▶ It's easiest to find files when you've placed them in properly named folders. That keeps everything organized and makes working with the computer much easier. Chapter 17 covers this subject in antagonizing depth.

Manipulate Them Files

Every so often, it comes time to practice some good old file manipulation. There are four basic things you can do to files: You can rename them, you can copy them, you can move them, and you can delete them. All this is done by using My Computer or the Explorer and various commands to manipulate the file icons you see.

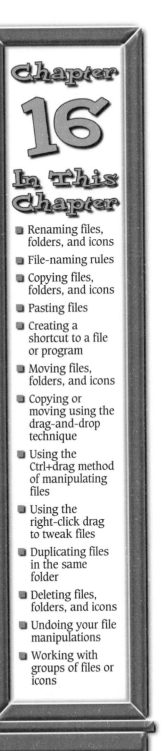

By the way, all the commands in this chapter apply to folders as well. You can rename, copy, move, or delete a folder if you like, just as easily as you can delete a file. You should be more careful, however, because folders typically contain lots of files and maybe other folders with even more files. Actually, if I were you, I'd check out Chapter 17, on the subject of folders, before doing any of this.

Blessing a File with a New Name

When you first save a file to disk, you give it a name. Maybe not the best name, because you can't always be creative and because maybe the file's contents change, warranting a name change. When that happens, Windows blesses you with the ability to change a file's name to something else.

To change a file's name or to change the name of a folder or just about any icon in a window, follow these steps:

1. Click on the icon.

   Just click once. This step highlights the icon, selecting it.

   ➡ You can rename only one thing at a time in Windows. Other file commands can work on groups of files at one time; see the section "Crowd Control, or Working with Groups of Files," near the end of this chapter.

2. Press the F2 key.

   F2 is one of your keyboard's function keys. Press that key, and the icon's name becomes selected, ready for editing or replacement.

3. Type a new name for the icon.

   Refer to the sidebar "Basic file-naming rules and regulations," later in this chapter, for more information about file-naming dos and donuts.

   ➡ You can edit an icon's name just as you edit any text in Windows. Normally, you just type a new name, which replaces the old one. But you can use the cursor keys, the Backspace and Delete keys, and other editing keys if you like. See Chapter 30, the section "Basic text-editing stuff."

4. Press the Enter key when you're done.

   The new name is in place.

Other, less handy ways to rename an icon

Pressing the F2 key is the best way to rename a file, primarily because you use the keyboard anyway to type a file's new name. Even so, there are three other ways to rename a file:

✗ You can choose File⇨Rename from the menu.

✗ Or you can choose the Rename command from the file's shortcut menu (see Chapter 5, the section "The Ubiquitous Pop-up Shortcut Menus").

✗ Another method, though somewhat tedious, is to click the mouse a second time on the file's icon. This method proves rather unreliable, though, because you have to be patient and wait for that second click (something you really don't have time for).

Don't rename programs. Sure, it would be cute to rename WordPerfect as DoodleWriter. Unfortunately, this may give you some problems when Windows claims that it can no longer find WordPerfect (because it was renamed).

Likewise, don't rename any file, icon, or folder you didn't create yourself.

Especially don't rename Windows' own folder or any of the folders or files inside that folder.

Don't bother trying to rename the Recycle Bin; it can't be done.

Another rename warning: You cannot rename a file with the same name of another file in the same folder. If you try, Windows displays an ugly warning dialog box. Press the Enter key to close the dialog box, and then rename your file.

On the other hand, you can give two files of different types the same name. It's possible, for example, to have both a WordPad file and a Paint file named Airplane Food in one folder. But two WordPad files named alike? No way.

Airplane Food   Airplane Food

Yet another warning: A few forbidden characters are not allowed in a filename. The nearby sidebar "Basic file-naming rules and regulations" lists them all. If you slip up and use one of these characters, an appropriate hand-slapping dialog box lets you know.

But you know what? You *can* rename disk drives. Not their letters, but their funky label-names. This subject is covered in Chapter 14, in the section "More than just a letter: Giving your disk a proper name."

Basic file-naming rules and regulations

You can name a file just about anything. You should concern yourself primarily with being brief and descriptive. For example:

Matt 14

This filename describes the 14th letter I've written to Matt. It could have been Letter to Matt 14, but the file lives in my Letters folder, so I already know that it's a letter (a good argument for proper organization, dwelt on extensively in Chapter 17).

Other than being short and descriptive, these are the technical rules for naming a file:

✗ A filename can be any number of characters long, from 1 to 255. A 256-character filename is one character too many and probably ridiculous as well.

✗ A filename can contain letters, numbers, and spaces.

✗ Uppercase and lowercase letters look different on the screen, but Windows doesn't notice any difference. So you can save a file as May Schedule, and Windows still finds it when you type **may schedule** or even **MAY SCHEDULE**.

✗ A filename cannot contain any of the following characters:

" * / : < > ? \ |

The naming rules for files also apply to folders. But with folders, I urge you even more to be brief and descriptive. It's just easier to read the names under the icons and to navigate the various directories' collapsible tree structures.

Ancient history on the old dot-three filename extensions

Windows 95 no longer requires you to type the optional filename extension when you name a file or save something to disk. For example, in the old days, you might have saved a document to disk with the following name:

PORB.DOC

You type the dot-D-O-C to flag the file as a "document." Whatever. In Windows 95, this is no longer necessary because Windows does it automatically. When you save a file, such as a document, you're given the chance to save it as a certain *type* in the Save As dialog box. When you choose a type, Windows automatically assigns the file the proper extension. You never have to type dot-DOC or dot-TXT or anything like that again.

See the section "Messing with File Types in an Application" in Chapter 15 for more information about file types.

"But I want to see the extensions!"

Windows does its best to hide the filename extensions from you. But if you want to see them in My Computer or the Explorer, follow these steps:

1. **Choose View⇨Options.** This step displays the Options dialog box.

2. **Click on the View panel to bring that forward.**

3. **Click on the box by Hide MS-DOS file extensions for file types that are registered.** If a ✔ appears in the box, the extensions are hidden. If the box is empty, you can see the extensions.

4. **Click on OK to close the Options dialog box.**

Copying, or Doop-Doop-Duplicating, Files

You need two things in order to copy a file. First, you need the file itself. Second, you need a destination, or the place you're copying a file to. Suppose that you create a graphics file that contains your signature. You want to copy it from your Graphics folder to your Letters folder. Here's how:

1. Click on the file once to select it.

   You can copy a file's icon from My Computer, the Explorer, or even the Windows desktop. Whatever, select the file by clicking on it once. The file becomes highlighted on the screen.

2. Choose Edit⇨Copy.

   Or you can right-click on the icon to bring up its shortcut menu and then choose Copy from the shortcut menu.

   Or you can even press the Ctrl+C key combination, which is the universal Copy keyboard shortcut key throughout Windows.

3. Find the destination.

   The file has been copied to Windows' Clipboard. Now you have to find a place to paste it. In the example, you would find and open the Letters folder by using My Computer. Open that folder to display its window on the screen.

   ◄▥ See Chapter 8, the section "Everything goes to the Clipboard," for more information about the Clipboard.

4. Choose Edit⇨Paste.

Or you can right-click on a blank part of the folder's window and choose the Paste command from the shortcut menu.

For keyboard enthusiasts, press the Ctrl+V key combination, the universal Paste shortcut key command.

If you're copying a large file (or many files), you see a Copy dialog box displayed while Windows copies the file. The file floats from one folder icon to another, one page at a time. It's rather silly to watch, but it assures you that the computer is still alive and functioning during large file copies.

Windows doesn't let you copy a file to a folder if a file with that name already exists in the folder. When that happens, the Confirm File Replace dialog box is displayed (see Figure 16-1). My advice is to click the No button when this happens, unless you're absolutely certain that you want to replace the existing file. (If you still want to copy the file but not replace the other file, rename the file before copying; see the section "Blessing a File with a New Name," earlier in this chapter.)

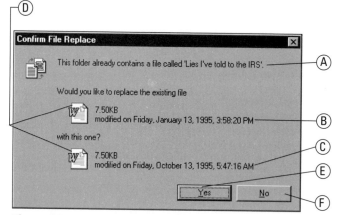

Figure 16-1
The Confirm File Replace dialog box warns that a file with that same name already exists.
A. A file with this name already exists in the folder. Oh, no! **B.** Is this file older? If so, go ahead and replace it. **C.** This newer file replaces the one above.
D. These are both Word documents. **E.** Click here if you want to replace the file — but only if you're certain. **F.** Click here to be safe.

Pasting file tips

Pasting a file into a window can be an ugly task; Windows usually tacks down the file wherever you clicked the mouse. Oftentimes, this doesn't bode well for the overall aesthetic look of the window. Some adjustments are necessary.

To arrange icons after a sloppy paste job, choose View⇨Line up Icons from the menu. (On the desktop, choose Line up Icons from the shortcut menu; right-click on the desktop to see the menu.)

If the icons line themselves up weird, choose View⇨Arrange Icons⇨By Name. This usually squares up the icons with the window's size.

And if you hate having to do this, choose View⇨Arrange Icons⇨Auto Arrange, and you'll never have to mess with rogue icons again.

You can even paste your file to the desktop, but if you plan to do so, I recommend reading Chapter 17, the section "Sticking stuff on the desktop."

---

5. Behold your copied file.

   A duplicate of the file is placed in the selected folder.

   ⮕ It's possible to copy a group of files at one time. See the section "Crowd Control, or Working with Groups of Files," later in this chapter, for more information.

 ⬅ A quick way to copy a file to a floppy disk is to pull up its shortcut menu and choose Send To⇨Floppy. See the section "Sending information to a floppy disk" in Chapter 14 for more information.

   ⮕ You can also drag a file with the mouse to copy it, as described in the section "The Old Drag-and-Drop," later in this chapter.

Taking a Shortcut Instead of Copying Files

Copying files takes up disk space. For example, a 32K file copied from one place to another takes up 64K of disk space, 32K for each file copy. Egads! A better solution is to create a shortcut to the original file rather than a copy.

A shortcut is essentially like a finger pointing elsewhere on the disk. It looks just like the original file, save for a little box with an arrow in it — the shortcut tattoo. It also works like the original: Double-clicking on a shortcut merely redirects Windows' attention back to the original file. That way, you can keep a copy of a file convenient — in another folder, on the desktop, wherever — without needing to bother with the original. You can also delete a shortcut without the guilt, because the original file isn't touched when the shortcut is killed off.

Shortcut to The old graveyard

Making a new shortcut

There are several ways to make a shortcut to a file, program, or folder on your computer. Here is the quickest and best way:

1. Use My Computer to find the original file.

   Open folders and windows until you locate the file, program, or folder you want to make into a shortcut.

   If you want to make a shortcut of your printer, you have to open the Control Panel and then the Printers folder to find your printer's icon.

2. Right-click drag the file.

   Click on the mouse by using the right mouse button — the one you use to bring up a shortcut menu. Then, keeping the mouse's button down, drag the file to a new location, another folder, the desktop, or in the same window. Release the mouse's right button.

   Please see the section "The old right-click drag gag," later in this chapter, for a more detailed description of this action.

3. Choose Create Shortcut(s) Here.

   From the menu that appears when you release the mouse button (see Figure 16-4, later in this chapter), choose Create Shortcut(s) Here. This step plops down a shortcut right where you released the mouse button.

4. Drag the shortcut icon to its proper place.

   If you need to, drag the shortcut icon to another folder, the desktop, or wherever at this point. Or you can cut and paste it, according to the instructions in the section "Deeply Moving Files," later in this chapter.

You might also consider renaming the shortcut; each shortcut icon is given the new name Shortcut to plus the original icon's name. Renaming is fine because the little arrow guy on the icon always lets you know what's a shortcut and what's not.

The second runner-up: Copy-and-paste as a shortcut

If you're going to paste your shortcut file elsewhere, it makes more sense to fake a real file copy-and-paste and then just paste a shortcut rather than a true copy of the file. Here are the brief steps:

1. Follow the steps for copying a file, as outlined in the section "Copying, or Doop-Doop-Duplicating, Files," earlier in this chapter.

2. But, in step 4, choose Edit➪Paste Shortcut.

   Or you can choose Paste Shortcut from a shortcut menu. To choose that command, right-click in the window or on the desktop where you're pasting the file.

   Whichever technique you use, the shortcut is pasted down instead of a bulky copy of the original file.

One to avoid

The worst way to create a shortcut is to choose New➪Shortcut from the various File menus in My Computer or the Explorer or from a shortcut menu. When you do this, you're faced with a dialog box that forces you to manually type the original file's pathname (barf!) or use a Browse dialog box to hunt down the original file.

What a colossal waste of time!

Use the methods outlined in the preceding two sections rather than bother with this hackneyed approach.

A shortcut to where?

To find out information about the original file that a shortcut points to, you have to examine its Properties dialog box:

1. Locate a shortcut icon.

2. Click on the icon once to select it.

   Click.

3. Press Alt+Enter to bring up the icon's Properties dialog box.

4. Click on the Shortcut tab to bring that panel forward (see Figure 16-2).

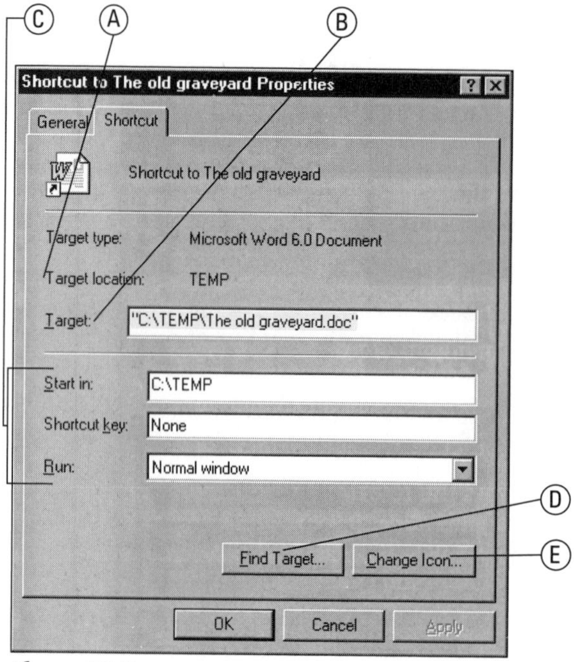

Figure 16-2
The Shortcut panel in a shortcut icon's Properties dialog box.
A. Where the shortcut currently resides. **B.** The pathname to the original file. See Chapter 17, the section "Beating a pathname to a file's door," for more information about the horrid pathnames. **C.** Miscellaneous info about how to run the shortcut as a program. **D.** Click this button when Windows loses track of the original file's location — which happens often. **E.** You can even assign a new icon to the shortcut, though I won't explain the details of how this works because it's not really necessary.

Look for the first text-input box named Target. It displays a pathname that tells you where the original file is located.

If you don't understand the pathname (and who really does?), you can click on the Find Target button. If Windows hasn't lost track of the original file, clicking on that button brings up a My Computer window that shows you the folder where the original file lives and highlights that file. Click the × Close button on that window when you're done gawking at the original file.

5. Click on the OK button in the shortcut's Properties dialog box.

Do this when you're done with the process of discovery, enriching yourself because you now know where the shortcut leads. Cool. Great. Aren't you glad that you buy Microsoft software?

Deeply Moving Files

Most of your file manipulations come in the form of moving them. Ideally, this happens during the throes of disk organization: You realize that your Misc folder contains a number of doodles you draw while you're on the phone. So you move them out of that folder and into a special Doodle folder, where you keep them until one day they'll be published and you'll be famous (but that will happen after you're dead, so you'll never see any money from it).

To move a file, follow these steps:

1. Click on the file's icon once to select it.

    The icon can be on the desktop, in a folder's window in My Computer, or in the Explorer. After you click it once, the file becomes highlighted. It's selected.

2. Choose Edit⇔Cut.

    Or right-click on the icon, and from its shortcut menu choose Cut.

    Or use the keyboard-friendly Ctrl+X shortcut key.

    The Cut icon appears dimmed on the screen. This lets you know that it's been "cut," though it won't be moved until you paste it somewhere.

    By the way, you can cancel the whole cut-and-move operation here by pressing the Esc key.

3. Find the destination.

    You're moving the file to a new location, so find it now. Use My Computer or the Explorer. For example, you open the new Doodle folder for your art projects.

    When you find the folder, open it so that its contents are visible in a window on the screen.

    For more information about creating folders, see Chapter 17, the section "Conjuring up a new folder."

4. Choose Edit⇔Paste.

    Or right-click in the folder's window, and choose Paste from the shortcut menu.

    Or press the Ctrl+V Paste command shortcut key.

Windows moves the file; the ghostly image is gone, and the file's icon appears in the current folder's window or on the desktop — wherever you pasted.

When you move larger files, a Cut dialog box is displayed, similar to the one displayed for copying files. It's entertainment like this that makes Microsoft software retain its value.

If you try to move a file to a folder but a file with that same name already lives there, Windows warns you with a proper dialog box (refer to Figure 16-1). Make it your first instinct to click No. Only if you're absolutely certain that you want to replace the existing file should you click Yes.

5. The file done be moved.

The file now lives in the new folder.

➠ Before you repeat these steps a dozen times for a dozen files, know that you can cut and paste a whole gaggle of files all at one time. See the section "Crowd Control, or Working with Groups of Files," later in this chapter.

The Old Drag-and-Drop

A quick way to move or copy a file is to take advantage of that graphical user interface and use the mouse to move the file's icon. This is about as easy as moving someone else's Monopoly piece back a square to Boardwalk when they're not looking.

The only requirement for the old drag-and-drop is that you must be able to see both folders' windows before you move or copy anything. This limits you to using this trick only in My Computer and only when you're using multiple windows to view the stuff on your hard drive. Figure 16-3 shows sort of how you set things up.

There are certain places you cannot drag a file. I can't name them off the top of my head, but Windows has darn good reasons why you can't drag anything there. When you make the attempt, the dragged file's icon has the universal "no" thing on it. Uh-uh. No way. Forget it. Start over.

No! I don't want to go!

⬅ See Chapter 2 for more information about using My Computer and its windows. See the section "The 'single window' approach to using My Computer," and don't do what it says there before you drag and drop.

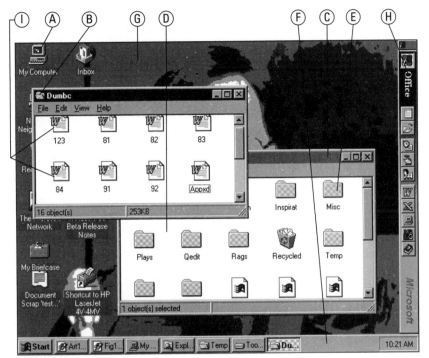

Figure 16-3
Preparing two folders' windows for a drag-and-drop.
A. You have to use the My Computer program for this; you cannot see two folders at one time in the Explorer. **B.** The folder containing the file you want to cut or copy. **C.** The destination folder, where the cut or copied files will end up. **D.** You don't have to see all of the destination folder. **E.** You can even drag to a folder within that window. **F.** If you do want to see all of the destination folder, right-click here to bring up the taskbar's shortcut menu and then choose Tile Vertically to neatly arrange both windows. **G.** You can also drag the folders to the desktop, if you can see part of it on the screen. **H.** See Chapter 24, the section "Moving the Office Bar," for information about moving the Microsoft Office toolbar. **I.** Word for Windows document icons, which also look like WordPad document icons.

It's a drag to move a file

To move a file, click on it with the mouse. Keep the mouse button down, and drag the file from its current folder's window to a new folder's window. Behold! The file has been moved.

The only time this doesn't work is when you drag the file to a folder on another disk drive. In that case, you see a plus sign (+) appear on the file's icon as you drag it over the other folder's window. That's because Windows only lets you drag-copy files between different disk drives. A curious thing, but worth noting.

Plus+⊞

The same limitations on moving a file with cut-and-paste also apply here. Refer to the section "Deeply Moving Files," earlier in this chapter.

It's a controlled drag to copy a file

To copy a file by using the drag-and-drop method, you must first press and hold the Ctrl (Control) key. This is known as a "Ctrl+drag" — a control drag. Otherwise, if you don't hold down the Ctrl key before you click on the file's icon, you move, not copy, the file. Here are the steps:

1. Locate the file you want to copy.

2. Press and hold down the Ctrl key.

3. Drag the file to its new destination.

   Click on the file by using the mouse, press and hold down the mouse's button, and move the icon.

   You'll notice that the mouse pointer dragging the icon has a little plus (+) on its tail. The plus sign means that whatever is being dragged is being copied, not moved — a sure sign that you're doing things properly.

Plus+⊞

4. Release the mouse button.

   This step drops the file into the new folder's window.

5. Release the Ctrl key.

The same rules and regulations for copying and pasting a file apply to the drag-and-drop method. See the section "Copying, or Doop-Doop-Duplicating, Files," earlier in this chapter, for the lowdown.

The old right-click drag gag

Most dropping-and-dragging is done with the mouse's left button, the main button. If you drag and drop with the right mouse button, you see a nifty pop-up menu appear when you release the mouse's button. It works like this:

1. Right-click on a file's icon, but keep the mouse button down.

2. Drag the icon to a new location.

    You don't really have to drag the icon to a new location; you can drag it to a different spot in the same folder's window if you like.

3. Release the right mouse button.

    A shortcut menu appears, as shown in Figure 16-4. This menu may seem rather silly, but it gives you all the options for drag-and-drop file manipulation — and it's the quickest way to duplicate a file inside a folder (see the following section).

4. Choose an option for the file: move, copy, shortcut, or cancel.

    For example, choose Move Here if you want to move the file. Or if a copy is more in line with your thinking, choose Copy Here. If you're baffled, write Cancel on the receipt, and you owe nothing.

As with regular move and copy operations, some limitations apply, and your mileage may vary. Windows still forbids you to move or copy to some destinations, and you are warned if a file of the same name already exists — the usual.

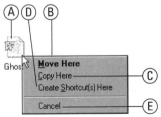

Figure 16-4
The right-click drag shortcut menu.
A. The ghost of the file waits here until you make your decision. **B.** Moves the file to this location — just like a regular drag. However, this option can be used if you want to move a file to another disk drive. Unlike the normal drag, this one here is a definite move. **C.** Copies the file to this location, which is a quick way to make a duplicate of a file in the same folder (see the following section). **D.** The best way to create a shortcut copy of a file; see the section "Making a new shortcut," earlier in this chapter, for details. **E.** The "I give up" option is the same as pressing the Esc key at this point.

Duplicating a file in the same folder

Often it's nice to have a backup copy of a file, especially if you think that something dreadful is going to happen to it and you want a copy of the original just in case. In those instances, you can make an instant copy of the file by using the right-click drag gag.

Here's how to make a backup copy of a file:

1. Right-click the file's icon, and keep the mouse button down.

2. Drag the icon a little above or below its current location.

   Keep the icon in the same window; you're making a duplicate copy of the file in the same folder here.

3. Release the right mouse button.

   The shortcut menu appears (refer to Figure 16-4).

4. Choose Copy Here.

5. Release the mouse button.

   A duplicate of the file appears. It's given the same name as the original file but is prefixed with Copy of. So the file named 1996 Tax Stuff is duplicated, and the new copy is given the name Copy of 1996 Tax Stuff.

➡ The backup copy is identical to the original; the only difference is the name. That way, you can mess with one and the other will remain intact. This is a handy trick for saving information that you may fear will get changed or corrupted. But a better way to be safe is to back up your hard drive, which is covered in Chapter 18.

Some Files Just Hafta Go, or Deleting Files

It may seem like a scary proposition, but deleting files is part of computer life. You delete files because you no longer need them, to free up disk space, or because they're old and useless. It's all a part of routine file maintenance, which, like sweeping the floor, is something you'd rather have someone else do.

To blast a file to kingdom come, follow these steps:

1. Click the file's icon to select it.

   Click once. This step highlights the icon, telling the universe that you're about to do something with it.

   The icon can be stuck on the desktop, nestled in a window in My Computer or lurking in the Explorer.

2. Choose File⇨Delete (see Figure 16-5).

   Or right-click to bring up the icon's shortcut menu, and choose Delete.

   Or you can just whack the Del key on a keyboard near you.

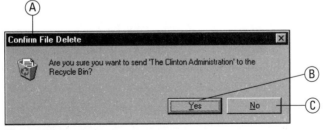

Figure 16-5
The Confirm File Delete dialog box.
A. This dialog box appears only if you've configured Windows to alert you every time you delete a file. See the section "Displaying those warning boxes for the timid file-deleting person" in Chapter 5 for more information. **B.** Click on Yes to delete the file. **C.** Click on No if you chicken out and change your mind.

The Confirm File Delete dialog box appears (refer to Figure 16-5), questioning your sanity about whether you really want to delete the file.

3. Click Yes.

The file is gone, gone, gone. A dialog box appears (refer to Figure 5-7) detailing how the file is being thrown from its cozy, little folder into the cold, harsh world of the Recycle Bin.

◀▬ You can also drag the icon directly into the Recycle Bin, but only if you can see it on the screen. When you do this, no warning dialog box is displayed before the file is deleted; Windows assumes that you don't drag wantonly. Refer to the tutorial in Chapter 5, in the section "Using the Recycle Bin just once to see how it works," for more information.

◀▬ Be careful with what you delete! Just because Windows lets you recover files from the Recycle Bin is no excuse to be lazy. And if you delete an important file, such as a program file, Windows warns you. Refer to the section "But the file *whatever* is a program!" in Chapter 5.

◀▬ Also refer to the section "A quick, odorless peek into the Recycle Bin to restore something" in Chapter 5 for information about recovering a file you may have accidentally deleted. This does not apply to anything you Shift+Del, because those files are not put in the Recycle Bin and are gone for good.

The super deadly Delete command

When you delete a file, Windows places it in the Recycle Bin. This doesn't mean that the file is really deleted, because you can recover it later if you like — just like pulling that old, black banana out of the Dumpster when you change your mind and decide to make banana nut bread. However, you can utterly erase a file from your disk and avoid the Recycle Bin altogether. This is done by pressing Shift+Del (as in the preceding step 2) to delete the selected file. But be careful here because there is no possibility of recovery.

Why use this command? The Recycle Bin doesn't delete things as much as it stores them. Therefore, if you're deleting files to free up disk space, you might consider Shift+Del rather than drag icons to the Recycle Bin. Or you can consider moving the files to a floppy drive or backing them up instead of deleting.

Undo Thy File-Manipulation Sins!

Almost anything you do to a file can immediately be undone. Simply choose Edit⇨Undo from the menu. That will undo a copy, move, delete, or even a rename command.

You can also use the handy Ctrl+Z keyboard shortcut, if your hands just happen to be lying there.

Don't be confused by some rogue dialog boxes that may appear after you undo something. If you undo a file copy, for example, Windows may ask whether you really want to delete a file. What it's asking is whether you want to delete the file's *copy,* not the original. Click Yes in all these instances to finish the Undo operation.

← Well, not everything can be immediately undone. You cannot undo a Shift+Del command. See the sidebar "The super deadly delete command," at the top of this page.

Crowd Control, or Working with Groups of Files

Everything that can be done to a single file can also be done to a group of files. The only difference is that you have to select more than one file in the first step. That way, you can treat the files as a group for a gang-copy, gang-cut, or gang-delete. This is obviously much more efficient than doing things one file at a time.

The best way to select a ragtag rogue group of files

There are many ways to select more than one object on the screen. The best way is the Ctrl+click:

1. Point the mouse pointer at the icon you want to select.

2. Ctrl+click.

   Press and hold the Ctrl (Control) key. You can use either Ctrl key, though I use the one on the left because my right hand is on the mouse. Click the mouse's button while keeping the Ctrl key held down.

3. Repeat steps 1 and 2 for every file you want to select in the group.

   Just keep Ctrl+clicking. Every file you select appears highlighted on the screen (see Figure 16-6).

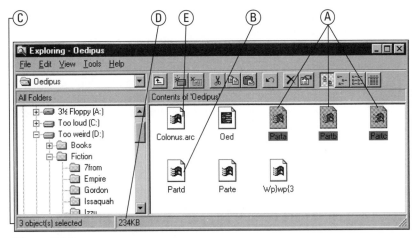

Figure 16-6
Several files are selected in this window.
A. These highlighted files are selected. Choosing the Copy, Cut, or Delete commands affects all of them together. **B.** Point at another icon, and Ctrl+click on it to make it part of the gang. **C.** The status bar tells you how many files have been selected. It uses the word *objects* because you can also select folders or other items floating in a window. **D.** This value tells you the total size of all the files you selected in bytes. Here, 234KB of information has been selected. **E.** These are actually old WordPerfect documents, though Windows doesn't recognize them and gives them the "generic" icon.

You can even use the scrollbars to scroll the window and select more files.

You cannot, unfortunately, select files in another window. This trick works only on files in the current window.

4. Choose a file command for the group.

You can choose Edit⇨Copy to copy the group of files.

You can choose Edit⇨Cut to cut the group.

In either case, when you paste, you paste the entire group.

You can also choose File⇨Delete to zap the group to the Recycle Bin.

You cannot, unfortunately, choose File⇨Rename; Windows lets you rename only one file at a time.

◀▥ Refer to the various sections earlier in this chapter for more information about cutting, copying, pasting, and deleting files.

Calf-ropin' files

A wholly graphical way to corral a bunch of files into a group is to drag the mouse around them (see Figure 16-7). Start by clicking above and to the left of the group of icons, and then drag the mouse down and to the right. Dragging creates a line-of-ants outline, and then all the files inside the outline are tagged and selected for copying, cutting, or deleting.

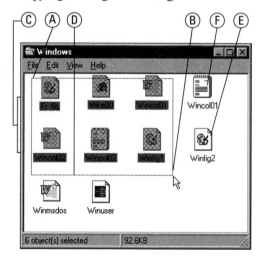

Figure 16-7
A group of files is selected at one time.
A. Begin dragging the mouse here; press the mouse's button and keep the button down.
B. Move the mouse to here, and then release the mouse's button.
C. All these icons are selected for group activities. **D.** The line of ants. **E.** A bitmap graphics icon (old style). **F.** A plain text file icon.

Oftentimes, you're not blessed with having all your file's icons in a neat and nifty group. If so, you can rope as many as you can and then you can still Ctrl+click other rogue icons to make them part of the group.

Selecting scads of files with Shift+click

In the Details view, files can still be clicked one a time, Ctrl+clicked, or calf-roped. But another trick you can try is the Shift+click. This keystroke selects a whole lotta files in a row, which can be handy in a Details view:

1. Select the first file in the group.

   From Figure 16-8, suppose that you're selecting bitmap image files. You click on the first one in the list, samicon, to select it.

2. Shift+click on the last file in the list.

   Find the last file. You can use the scrollbars to move the window if you can't see it on the screen.

   When you find the file, press and hold the Shift key and then click the mouse on the file's icon. This selects that file and all the files between it and the first file you selected.

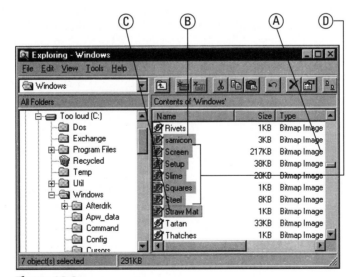

Figure 16-8
Selecting a list of files with Shift+click.
A. Details view is selected. **B.** Click on the first file in the list to select it.
C. Shift+click on the last file in the list to select it and all the files in between.
D. All these files are selected for group activities.

If you're trying to tag files of a similar type, sort the Details view first by that type. Click on the Type heading with the mouse. That sorts all the files by their type. (Click a second time to sort in reverse alphabetical order.) That way, you can find groups of similar files in a Details view window. See the section "The Details view (nerds love this)" in Chapter 2.

Selecting the whole dang doodle

If you're not discriminating about which files you select, it's possible to select them all — the whole dang doodle — all the files in a folder or window on the screen. Here's how you do that:

1. Go to the window containing the hoard of files you want to select.

2. Choose Edit⇨Select All.

   Or you can press the handy Ctrl+A shortcut key combo. Whatever, everything in that window is selected.

Suppose that you choose Edit⇨Select All, but in addition to all the files in the window, some folders and other whatnot are also selected. If so, you can deselect various items by Ctrl+clicking on them. When you Ctrl+click on a selected item, you unselect it without affecting anything else selected in the window. Refer to the section "The best way to select a ragtag rogue group of files," earlier in this chapter, for more information about Ctrl+clicking.

Here's a fancy way to select all but one file in a window. First, click on the one file you *don't* want to select. Click on the file's icon once to highlight it. Then choose Edit⇨Invert Selection. That causes all deselected files to become selected and vice versa. The end result is that your only selected file becomes the only unselected file.

Organizing Files, Folders, and the Desktop

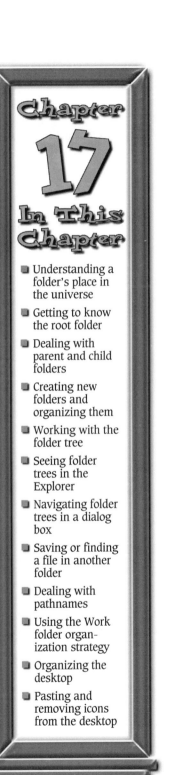
When it comes to using a computer, a certain portion of your sanity is at risk. Unfortunately, few people accept the notion that it's their laziness that makes using a computer so frustrating. The problem is *organization.* It requires effort. It requires a plan of attack. It requires making new folders on your computer and putting files into them according to some Grand Organizational Scheme. It's being neat and tidy with the desktop. It's ending up with a computer that's much more fun to use.

But organizing folders and the desktop only once isn't enough; you must be vigilant in this effort, constantly arranging your files and folders to maintain order. The end result is a (what else?) logically organized computer with a sane human attached.

How Folders Helped Tame the Wild West

A hard drive can be a big, wild, and unforgiving place. The problem is the massive amount of storage space. Although acres and acres of empty space seems ideal, because space is always at a premium, great care must be taken to use the storage space wisely. Imagine a huge closet the size of an Olympic swimming pool. Then imagine putting all your stuff in the closet, with no hangers, no drawers, no California Closet Organizer. Just use a dump truck, and load it all in. You'd have a mess! The same thing can happen on a hard drive, if you don't organize.

The organization of files and programs on a hard drive is done by shoving everything into its own unique storage bin. In Windows, these storage bins are called *folders.* They used to be called "directories," but that was deemed too technical because it has four syllables and "folder" has only two.

Hi! I'm just a happy little storage bin for your stuff in Windows!

A folder is merely a place to put files and programs on a hard drive. All those files and programs live by themselves, not seeing or touching any other files or programs elsewhere on the disk.

Folders can also contain more folders, which means that organization is carried one level deeper (see Figure 17-1). On drive C, for example, you can have a Games folder. Inside that folder, you may have an Arcade folder. And inside the Arcade folder may live a CapMan folder. Inside the CapMan folder is your CapMan game program and all its files. That's organized.

If you don't organize folders, you get a cosmic mess. Who knows where the CapMan game is? Or worse, imagine 2,000 files and programs all stored sloppily in one place. Even if the files are all well-named with pretty icons, it would still be a major bother to find anything.

The only drawback to this scheme is that Windows, frankly, doesn't care how you organize folders. There are no rules, no regulations. It's up to you to be the sheriff and organize the wild, untamed hard drive territory. This isn't as hard as you might think. And you don't even need a gun.

Figure 17-1
The concept of organizing folders.
 A. The Drive C icon actually represents the main folder on your disk, the root. **B.** Games is a child folder of the root folder and a parent of the Arcade folder. **C.** Arcade is a child of the Games folder and a parent of the CapMan folder. **D.** CapMan is a child of the Arcade folder. **E.** The CapMan program lives in the CapMan folder. No more offspring.

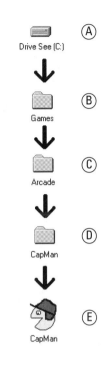

What's up with the root folder?

No matter what, every disk has one main folder, called the *root* folder. You see this folder's contents every time you open a disk drive for viewing. That first window displays the contents of the root folder for that drive. Figure 17-2 shows the root folder for drive C in My Computer.

Of all the folders in your computer, the root is the one most likely to be called a *directory*. Old habits die hard, and calling this folder the *root directory* is a PC tradition. Just know that it means the first folder on a disk, the one you see when you peer into a disk drive's icon in My Computer or the Explorer.

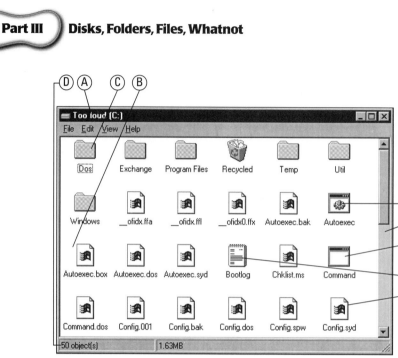

Figure 17-2
The root folder on drive C.
A. When the disk's name and letter appear here, you know that you're looking at the contents of the root folder. Sometimes the letter appears by itself if the disk has no name. (See the section "More than just a letter: Giving your disk a proper name" in Chapter 14.) **B.** These folders and files live in the disk's root folder. See Chapter 2, the section "Different Ways to Look at the Stuff in My Computer." **C.** Open one of these folders, and you'll see its name at the top of the window. **D.** This tells you information about the files and folders in this folder. **E.** See Chapter 27 for information about using the scrollbar to view the rest of the window. Or you can resize the window by using other gizmos. **F.** DOS batch file icon. **G.** DOS generic program file icon. **H.** Text file icon. **I.** General "I dunno" icon.

Why some folders look strange or ugly

Control Panel   Printers   Dial-Up Networking   Fonts   Programs

A few of Windows' folders are used for special purposes. For example, the Control Panel, Printers, Dial-Up Networking, and other folders have cute little icons on them. In the Start Menu folder, which is really where the items on the Start Thing's menu are kept, each folder looks stranger still.

Why so weird? Because those things aren't really folders.

The Control Panel isn't a folder, and neither is anything else that looks like a folder but that has something graphical on it. Windows uses the folder metaphor because you can open whatever it is to look inside. Other than that, they aren't folders (even their shortcut menus are different).

The folders in the Start Menu folder are different, however. Windows wants you to recognize that the program shortcuts and folders which live there are really menu items. To make you aware of this, those folders appear differently.

See Chapter 6, the section "Moving things around between the menus," which discusses modifying the Start Menu folders by using the Explorer.

Crazy folder terminology

Folders should be everywhere on your computer. Windows is in its own folder, surprisingly named Windows. Inside that folder are other folders in which Windows has organized all its various pieces parts (take a look sometime).

The folders in the Windows folder are its children. This isn't biological; it's just the term that is used. (Some nerds call them subfolders.) The root folder, of which the Windows folder is a child, is said to be Windows' parent folder.

A folder in a folder is a *child.*

A folder "above" the current folder is the *parent.*

There are no brother, sister, aunt, uncle, cousin, or grand-anything folders.

Observe Figure 17-1, which illustrates this concept.

Checking out a folder's shortcut menu

Like every other icon in Windows, folders have shortcut menus (see Figure 17-3). You see the Open, Rename, Cut, Copy, and other common shortcut menu commands living there. Plus, a few other folder-specific commands exist.

Figure 17-3
A typical folder's typical shortcut menu typically looks typically like this.
A. This command opens a window detailing the folder's contents in My Computer. **B.** Here you can start a custom window by using the Explorer, in which you can explore the files and whatnot stored in the folder. (Disk drive icons also have this command.) **C.** Network malarkey; see Chapter 22. **D.** Same, same, same.

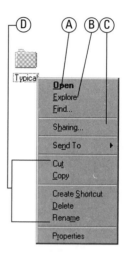

⟶ See the section "Let's go Explorering," later in this chapter, for more information about the Explorer. It's a little more limiting than using My Computer, but it can be an excellent tool for folder spelunking.

⟵ The Cut, Copy, Delete, and Rename commands work the same for a folder as they do for single files; all the commands and steps presented in Chapter 16 also apply to folders. But . . .

When you copy, move, or delete a folder, keep in mind that you might be working with more than one item. Folders can contain files and even other folders (with even more files). You may think that you're innocently deleting a single folder icon, but in fact you may be zapping 1,000 files to The Great Beyond.

⟵ The Properties dialog box for a folder looks and works the same as one for a single file. Additionally, it tells you how many files and folders are inside the folder (see Figure 15-6 in the section "Gawking at a file's properties," in Chapter 15). There's also an extra panel in the dialog box for sharing the folder over the network.

Conjuring up a new folder

Making a new folder is a part of computer life, something you shouldn't be timid about and something required if you're to keep your hard drive organized. Follow these steps:

1. Find a place for the new folder.

   This all depends on your hard drive organization. New folders can be placed anywhere, however. But before you make the new folder, you must open up its parent's window.

   If you want to create a My Documents or Work folder, for example, start in the root folder; go to My Computer and open drive C. The window you see is the root folder, the parent of your new folder baby.

   Refer to Chapter 2, the section "Opening up stuff inside My Computer," for more information about opening windows and other routine tasks in My Computer.

   Hard drive organization is the art of taming the wild disk wilderness. Chapter 18 has the lowdown, which I recommend that you read before you start hatching new folders all over town.

2. Choose New⇨Folder.

   You can choose New⇨Folder from the window's menu or from a short-cut menu. In fact, this is how you create a new folder on the desktop: right-click the mouse on the desktop and choose New⇨Folder from the shortcut menu.

   The new folder appears in the window, ready for you to give it a new name (see Figure 17-4).

3. Type a new name for the new folder.

   Type a proper name for the folder, keeping in mind the short-and-sweet rule. For example, you can name the folder Projects or Work and let it be your main project folder.

   Press the Backspace key to back up and erase if you make a mistake.

   Press the Enter key when you're done, which locks in the new name.

   You can always rename the folder at a later time. See the section "Blessing a File with a New Name" in Chapter 16 for more information. (Both files and folders are renamed in the same manner.)

4. You're ready to go.

   Now take a look at the hard disk organization strategies offered at the end of this chapter, in the section "Setting Up Folders Just So." Keep in mind that this is the reason for making folders: to keep your stuff organized.

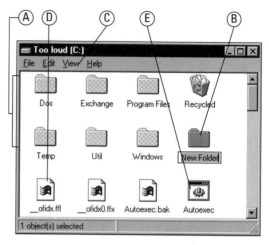

Figure 17-4

A new folder is hatched. **A.** The new folder's parent window. **B.** The new folder, ready for renaming. **C.** When the new folder is placed in an ugly position in the window, you can choose View⊅ Arrange Icons⊅By Name. This sorts the icons alphabetically, adjusts their position within the window, and adjusts the window's size somewhat so that you can see all the icons. **D.** The Windows "I dunno" icon, slapped on any file type it doesn't recognize. **E.** The DOS batch file icon, indicating a special program file run by DOS.

Creating a new folder as you save something to disk

The Save As dialog box you use when you first save a file to disk has a special button in it (shown later in this chapter) you can use to create a new folder. Clicking on that button plops a new folder down in the current window, the same as working through steps 1 and 2 in the preceding section.

After creating the new folder, you should type its name. Then go on and save your file to disk.

◄▬ See Chapter 4 for more information about working with the Save As dialog box. The section "Setting Up Folders Just So," later in this chapter, also has some information that comes in handy for finding a proper place for the new folder.

Climbing the Folder Tree

With all its folders and files, a disk drive is organized like a tree, which is one way to look at it. At the base of the tree is the main folder, the root. (Ah — a pun. Get it?) Then come more folders, branching [sic] off into other folders, and eventually you have files and programs, which are the leaves. Figure 17-5 shows one way you can look at this, though it's an upside-down tree.

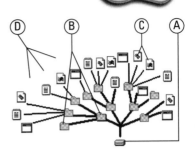

Figure 17-5
The folder tree structure of a hard drive.
A. The root of the tree is your disk drive, the root directory. **B.** Other folders branch from the root. **C.** Files and folders even farther up the tree structure. **D.** It looks like a mess, but really it's organized. The Explorer uses a collapsible tree structure thing to help you view how it all works.

With all this negotiation comes the job of going from one folder to another, sort of like climbing a tree. For example, you may have your projects in a Tahiti folder that lives inside your Work folder. However, the report you just scammed from the Internet is in your Internet Stuff folder, which lives in your Communications folder. That's being organized, but it presents a problem in getting information from one place to another.

Fortunately, climbing the folder tree doesn't require hairy arms, feet with thumbs, or a long tail. All you have to know is how to manage a collapsible tree structure, which is the graphical doojobbie Windows uses to represent folders on your disk drives. The main tool for that is the Explorer.

Let's go Explorering

Many Windows users prefer the Explorer for working with files over My Computer. It's all a matter of taste. I like My Computer because you can have two folder windows open at a time. Windows geeks like the Explorer because it reminds them of the old File Manager program. Whatever. The Explorer remains the best way for looking at your hard drive's tree-structured directories.

To explore the bowels of the folder tree on your C drive by using the Explorer, follow these steps:

1. In My Computer, bring up the shortcut menu for drive C.

   Right-click the mouse on your C drive icon.

2. Choose Explorer from the menu.

   The Explorer starts. It appears in a window with many elements similar to those in My Computer (see Figure 17-6). The main difference is that you have only two windows to work with. The one on the left, All Folders, shows the folder tree on your hard drive (actually, for your entire computer); the window on the right, Contents, shows the contents of a specific folder.

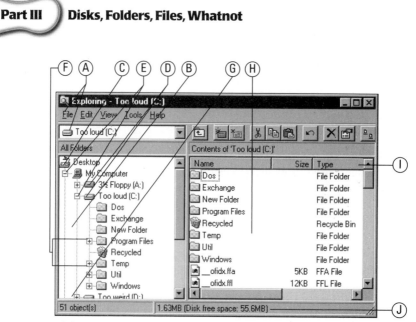

Figure 17-6
The Explorer

A. These menus and this toolbar work identically to their counterparts in My Computer. See Chapter 2, the section "Whip out the toolbar." **B.** This is the All Folders part of the window. **C.** The desktop is the main level, containing things you see on the desktop. On this computer, My Computer, Network Neighborhood, Recycle Bin, and My Briefcase are icons on the desktop. **D.** These are drives on the computer. **E.** The minus (–) means that this branch of the tree is already open. Click here again to close it. **F.** The plus (+) tells you that this part of the tree is hidden. You can click here to open up the drive or folder and see its contents displayed as part of the tree structure. **G.** If another folder were dragged to the desktop, it would appear here in the list. **H.** The Contents part of the window. **I.** You can click on these titles to sort the items in the window. Click again to do a reverse-order sort. For example, click once on Name to sort the window's contents alphabetically; click again to sort them from Z to A. **J.** The items shown here are located in the highlighted drive or folder in the All Folders part of the window. Here you see the contents of the drive named Too loud.

← You can also start the Explorer by choosing its command from the Start Thing's menu; press Ctrl+Esc to pop up the Start Thing, and then choose Programs⇨Windows Explorer. See Chapter 3 for more information about starting programs in Windows.

Other than the presentation, the Explorer behaves much like My Computer. The toolbar is the same, the menus are the same, and you can do the same things to the files shown in the Contents window.

The general approach to using the Explorer is as follows:

1. Use the All Folders side of the window to locate the disk drive you want to examine. (You can even look on other computers by using the Network Neighborhood icon.)

2. Open the folders on that disk drive until you get to the one you want.

   You can view the files in the Contents window as icons in a list, though the Details view is most popular. You can double-click on an icon to open it. You can drag an icon to another folder (though the folder must be visible in the tree, which is why I recommend My Computer for this trick). You can check out a file's shortcut menu or view its Properties dialog box. You can even select a group of files and work with them en masse.

   ➡ For information about working the collapsible tree folder thing in the Explorer, see Chapter 28, the section "The collapsible tree-structure thing."

3. When you're done messing around, close the Explorer.

   Choose File⇨Close, or click on the × Close button in the window's upper right corner.

Working with folder trees in the Save As, Open, and Browse dialog boxes

Most Windows programs use the Save As dialog box to help you save a file in a proper folder on a specific disk drive. Three tools in that dialog box help you do so:

✗ A Save in or Look in drop-down list

✗ An up-one-level button

✗ Folders that appear in the dialog box's main window

Look in:	📁 Windows	▼

The Save In or Look in drop-down lists enable you to jump to another hard drive or another computer on the network.

The up-one-level button lets you move to a parent or even grandparent folder somewhere on the current hard drive.

And you can open folders visible in the dialog box's window to go "down one level" and store files there.

📁 Look in me!

📁 No! Look in me!!

This all makes perfect sense, providing you have a good organizational strategy to begin with.

See Figure 17-7 to identify these three items in a typical Save As dialog box. In the Open or Browse dialog boxes, the Save in drop-down list is called Look in.

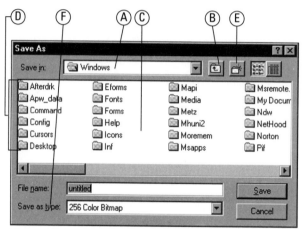

Figure 17-7
The Save As dialog box.
A. Use this drop-down list to move to a parent folder or to another disk drive.
B. You can also use this button to move up one level to the parent folder. **C.** Files and folders in the current folder are shown here. **D.** If any folders appear here, you can double-click on them to open them up. **E.** Use this button here to create a new folder, but only after you've found a proper location for it. **F.** Only files that match the file type specified here appear in the window, along with any folders. See Chapter 15, the section "Saving a file as a specific type," for more information.

The "Let's save something to disk" quasi-tutorial

You yearn to save something to disk. Suppose that you're in the Paint program and you want to save your creation in the Art folder inside your Projects folder on drive D. Here are the steps you take to get that done:

1. Choose File⇨Save As.

   This step displays the Save As dialog box, as shown in Figure 17-7.

2. Find the disk drive on which you want to save your file.

   If you want to save the file on another disk drive, click on Save in the drop-down list. Choose the drive letter from that list.

Suppose that the Save As dialog box shows you files in the Windows folder on drive C but that you want to save your file on drive D. If so, click on the down arrow by the Save in drop-down list. This displays the list of disk drives on your computer. Click the mouse on drive D to "move over" to that drive.

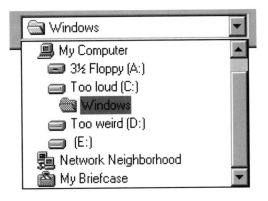

3. Choose the folder in which you want your file saved.

If the folder is a parent folder, you can click on the parent folder button. This step moves you up one level.

If you're using the keyboard, the quick way to get to a parent folder is to press the Backspace key.

You can also click on the Save in drop-down list to move to a "grand-parent" or "great-grandparent" folder.

If the folder is a child folder shown in the window, double-click on it to open it. If you see the Projects folder displayed in the window, for example, double-click on it to open it up and view its contents. If you then see the Art folder, double-click on it, and you're where you want to save your file.

Sometimes the folder may be elsewhere on the hard drive, in which case you have to do a little tree climbing to get there. Figure 17-8 outlines the steps required to move from an Internet Stuff folder to a Tahiti folder on the same disk drive. Basically, you climb the tree to the root folder, and then you open various folders that appear in the Save As dialog box's window until you get to where you want.

You can save the file to another spot on the network by choosing Network Neighborhood from the Save in drop-down list. Just open the computer on which you want to save the file, and then keep opening disk drives and folders until you get to the proper spot. See Chapter 22 for more information about networking.

4. Save the file.

Type a name for the file, and click on the Save button.

 For more information about saving files, refer to Chapter 4, "Saving your stuff."

Figure 17-8
Moving to another branch on the folder tree.
A. 1. Start here. **B.** 2. Choose drive C from the Save in drop-down list to move right here. **C.** 3. Open the Work folder that appears in the window. **D.** 4. Then open the Tahiti folder that appears in the window.

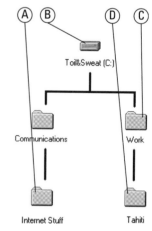

Beating a pathname to a file's door

Pathname is an ugly computer term you encounter all too often. It's used to describe the exact location of a file in your computer, on which disk drive and in which folder (or folders) the file happens to live. In a way, it's a path to a file's door, which is sort of where the term comes from.

The following is a typical pathname:

C:\WINDOWS\SYSTEM\PASSWORD.CPL

This pathname is broken down into several parts:

C:	The drive on which the file lives
WINDOWS	The name of a folder; here, a folder right off drive C's root
SYSTEM	The name of a folder in the WINDOWS folder
PASSWORD.CPL	The name of the file or program inside the SYSTEM folder

The "backslash (\)" characters are used to separate the various folder names and the final filename. Be careful not to confuse this character with a forward slash (/).

There's no need to memorize the preceding format. Don't bother with it. If you're ever told to type it, don't. You can always use a Browse button in Windows to find the file without having to type a pathname. Both methods direct Windows' attention toward the file you want.

If you find the C:\WINDOWS\SYSTEM\PASSWORD.CPL file by using a Browse button, for example, you take these steps:

1. Use the drop-down list to go to drive C.

    Choose the drive C icon from the list.

2. Open the WINDOWS folder.

3. Open the SYSTEM folder.

4. Look for the PASSWORD file in the window.

    When you find the file, click on it once to highlight it and then click on the Open button.

Note that full pathnames include the cryptic three-letter acronyms that end most DOS filenames. This is yet another reason to avoid pathnames: Windows tries hard to hide the acronyms from you. Don't let the fact that you can't see the acronyms in My Computer or the Explorer confuse you.

Setting Up Folders Just So

Windows and most of its applications know that you hate to organize folders on your computer. That's nice, because most of these programs do some form of organization for you. Inside Windows' own folder, for example, you find dozens of other folders, each of which contains some aspect of Windows, all organized neat and tidy. The same thing happens with Microsoft Office, which also organizes itself into a clean branch of folders. But your own stuff? That organization job is up to you.

The useful Work folder organizational strategy

The best way to organize your stuff is to create one central folder. Call it Projects, Work — what-have-you. (Microsoft Office creates a folder called My Documents for the same reason.) This folder, created right off the root of your C drive, contains all the stuff you do on your computer.

My personal preference is a Work folder. Figure 17-9 illustrates how the Work folder works on my computer.

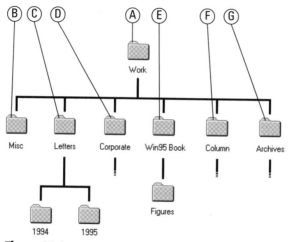

Figure 17-9
A Work folder strategy.
A. The folder Work is right off the root, right where it's easy to get to. **B.** Misc contains miscellaneous stuff, projects in progress, and other "junk." **C.** Letters contains my correspondence. Additionally, folders beneath this one store correspondence from previous years 1994 and 1995. At the end of the year, I'll have to create another folder for 1996 and then move all my letters to that new folder. **D.** Corporate contains typical corporate b.s., accounting files, and such. Though they're not pictured here, 1993, 1994, and 1995 folders live beneath this one, storing information for those years. **E.** Win95 Book contains the text files for this book plus related materials. The Figures folder contains figures for the book. **F.** Column contains material I write for various magazines. Though they're not shown here, there are seven folders beneath Column, each of which contains material for a specific magazine. **G.** Archives contains numerous folders, one for each of my book projects. It has quite an extensive structure of folders beneath it, yet everything is named properly, so I know what each folder contains. For example, beneath Archives is a *DOS For Dummies* folder, with folders beneath it for each edition.

You should set up something similar on your PC, a place where you can store other folders related to other projects on your computer.

Below the Work folder you should have other folders. Each of them should contain information pertaining to one of your projects. And if your project has different elements to it, you can create separate folders for each element.

Above all, never be afraid to create a new folder. When I start a new book, I immediately make a new folder in my Work folder for it.

← Sometimes material for a new folder comes from a Misc or Temp folder. I just pull together all related files and move them over to the new folder. Refer to the section "Deeply Moving Files" in Chapter 16 for more information about moving files.

Random folders for random stuff

In addition to a Work folder for your projects — or a Projects folder for your work — you should have a random folder for "junk" you collect. Call it Misc, call it Temp, call it Junk, whatever. Creating such a folder off the root is ideal for storing ne'er-do-well files and other information that just doesn't seem to have a place elsewhere on your disk.

← My ugly folder is called Temp, and I put it right off the root. That's where I put new files I download or steal from the Internet, plus other stuff that just doesn't go anywhere else. Refer to the section "Conjuring up a new folder," earlier in this chapter, for information about how to make a new folder.

← Don't forget to clean out your Temp or Junk folders! Make liberal use of Cut and Paste to put files you want to keep in a more permanent location. And don't forget the Delete command for scrubbing off files you didn't really want to keep in the first place. Both commands are detailed in Chapter 16.

Bringing Order to the Desktop

The desktop is entitled to a wee bit of organization, just like everything else in your computer. You should set things up just so, making sure that everything works well with the way you work.

Organizing the desktop isn't as crucial as keeping your files organized in folders. The purpose of organizing the desktop is really twofold: First, it helps to keep certain things handy as icons on the desktop. Second, a cluttered desktop can be a major pain, just like a cluttered folder. Files and programs you no longer use should be cut and pasted back into their proper folders; old shortcuts should be deleted and new icons arranged in an orderly manner that would please the most anal-retentive of neatniks.

➠ Aside from organizing icons on the desktop, you can also change the desktop's background and mess with the taskbar. These two items are covered in Chapter 24, in the sections "Background information" and "Whipping about the taskbar."

➠ The way the icons appear on the desktop can also be changed. You can make the icons appear bigger or smaller and adjust the way they lay out in a grid. See Chapter 25, the sidebar "Some funky things you can change that have nothing to do with color," for more information.

Uncluttering your desktop

I've always said that a cluttered desktop (the real-life kind) is the sign of a highly intelligent, creative mind. Of course, that's just my excuse. On a computer, there's no excuse for having icons cluttering your desktop.

First, organize the icons. Right-click on the desktop (if you can find a clean spot), and choose Line up icons from the menu. This "snaps-to" all the icons, making them line up in a neat grid. It doesn't move them far from their current positions, but it does line them up nicely.

If you want everything lined up starting on the left side of the screen, right-click on the desktop and choose Arrange Icons➪by Name from the shortcut menu. This organizes your icons from top to bottom, left to right, alphabetically. (My Computer remains the first icon, however.)

Another shortcut menu item to choose is Arrange Icons➪by Type. That puts your programs first, folders next, and so on.

If you want to get fancy, you can create a special desktop background, similar to (and hopefully better than) the one shown in Figure 17-10. Use the background to enforce how the icons are organized on your desktop. You can also type notes reminding you of shortcuts and other cool tricks.

➠ To set a new background — or "wallpaper" — for the desktop, you use the Display Properties dialog box. This is all explained amidst the fun and excitement of Chapter 24.

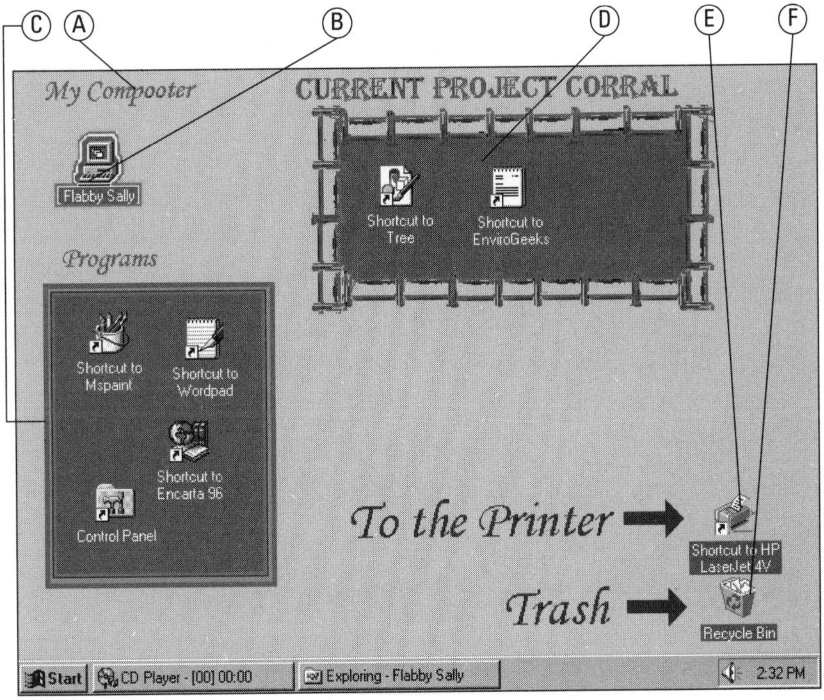

Figure 17-10
An interesting wallpaper pattern for organizing the desktop.
A. This wallpaper was created in the Paint program; see Chapter 9 for more information about using Paint to create wallpaper. (Maybe you can make one that looks less cheesy.) **B.** Renaming My Computer makes a lot of sense. See Chapter 2, the section "My Computer, Your Computer," and also Chapter 16, the section "Blessing a File with a New Name," for the how-to. **C.** Just drag programs to this area, keeping them together. **D.** Drag document icons here to keep your current projects in one place. **E.** Here's a shortcut to the printer for easy drag-and-drop printing of icons. See Chapter 16, the section "Making a new shortcut," for information about creating a shortcut. **F.** The Recycle Bin was dragged here to annoy Apple Computer, because its Macintosh Trash can goes here as well.

Sticking stuff on the desktop

A few things belong on the desktop, and there's no way to move them: My Computer, the Recycle Bin, the taskbar, maybe the Microsoft Office bar, the Network Neighborhood, and a few other goodies. Still the desktop must be a popular place. Files, folders, and programs hang out there like mall rats around a 7-11.

There's nothing wrong with adding a few things to the desktop. Having them there makes getting at them handy. In fact, some people have *everything* they need on the desktop, avoiding the Start Thing menu and My Computer altogether.

← To place an icon on the desktop, copy and paste it there. Or, better still, paste a shortcut to that item. See Chapter 16, the section "Taking a Shortcut Instead of Copying Files."

To paste a shortcut to the printer on your desktop, open the Control Panel in My Computer and then open the Printers folder. Right-click on your printer, and choose Create Shortcut from the shortcut menu. Click on Yes in the warning dialog box to place the shortcut to the desktop.

← Shortcuts to programs are popular on the desktop. To place one there, first find your program by using My Computer or the Explorer. Then use the instructions in Chapter 16, in the section "Making a New Shortcut," to right-click drag the program out onto the desktop, making a shortcut.

Peeling an icon from the desktop

Don't be timid about removing something from your desktop. I'm not talking about My Computer, the Recycle Bin, or the Network Neighborhood. I'm talking about random icons and shortcuts that tend to accumulate on the desktop.

For shortcuts, simply drag them into the Recycle Bin. Because they're shortcuts, you won't delete the original files — just the feeble copies.

For real files, you should drag (or cut and paste) them into a proper folder elsewhere on your hard drive. For example, create a new project folder in your Work folder for the stuff you've been working on. Then gang-select the icons on the desktop and drag them off into the new folder.

See Chapter 16, the section "Deeply Moving Files," for more information about moving files. Also check out the section "Setting Up Folders Just So," earlier in this chapter, for information about placing files in a proper folder.

Regional Settings

Multimedia

Display

Mail and Fax

Part IV

Microsoft Mail Postoffice

Add/Remove Programs

System

Dinking

Date/Time

Add New Hardware

Joystick

Fonts

Accessibility Options

ODBC

Passwords

Keyboard

Modems

Sounds

Printers

In this part

- Keeping Mr. Disk Drive healthy and happy
- Messing with your printer
- Dinking frenzy at the Control Panel
- Fun with fonts
- Windows and everyone else's PC (the joys of networking)
- Installing new hardware

How do I... ?

Make sure that my disk drive is up to snuff?

Disk drives need periodic maintenance. If you avoid it, the drive runs slower, you're plagued with problems, and eventually you begin losing some of your precious stuff.

➡ Every so often you have to back up all the files on your hard drive. Chapter 18, the section "Backup Drudgery," tells you about Microsoft Backup, which comes with Windows (though it's not the best backup program available).

➡ You should also run the ScanDisk program on your hard drive, to fix any creeping errors. See the section "Weaseling Out Errors with ScanDisk" in Chapter 18.

➡ The Defragment program should also be run (but not that often) to remove fragmented files and greatly improve hard disk speed. See the section "Removing Those Nasty Fragments from Your Disks" also in Chapter 18.

Switch between my computer's printer and a network printer?

Windows lets you have several printers installed, though you can use only one of them at a time — your "main" printer.

➡ To switch from one printer to another, see the section "Yo, my main printer" in Chapter 19.

➡ Also see Chapter 19 for information about the Printers folder, a special place where everything about printing is done in Windows.

Stop a document from printing?

Even after you've used the Print command, it's possible to stop a document from printing — but only if you're quick. The reason is that Windows stores documents waiting to be printed in a *queue*.

➠ To delete a document from the printing queue, see the section "Killing off documents in the queue" in Chapter 19.

Dink! Dink! Dink?

All major dinking takes place in the Control Panel, which contains a cluster of icons and programs for adjusting various parts of Windows or pieces of hardware attached to your computer.

➠ Chapter 20 covers the Control Panel in detail. Some of the Control Panel's items are covered elsewhere in this book; Chapter 20 contains all the cross-references.

Use my keyboard with only one hand?

If you're physically impaired (or maybe you just always itch), you can use Windows with only one hand, including all the Alt+, Shift+, and Ctrl+key combinations. This is possible by using the Accessibility options as set up in the Control Panel.

➠ See Chapter 20, the section "Accessibility options, or making Windows friendly to everyone," for more information.

Add some cool new fonts to my computer?

You can buy disks full of fonts, or you can download them from the Internet or CompuServe. But after they're on your disk, you have to install them by using a special command in your computer's Fonts folder.

➠ See Chapter 21 for more information about fonts.

➠ See the section "Adding fonts to your collection" in Chapter 21 for information about installing new fonts.

Use another computer's disk drives?

You can save files on another computer, open files you find there — and even run programs — if both your computers are hooked up to the same network.

➠ See the section "Messing with Someone Else's Computer" in Chapter 22 for information about using disk drives and printers on other computers.

➠ Chapter 22 covers general networking stuff, including sharing your disk drives and printer with others, sending mail in the Network Neighborhood, and other cool stuff.

Install a new adapter-card thing?

Installing new hardware in your computer is the mechanical part, which you do yourself. After that, you have to let Windows and your applications know about the new hardware doojobbie. That's done by using Windows' amazing new Add New Hardware Wizard, which takes you step-by-step through the hardware's software setup.

➠ See Chapter 23 for information about what to do after you install new hardware.

➠ Installing a new printer is different from installing other hardware. See the section "Installing a Brand-New Printer" in Chapter 23 for the details.

Keeping Mr. Disk Drive Healthy and Happy

Chapter 18

In This Chapter

- Finding the disk tool programs
- Using the Backup program
- Using the Restore part of the Backup program
- Eliminating disk errors with ScanDisk
- Defragmenting your hard drive
- Compressing a hard drive

There are three common disk chores you must occupy yourself with from time to time. They are: Backup, Defragment, and ScanDisk. All these tasks are necessary, and each of them is universally proclaimed as a pain in the rear. It's true: It takes *effort* to keep your system up to speed. And though I've been writing about it for more than ten years now (and each time it gets more clever), most people still don't practice what I call "disk housekeeping." This is really sad because the benefits offered by these cute little programs far outweigh any inconvenience they may cause you.

Some Mild Ranting

Somewhere out there, out in the electronic ether, are several unique programs that may, someday, sometime, in the future, really save your butt. They are listed in Table 18-1.

Each of the special disk tools — or *utilities* — does something to your hard drive, fixing some problem you may have. Isn't that

wonderful? The problem is that you have to motivate yourself to use them. That backup copy isn't any good to you if it's three months old. You have to backup, defragment, and scan your disk on a regular basis for any of these handy tools to be effective.

Enough finger wagging!

Table 18-1 Butt-Saving Disk Tools	
Program ("Utility")	**How It Saves Your Keister**
Backup	Creates a second, emergency copy of the stuff on your hard drive. Even if your hard drive goes poof!, the second copy helps you get your stuff back.
Defragment	Removes nasty fragments from your disk, greatly speeding up disk access. A boon to mankind.
ScanDisk	Detects and fixes any errors that creep into your hard drive. A must.
DriveSpace	Almost doubles your disk storage capacity. Ideal for when space is tight (but not truly the best solution; keep reading).

Finding the Disk Tools Tool Shed

Windows' disk tools can be grabbed from one of two places. First, from the Start Thing's menu, follow this path:

1. Press Ctrl+Esc to pop up the Start Thing's menu.

2. Choose Programs➪Accessories➪System Tools.

   You see a menu of several disk tools, maybe some network tools and other stuff, but the four biggies discussed in this chapter are there (see Figure 18-1).

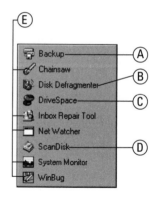

Figure 18-1
The System Tools sub-sub-submenu.
A. Backup program. **B.** Defragment program.
C. DriveSpace. **D.** ScanDisk. **E.** Other stuff.

The three tools most central to your hard drive's health are found right in your hard drive's Properties dialog box. Follow these steps:

1. Find a disk drive.

   You can look in either My Computer or the Explorer.

2. Bring up that drive's shortcut menu.

   Right-click on the drive by using your mouse.

3. Choose Properties.

   The Properties dialog box appears.

4. Click on the Tools tab to bring that panel forward.

   The Tools panel in the dialog box appears, similar to what you see in Figure 18-2. The three tools are ScanDisk, Backup, and Defragment. The buttons are just shortcut links to those programs.

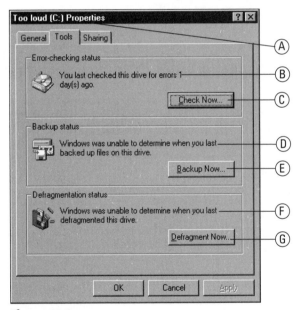

Figure 18-2
Disk tools galore in the Properties dialog box.
A. The disk drive you're examining. **B.** Hey, just used ScanDisk yesterday.
C. ScanDisk checks the disk drive here. **D.** Oops! I've never backed up this drive. Naughty me. **E.** Back up (yech!) here. **F.** Haven't defragmented today. (Actually, the drive doesn't need it. Yet.) **G.** Runs Defragment.

Another nice thing about this dialog box is that it tells you when you last used the tools on your hard drive (the hard drive indicated at the top of the Properties dialog box). That way, you can get a gauge on whether you have to run the program again.

How often should you run these tools? For Backup, it should be done at least once a day. ScanDisk should be run every few weeks or so and always right after a system crash or accidental reset. Defragment should be run every few months, though you don't have to defragment your disk unless the tool tells you that it's necessary. On one of my hard drives, that was about once a year.

➠ The remaining sections in this chapter describe each of the tools and how and when to use them.

Backup Drudgery

No one likes to back up. Honestly, it is a pain. It takes time, and it requires you to sit there and physically exchange floppy disks for what seems like hours, sometimes days and weeks. It's such a pain that few people bother with it. Most would rather have a root canal — without the Novocain.

The drudgery aspect of Backup seems so ironic, given how a recent backup copy can save your hard drive. I had a disk crash recently and got 100 percent of my files back because I had backed up the day before. Yeah, the backup was a pain, but I was glad that I did it. Backing up is also the only way to recover a file you may accidentally overwrite with a Copy or Save As command.

So what's the solution? The solution is to buy a tape-backup unit. It looks like a little cassette or 8-track player, and it sticks in a special drive. You can then back up to that tape rather than to a stack of floppy disks. You don't even have to sit there and watch. And if you keep the tape in the drive all the time, you can back up every day without ever having to fuss over it. That's what we do around my office. No one complains.

There is only one problem with the tape-backup stuff. You really need a third-party program in order to run it. Windows can back up to tape-backup units but only by using its cruddy Backup program. The third-party backup programs come with special scheduling software that makes backing up automatic — at 2:00 A.M. around these parts. But be sure that you get *Windows 95*-compatible backup software. The older stuff doesn't know how to handle Windows' long filenames.

What to back up and when to do it

You should have a backup schedule that works like this:

✗ Every day, back up the work you did that day.

✗ Every week, back up your entire hard drive.

The first backup is called an *incremental* backup. It backs up only those files that have been changed or created since the last time you backed up. For most of us, that's just a handful of files.

The weekly full hard drive backup copies all the files — everything — from your hard drive. That takes a bit longer, but it keeps that valuable second copy of your information up-to-date. If things don't change on your hard drive that much, you can postpone the full backup to once every two weeks, 15 days, or maybe just monthly. It really depends on how safe you want your data to be.

I always keep my backup tapes in a fire safe. It's not a real safe, just a thick box with a locking lid. Supposedly, whatever's inside stays nice and comfy while outside there can be 1,200 degrees of flames. That's the ultimate way to keep your data safe.

How it's done

The following steps briefly outline the backup process. You're probably not going to do this anyway, so I see no reason to go into any details. About the only advice I can give you is to have a *big stack* of floppy disks ready, and be prepared to sit there disk-swapping for a few hours. Put on some headphones or turn on a handy TV, and then follow these steps:

1. Start the Backup program.

←ıı   It can be found in one of two places; see the section "Finding the Disk Tools Tool Shed," earlier in this chapter.

←ıı   And if it can't be found, you may not have Backup installed on your computer. See Chapter 13, the section "Adding the Rest of Windows" for more information.

The name of the button you're supposed to click in the disk Properties dialog is Backup Now.

After starting the Backup program, you see the first Welcome screen. It outlines the process; see Figure 18-3.

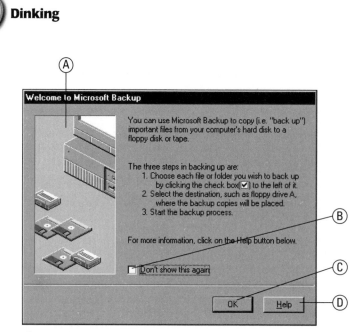

Figure 18-3
The Welcome to Backup screen. Rah.
A. What? No pencil? **B.** Click here to avoid seeing this thing in the future.
C. Click to continue. **D.** This doesn't make it any easier.

2. Click on OK.

   You might see a dialog box saying "Backup has created the following full backup set for you." If so, click on the OK button. You can optionally put a ✔ check mark in the box so as not to see that screen again.

3. The Main Backup Screen.

   The main Backup screen appears (see Figure 18-4). It looks much like a typical Explorer window, with a collapsible tree-structure thing on the left and a list of files on the right. This is where you choose files to back up.

4. Put a ✔ in the box by all your hard drives.

   To back up every file on your system, click the mouse in the box by each one of your hard drives. This step selects all the files on your system for backup. (A cute dialog box appears while Windows counts the files to back up.)

   You can select any or all of your files. If you don't want to back up files in one folder, for example, find that folder and remove the ✔ from its box.

   If you select only part of a disk drive or a few of a folder's files, the ✔ ☑ appears inside a gray box.

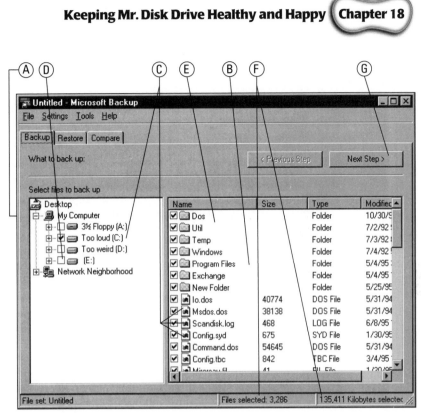

Figure 18-4
The main backup screen.
A. Collapsible tree-structure thing. **B.** Files and such. **C.** Item chosen for backup.
D. Put a ✔ in here to back up this item. **E.** Each of these folders and files is
selected for backup. **F.** Trivia about the files you chose. **G.** Click here to move
on to the next step.

5. Click on the Next Step button.

   Click.

   In the next screen, you tell Windows where to back up your files. You
   can choose a floppy drive, another disk drive on your computer (or
   elsewhere on the network), or any tape drives that Windows has found.

   If you have a tape-backup unit, click on it. Windows backs up to the
   tape unit, which saves you some (but not much) time.

   If you want to back up to another hard drive, pick it.

   If you want to back up to a hard drive elsewhere on the network, pluck it
   out of the Network Neighborhood.

   See Chapter 22 for more information about the Network Neighborhood.

   If you just don't have any other options, choose your floppy drive. Oy.

6. Click on the Start Backup button.

   Windows asks you to type a Backup Set Label. Try to describe the backup here. Type something like this:

   It's Friday and it's time to back up the whole hard drive

   Or you can be nerdy:

   Friday, 10/18, full backup of C

➠   This name doesn't come in handy now, but it helps you identify the backup "set" later if you ever have to restore. See Figure 18-8, later in this chapter, where the name you give the backup appears on the title and inside the Restore window.

7. Stick the first backup disk or tape into the proper PC orifice.

   Put your first backup disk into your drive A, or make sure that a formatted tape is in your tape-backup unit.

   If you don't do this now, Windows warns you after you click on OK in the next step. I would hate for that to happen.

8. Click on OK.

   The backup begins. You are entertained while this happens (see Figure 18-5).

   If the disk already contains files, you see a warning dialog box. Oops! Better use another disk. There's no sense in erasing a disk that may have important files on it.

9. You might be asked to switch disks.

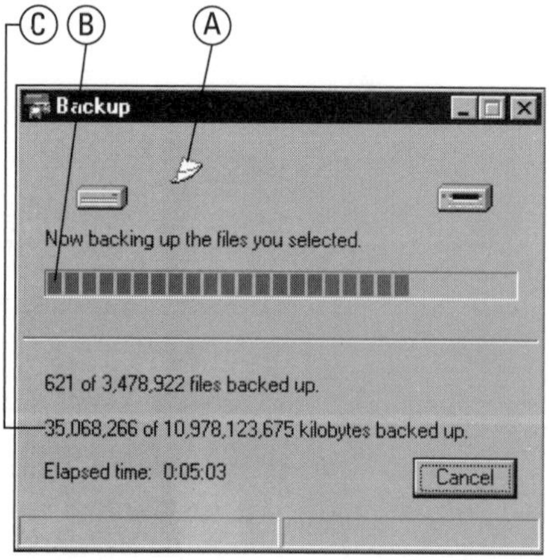

Figure 18-5
Backing up is hard to do.
A. This paper flies from the hard drive to the backup device thing.
B. The progress thermometer.
C. Trivia.

If you're backing up to floppy disks — and face it, one floppy disk doesn't hold a whole hard drive's worth of information — you have to switch disks. You see a message displayed (see Figure 18-6).

Remove the current disk. Yank it out of your disk drive and set it aside.

Insert the next disk. Close the drive-door latch if it's a 5¼-inch drive.

Figure 18-6
Feed me, Seymore!
A. Well, do it! **B.** Click here *after* removing the old disk and inserting a new one.

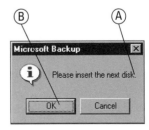

When you set aside the disk, number it. Write the disk's number on the sticky label. This keeps your backup disk set organized. You might also want to write the date, time, your name, company name, astrological sign, and blood type.

10. The backup is complete. Close stuff.

    A dialog box appears, congratulating you for completing your hard disk backup (see Figure 18-7).

Figure 18-7
A happy dialog box to see.
A. It's about time! **B.** It's OK.

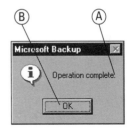

Don't forget to remove and number the final disk. If you did a tape backup, remove it and label it as well.

Click on OK to close the backup complete dialog box.

Then click on OK to close the other dialog box.

Then close the Microsoft Backup application window.

Whew! You're done.

Restoring something you backed up

Backing up is pretty useless without its other counterpart, Restore. You use Restore to take the files stored on backup disks and recopy them to your hard drive.

After a massive hard drive heart attack, you'll probably restore all your files from a full backup set. But sometimes you may just want to restore one file. For example, the other day Windows ate this book's table of contents file. I got it back immediately from the preceding day's backup. And I kind of, sort of followed these steps:

1. Start the Backup program.

   Lead yourself to it. Heed the instructions earlier in this chapter, in the section "Finding the Disk Tools Tool Shed."

2. Click on the Restore tab to bring that panel forward.

   The Restore panel is where you pluck out files from a backup set of disks to be restored to your hard drive (see Figure 18-8).

3. Put your first backup disk or tape into the proper PC orifice.

   Kee-lunk!

4. Click on that backup device in the Restore panel.

   For example, if you backed up to floppy drive A, you click on drive A. In a few moments, you see your backup set (the one you named when you first created the backup) appear in the right half of the window, along with the time you last backed up (refer to Figure 18-8).

5. Choose the files you want to restore.

   Just like backing up, the next screen details all the files saved on your backup set. Go through the collapsible tree structure, and put a ✔ check mark in all those files you want to restore.

   In my case, I simply looked for my TOC document file and put a ✔ in that file's box.

   To restore the entire hard drive, put a ✔ in its box.

6. Click on the Start Restore button.

   Windows flies the file from the backup disks back to your hard drive.

7. Swap disks (if necessary).

   This is the boring step. Windows lets you know whether you need to switch disks.

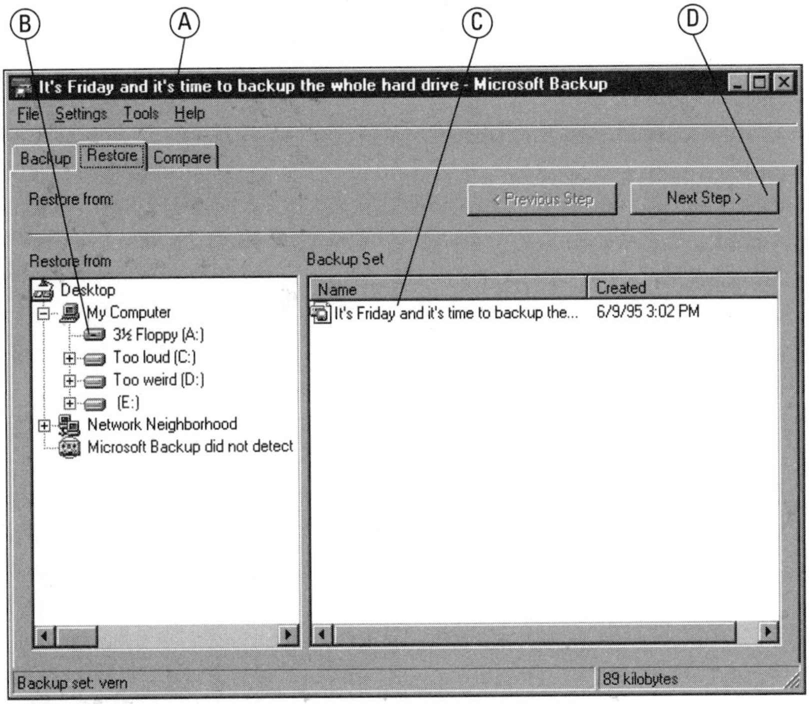

Figure 18-8
The Restore panel, ready to recover files.
A. The name of your backup set. **B.** Since the first disk was in drive A, I clicked here. **C.** This appeared after choosing drive A. **D.** Click here to continue.

8. And suddenly . . . you're done.

    Aren't you glad you had a backup in the first place?

Weaseling Out Errors with ScanDisk

Disk errors happen. It's ScanDisk's job to look for them and fix them where it can. Although it doesn't work miracles, it can patch up many problems and fix such things as broken long filenames and errant shortcuts. Because of this, you should run ScanDisk at least once a week, and more often if it always reports a few errors.

Follow these steps to run ScanDisk:

1. Start the ScanDisk program.

← Follow the directions posted earlier in this chapter, in the section "Finding the Disk Tools Tool Shed."

It's not called ScanDisk in the disk drive Properties dialog box; look for Error Checking status (refer to Figure 18-2).

Click on the Check Now button if you're running ScanDisk from the Properties dialog box.

When ScanDisk starts, you see its window displayed, similar to what Figure 18-9 looks like.

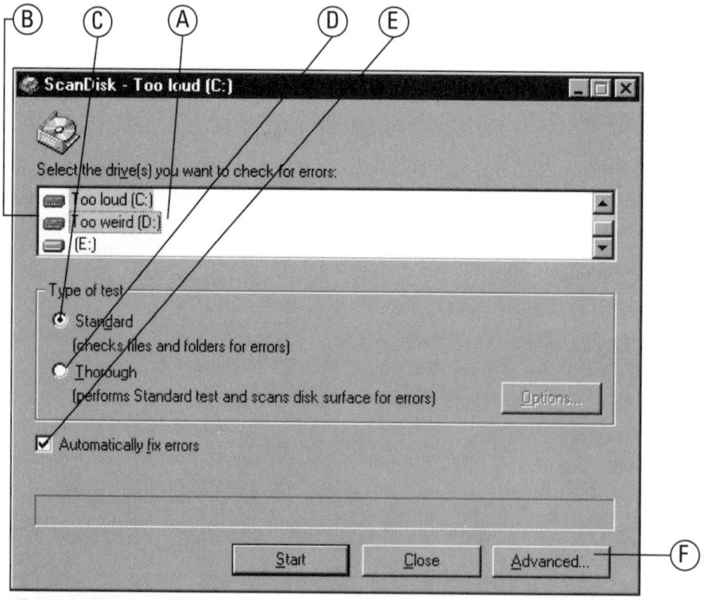

Figure 18-9
ScanDisk is about to go error-hunting.
A. Pick a drive here. **B.** You can Ctrl-click on more than one drive. ScanDisk scans them all. **C.** Standard is okay if you're just checking. **D.** Choose this option if you've been experiencing lots of disk errors. **E.** Check here. **F.** Click here to set options before starting.

2. Pick a drive to scan.

Choose a disk drive to scan from the scrolling list. You can drag through all of them with the mouse to select every drive. Or you can Ctrl+click on only those drives you want to check.

3. Set some "Advanced" options.

   The idea is to run ScanDisk as efficiently as possible. To do that, click on the Advanced button. (There's nothing really "advanced" there, not like the advanced section of the math SAT you skipped over.) Figure 18-10 shows you which options you should click. This enables ScanDisk to do a proper job without any extra bother on your behalf.

Figure 18-10
Save yourself some time with these options.
A. Bother with the summary only if anything went wrong. **B.** Tech-support personnel may ask for log files . **C.** Delete 'em. **D.** Free 'em (no sense in keeping them). **E.** Better check all these to be safe. **F.** DriveSpace compressed drive option.

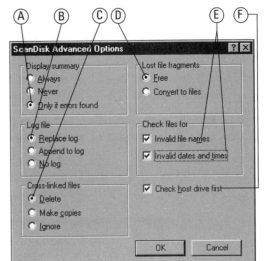

4. Click on OK to close the Advanced Options dialog box.

5. Click on the Start button.

   Scan disk examines all sorts of technical things about your hard drive. It checks this. It checks that.

   If you encounter any errors, ScanDisk should fix them automatically — if you checked the Automatically fix errors box in step 1 and set the proper advanced options in step 3.

6. ScanDisk is done.

   If any errors were encountered, you see a summary of them now (see Figure 18-11). Because you set the proper options in previous steps, ScanDisk didn't alarm you when it found them, and it fixed them all automagically. (Aren't computers wonderful?)

Figure 18-11
ScanDisk found and fixed
a bunch of errors.
A. Yeah! ScanDisk worked!
B. Whatever.

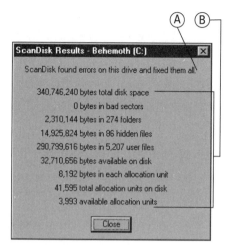

You can go back and repeat these steps to scan another drive, or you can close ScanDisk now by clicking on its Close button.

Trivial information about file fragments

Windows tries to use disk space as efficiently as possible. In a perfect world, all the files and stuff you save to disk would be put on the disk end-to-end, just as you neatly pack a suitcase or stack a load of bricks. The problem is that files are deleted and moved, which leaves "holes."

Windows makes the best use of the holes by filling them in with new files saved to disk. The problem is that the files don't always fit into the holes, so Windows breaks up the files into pieces for a more proper fit. There's nothing to worry about here; Windows keeps track of everything and pieces the fragmented files back together again when you use them. But that takes time, which is why file fragmentation is a curse.

The blessing part comes in from the efficiency of breaking up (or fragmenting) files. If you didn't, your hard drive would contain lots of file "holes," and eventually some files may not fit into any of them. So it's a good and bad thing, but the defragmenting disk tool keeps the bad part to a minimum.

Removing Those Nasty Fragments from Your Disks

File fragmentation is a blessing and a curse. It's a blessing because, without it, your hard drive would fill up faster than an unattended litter box. The problem is that all those little file fragments take time for Windows to manage. Too many of them really turn your hard drive into a frozen slug pig.

To end the fragmentation curse and put a little pep back into your hard drives, follow these steps:

1. Start the Defragment program.

   There are two places you can look. The instructions at the beginning of this chapter show you both of them. See the section "Finding the Disk Tools Tool Shed."

   Click on the Defragment Now button if you're running the defragment program from a disk's Properties dialog box.

2. Decide whether you really have to do this.

   The cool thing about the Disk Defragmenter is that it immediately lets you know whether you're wasting your time. Figure 18-12 shows you the first screen. When the fragmentation level of a drive is low, there's no point in going on. Just click on the Exit button, and you're done.

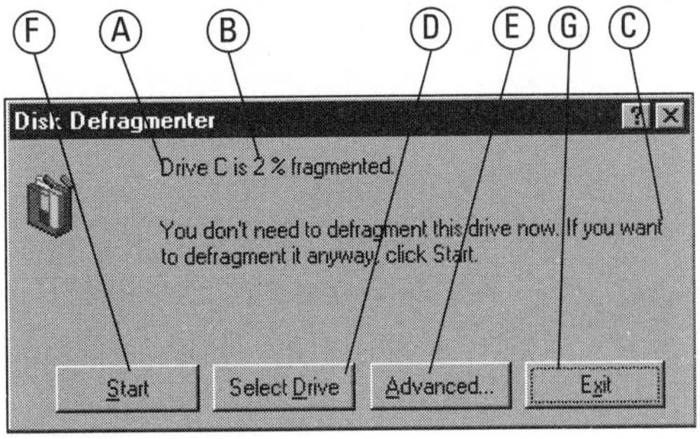

Figure 18-12
To defragment or not defragment, that is the question.
A. The drive being examined. **B.** Anything less than 8 or 10 percent, no way! **C.** Good advice. **D.** Pick another drive to check, or choose All Hard Drives to do everything.
E. Nothing valuable here. **F.** Go ahead and defragment. **G.** Get back to work.

If Windows suggests that you defragment your drive or if you just want to do it for the heck of it, click on the Start button.

If you choose All Hard Drives from the Select Drive button's list, Windows immediately goes ahead and defragments all your hard drives — whether they need it or not — skipping the "press the Start button step."

3. Click on the Start button.

   Windows moves into defragmenting mode. While this is going on, I advise you not to really do anything else with your computer. Sure, you can. But defragmenting moves much quicker if you just sit and watch until it's done. While you wait, a progress dialog box entertains you (see Figure 18-13).

Figure 18-13
I'm defragmenting now.
A. Pretty graphics to entertain you while you wait. **B.** Progress thermometer. **C.** Stop defragmenting now. **D.** Just pause. **E.** Displays a larger, more detailed busy screen.

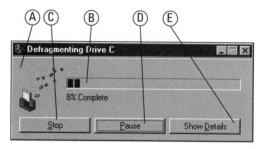

   If you click on Pause, Windows temporarily halts defragmentation.

   If you click on Stop, Windows first asks whether you really want to stop, and then it stops if you claim to be serious.

4. Wait.

   If your screen saver kicks in, just press the Ctrl key or wiggle the mouse to get rid of it. Or you can take a nap because this does burn up a little time.

   See Chapter 25, the section "Saving the Screen from Boredom," for more information about Windows screen savers.

5. You're done!

   Windows announces that defragmentation is complete and asks whether you want to defragment another drive.

   If you click on Yes, pick a drive from the drop-down list, and then go back to step 2.

   If you click on No, you're really done.

Blowing Up Your Disk Drive with DriveSpace

DriveSpace is Windows' own Stacker solution. In fact, since they sued each other and then kissed and made up, DriveSpace is very similar to the Stacker disk compression product. Very similar.

What disk compression does is to give you more disk space for storing your stuff. It does this through various plots and devices, which only scientists and computer programmers need to fuss over. The nitty-grittys aren't important; what is important is that it works and that it gives you more disk space.

Of course, the really big question is whether you need DriveSpace. In my honest opinion, you don't. Just don't bother with DriveSpace, because there are other, better disk storage solutions available. The best option is always to buy a second, larger-capacity hard drive. These things are dirt-cheap and a cinch to install, plus they give you megabytes of extra storage.

About the only time you really should use DriveSpace is when you honestly cannot afford another hard drive. (But you should look at those prices, getting cheaper all the time!) DriveSpace, like Stacker and other disk compression programs, is a stopgap measure. In a few years, massively huge hard drives will be common, and few people will ever run out of disk space.

Nasty disk-compression issues

If you decide to go ahead with DriveSpace (even though I don't recommend it), this section describes some issues you should confront yourself with:

Nerdy terminology. There are only three new terms you should acquaint yourself with when you're dealing with DriveSpace: *Compressed drive, Host drive,* and *CVF file,* detailed in Table 18-2.

Backing up. Backing up a compressed drive works just like backing up any other drive. The only difference is that you don't have to back up the host drive or the CVF file.

Don't delete DRVSPACE files! You may see special DRVSPACE or DBLSPACE files listed in My Computer or the Explorer. Never, under any circumstances, should you mess with, alter, or delete these files. The consequences would be drastic for your compressed drive.

Don't format your compressed drive! Like, duh. You shouldn't format any hard drive. Format only floppy drives.

Table 18-2	**Nerdy DriveSpace Terminology**
Term	*What It Means*
Compressed drive	A drive you compressed or made with DriveSpace. You use this drive like any other disk drive in your system.
Host drive	The original disk drive you compressed. It contains the CVF file.
CVF file	The secret to DriveSpace. This file is really — shhh! — the compressed drive. DriveSpace fools Windows into thinking that it's another disk drive, though. Alchemy makes it happen.

See? If you don't bother with compressed drives and DriveSpace, you never have to clutter your head with this information.

Compressing a disk drive

1. Start DriveSpace.

   You can start DriveSpace only from the Start Thing's menu (or if you find the icon in My Computer or the Explorer). From the Start Thing's menu, choose Programs⇨Accessories⇨System Tools⇨DriveSpace. DriveSpace's main menu appears on your screen (see Figure 18-14).

Figure 18-14
DriveSpace is about to squeeze one of your hard drives.
A. Disk drives in your computer. **B.** Pluck out a drive to compress. **C.** Any drives you already have compressed would be flagged down here.

Ⓑ   Ⓒ Ⓐ

DriveSpace

Drive / Advanced / Help

Drives on this computer:

3½ Floppy (A:)	3.5" Floppy drive
Too loud (C:)	Physical drive
Too weird (D:)	Physical drive
(E:)	Physical drive

2. Click on a disk drive to compress.

    Suppose that drive E is getting awfully full: Click once to highlight it.

3. Choose Drive⇨Compress.

    Windows displays a summary of how compression will affect your drive. In Figure 18-15, you see that drive E has only 30MB of disk space left. After compression, drive E will have a whopping 221MB of disk space available. Amazing. Don't ask me how it works.

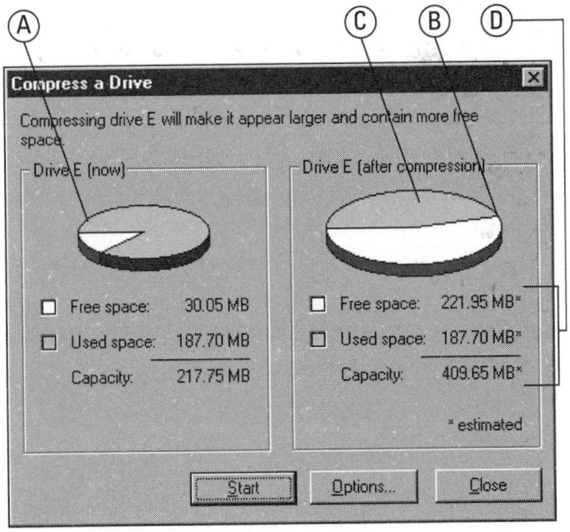

Figure 18-15
The stats on drive E before and after compression.
A. The before picture. **B.** The after picture. **C.** Blueberry filling. **D.** These figures are all estimated, yet very impressive.

4. Click on the Start button.

    A drastic "Are you sure?" warning box appears. It tells you three things:

    ✘ Windows will run ScanDisk on your disk drive first, to ensure that there aren't any drastic errors.

    ✘ You may be sitting here a long time.

    ✘ Because this is so unreliable, you had better back up first.

◄━━ See the section "How it's done," earlier in this chapter, for information about backing up your hard drive.

◄━━ See the section "Weaseling Out Errors with ScanDisk," elsewhere in this chapter, for information about ScanDisk.

5. Quit everything.

   If you're running any other programs in addition to DriveSpace, quit them now. That means WinPopup, the CD player, Word, any games you have minimized, and so on. If you don't do this now, Windows insists that you do it later.

   Before you do the next step, be aware that after you start compression, there is no way to stop it. You cannot use your computer until Windows is done compressing the drive. (Ugh.)

6. Click on Compress Now.

   First, Windows scans the drive for errors. If any are found, they're repaired. If they're irreparable, Windows lets you know about it, and, alas, you cannot compress the drive.

   Second, Windows checks to see whether you have any programs using your hard drive. If so, you are asked to shut them down (you were warned about this in step 5). If the error message persists, Windows has you reset. (See? This gets worse and worse. You really should question your motives for using DriveSpace.)

   If you have to restart Windows, it starts up again and immediately continues with disk compression.

   Third, Windows does some fancy stuff: resizing the compressed dojobbies. Whatever.

   Fourth, you see a parade of your files march by as they're compressed: "Now compressing anything." A progress thermometer lets you know that things are going as scheduled.

   Fifth, you sit and wait.

   Sixth, you wait some more. (It took three hours to compress my drive E, the one you see in Figure 18-15.)

   Seventh, you think that you're done, but Windows begins defragmenting the drive. This is okay; it's trying to squeeze out even more space.

   Eighth, even more compressing and resizing takes place.

7. *Ah.* Compression is finished.

   Didn't think that it would happen, eh? A final summary screen appears, giving you the before and after details. It's very similar to Figure 18-15.

8. Click on the Close button.

   Windows now insists that you restart your computer.

9. Click on Yes.

   It's best to restart, so you can now start enjoying your new compressed drive.

Working with your compressed drive

Your compressed drive shows up in My Computer and Explorer just like it did before. The only difference is that you find more room on the drive for storing your stuff. Otherwise, all of Windows' disk tools work the same or nearly similar enough that you aren't constantly reminded that the compressed drive is any different.

As with other drives, you should occasionally run the ScanDisk and Defragment tools on your compressed drive. Refer to the proper sections earlier in this chapter for the details.

If you need to adjust your compressed drive, you have to run the DriveSpace program again. There really isn't anything there that you'd want to mess with, because Windows automatically handles all the details of your compressed drive; you can poke around there, however, to see which options are available if that amuses you.

 **Part IV** Dinking

Messing with Your Printer

One of the major joys of Windows is that it takes care of all the printing hassles for you. In the olden days of DOS, you had to muss with each program to get it to work with your printer. In Windows, you muss only once. After that, everything that works with Windows works with your printer. And not only that, because Windows is in charge of printing, there is no more waiting for a slow printer. Windows sits and *spools* information out to the printer while you're off doing something else. This is truly one of the miracles of the 20th century.

This chapter talks about using your printer but doesn't mention how to print something in Windows. That subject is covered in Chapter 4, in the section "Printing your stuff."

By the way, Windows' capability to do more than one thing at a time — such as printing while you're off doing something else — is called multitasking. The subject is broached in Chapter 8.

Where the Printer Lurks

Obviously, the printer lurks somewhere nearby your computer, tethered there by some sort of printer cable. Or there's an off chance that the printer is down the hall and you print on a network. But that's only where the printer *physically* lives. Mentally, you can find your printer by looking for its handy icon located somewhere in the bowels of Windows.

My li'l LaserJet

I found the printer in the Control Panel

To find your printer's icon, you can always look in the Control Panel. Open up My Computer to find the Control Panel's folder, or you can choose Settings⇨Control Panel from the Start Thing's main menu.

Control Panel

After opening the Control Panel, look for the folder named Printers. Open that folder by double-clicking on it, and you've found your printer, or, more accurately, you've found the Printers folder, which may contain your printer, network printers, faxes, and other goodies, all related to printing (see Figure 19-1).

Printers

Figure 19-1
Treasures in the Printers folder window.
A. The add-a-printer wizard (see Chapter 23, the section "Installing a Brand-New Printer").
B. A printer installed but no longer connected to your computer. **C.** A typical printer (probably the main printer).
D. A network printer. **E.** A fax something.
F. Another fax something.

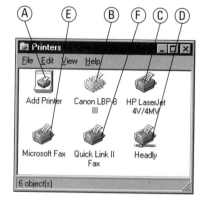

I found the Printers folder right in My Computer

A more direct route to the Printers folder is through My Computer, where it sits as a folder right alongside the Control Panel. Just double-click to open it, and you see something similar to Figure 19-1.

Printers

I found the Printers folder there on the Start Thing's menu

Another place to find the Printers folder — an almost guaranteed instant abduction — is off the Start Thing's menu. Choose Settings⇨Printers. Voilà! Instant Printers folder (refer to Figure 19-1).

I found a printer stuck on the desktop

Although you may not find the Printers folder stuck on your desktop, odds are pretty good that you'll find a printer stuck there. This is a good way to access your printer directly, for adjusting the queue, pausing printing, and so on, but you still have to try one of the already mentioned techniques for access to the Printers folder.

⬅ The idea behind sticking a shortcut to your printer on the desktop is that you can print by way of the old drag-and-drop. See the sidebar "Printing can be such a drag" in Chapter 4 for more information.

⬅➡ If you want to stick a shortcut of your printer on the desktop, see Chapter 17, the section "Sticking stuff on the desktop." You have to right-drag the printer's icon from the Printers folder out on the desktop; see Chapter 30 for more information about the right-drag.

Yes, you can rename your printer

Better than knowing your printer as "Toshiba P351SX," you can give your printer a real name. This is as easy as changing the name of any other icon. Follow these steps:

Ed's big, fast printer that no one else can use

1. Locate your printer's icon.

   Wherever your printer lurks (see the previous sections), find it.

   If you have more than one copy of your printer, you have to rename each one. If you have "Shortcut to Toshiba P351SX" on the desktop, for example, you have to rename it separately.

2. Click on the printer's icon once to select it.

   Click. The icon becomes highlighted.

3. Press the F2 key.

   The F2 function key is the rename key. Now you're ready to type a new name for the printer.

4. Type a new name.

Carefully type something clever. Press the Backspace key to back up and erase.

← You can type spaces, upper- and lowercase letters — just about anything. But see the sidebar "Basic file-naming rules and regulations" in Chapter 16 for more information about what's proper and what's not for a file's name.

Here are some clever printer-name examples:

> Eventually
> Firecracker
> Gutenberg
> Jammer
> Kinko
> Mr. Slug
> Shredder
> Smudgy
> The Hammer

5. Press the Enter key when you're done.

This step locks the new name into place. No biggie, but you've made things a little more interesting.

➡ If you're sacrificing your printer for use on a network, you can give it another name as well. See Chapter 22, the section "Sharing your printer," for more information about naming your network printer.

Peeping at the Printers Folder

The Printers folder is merely a waiting room for anything to do with printing in Windows. Honestly, there really isn't much you can do there. Most of the real action happens in your own printer's window, in something called the *queue,* which the section "Playing with the Queue," later in this chapter, goes into in detail.

Yo, my main printer

Odds are that you have only one printer. If so, it's your main and only printer. But if your PC is hooked up to two printers (which is possible) or you have printers available on a network, you have to choose one of them as your main printer.

To pick a main printer, follow these steps:

1. Mosey on over to the Printers folder.

   Use any of the paths to the Printers folder, as described in the first part of this chapter.

2. Point the mouse pointer at the printer you want to choose as your main printer.

   Make sure that it's a printer and not a fax machine thing.

3. Bring up the printer's shortcut menu.

   Right-click the mouse. The shortcut menu appears.

4. Choose Set As Default.

   If there is already a ✔ check mark by this item, that printer is your main printer. If not, choosing Set As Default makes it your main printer. That is now the printer Windows uses whenever you print anything.

It's possible to change your main printer at any time; just repeat the preceding steps. However, you can also change "on the fly" whenever you print something. You do this by choosing an alternative printer in the standard Print dialog box (see Figure 19-2). Use the drop-down list to pluck out another printer. From then on, Windows prints using that printer as your main printer; you must repeat these steps to reestablish your original main printer.

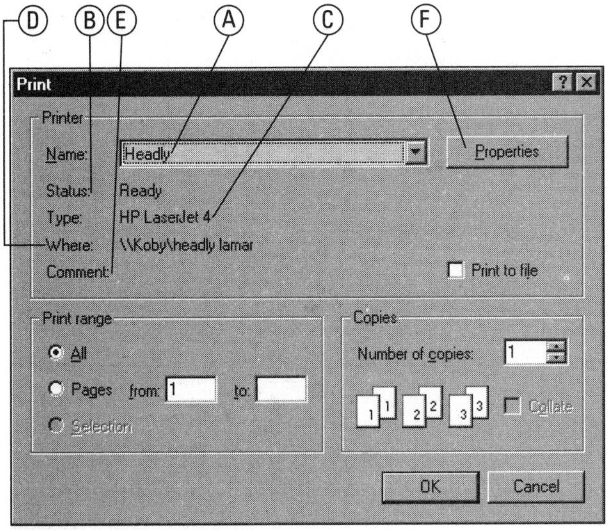

Figure 19-2
The standard, boring Print dialog box.
A. Choose a new printer from this drop-down list. **B.** How the printer feels. **C.** The printer's brand name. **D.** Where the printer sits (this is a network printer). **E.** Rude comments (optional). **F.** Click here to see the printer's Properties dialog box.

By the way, you must do this with the File⇨Print command or by pressing Ctrl+P. You cannot access the Print dialog box when you use the printing button on the toolbar.

◀▥ See the section "Printing your stuff" in Chapter 4 for more information about the standard Print dialog box.

Printer setup and properties nonsense

Like almost everything else in Windows, your printer has its own Properties dialog box, chock-full of interesting options and gizmos. Honestly, I can tell you that most of it is pretty useless. The following illustrates some of the highlights.

Display your printer's Properties dialog box by finding your printer (see the beginning of this chapter), right-clicking on it, and choosing Properties from the shortcut menu. In the Print dialog box, you can click on the Properties button to bring up your printer's Properties dialog box, looking something like Figure 19-3.

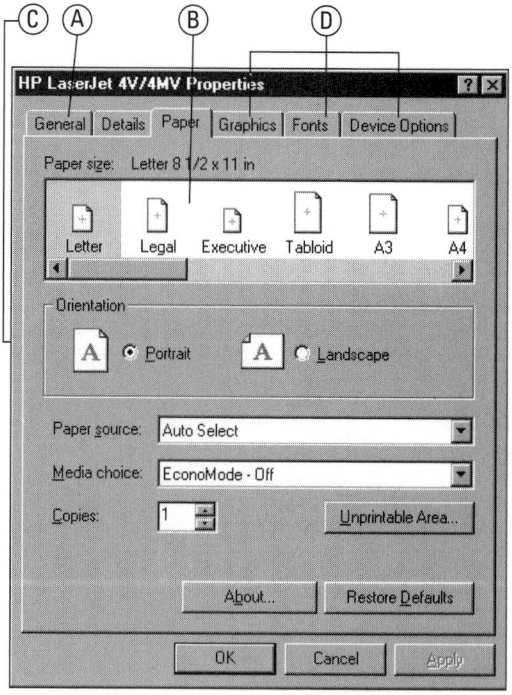

Figure 19-3
Any old printer's Properties dialog box.
A. Not all these tabs appear for every printer. **B.** Set the paper type here. **C.** Set which way the paper prints here. **D.** These tabs are specific to this HP printer.

You must choose the Properties command from the printer's icon itself, not from a shortcut. When you choose the Properties command for a printer shortcut, such as one that may live on your desktop, you see the Properties dialog box for that shortcut, not for the original printer.

Some printers have a special configuration button, located in the Details panel. Click on the Details tab to bring that panel forward and look for the Setup button in the lower left corner. Click on that button to run special setup software for your printer. Figure 19-4 shows what happens when you click on the Setup button for an HP DeskJet 500 C, a color printer.

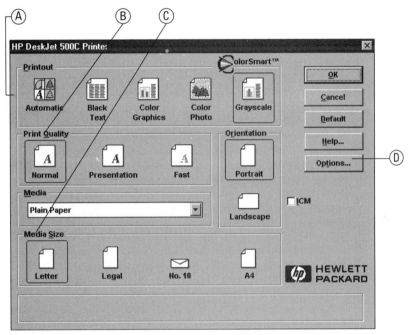

Figure 19-4
A cool Setup dialog box for a color printer.
A. Settings. **B.** More settings. **C.** Even more settings. **D.** Oh, gosh, and there are options too!

Network printers may lack certain control features in their Properties dialog box. In some cases, you can set only specific printer options at the computer directly connected to that printer.

Playing with the Queue

The word *queue* means a waiting line. When you're waiting to buy tickets in Britain, you're standing in a queue. In America, you stand in a line. Queue (pronounced "Q") is actually correct; compare its definition in the dictionary with that for *line,* and you'll see what I mean. And this does have something to do with printing in Windows.

The theoretical hockey puck of a printing queue

When you print something in Windows, the application sends it off to a special place in memory. There it sits and waits to be printed. When the time comes, Windows prints a little bit of your document at a time, sending small bits of it out to the printer so as not to disturb anything else you're doing in Windows. This process, known as *spooling,* is what enables you to keep working while Windows prints. (Oftentimes your stuff prints quickly, but, relatively speaking, Windows doesn't give printing a high priority.)

So you could, theoretically, print 100 documents and, while they're printing, be off playing the Minesweeper game. The 100 documents sit and wait in the printing queue (British), which is a line (American) of documents waiting to be printed. To see the line, open up a handy printer icon near you.

Looking at the printing queue

To see the printing queue, you have to open your printer's icon. Double-click on it, and the queue appears. Of course, if you have a quick printer, you may never see anything there (see Figure 19-5). But print several complex documents in a row, and you may see them lurking in the queue; the document at the top of the list is printing, and the others are waiting in the queue.

Pausing your printing

If you need to get at the printer or you want to pause printing for any reason, choose Printer⇨Pause Printing from the menu in your printer's dialog box (the queue box). I've done this a few times to change paper or just to keep things inside the queue waiting until I had a whole boatload of things to print all at one time.

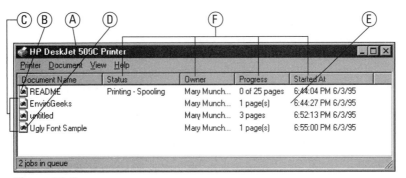

Figure 19-5
A typical printing queue.
A. This is a slow printer, which is the only way I could get four documents to show up. **B.** First document, the one printing. **C.** Things waiting in the queue. **D.** You can drag these things to change their order. **E.** Other information. **F.** You can adjust these column widths by dragging here.

Note that although pausing printing stops Windows from sending something to the printer, your printer has its own memory and continues to print a little after you've paused printing. Sometimes that's maybe half a page, and sometimes six pages print before things are "paused."

You can pause individual documents by clicking on them in the queue and choosing Document⇨Pause Printing from the menu.

Moving documents in the queue

Things print in the order in which you printed them. This makes sense; the people who ordered food ahead of you in the line, er, queue at McDonald's get their food before you do. But if you're really hungry, or if you want one document to print before another, simply drag it up toward the top of the queue; click on the document's icon, and drag it up. Easy enough.

Killing off documents in the queue

Sometimes you may not want something to print. For example, you just pounded out a steamed letter to your department head about what an incompetent twit she is, and then she phones to say that you got that big raise. Oops.

Immediately, you can open your printer's windows to see the queue. Locate the offending document, and click on it once with the mouse to highlight it. Then choose Document⇨Cancel Printing. ZAP! The document is gone.

If you choose Printer⇨Purge Print Jobs from the menu, every print job is purged.

Needless to say, you should be quick with this one. Only if something is waiting to print can you yank it back. Otherwise, like words uttered, there's no way to stop it.

If you cancel a document that's printing, you may end up with part of it stuck in the printer. To clear the document from the printer, press your printer's Page Eject or Form Feed button. That spits that final page out of the printer and clears the document from memory.

Basic Fax

Faxing is similar to printing. All you have to do is think of a fax machine as another type of printer. The only difference is that the printer is miles away and you have to dial up a phone to get it to print. Other than that, faxing is very similar to printing, which is why I've hidden it here in this chapter.

To send the fax, you simply follow a similar set of steps as you would to print a document:

1. Create the document to be faxed.

   In your word processor or wherever, create the document you want to fax.

2. Choose File⇨Print.

   Or press Ctrl+P, both of which bring up the Print dialog box. This is important: You cannot use the Print icon on a toolbar to print your fax. You need access to the Print dialog box for the next step.

3. Choose the fax machine as your printer.

   In the Name drop-down list, choose your fax machine as installed by WinFax or whatever fax software you're using.

   As an example, choose Microsoft Fax. That's the name Windows gave your fax/modem when it was first detected.

4. Click on Print.

   This step prints your document, but with a fax machine what happens next is that your faxing software takes over. In the case of the Microsoft Fax, the Compose New Fax Wizard dialog box is displayed, as shown in Figure 19-6.

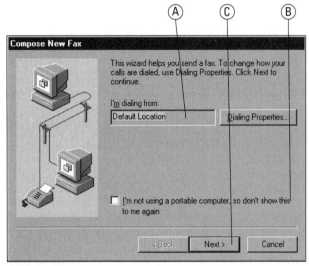

Figure 19-6
Here we go a-faxin'.
A. Change only if you're using a laptop somewhere on the road. **B.** Hey! Good idea to check this if it's true. **C.** Moving right along . . . .

5. Click on Next.

   Now it's time to type the phone number. If you're sending a fax to the Pope, for example, you type his private fax machine number, which is [censored by publisher]. Figure 19-7 describes the current Fax Wizard dialog box in more detail.

6. Click on Next.

   The next dialog box in the Fax Wizard suggests a cover page (see Figure 19-8). Pick one from the list. It will be filled in according to the information you've already given this dialog box.

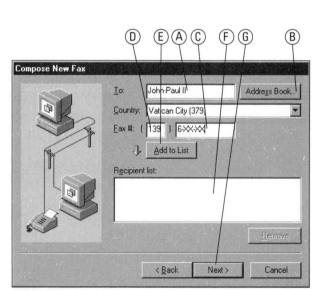

Figure 19-7

The Fax Wizard wants to know where to send your fax.

A. Type the recipient's name here. **B.** You can select their info from your Address Book here (though I personally find the Address Book massively confusing to use). **C.** Type the phone number here. **D.** Windows suggests your current area code here. **E.** You can click on this button to send the fax to multiple recipients. **F.** Multiple recipients appear here. **G.** Moving right along.

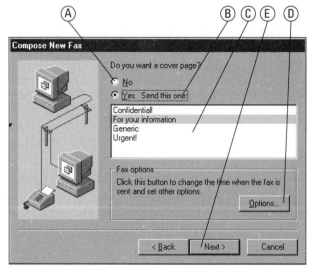

Figure 19-8

Pick a fax cover page here.

A. Click here for no cover page. **B.** Click here and then . . . **C.** . . . choose a cover page here. **D.** Don't bother. **E.** Moving right along.

There is a program called Cover Page Editor that you can use to modify or create your own fax cover pages. It's located off the Start Thing's menu; choose Programs⇨Accessories⇨Fax⇨Cover Page Editor. It's too complex to describe in this paragraph, but you can use it to view, modify, or create your own interesting fax cover letters.

7. Click on Next.

    The next dialog box allows you to fill in additional information about the fax, info that is stuffed into the cover page (if you elected to send one).

    Fill in the Subject field.

    Fill in a Note if you want.

    Make sure that a ✔ check mark is in the box by Start note on cover page.

8. Click on Next.

    A-ha! You're done.

9. Click on Finish.

    The little "I am printing" dialog box appears; Windows assembles your document and prepares to send it.

    You see a Microsoft Fax Status dialog box appear (see Figure 19-9).

    You hear the modem dialed.

    The other fax picks up.

    Tension builds . . . .

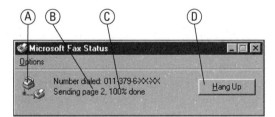

Figure 19-9
Fax-sending dialog box.
A. Pretty to watch. **B.** Page being sent. **C.** Percentage of page being eaten by other fax machine. **D.** Oops!

10. Your fax has printed.

    No fanfare. Nothing really special. Your modem has sent the fax — along with your cover page — to a fax machine elsewhere on the planet.

It may be a good idea to reactivate the Print dialog box at this time to reset your main printer: Press Ctrl+P to bring up the Print dialog box, and then choose your original, favorite printer from the Name drop-down list. That way, the next time you go to print something, it prints on the printer and Windows doesn't try to send another fax.

Dinking Frenzy at the Control Panel

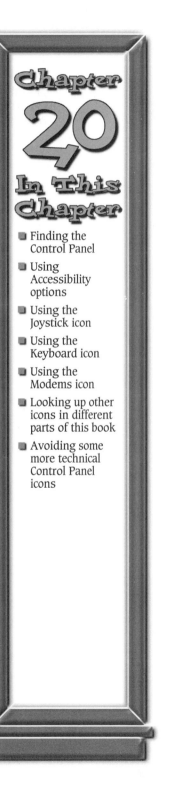

chapter

20

In This chapter

■ Finding the Control Panel

■ Using Accessibility options

■ Using the Joystick icon

■ Using the Keyboard icon

■ Using the Modems icon

■ Looking up other icons in different parts of this book

■ Avoiding some more technical Control Panel icons

The Control Panel is a dinker's paradise. It's where you have direct access to tweak, twiddle, or tangle with any or all of Windows' various settings and options. You could spend weeks there. You may have already. This chapter discusses the various icons and programs in the Control Panel, how they work, and why bother.

The Great Control Panel Hunt

The Control Panel lives as a special folder icon. You can find it right in the main My Computer window, or you can pluck it from the Start Thing's menu: Choose Settings⇨Control Panel.

Control Panel

⬅ ▥▥ If dinking is your passion, you might consider pasting down a shortcut copy of the Control Panel on the desktop. Chapter 17, the section "Sticking stuff on the desktop," tells you how.

Open the Control Panel folder by double-clicking on it — just as you open any folder. Its window appears, looking something like Figure 20-1. What you see may be different; certain programs may add their own icons to the Control Panel, and you may not see some specialty items, such as the Accessibility Options, as shown in Figure 20-1.

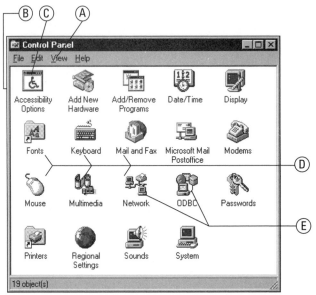

Figure 20-1
A typical Control Panel window.
A. You can change the view here — just as you can change any My Computer window; see Chapter 2, the section "Different Ways to Look at the Stuff in My Computer." **B.** This is the Big Icon view, most popular. **C.** This goodie appears only if you've installed it specifically; see the section "Adding the Rest of Windows" in Chapter 13. **D.** Double-click on any of these icons to open them. **E.** These icons appear only if you have special networking software installed.

The way the Control Panel works is just like any folder: You double-click on an icon to run a special control gizmo. The icon usually opens up a window or dialog box in which additional settings are made.

The remaining sections in this chapter detail what the various components in the Control Panel do.

➡ Working the various icons in the Control Panel presents you with a smorgasbord of various dialog box options, gizmos, and gadgets. See Chapter 28 for more information about how they all work.

Items Not Covered Elsewhere in This Book

This section outlines various Control Panel icons and their functions. This group consists of icons not covered somewhere else in this book, which you can probably take to mean that their function isn't that crucial or that what they do just isn't exciting enough to appear elsewhere.

Accessibility options, or making Windows friendly to everyone

The Accessibility Options icon is used to assist handi-capped or physically impaired folk with using Windows. It contains options for using a keyboard with one hand, having visual clues rather than sounds appear, a keyboard-simulated mouse, and other settings to make using a computer more pleasurable.

Accessibility Options

◄⊪ You must install this icon as an optional extra. Refer to the section "Adding the Rest of Windows" in Chapter 13.

Double-click on the Accessibility Options icon to open its window. The Accessibility Properties dialog box appears with several tabs and panels for making various adjustments to the way Windows works. I won't tread through each of them here because most of them are pretty obvious in function and use. Here are some highlights:

If you have to use the keyboard with only one hand, consider turning on the StickyKeys option. This option enables you to press Shift+, Ctrl+, or Alt+key combinations one key at a time. So you can do a Ctrl+P by pressing the Ctrl key and then the P key one after the other. To set this up, go to the Key-board tab and put a ✔ check mark in the Use StickyKeys box and then click on the Settings button for more options and information.

The SoundSentry option can be used to have Windows offer visual clues when it would normally bleep the speaker. (I like this option because loud computers annoy me.) Go to the Sound panel and put a ✔ check mark in the Use SoundSentry box. Then click on the Settings button to make more adjustments and get an explanation of what's going on. The ShowSounds option is also pretty cool.

If you're visually impaired, you might want to check out the Display panel. There you can set up Windows to splash things on the screen in

high contrast mode. A bizarre key combination sets this up: left Alt+left Shift+ Print Screen. I suppose that they don't want anyone accidentally falling into that mode.

➡ Also check out Chapter 24 for information about changing the Windows color scheme in other ways; Chapter 25 discusses how you can make the mouse pointer larger and easier to find.

As usual, after making any changes here, Windows may beg you to let it restart your computer. Click on Yes because it's better to do that now than dawdle around and forget about the changes.

Happy, happy, joystick

The Joystick icon appears only if you have a joystick attached to your Windows computer. This is really silly because most Windows games use a mouse. And DOS games that use a joystick typically require that you calibrate them when you start the DOS game. Even so, you can double-click on the Joystick icon to do some in-Windows calibration.

Joystick

Supposedly, Microsoft has included splendid Windows game technology that's supposed to allow for nifty Windows games in the future. This is the reason that the Joystick icon is included in the Control Panel. But I wouldn't hold your breath, if I were you.

Your joystick may have come with its own Control Panel icon for making adjustments, or it may have a separate utility you can run from the Start Thing's menu. In all cases, it's better to use that program than the generic Joystick icon.

➡ See Chapter 26, the section "Wrestling with DOS Games," for more information about playing DOS games in Windows.

Spicing up a keyboard

The Keyboard icon enables you to make minor adjustments to your keyboard. Nothing major can be done there — it's not like you can rearrange the keys to a more proper pattern or speed up your fingers. And here is where you can set up a foreign-language keyboard, if typing in French is your thing.

Keyboard

To display the Keyboard Properties dialog box, double-click on the Keyboard icon. You see something similar to Figure 20-2. Honestly, unless you're having trouble with your typing, don't bother with anything there.

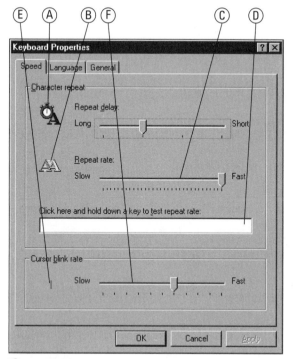

Figure 20-2
The Keyboard Properties dialog box thing.
A. The press-and-hold-until-it-repeats delay. **B.** The repeat-rate delay. **C.** Move the slider over here if you're getting a bunch of ddoouubblleedd-uupp characters.
D. Practice doesn't make perfect; *perfect* practice makes perfect. **E.** It's a blinkin' toothpick cursor! **F.** Make blink faster or slower.

The Language panel can be used if you ever plan to use your keyboard to type in a foreign language, such as English. Seriously, if you occasionally type letters to French people, for example, you can configure Windows to have a French keyboard ready for you, complete with various letters French. To do this, follow these steps:

1. Summon up the Keyboard Properties dialog box.

   Follow the steps in this chapter for locating the Control Panel, and then double-click on the Keyboard icon to open it up.

2. Click on the Language tab to bring that panel forward.

   If you already have two or more languages selected, skip down to the last step (but don't click on OK).

3. Click on the Add button.

   The Add Language dialog box appears.

4. Choose French (Standard) from the drop-down list.

5. Click on OK.

You return to the Keyboard Properties dialog box. Notice that you now have two languages listed and that the Switch Languages region is activated. You can now use the key combination marked with a dot to switch keyboard language layouts.

To switch over to a French keyboard, for example (with special French characters available), as set up in Figure 20-3, you press the Alt+Shift key combination. Voilà. Vous pouvez maintenant taper des mots doux à votre chère Française secrète.

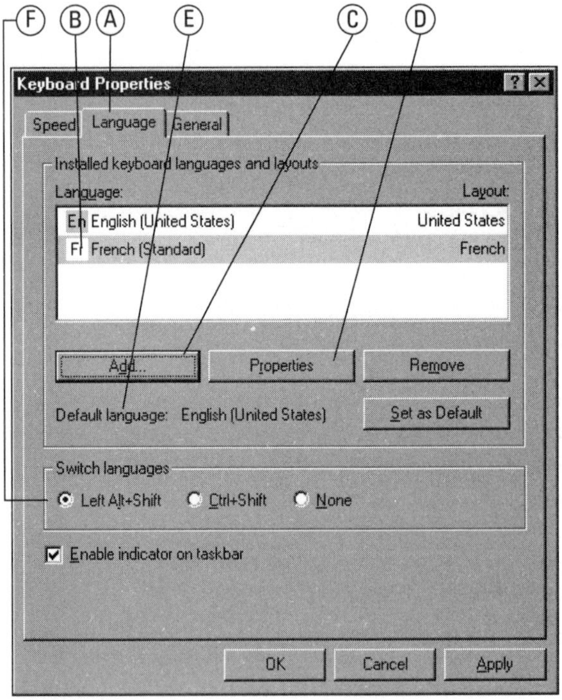

Figure 20-3

Oui! Oui! Vous avez selectionné un clavier français!
A. Click on this tab to bring the Language panel forward. **B.** The French keyboard layout was added. **C.** Click on this button to add more keyboard layouts. **D.** This button doesn't do much of anything. **E.** Make sure that English is still your first keyboard. **F.** Key combinations you can use to switch keyboard layouts.

6. Click on OK to exit the Keyboard Properties dialog box.

You're asked to insert your Windows setup disk (or disks) to copy over the files for the new keyboard layout — so be prepared when asked! (You don't have to reset your computer, though.)

With this option set, you see a little icon in the Loud Time area, letting you know which keyboard is selected. It's really boring: En for English, for example. When you can press the proper key combination to switch to French, for example, the En changes to Fr for French. Boring, but informative.

No, I'm sorry, but just switching to a French keyboard doesn't mean that you instantly become a master of the French language.

Hey: And you have to look up the French (or whatever) keyboard layout in your Windows manual. That tells you where all the funny franc keys are located.

Merry modems

The modem guy in the Control Panel gives you access to a configuration panel for your modem. You can also get there by choosing Modem Setup from any of a number of other places: from a communications program, the Phone Dialer, or the little modem guy who appears in the Taskbar's Loud Time when you're using your modem. Whatever, when you open the Modems icon in the Control Panel, you see the Modems Properties dialog box, similar to the one shown in Figure 20-4.

Modems

There really isn't anything radically important in the Modems Properties dialog box; don't be seduced into wasting any time there.

You may want to configure the Dialing Properties information. If you don't do it now, you're asked about it later, when you use your modem. Click on the Dialing Properties button to see the Dialing Properties dialog box (see Figure 20-5). That helps your modem programs dial numbers, and it also comes in handy when you're faxing. The information in the figures helps you get around.

Figure 20-4
The illustrious Modems Properties dialog box.
A. Various modems you may have attached to or inside your computer. **B.** Here is where you can add more modems. **C.** Get rid of modems. **D.** Modem properties, set connections, speed, and so on. **E.** Click here to move to the exciting Dialing Properties dialog box. **F.** Nothing interesting back here.

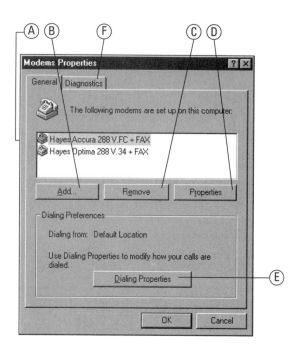

Figure 20-5
The even more exciting Dialing Properties dialog box.
A. Choose your location here. **B.** Add new locations here.
C. Type your area code. **D.** Where you live (like, uh, internationally).
E. Need to dial a 9 first? Type it here.
F. Special long-distance access number here.
G. Calling-card info (if you need to dial it when you call).
H. Check here to turn off annoying call-waiting feature.
I. Tone and pulse dialing selection.

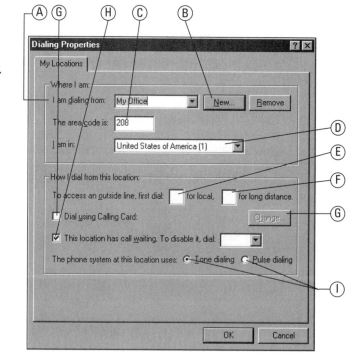

Other strange and wonderful goodies

There's no limit to the madness you may encounter in the Control Panel. Often there are lots of interesting things to tweak and dink there, each of which controls something interesting in Windows or some hardware attached to your computer.

My best advice for this is to *be careful.* Some settings you shouldn't mess with. Always be sure to read the Help file or any documentation before setting various options. Also be aware that choosing a new option may require your computer to reset. Therefore, it's best to do all your dinking at one time. Keep your dinking time separate from your work time.

Items Covered Elsewhere in This Book

Much of the dinking that takes place in the Control Panel is covered elsewhere in this book, in chapters devoted to the subject at hand. The following sections tell you where to look for various Control Panel icons.

Oh, to add new hardware

The Add New Hardware icon opens up the Add Hardware wizard. Use this thing whenever you add new hardware to your computer. The wizard examines your system and discovers what it is you've installed. It's all part of Windows' Plug-and-Play feature, which supposedly saves you setup time.

Add New Hardware

➠ See Chapter 23 for more information about installing new hardware.

➠ Setting up your printer is done by using the Add Printer icon in the Control Panel's Printers folder. This subject is also covered in Chapter 23.

Oh, to add and remove programs

This icon is used to help you install software (though all it really does is hunt for the Setup or Install program on a floppy disk or CD-ROM drive). Anyway, it's an improvement over the way things worked in the olden days.

Add/Remove Programs

◀━ıı See Chapter 13 for more information about adding new software. Removing old software is also covered there.

Up to the second with Date/Time

The Date/Time icon fires up the Date/Time Properties dialog box, which you can also get to from the Loud Time on the taskbar.

Date/Time

◀━ıı See Chapter 7, the section "Fooling with the time (or, setting the time on your PC)," for information about how to work the Date/Time Properties dialog box.

What's on display?

The Display icon in the Control Panel is a shortcut to the Display Properties dialog box, which you can get to right from the desktop as well: Bring up the desktop's shortcut menu, and choose Properties.

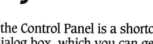

Display

ıı━▶ See Chapter 24 for information about the Desktop Properties dialog box. Look for the sections "Background Information," "The Screen-Resolution Revolution," and "Making the Windows Color Scheme Match Your Office."

ıı━▶ You also should look in Chapter 25 for information about the screen saver, also located in the Display Properties dialog box. See the section "Saving the Screen from Boredom."

Fabulous fonts

The Fonts folder opens up to reveal all the fonts (or most of them, at least) installed on your computer. There you can look at the fonts, print previews, delete fonts, or install new fonts.

Fonts

ıı━▶ See Chapter 21 for more information about fonts (it's just a barrel of fun).

Mouse messing

The Mouse icon opens up the Mouse Properties dialog box, where you can mess with the mouse, change its pointer, adjust the buttons, speed, and so on. Eek! Eek!

Mouse

➥ See Chapter 25, the section "A More Lively Mouse Pointer," for some pointers on mouse pointers.

➥ Chapter 29 also contains information about using the mouse and some Mouse Properties dialog box stuff as well.

Network work

The Network icon in the Control Panel is something you probably don't want to mess with. Network stuff is such voodoo that no one should really bother.

Network

➥ There are a coupla things you can mess with in the Network Properties dialog box that appears when you open the Control Panel's Network icon. Chapter 22 discusses them briefly, in the section "Giving your PC a network name."

Needless to say, this icon appears only if you're using Windows on a network.

And the password is . . .

The Passwords icon isn't really where you change your password. In fact, Windows doesn't rightly care about your password; just type a new one if you forget the old one, and Windows, doh-de-doh, changes it right like that.

Passwords

There's no way to recall your password when you forget it, so this part of the Control Panel won't help you anyway.

➥ One piece of the Passwords puzzle covered elsewhere is the capability of Windows to configure itself differently for different users. Mosey on up to Chapter 22, the section "Logging Off and Logging in As Another User," for more information.

➥ If you're using a screen saver, it can also be password-protected, which essentially locks up your entire computer (and there's no way to get your password back if you forget). See the section "Shhh! Using the password option" in Chapter 25.

The proof is in the printers

The Printers folder in the Control Panel opens up a special window where your printer (or printers) lives, along with its cousin the fax machine and a special icon for installing new printers.

Printers

←ııı See Chapter 19 for anything to do with your printer . . . .

←ııı . . . except for the actual task of printing, of course, which is covered in Chapter 4, in the section "Printing your stuff."

Solid walls of sounds

Obviously, you need a sound card to make sounds really happen, but the Sounds icon still appears in the Control Panel whether your PC has sound equipment or not.

Sounds

ııı⟶ Using the Sounds Properties dialog box is covered in Chapter 25, in the section "A More Euphonious PC."

Items You Need Not Bother with

Some stuff is just too hairy to mess with. The following list includes several items you may find lurking in the Control Panel, ones that I'd never bother changing because either they're too complex or changing them just isn't done by us mere mortals.

The Mail and Fax icon contains various advanced and confusing settings for using the Microsoft Exchange. Although it wouldn't kill you to wander through that dialog box and ogle at the settings, it all seems like a colossal waste of time.

Mail and Fax

The Microsoft Mail Postoffice icon doesn't need to be messed with unless you plan to tweak the network mail system. This job is best left for those who know how mail works; although the Mail Wizard that runs when you open this icon seems friendly enough, I'll bet that your network administrator would rather not have you tweak it.

Microsoft Mail
Postoffice

The Multimedia icon is a locus for various multimedia things in your computer, all of which you don't really need to mess with. The settings there were customized by Windows when it was installed or by the Add New Hardware wizard when you upgraded your PC. There's no reason to tread those waters now — unless you're directed to do so by some hardware or software manual that makes *specific* suggestions.

Multimedia

➡ See Chapter 23 for more information about installing new hardware on your PC.

Who really knows what ODBC means or what it does? You'd think that, in its effort to make Windows easy to understand, Microsoft would come up with something a little more pleasant for this item. Alas, it just has "don't touch me!" written all over it.

ODBC

The Regional Settings icon opens up an interesting dialog box that's kind of fun to examine. There are options there for changing various cultural and national settings for different parts of the world. Weird and wacky, but not worth frustrating yourself with.

Regional Settings

The System icon opens up the System Properties dialog box, which is the same dialog box you'd see if you chose Properties from My Computer's shortcut menu. The items there are very complex and should not be messed with.

System

◄ This dialog box is ventured into in Chapter 14, in the sidebar "So how much memory does this beast hold?"

If you don't have the Telephony icon, you're lucky. This one is a fine example of something that average folk should not mess with. Heck, filling out your income-tax form is much easier than understanding how this sucker goes about its business.

Telephony

(You may not have this icon in your Control Panel; it's available with only certain Windows configurations.)

Part IV Dinking

Fun with Fonts

There really isn't anything fun with fonts. They're basically different styles of type you can see on the screen, use in documents, and send off to the printer. Hubcaps are more interesting (especially when they pop off on the freeway and transform themselves into spinning, metal disks of death).

Fonts add pizzaz, but that's not the subject of this chapter. With Windows 95, fonts have collected themselves into one location. Now working with and organizing fonts is much easier, and much more sane, than it ever was. It's all worthy of a good look.

Where the Fonts Folder Lurks

All Windows fonts (well, almost all of them anyway) are kept in their own Fonts folder. It's a special folder sitting right beneath Windows' own folder on your hard drive. But you don't have to wade through My Computer or the Explorer to get there; a handy shortcut to the Fonts folder lives inside the Control Panel. Take these steps:

1. Open a handy Control Panel near you.

   You can find a Control Panel icon located right

Control Panel

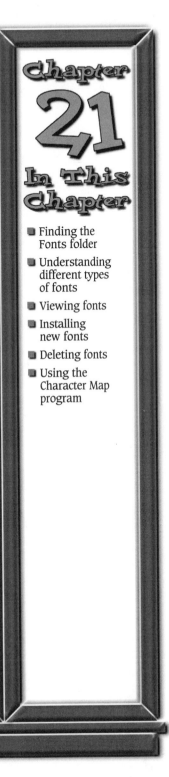

in My Computer's main window. There's also one you can grab from the Start Thing's menu: Press Ctrl+Esc, S, C.

2. Open the Fonts folder.

   Double-click on the Fonts folder to open it. You see its contents displayed, similar to Figure 21-1. That's the Big Icon view in the figure; like any other My Computer window, you can change the view to something else.

Fonts

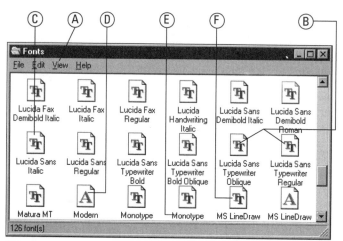

Figure 21-1

A typical Fonts folder window.

A. The Big Icon view. **B.** You choose View⇨Hide Variations to cut out the similar fonts. **C.** TrueType font icon. **D.** Older-style "fixed font" icon. **E.** Font name. **F.** Double-click on a font icon to see its preview window.

← See Chapter 2, the section "Different Ways to Look at the Stuff in My Computer," for more information about the different ways to view stuff in a My Computer window.

← See Chapter 20 for more information about the Control Panel, though all the Fonts stuff is covered right here in this chapter.

Missing and AWOL fonts

Only Windows TrueType fonts live in the Fonts folder. Other types of fonts, such as those supplied by Adobe for use with its ATM software, will probably live in another folder. This chapter doesn't cover the use of ATM fonts or the ATM software.

Playing with the Fonts Folder

The Fonts folder is the center of font activity on your computer. I know, "Big deal." But it's extremely nice to have a central place for fonts, especially a way to preview and print them before you use them. That's what the Fonts folder offers, which makes it handy for those times you sit and antagonize over fonts (which is much more often than you'd think).

Here a font, there a font, everywhere a font font

Fonts in Windows are used to form the text you see on the screen and the text that's printed. Primarily there is one type of font: the *TrueType font.* These fonts are earmarked by the T-T icon in the Fonts folder (refer to Figure 21-1).

Matura MT

Another type of font is the *screen font,* or *fixed font.* This type of font, marked by the letter *A* (as shown in Figure 21-1) is an older-style font, used primarily by old Windows applications.

Modern

Both the TrueType and system fonts appear on the screen as they do on your printer. The TrueType font is best because it can be any size, big or little, and still look good. The fixed fonts look good in only a handful of sizes; when you try to make the font too big or too little, it looks terribly disgusting.

A third type of font is the *printer font,* which is a font your printer can produce with ease. In most cases, your printer comes with a disk full of TrueType counterparts you can see on the screen — but not all printers come with such a disk. An older Canon printer of mine has a beautiful set of fonts, but on the screen they all look dorky; Windows doesn't know about the printer fonts, so it *substitutes* on the screen what it thinks is a similar font. Because the result is kind of maddening, most people (obviously) tend to avoid printer fonts, except for those that have TrueType counterparts for the screen.

Figure 21-2 shows a typical Fonts drop-down list in a word processor. There you can get some kind of clue about which type of font you're using; in addition to the font's name, a small icon appears next to the font, telling you which type it is. There are three: TrueType, Printer, and fixed font (no icon).

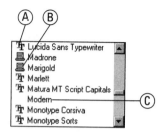

Figure 21-2
A typical Fonts drop-down list thing.
A. A TrueType font. **B.** A printer font (tiny printer icon). **C.** A fixed font.

Use TrueType fonts rather than other fonts when you can. True Type fonts look good at any size and on any printer.

My font's uglier than your font!

To see what a font looks like — the sneak preview — double-click on its icon in the Fonts folder. You see a special Quick View window displaying all sorts of details, as shown in Figure 21-3.

Figure 21-3
A sneak peek at the Bookman Old Style font.
A. Click here when you're done (which should be obvious). **B.** Meaningless font trivia. **C.** A sample of the character set. **D.** Sample text at different sizes. **E.** Click here to print a sample page. **F.** Scroll down to see the grotesquely huge font sizes.

Go ahead and print a few of your fonts — those you plan to use most of the time. Keep them in a little folder or three-ring binder by your computer. That will help you pick out a proper font for your designs.

When you examine a font, look for certain special characters. Admittedly, every font uses the English alphabet, but subtle differences appear in the letters. Pay close attention to the lowercase *g,* for example. Also look at the big *W* and the big *Q.*

For more exact font differences, plus some suggestions on how to use them, you have to refer to a book about desktop publishing and design. My favorite is anything by Roger Parker. His *Looking Good in Print* is a classic for any budding desktop designer.

Adding fonts to your collection

New fonts are added to your system by using a special command in the Fonts window — a command that doesn't appear in any other My Computer window. To add new fonts to your system, follow these steps:

1. Open up the Fonts window.

   See the section "Where the Fonts Folder Lurks," earlier in this chapter.

2. Choose File⇨Install New Font.

   The Add Fonts dialog box appears (see Figure 21-4).

3. Use the Drives and Folders windows to locate your font files.

   If you have a disk full of fonts, for example, stick it in drive A and choose that drive from the Drives drop-down list. It takes Windows a while to read in the font names and such. Be patient.

   You can also look in any folder on your hard drive for the fonts. Use the folders window for that.

   Don't bother with the Network button. It brings up one of those "You have to know the network pathname first" type of dialog boxes — a waste of time.

4. Select the fonts you want to install.

   Choose the fonts you want to install from the List of fonts list.

   You can select groups of fonts at a time to install. The method here is the same as for selecting a group of files. Refer to the section "Crowd Control, or Working with Groups of Files" in Chapter 16 for the how-tos.

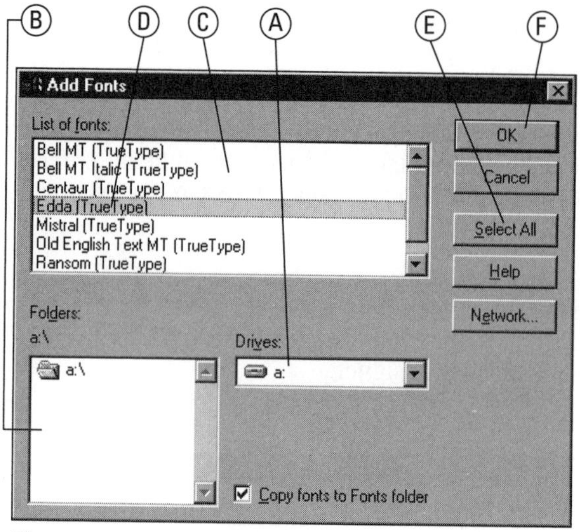

Figure 21-4
The crude Add Fonts dialog box.
A. Start here. Pick a disk drive. **B.** Optionally choose a folder full of fonts. **C.** The fonts you've found. **D.** Click on fonts to install them. **E.** You can click here to select all the fonts for installation. **F.** Go for it!

5. Click on OK.

   Chugga-chugga. Soon the fonts are copied to the Fonts folder window, where they live safely on your hard drive. There's no need to reset; the fonts are ready to use.

Removing an old, cruddy font

Font glut happens. Fonts can sprout up on your computer thicker than a clump of Canadian thistle. Although this gives you endless variety, many of the fonts you never really use. Also, font glut tends to slow down you and your computer; it can take days to scroll through a font-laden drop-down list.

Killing off old, unused fonts is a breeze:

1. Open up the Fonts window.

   Follow the directions in the section "Where the Fonts Folder Lurks," earlier in this chapter.

2. Select the font (or fonts) you want to kill off.

   Just click on the offending font. That selects it, ready for action.

Follow the instructions in Chapter 16, in the section "Crowd Control, or Working with Groups of Files," for information about selecting a group of fonts.

3. Choose File⇨Delete.

   A warning box appears, asking whether you're sure that you want to delete the font.

4. Click on Yes.

   The font is rubbed out.

Now though the Undo command isn't available, you can undelete the font. This is done just as you'd undelete anything, by restoring the zapped font from the Recycle Bin. See Chapter 5, the section "A quick, odorless peek into the Recycle Bin to restore something," for the details.

Weeding Out Cool Characters with the Character Map Program

Although you can preview in the Fonts folder what a font will look like, you really can't get at any of the interesting characters it offers. I'm not talking about the regular alphabetic characters. No, I mean the strange and wonderful characters that are included with such special fonts as Wingdings and Zapf Dingbats. These fonts contain all sorts of fun stuff you may want to use to spice up dull documents. To get at those fun characters, you need the Character Map program.

Start the Character Map program. From the Start Thing's menu, choose Programs⇨Accessories⇨Character Map. The Character Map program appears, looking similar to Figure 21-5.

◄═ On the off chance that the Character Map isn't installed on your computer, see the section "Adding the Rest of Windows" in Chapter 13 for information about getting it.

Begin by choosing a font from the drop-down list. That displays all the characters available with that font, especially the bonus characters in addition to the standard alphabet.

To enlarge a character for better viewing, click the mouse on that character, but keep the mouse button down (see Figure 21-5).

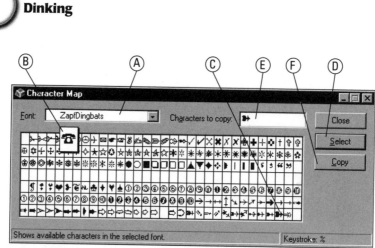

Figure 21-5

The Character Map program.

A. Choose a font here. **B.** Click on a character to see it magnified. **C.** Double-click to "paste" the character. **D.** Same thing as double-clicking on the highlighted character. **E.** Characters are pasted here for copying. **F.** Click here to copy the character into the Clipboard.

If you double-click on a character, it's sent up the paste zone. You can double-click on any number of characters from any number of fonts. Click on the Copy button to copy them to Windows' Clipboard. From there you can paste them into any application capable of receiving pasted text.

Remember to close or minimize the Character Map window when you're done playing around.

Microsoft Word has a special command that works just like the Character Map program. If you choose Insert⇨Symbol from Word's menu, you see a dialog box similar to the Character Map. You can use that dialog box to insert special characters right into your document; just click on the Insert button.

◄ιιι If you find yourself using the Character Map often, consider making it one of those programs Windows starts automatically every time you turn on your computer. See Chapter 6, the section "Applications that Amazingly Start Automatically."

Windows and Everyone Else's PC (The Joys of Networking)

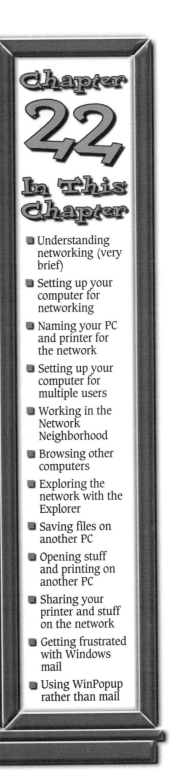

Chapter 22

In This Chapter

- Understanding networking (very brief)
- Setting up your computer for networking
- Naming your PC and printer for the network
- Setting up your computer for multiple users
- Working in the Network Neighborhood
- Browsing other computers
- Exploring the network with the Explorer
- Saving files on another PC
- Opening stuff and printing on another PC
- Sharing your printer and stuff on the network
- Getting frustrated with Windows mail
- Using WinPopup rather than mail

Happiness is a network that works. When they work, networks can be a joy. For example, I have three computers hooked up into one printer. Not all the computers are even in the same office, yet they all *share* one printer. That's the joy of networking: It's all about sharing, offering your disk drives up for use by others and, likewise, stealing things from their disk drives.

Windows comes with built-in networking. It's the simple form of networking, called *peer-to-peer* in the computer biz. This isn't file server networking, but the freebie stuff Windows offers. And this chapter goes into only light detail about using Windows' network to get your work done. There's just too much technical stuff to bother with anything more complex than that.

Networking Nonsense

If your computer is hooked up to some type of network, Windows saw it when it was installed, and everything is set up for network activity. Windows saw your network card. It saw the network hose leading out the back of your computer. Everything is done. Now you have to worry only about using the network to get work done.

How you can tell that you're on a network

Your first major clue that your computer is hooked up to a Windows network is the Network Neighborhood icon floating on your desktop, probably right under My Computer.

Network   Network
Neighborhood

Another way to determine whether you have a network is the telltale Network icon in the Control Panel.

➡ The Network Neighborhood is a window to other computers up on the network, just as My Computer is a window to your own PC's disk drives and folders. See the section "Prowling around the Network Neighborhood," later in this chapter, for more information.

⬅ Chapter 20 talks at length about the Control Panel, though all the pertinent stuff about networking can be found in this chapter.

Making your PC network happy

Networks are about sharing *resources,* or the goodies connected to your computer. The two most basic things you can share with others are your PC's disk drives (or specific folders) and any printers that are attached. This is just the nice, wholesome thing to do, just like they told you in kindergarten. Only nice people share.

To set up your computer to share on the network, follow these steps:

1. Open the Control Panel.

   You can open any Control Panel folder you see, either on the desktop or in My Computer's main window.

Control Panel

If you can't find a Control Panel folder anywhere, press Ctrl+Esc to pop up the Start Thing's menu and then choose Settings⇨Control Panel.

2. Open the Network icon.

Network

Double-click on the network icon to open it. The Network dialog box appears — ta-da.

3. Click on the Configuration tab to bring that panel forward.

It's probably already forward. Look for the File and Print Sharing button near the bottom of the panel.

4. Click on the File and Print Sharing button.

This step displays the File and Print Sharing dialog box, logically enough (see Figure 22-1). This is where you let Windows know what it is that you want to share on the network.

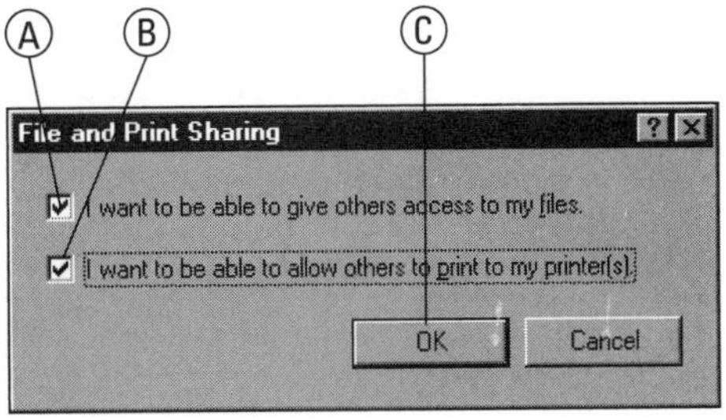

Figure 22-1
To share or not to share, that is the question.
A. A check mark here means that you want to share your disk drives.
B. A check mark here means that you want to share your PC's printers.
C. Click here when you're done.

(A) (B) (C)

File and Print Sharing

☑ I want to be able to give others access to my files.

☑ I want to be able to allow others to print to my printer(s).

OK   Cancel

5. Make the appropriate settings.

Choose whether to share your disk drives or printers. A ✔ check mark in the box means Yes; no ✔ means No.

There is some logic about not sharing your stuff. For example, I wouldn't want every bozo on the network to access the company's financial files. There are two options here: First, that computer doesn't have to share anything on the network. Or second, that computer's resources can be password-protected to limit access.

You can always change these settings later as your networking needs evolve.

6. Click on OK.

This step closes the File and Print Sharing dialog box.

7. Click on OK again.

This step closes the Network dialog box, but not before you're asked whether you want to reset your computer. Windows oftentimes must start again when you make networking changes.

8. Click on Yes to restart your computer.

This step resets your computer, which is what you want. If you click on No, you can keep on working, but you must reset in order for the changes to take effect. If you don't do it now, you may forget later.

9. Windows resets.

Time to get another cuppa java.

➠ See the section "Surrendering Your Hardware to the Network," later in this chapter, for information about password-protecting any disk drives you plan to share.

➠ See the section "Browsing other computers à la My Computer," later in this chapter, for information about password-protected access to other disk drives.

Giving your PC a network name

Three names are associated with your computer network:

✗ The workgroup name

✗ Your PC's network name

✗ Your login name

The workgroup name simply identifies a group of computers on the net. In a small-office situation, this probably means all the computers. Larger companies may have different workgroups, such as one for the production department, one for shipping, another for marketing, and so on. This is just a way of keeping things organized, not any evil plot.

Your PC has a *network name,* the name with which other computers recognize yours on the network. This name can be anything creative to designate your computer, though most offices are anal retentive when it comes to this subject, and they name computers things like E40003ZY. To give your PC a better name, follow these steps:

1. Open the Network thing in the Control Panel.

Follow steps 1 and 2 in the section "Making your PC network happy," earlier in this chapter.

Network

2. Click on the Identification tab to bring that panel forward.

   This is the panel where you can set various names for your computer. See Figure 22-2 for more information about what's what.

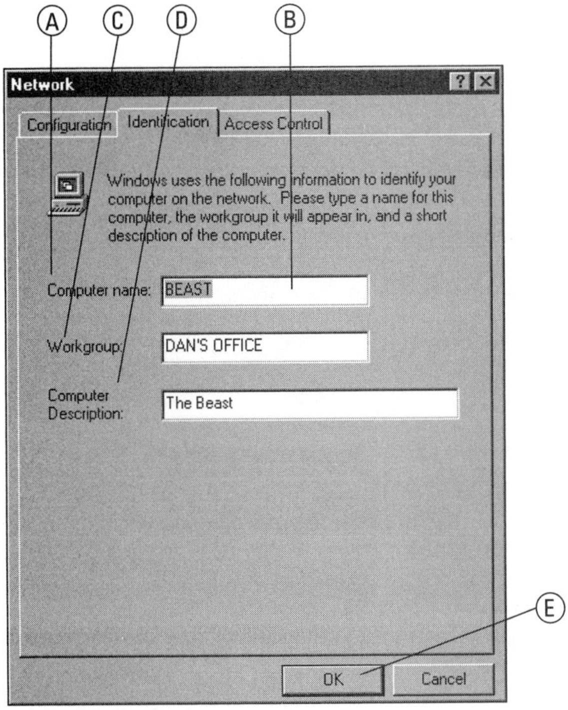

Figure 22-2
Changing names on the network dialog box.
A. Your computer's name on the network. **B.** Type a new name here. **C.** The workgroup name; don't mess with this. **D.** Something clever to say about your computer. **E.** Click here when you're done.

3. Type a new computer name.

   Enter your new computer name in the Computer name text box.

   You can type as many as 15 characters. Be descriptive.

   No, you can't use spaces. Sorry. Yes, even though you may see a computer named Monkey King in some of the figures, ignore it. Spaces. No way.

4. Optionally type a description.

   Click in the Computer Description box to type a description of your computer. This extra text is used to further pinpoint a computer's name on the network. For example, one computer in my office is named Koby, and its description is Financial stuff.

5. Click on OK.

   Windows thinks about it.

6. Click on Yes to restart your computer.

   Your computer must be reset in order for your naming changes to appear to others on the network. Reset now so that you don't forget about it later.

← Your computer's network name is different from the label you give your hard drive. See the section "More than just a letter: Giving your disk a proper name" in Chapter 14 for more information about disk labels.

Giving your printer a network name

If you plan to be nice and share your printer, you'll give it a name during the sharing process. It's like, "Here is my printer, Melvin. Abuse him."

Because sharing a printer and giving it a name are both one and the same, see this chapter's "Sharing your printer" section for more information.

Logging Off and Logging In As Another User

Though it really has nothing to do with networking (and everything to do with logging in), Windows makes it possible for two people to use the same computer and yet have wholly different setups. For example, Gerry may like a music scheme, and Mary may enjoy the Judge Lance Ito wallpaper. Both can use the same computer and enjoy their own personal settings.

To set up a computer this way, follow these steps:

1. Open the Control Panel.

   Find a Control Panel folder, and open it. Or you can press Ctrl+Esc to pop up the Start Thing's menu and choose Settings⇨Control Panel.

Network

2. Open the Passwords icon.

   This step displays the Passwords Properties dialog box.

3. Click on the User Profiles tab to bring that panel forward.

   The User Profiles panel is shown in Figure 22-3. You want to click on the second radio button (see the figure) to allow more than one person to use your computer.

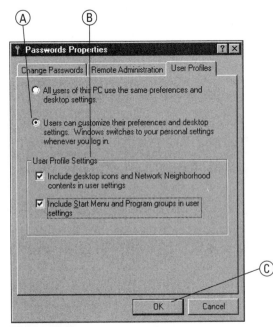

Figure 22-3
The lovely Password Properties dialog box.
A. Click here so that multiple people can have multiple personalities on this computer. **B.** Might as well check both of these, to be nice. **C.** "I'm done!"

Of course, anyone can use your computer now. But with this option set, they can change the desktop, the Start Thing's menu, and other items, each of which will be customized for them. Windows adjusts itself accordingly when they log in.

4. Click on OK.

   After clicking the OK button, Windows asks you to reset. Do it now.

5. Click on Yes to reset.

   The new settings can't take effect until Windows starts over again.

◀▥ By the way, when you're done using the computer, you should immediately shut down and let the other users log in on their own. Choose the Shut Down command from the Start Thing's menu, and click on the last option, "Close all programs and log on as a different user." See Chapter 1, the section "Quitting Windows and Turning Off Your PC," for more information about the Shut Down command.

◀▥ See Chapter 1, the section "Dialog box #1: Log in, mystery guest," for more information about logging in, which you do every time you start Windows. When you have a network, you log in on the network; otherwise, Windows logs you in just because it's nosy.

▥▶ See Chapter 26 for more information about music and sound schemes.

▥▶ Chapter 24 discusses the delicacies of Windows wallpaper on the desktop; you have to browse the Net for a handsome bitmap image of Judge Lance Ito.

It's a Beautiful Day in the Network Neighborhood

The Network Neighborhood is simply the name Windows gives the doorway into other computers on your network. Other than the fact that you're looking at other computers, it all works the same as My Computer. There are windows, My Computer's toolbar, different views, and so on.

◀▥ Refer to Chapter 2 for more information about My Computer. All the stuff about the various windows, views, and so forth applies also to the Network Neighborhood.

Prowling around the Network Neighborhood

Open the Network Neighborhood icon on the desktop. A window appears, looking something like Figure 22-4. That shows you all the computers up, running, and on the network in your workgroup.

Network Neighborhood

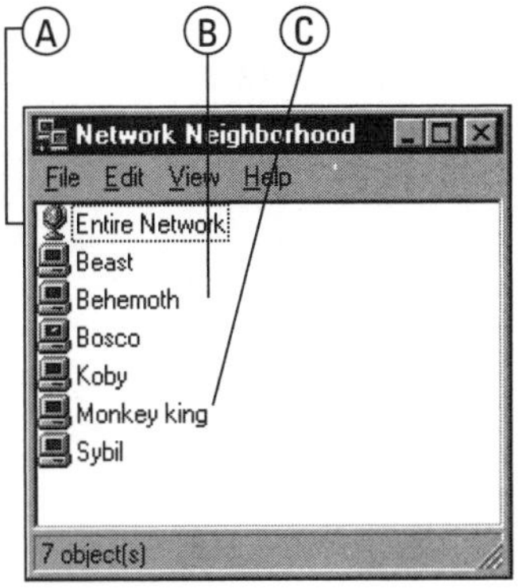

Figure 22-4
Other computers lurking in the Network
Neighborhood.
A. This represents every computer on your
network — the "globe." **B.** Other computers on
the network with their network names. **C.** Even
your own computer shows up on this list.

Figure 22-5 shows another view on the Network Neighborhood. As with My
Computer, you have all the options for looking at your computer groups in
different ways. Figure 22-5 also shows the Big Icon view, and the standard
My Computer/Explorer toolbar is also visible.

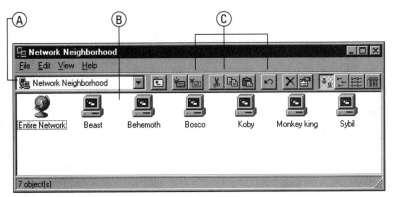

Figure 22-5
Network Neighborhood, different view.
A. Choose View⇨Toolbar to see the standard My Computer toolbar.
B. Big Icon view. **C.** All the buttons here work the same as they do in My Computer
or the Explorer.

◀ⅲ See the sections "Different Ways to Look at the Stuff in My Computer" and
"Whip out the toolbar" in Chapter 2 for more information.

Browsing other computers à la My Computer

To find out more about a computer on the network, open it up; double-click on the network computer's icon, and you see another window displaying what that computer has to offer. Again, everything appears as it would in My Computer; see Figure 22-6.

Figure 22-6
A view of what the network computer
Monkey King has to offer.
A. Monkey King is sharing its drive C root folder here.
B. Another folder named Figures is being shared.
C. Monkey King's printer, Mongo, is also up for grabs.

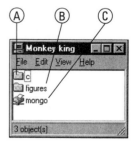

Anything you see in another computer's window is up for grabs. You can open folders, copy files, paste files, run programs, make shortcuts on your desktop — just about anything.

If a computer doesn't share anything, its window is blank when you open it up.

Some computers are password-protected; before you can peer into their shared folders, you must enter the proper password. When you try to open this type of folder, you see a dialog box similar to the one shown in Figure 22-7. Carefully type the password, cross your fingers, and click on the OK button. If you guessed correctly, you'll be able to use the computer.

➧ There are two types of passwords: a read-only password, which gives you access to merely browse through another computer's folders, and a full password, which gives you full access. See the section "Surrendering Your Hardware to the Network," later in this chapter, for information about setting the passwords.

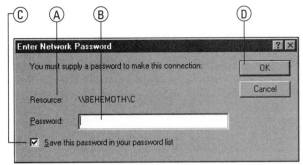

Figure 22-7
You must enter a password before you can access some network goodies.
A. This is what you're trying to access, drive C on the computer named Behemoth.
B. Type the password here. **C.** If you check here, Windows remembers the password in the future. **D.** Click here to continue.

Spanning the globe

If you open the globe icon in the Network Neighborhood, you see a window displaying all the different workgroups on your entire network (see Figure 22-8). That enables you to browse through them, though that's probably not a good idea because you were assigned to one workgroup for a reason, and network managers hate browsers.

Entire Network

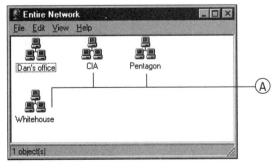

Figure 22-8
Open the globe to see various workgroups in your network.
A. Other workgroups I wouldn't mess with.

Using the Explorer/ Network Neighborhood connection

The Network Neighborhood also appears in the Explorer and in those little tree structures that appear in various drop-down lists. Using it there is no different from using other items on the Explorer, though you're opening up other computers to see what they have to offer rather than disk drives and folders on your own computer.

Figure 22-9 shows how the Explorer shows an open Network Neighborhood with the computer named Koby being examined. To continue to examine various items attached to another computer, keep Explorering them by using the collapsible tree structure — just as you would when you explore your own computer.

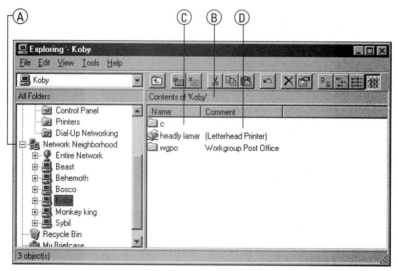

Figure 22-9
Exploring some other computer.
A. The Network Neighborhood is open. **B.** The right window shows the contents of the computer Koby. **C.** Koby is sharing two folders and a printer. **D.** The comments are entered whenever you name a shared resource.

Messing with Someone Else's Computer

When you're on a network, you're not limited to using only those goodies attached to your computer. You can save and open files on other computers as well as use another computer's printer. This is much easier than you may think.

Saving files elsewhere

Saving files is something that's pretty universal in Windows; just about every application uses the same steps (outlined in Chapter 4) for saving just about anything to disk. Saving your file on another computer is no different.

To save a file on another computer, follow these steps:

1. Choose File⇨Save As from the menu.

   The standard Save As dialog box appears.

2. Open the Network Neighborhood.

   Use the Save in drop-down list, and choose Network Neighborhood from the list. Windows displays a list of other computers available on the network (see Figure 22-10).

Figure 22-10
The Network Neighborhood is chosen for saving a file.
A. Pick Network Neighborhood from this list. **B.** Computers on the network.
C. Double-click on one of these to open it up.

3. Open the computer you want to save on.

   Double-click on the computer's icon. This step displays any folders shared on that computer.

   If no folders appear, that computer hasn't made its disk drives available for sharing. Oh, well. Try another computer if you're desperate.

4. Open the proper folder.

   Double-click on the folder you want to open. This step displays that folder's contents in the window, just as though that folder were opened on your own PC.

   You may be asked to enter a password here. Note that some folders have two passwords attached. You need the *full access* password in order to save a file on another computer. The read-only password does not let you save. See the section "Browsing other computers à la My Computer," earlier in this chapter.

5. Continue opening folders.

   Open folders until you find the one in which you want to save your file. At this point, using the Save As dialog box works exactly as it would for your own computer. In fact, it's often hard to tell the difference.

   Some computers share their root folder. For example, you see drive C's root folder up for sharing in Figure 22-6.

   Sometimes you may find an individual folder up for sharing. In Figure 22-6, for example, the folder Figures is shared on the Monkey King computer. Incidentally, that's the computer on my network where this book's figures are kept. Sharing a folder like that means that you have instant access to it from any other computer.

6. Type a name for the file.

   After finding the proper folder, type a filename. Do this just as you would on your computer.

7. Choose a file type.

   See Chapter 15 for more information about saving files as a specific type, in the section "Saving a file as a specific type."

8. Click on the Save button.

   The file is saved on another computer.

← You should also check out the section "Saving your stuff" in Chapter 4 for a general description of saving a file to disk.

Strange filenames on older Windows computers

Windows 95 can easily network with other computers running either the Windows for Workgroups or MS-DOS for Workgroups operating systems. You can use these computers just like any Windows 95 computer on the network. The only difference is that long filenames cannot be saved on them; instead of using a long name, the older operating system saves the file by using a *truncated name.*

The truncated name is merely the first six letters of the long name — no spaces — plus a tilde and a number. For example:

   Potato Salad

becomes:

   POTATO~1

on the non-Windows 95 computer. Unfortunately, when you go to open the file, it has that same name; the original, long name is forgotten.

My advice is to use only eight or fewer characters when you save a file on a non-Windows 95 computer. Furthermore, limit the filename to only letters and numbers; don't try any spaces, periods, or other fancy characters. That's easy enough to remember.

Opening files elsewhere

You can open any file anywhere on the network, if the other computer will grant you access to its disk drives. One of the best ways to find out is just to dive in to an Open dialog box and browse the Network Neighborhood to find out. Follow these steps:

1. Choose File⇨Open from the menu.

   One of those typical Open dialog boxes appears.

2. Open the Network Neighborhood.

   Choose Network Neighborhood from the Look in drop-down list. A list of other computers available on the network appears in the Open dialog box. (It looks like Figure 22-10, but the dialog box says Open instead).

The ordeal of mapping a network drive

In Chapter 14, Figure 14-2, you can see an illustration of a *mapped* network drive. That's a drive on someone else's computer that shows up just like one of the drives on your computer. To get one of these to appear, you have to go through the ordeal of mapping the drive, which is an about-face from the graphical ease of using something like the Network Neighborhood; to map a drive, you must know its cryptic network pathname. Yikes!

The only way to map a drive is to click on the Map Drive button on the toolbar in My Computer or the Explorer (so you must choose View⇨Toolbar first and then click on the button). This displays a dialog box in which you pick a drive letter for your computer (easy) and then type the network pathname for the networked drive (not so easy).

A network pathname looks like this:

   \\computer\resource

That's two backslashes, the name of the network computer, another backslash, and finally the shared resource. In Figure 22-9, for example, the network computer Koby is seen in the Network Neighborhood sharing its folder named C. Here is how that would look:

   \\koby\c

That's the network path you type in the Path input box to map drive C on Koby.

Click in the Reconnect at logon box if you want to have the mapped network drive always appear when you start your computer. A ✔ check mark appears in the box.

Whew! Like I said, this is no easy task. Maybe in a future version of Windows, they'll make it simpler to map a network drive.

3. Pick a computer to open.

   Find the computer you want to open a file on, and double-click on its icon. Any folders available on that computer are then displayed. If you don't see any folders, none is available; try another computer.

4. Open a folder.

   Double-click on a folder to open it. The folder's contents are then displayed in the window.

   ◄▥ Type a password if you're asked. See the section "Browsing other computers à la My Computer," earlier in this chapter, for more information.

5. Continue opening folders.

   Open folders and browse for that file you're looking for.

6. Double-click on the file you want to open.

   Eventually you find what you're looking for: a document, file, program, whatever. Double-click on it to open it. The file then appears in your application, ready for editing, or — if it was a program — the program runs, or whatever.

← Refer to the section "Opening stuff" in Chapter 4 for a general description of using the Open dialog box.

← If you open a file on another computer and then choose the Save command, the file is saved again on that computer. If you want to save it elsewhere, use the Save As command, as described in Chapter 4, in the section "Saving your stuff."

Using an alien printer

Your computer may not have its own printer. No problem — just steal someone else's from the network. Anyone who uses a computer with a printer attached and who is dopey enough to share it makes his printer available for anyone to use. In fact, you can even use his printer and use your own: Just make shortcuts to both printers on the desktop, and drag-and-drop stuff to print to either printer. It can really be quite swell.

To add a network printer to your hoard of printers, follow the steps outlined in Chapter 23, in the section "Tell me about your printer . . . ." There are only two differences:

   In step 4, choose the Network Printer option.

   Then, after step 4 and before step 5, you have to help Windows find your new network printer.

The new step after step 4 shows a dialog box asking you to find the network printer (see Figure 22-11).

← Use the Browse button to hunt down an available computer on the network. Follow the instructions in the preceding section, "Opening files elsewhere," for details about hunting down a shared printer; open various network computer icons until you find a printer. Click on that printer, and then click on OK.

After choosing your network printer, its ugly network name appears in the Network path or queue name box. For example:

   \\Koby\headly lamar

Be thankful that you didn't have to type that from memory. In Chapter 23, continue at step 5 in the section "Tell me about your printer . . . ."

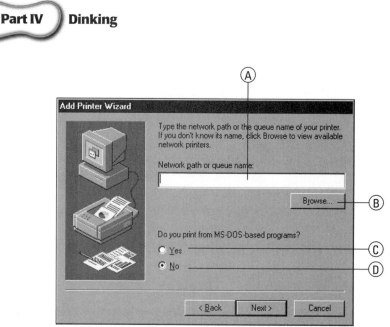

Figure 22-11
Where are you, O network printer?
A. Forget this! **B.** Use the Browse button to hunt down the network printer.
C. Click here if you're using any MS-DOS programs, such as the good old version of WordPerfect. **D.** No MS-DOS programs; click here.

Surrendering Your Hardware to the Network

If you want to be nice, you can have others use your PC's hardware, offering up your disk drives and printer for sharing on the network. There's really nothing to it, though you do have the option of slapping on various passwords and (my favorite) making your disk drives "read only" so that no one can alter or (gulp) accidentally erase anything on your system.

All the stuff you share on your computer is tagged with the little sharing-hand guy. He appears under disk drives, folders, or printers you've elected to share with your networking neighbors.

Sharing hard drives and folders

Sometimes you may want to let everyone else play with your entire hard drive. If so, just surrender the entire thing by sharing the disk drive itself. Other times, it's better just to share a folder or two. This not only limits the access others have to your computer but also makes it easier for them to find those folders, because they appear right there when your computer is opened in the Network Neighborhood.

To offer up any hard drive or folder to the net, follow these steps:

1. Locate the disk drive or folder you want to share.

   Use My Computer or the Explorer to find that special disk drive or folder.

   Keep in mind that when you choose a disk drive, you're sharing the entire drive.

2. Click on the folder or disk drive once to select it.

3. Choose File⇨Sharing.

   This step brings up a Properties dialog box for whichever drive or folder you chose, with the Sharing panel forward — sorta like Figure 22-12.

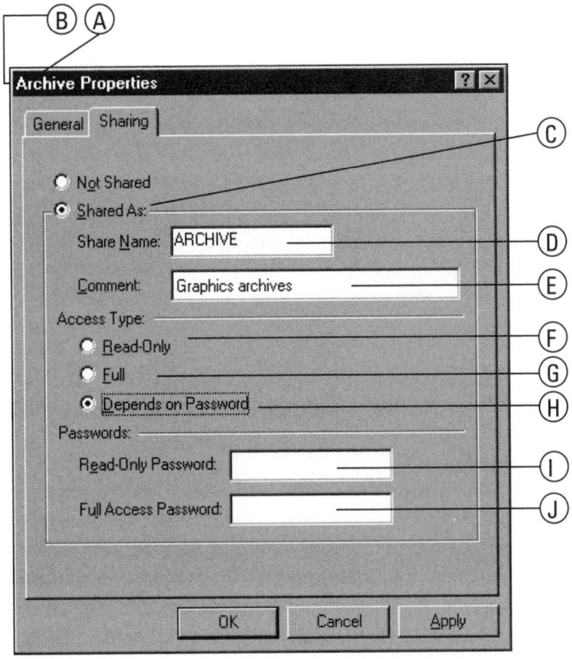

Figure 22-12
Surrendering something to the network gods.
A. The folder Archive is being shared. **B.** A disk drive letter would appear here if you were sharing an entire drive. **C.** Click here to share. **D.** The name others will see on the network. **E.** A comment, visible in the Details view in the Network Neighborhood. **F.** Others can only read information; no changing or deleting. **G.** Others have full access, just like you do. **H.** Access depends on which password they type. **I.** Optional read-only-access password. **J.** Optional full-access password.

4. Click on Shared As.

   This step surrenders the disk drive or folder for sharing.

   That's really it. Anything else you set in the dialog box is optional at this point. The disk drive or folder is shared and everyone else has full access when you click on OK. But . . .

   . . . click on Read Only to permit others to only browse your disk drive and not allow them to add, change, or delete anything. This is a safe bet. You can even limit access further by typing a password in the Read-Only Password input box. That way, they can access the drive only if they type the proper password, and then they still can't change anything.

   Click on Full only to give everyone else the same access you have. You can optionally enter a password in the Full Access Password input box. That way, they can have full access only if they type the proper password.

   Click on the Depends on Password option to grant access depending on which password they type. In this case, you have to enter a password in each input box. Whoever tries to play with your computer will have either read-only or full access, depending on which password they guess correctly.

   You can still access your disk drives from your own computer, no matter what the password.

   The name you type in the Share name text box is the name others see attached to that folder in the Network Neighborhood. Normally this should be just the name of the disk drive or folder that's shared, but you can type anything you like. And as a secret, if you stick a dollar-sign character ($) at the end of the name, that folder does not appear in the Network Neighborhood — even though it's still shared. Type **C$** rather than **C**, for example, to share drive C secretly.

5. Click on OK.

   Humma-humma-humma. Eventually you see the sharing hand appear under whatever it was you shared. It's now up and on the net.

By the way, you can reverse this process at any time. All you have to do is repeat the preceding steps and choose Not Shared from the dialog box in step 4.

Sharing your printer

Surrendering your printer to everyone else on the network is almost as cinchy as sharing a disk drive:

1. Open up the Control Panel.

   Find a Control Panel near you, or choose it from the Start Thing's menu: Press Ctrl+Esc, S, C.

   Control Panel

2. Open up the Printers folder.

   Double-click on the Printers folder to open it. You see the Printers window, in which all sorts of printers and faxes live.

3. Choose the printer you want to share.

   Click once on your printer's icon.

   Printers

4. Choose File⇨Sharing.

   This step brings up the printer's Properties dialog box with the Sharing panel up front and ready for action, similar to what you see in Figure 22-13.

5. Click on the Shared As radio button.

   This step shares the printer. That's really it, though you can toy around with the other options in the dialog box.

   My advice is not to password-protect any printer. Having to enter a password every time you print is a major pain in the butt; if there's any reason to give your printer a password, just don't share it on the network.

6. Click on OK.

   You're done. The printer is up on the network, and soon you see the little sharing-hand guy under it, meaning that it's all cozy and ready to go.

If there's any reason you want to stop sharing your printer on the network, just choose Not Shared in step 5. Be sure to let others on the network who might have been using your printer know that it's no longer available.

Also check out Chapter 19, which discusses in depth the use of a printer on your PC. Everything in there that applies to a local printer applies also to a network model.

Stop! Oh, Yes, Wait a Minute, Mr. Postman!

Network mail can be a pain. In fact, I'm not even going to mention how it gets configured and all that, because most people who configure such things are paid lots of money and don't want their secrets revealed. (Truthfully, network mail is a whole book unto itself.)

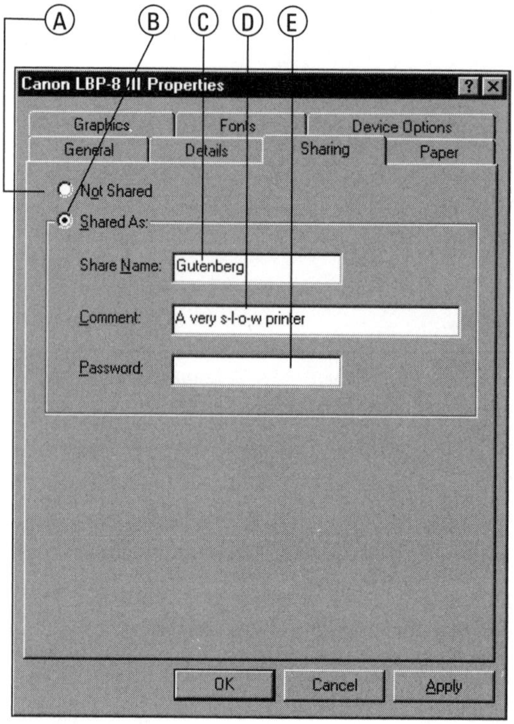

(A) (B) (C) (D) (E)

Canon LBP-8 !II Properties

| Graphics | Fonts | Device Options |
| General | Details | Sharing | Paper |

○ Not Shared

◉ Shared As:

Share Name: Gutenberg

Comment: A very s-l-o-w printer

Password:

OK   Cancel   Apply

Figure 22-13
A printer's Properties dialog box.
A. Click here to stop sharing a printer. **B.** Click here to share a printer. **C.** The printer's name as others will see it on the network. **D.** Optional rude comments. **E.** Optional pointless printer-access password.

There are really only two things you want to do with mail: Read any mail you get, and send mail to other people. Before doing that, you have to get acquainted with the Exchange program, which is Windows' mail-manager program.

Odds are real good that you may have a different mail program from the Exchange program provided "free" with Windows. You should consult with your office's network manager for tips about using your mail system.

If your office is small enough, I recommend using WinPopup for most of your messaging. WinPopup is covered in the section "The joys of WinPopup," at the end of this chapter.

Fussing with the Exchange program

Windows mail is brought to you by the Exchange program. I hate that name. It sounds like those little booths in international airports where they over-charge you to swap money. I suppose that they can't call it just "mail" because you can't copyright that name. *C'est la guerre.*

There are two versions of Exchange: the cheapie version that ships with Windows and a more expensive version available from Microsoft. Both of them are horrid, and the more expensive one even more so.

Exchange can be found off the Start Thing's menu; choose Programs➪Microsoft Exchange. You may also see the Inbox icon on your desktop, in which case you can click on it to start Exchange.

Inbox

After you start Exchange, you'll probably want to minimize it; click on the Minimize button in the window's upper right corner. You can keep Exchange as a button on the taskbar until you're ready to compose new messages or read your mail.

All the following sections assume that you've started Exchange and that it sits waiting as a button on the taskbar.

← Exchange is a great program to have start automatically every time you start Windows. Refer to the section "Applications that Amazingly Start Automatically" in Chapter 6 for more information.

Checking your mail

When new mail arrives, your computer beeps, and you see the friendly mail guy appear near the Loud Time on the taskbar. Double-click on him to pop up the Exchange and read your new mail (see Figure 22-14).

Any unread mail you have appears in your Inbox mail list in bold type; double-click on it to read it. This displays the mail reader, where you can view the message, reply to it, or forward it to someone else. Figure 22-15 shows where the buttons are that you push.

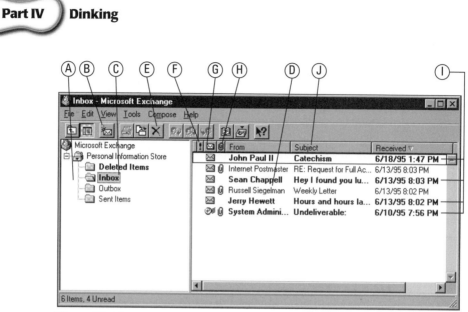

Figure 22-14

The joys of getting new mail in the Exchange program.

A. Your mail folder list. **B.** Click here to compose a new message. **C.** The Inbox is highlighted. **D.** Messages in your Inbox. **E.** Click here to delete a message (move it into your Deleted Items folder). **F.** Priority-message flag. **G.** Type of message (e-mail or return receipt). **H.** The paper clip means that there's an "attachment" to the message. **I.** Unread messages; double-click to read them. **J.** Click on a heading to sort your Inbox by that item.

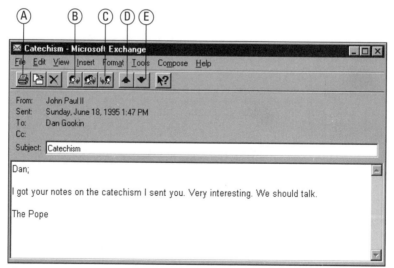

Figure 22-15

The mail reader window.

A. Print the message. **B.** Reply to the sender. **C.** Forward this message to someone else. **D.** See the preceding message in your Inbox. **E.** See the next message in your Inbox.

Sending mail

To send a new message, choose Compose⇨New Message from the Exchange's menu. Or you can click on the wee little New Message button on the toolbar. This starts up a text editor for you to type your message (or it may start a special version of Microsoft Word, if you have Word). The New Message editor is shown in Figure 22-16.

Unlike a normal text editor, however, you have to fill in the To, Subject, and optionally the CC (carbon copy) input boxes.

Fill in the body of the message just as you would when you're writing a letter. Keep in mind that most people tend to write e-mail casually, yet people tend to take e-mail just as seriously as they do any business letter. Try not to be clever or quirky when it can easily be misinterpreted. Save the humor for the phone.

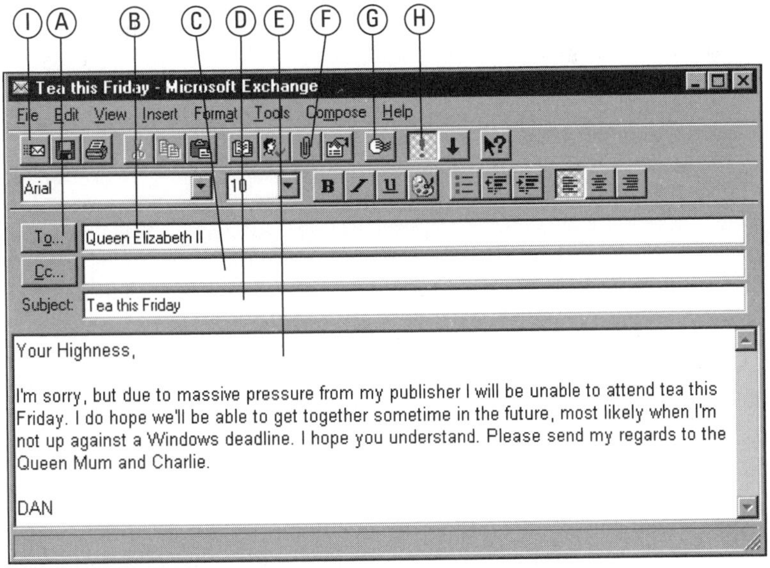

Figure 22-16
The new message text editor.
A. Click here to pull a name from your personal address book. **B.** Or just type the name here. **C.** Carbon copies are entered here. **D.** The message subject. **E.** Body of the message. **F.** Click here to add a file attachment. **G.** Click here if you want a receipt (an indication that the message was received). **H.** Click here to make it a priority message. **I.** Click here to send the message.

Choose File➪Send to send your message, or click on the wee little Send button on the toolbar.

The Joys of WinPopup

WinPopup can be really handy and much simpler to use than a full-on mail program. In a two-person office, it's about all you need. The only thing you can't do with it is send files back and forth.

◀━━ You may not be blessed with WinPopup's presence on your computer. If so, you have to install it manually. Refer to the section "Adding the Rest of Windows" in Chapter 13 for information about adding WinPopup.

Start WinPopup by choosing it from the Start Thing's WinPopup menu. It should be in the Programs➪Accessories submenu. WinPopup appears in Figure 22-17.

Figure 22-17
WinPopup is used for instant messaging.
A. Click here to send a message.
B. Trashes the current message.
C. See the preceding message.
D. See the next message.
E. Who sent what. **F.** The message. **G.** When WinPopup is active, you're alerted when network printing jobs are printed.

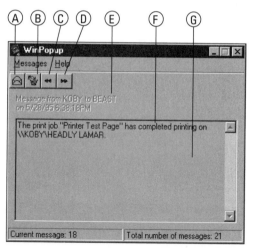

━▶ If you can't find WinPopup, see Chapter 32 for information about tracking down lost programs. When you find WinPopup, add it to the Start Thing's Startup submenu, as described in Chapter 6, in the section "Adding WinPopup programs to the Startup menu."

To send a message, click on the little envelope button. Type the user's name (how she's logging in to her computer), or type the computer name. Press the Tab key, and then type the message (see Figure 22-18). Click on OK to send it.

Figure 22-18
Sending a message in WinPopup.
A. Type the user's name or computer name here. **B.** If you click here, you send a message to everyone in the workgroup. Oops! **C.** Message goes here. **D.** Click here to send.

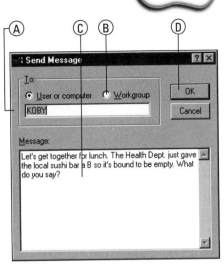

Unlike a real mail program, there's nothing fancy with a WinPopup message. You can't send files, you can't schedule mail, and you can't get your mail at another computer. But it's not a big hassle to install or use, either.

Remember to minimize WinPopup when you're done; don't quit. If you quit, you can't get any new messages. WinPopup warns you about this if you do try to quit.

Part IV Dinking

Installing New Hardware

Chapter

23

In This Chapter

- Setting up new hardware (the software side)
- Configuring for a new printer
- Removing an old printer

Installing new hardware isn't really a hassle. Anyone with a screwdriver, a few minutes of time, and a good book of instructions can add any component to a PC. No problem. What was a problem, however, was getting that new something to work properly with your software. That's no longer a problem because Windows now comes with a Hardware Installation Wizard, which automatically does the software part of your hardware setup for you.

This chapter does not go into detail about the hardware side of installation. It's assumed that you've already set up, screwed in, or attached some new hardware gizmo to your PC and have just replugged it in and turned on the power. Only after doing that do you need to follow the instructions in this chapter.

Adding a New Something to Your Computer

Pretty much anything you add to your computer can be detected by Windows and configured automatically. This is all part of the new *Plug-and-Play* standard, a feature of

Windows that enables it to scrutinize, identify, and properly set up your software to work well with your hardware.

On the up side, Plug-and-Play means that you don't have to mess with a CONFIG.SYS or AUTOEXEC.BAT file or any of the INI files that plagued earlier versions of Windows. On the down side, Microsoft admits that its software will recognize and properly configure only 95 percent of the hardware out there. The other 5 percent consists of old stuff that you probably don't have. But in the future, just about anything will be easily detected and set up by Windows, all thanks to Plug-and-Play (which the wags have dubbed "Plug-and-Pray").

⟶ If you've just added a printer, see the section "Installing a Brand-New Printer," later in this chapter.

⟶ If you've just upgraded to a new monitor, you should turn to the sidebar "Picking a monitor" in Chapter 24. It's not really necessary to choose a monitor type unless you're messing with your screen resolution, which is also covered in that chapter.

If you've just set up an external piece of hardware, such as a modem or external CD-ROM drive, turn it on before you go through the following steps. Windows can't find your hardware unless you turn it on first.

After setting up your hardware and restarting Windows, follow these steps to complete your hardware installation:

1. Open the Control Panel.

   There are many ways to find a Control Panel near you. There's a Control Panel folder icon right in My Computer's main window. You can also fire up the Control Panel from the Start Thing's main menu: Press Ctrl+Esc, S, C to see its lovely window displayed.

   Control Panel

2. Open the Add New Hardware icon.

   Double-click on the Add New Hardware icon. This step starts the Add New Hardware wizard, and because this chapter is kind of thin, I'm going to show you all the steps with figures attached. The opening dialog box is shown in Figure 23-1, though it's dull and truly boring.

   Add New
   Hardware

3. Click on Next.

   Moving right along, Windows next asks whether you want do this manually or automatically. No masochists here, so keep the dot in the Yes radio button (see Figure 23-2).

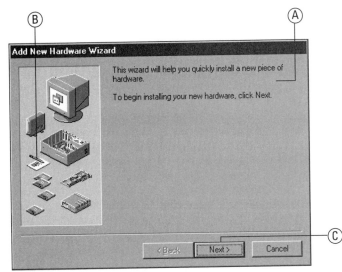

Figure 23-1
The boring opening dialog box.
A. Yeah, yeah. **B.** Why is there always a pencil? **C.** Click here to move forward.

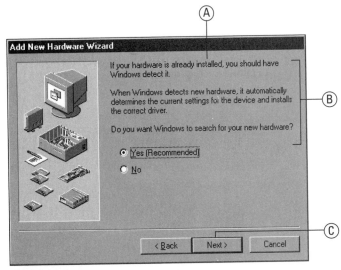

Figure 23-2
Another boring dialog box.
A. Of course, there is no option if your hardware *isn't* already installed.
B. Yes, Yes, Yes. **C.** Click here to move forward.

If you click on No, Windows merely presents you with a list of new items that *could* have been installed. You pick one and then pick the brand name and model number in additional dialog boxes. Eventually Windows confirms your choices and sets things up. But because this is a computer and because they're *supposed* to make life easier, you should stick with the Yes option.

4. Click on Next.

   Windows warns you that it might seize on you while it's looking for your new hardware. Hey, if you want perfection, you should have bought a Macintosh. Figure 23-3 echoes these sentiments.

5. Click on Next.

   It's the detection stage, similar to the last stage but with a progress thermometer along the bottom of the dialog box (see Figure 23-4). Now Windows is searching high and low for any hardware changes you've made.

   This will take a few hundred moments.

   Like the instructions say, if your computer stops working for a while — meaning that you don't see the thermometer move or that the hard drive chipmunks seem to have died — then you have to reset your computer. Please wait an *extra* two minutes after you've made this decision before you really do reset.

   If you have to reset: Turn your computer off. Wait about 40 seconds. Then turn the computer on again. Start over with your installation procedure, but do it manually (choose No in step 3.)

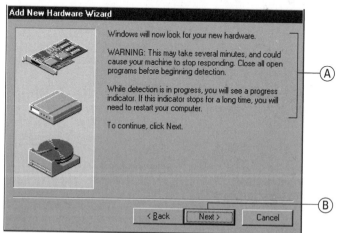

Figure 23-3
Nothing to do here.
A. Our software is unreliable, so you take a chance here. **B.** Moving right along.

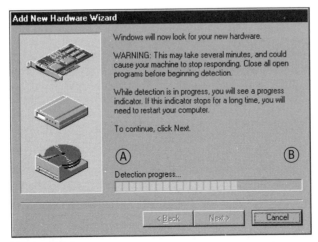

Figure 23-4
Windows is looking, looking, looking.
A. This moves from here . . . **B.** . . . to here.

6. Windows found your hardware!

   The very next dialog box (see Figure 23-5) shows that Windows has found something new and has set it up. To see the new something (or somethings) displayed, click on the Details button, as was done in the figure.

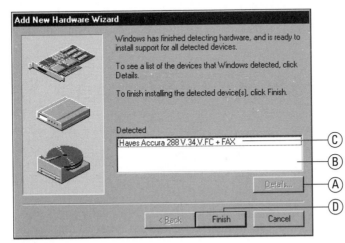

Figure 23-5
Alors! Some new hardware thingy was installed.
A. Click here. **B.** To see this. **C.** Windows found my new modem. **D.** Click here when you're done ogling.

7. Click on the Finish button.

   You're done.

Well, not really. Depending on what was installed, there may be additional verification or configuration. What happens next really depends on what was installed. With my modem, for example, Windows next went through verification of the modem (whatever that means; the dialog box just said "OK," and that was it). Your hardware may require additional setup, depending on what it does.

Just keep working your way through the end of the wizard. When it disappears from the screen, or in those rare instances in which you may have to reset, you'll be ready to begin using your new hardware.

➡ If you have any trouble with your new hardware, you can use Windows' Hardware Troubleshooting Wizard. This subject is covered in Chapter 31, right up front.

Installing a Brand-New Printer

Windows probably asked you a dozen questions about your printer when it was installed. Great. But if you bought your PC with Windows already on it or if you just added a new printer, you have to tell Windows about it. This is a must; after Windows knows about your printer, you can print anything you can see on the screen. It's really much easier than the bad old days, when you had to go through these steps for every piece of software you used. Yech.

Tell me about your printer ...

To set up Windows to use your printer, follow these steps:

1. Open up the Control Panel.

   Find a Control Panel near you, or choose it from the Start Thing's menu: Press Ctrl+Esc, S, C.

   Control Panel

2. Open up the Printers folder.

   Double-click on the Printers folder to open it. You see the Printers window, where all sorts of printers and faxes live.

   ⬅ See Chapter 19 for more information about the printing thing.

Printers

3. Double-click on the Add Printer icon.

This step opens a Hardware Wizard thing, which enables you to set up a printer on your computer. It's basically a step-by-step thing with lots of purty pictures. (The steps here point out only the highlights; no sense in echoing all those splendid graphics.)

Add Printer

4. Click on the Next button.

The How is this printer attached to your computer? panel appears, as shown in Figure 23-6. Click on Local printer unless you're shackled to a network.

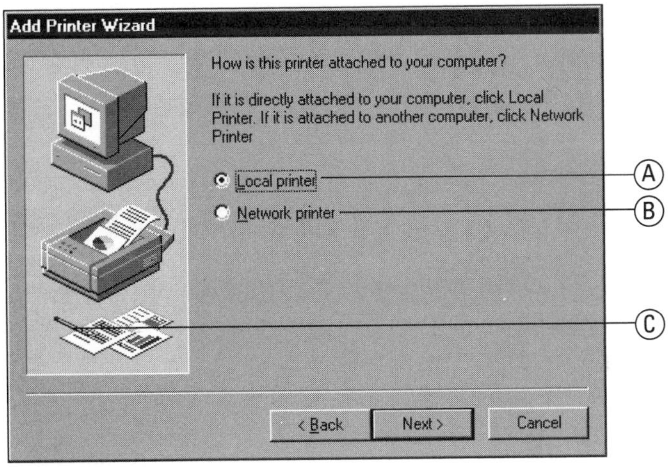

Figure 23-6
How is my printer attached?
A. Click here if the printer is right there next to your computer. **B.** Click here if the printer is on a network somewhere. **C.** The damn pencil again.

Even if your computer is going to be available, or "shared," on the network, click on Local printer if it's directly connected to your computer.

If you're installing a network printer, refer to Chapter 22, the section "Using an alien printer," for another step that goes right here.

5. Click on the Next button.

Now you get to tell Windows which brand and model of printer you have. There is quite a list to choose from (see Figure 23-7).

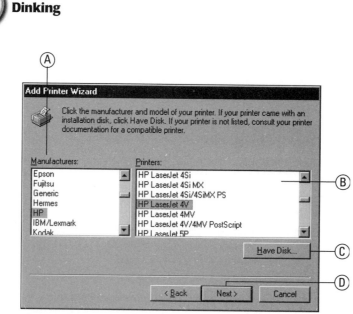

Figure 23-7
Pick your printer from the list.
A. Pick the brand name first. **B.** Choose a model number from this list. **C.** If you can't find either but your printer came with a disk, click on this button. **D.** Click on Next after you're done.

Pick the brand name first.

Pick the model number second. You should look on your computer for hints about a brand name and model; most are pretty obvious. Sometimes you may have to look at the printer's rump for a name and model number.

If your printer isn't on the list but came with an installation disk, stick the disk in drive A and click on the Have Disk button.

6. Click on the Next button.

Choose how the printer is connected to your computer. Normally you pick LPT1, your computer's first printer port. This option is, thankfully, already highlighted on the screen for you.

7. Click on the Next button.

Now you get to give your printer a name. Trudge through the dialog box, as shown in Figure 23-8.

Windows lets you have several printers installed, but you can choose only one as your main printer (the, ugh, *default* one). Refer to the section "Choosing your main printer" in Chapter 19 for more information about setting your main printer from a gaggle of other printers.

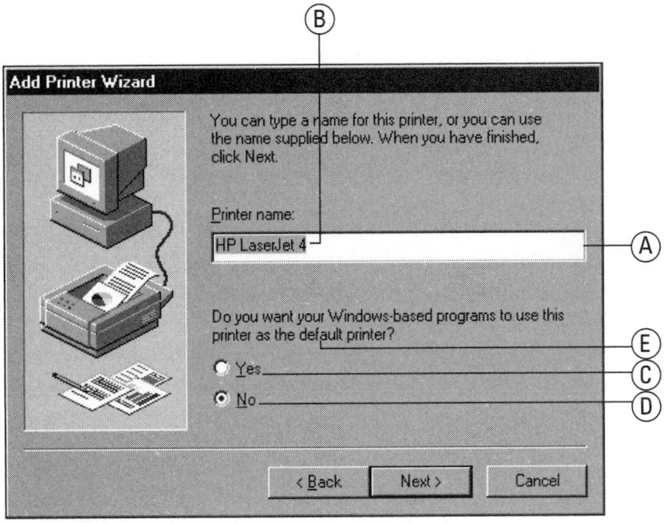

Figure 23-8
Name that printer!
A. Type a cute name for your printer here. **B.** Already entered is the printer's brand name. Bor-ing. **C.** Click here if you want to use this as your main printer. **D.** Click here only if you're installing a secondary printer. **E.** I hate this word.

8. Click on the Next button.

   Would you like to print a test page? This can be fun. Make sure that there's a dot in the Yes radio button, and then do the next step.

   The test page ensures that your printer is hooked up properly and working just fine. Frame it as the first thing you printed in Windows on your printer.

9. Click on the Finish button.

   You're done. If you've chosen to print a test page, it prints now. A dialog box announces that the page has printed. Click on the Yes button if everything was okay. If not, click on the No button to run through some troubleshooting.

If you've installed a network printer, the page prints elsewhere on the network. Run around madly looking for it, and, when you find it, hold the test page up over your head and grin with glee.

"There's a stupid printer installed here, and I want to get rid of it"

If you've just changed printers, you'll probably want to get rid of the old one. This is just too silly; to get rid of the old printer, simply delete it from your Printers folder. Poof! It's gone.

My advice is not to delete the printer. You can leave it hanging around "just in case." Suppose that your new printer breaks and goes back to the shop, or maybe someone else (some manager doody-head) in the office steals your newer printer and gives you back the old one. Then it's merely a matter of switching your "main printer" in the Printers window; no reinstallation is required.

See Chapter 19, the section "Yo, my main printer," for information about making one printer out of the hoards in your Printers window your main printer.

Part V

Mouse

Control Panel

Sounds

Having Fun

In this part

- Changing Windows' look
- Interesting, weird, and neat stuff
- Fun, games, and frivolity

How do I...?

Put that trendy picture of Judge Lance Ito on my desktop?

Windows enables you to change the way the desktop looks so that, even when Judge Ito isn't trendy anymore, you can change your desktop to the next, latest fad.

➤ See the section "Wallpaper without the glue" in Chapter 24 for more information about slapping an image into Windows' desktop.

Change the ugly colors Windows uses?

Windows colors don't match everyone's appetite, so you can change them. Want a green menu? Got it. Brown highlights? Sounds great. Or maybe change the whole scheme at once to something more like ice cream. Yeah. That's the ticket.

➤ Chapter 24 discusses changing Windows' looks at length. See the section "Making the Windows Color Scheme Match Your Office" for more information.

Make Windows more fun?

There's so much you can do, from animating the mouse pointer to assigning a special sound to everything Windows does. It's all covered in Chapter 25.

➤ To add sounds to Windows' normal activities, see the section "Making Windows noisy" in Chapter 25.

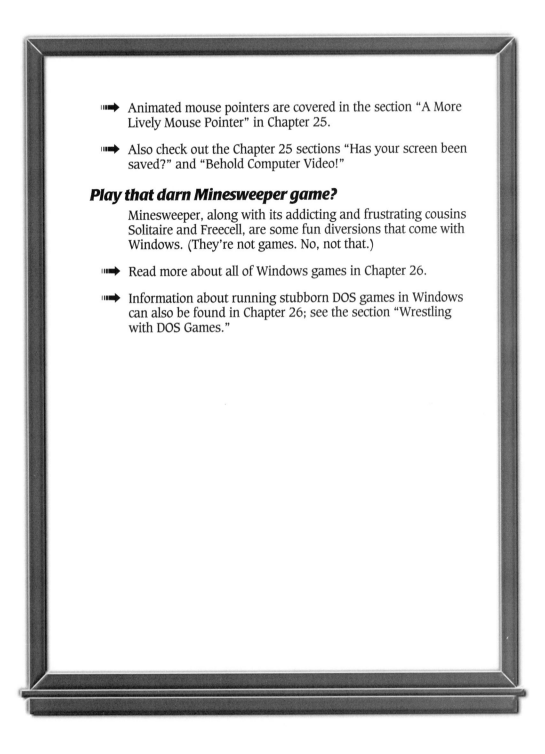

➡ Animated mouse pointers are covered in the section "A More Lively Mouse Pointer" in Chapter 25.

➡ Also check out the Chapter 25 sections "Has your screen been saved?" and "Behold Computer Video!"

Play that darn Minesweeper game?

Minesweeper, along with its addicting and frustrating cousins Solitaire and Freecell, are some fun diversions that come with Windows. (They're not games. No, not that.)

➡ Read more about all of Windows games in Chapter 26.

➡ Information about running stubborn DOS games in Windows can also be found in Chapter 26; see the section "Wrestling with DOS Games."

Changing Windows' Look

Chapter 24

In This Chapter

- Understanding the desktop background
- Summoning the Desktop Properties dialog box
- Changing the desktop pattern
- Changing the desktop wallpaper
- Altering the screen resolution
- Choosing a new color scheme
- Moving the taskbar
- Adjusting the taskbar's behavior
- Working with the Microsoft Office toolbar ("MOM")

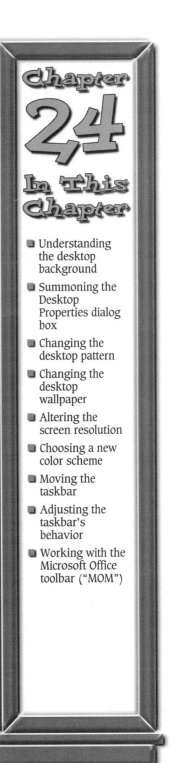

Windows has some basic parts that don't change: The gizmos on a window and the gadgets in a dialog box are pretty much there for good. But you can change certain aspects of Windows, primarily the way it looks. Specifically, you can change the screen resolution, the color scheme, and the graphics you see in the background. You can also move around the taskbar and even rearrange your MOM (if you have one on your screen). All this is covered here. And all rather tastefully too.

Background Information

The background you see when you work in Windows is called the desktop. But how the desktop looks can be changed. You can choose either an exciting pattern for the desktop or an interesting graphical image, appropriately called *wallpaper.* Figures 24-1 through 24-3 show several examples of background wallpapers and patterns.

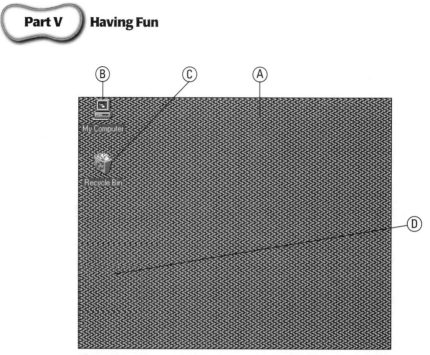

Figure 24-1
The Dizzy pattern (as though using a computer isn't annoying enough).
A. This is a pattern: black and green over and over. **B.** My Computer (see Chapter 2). **C.** Recycle Bin (see Chapter 3). **D.** Everything else on the desktop is optional.

Since you're curious about it, the image of Judge Ito in Figure 24-3 was stolen from the Internet. I downloaded the image (which is probably copyrighted, so this is the only edition of this book that will contain it) and then saved it to disk as a Windows bitmap graphics file in the Windows folder. Any bitmap graphics file you save in the Windows folder appears available for wallpaper duty on the desktop; keep reading.

You can create your own wallpaper lickety-split by using the Windows Paint program. This is how the background image in Figure 17-10 was created. In fact, when you use Paint, you see two items in the File menu: Set as Wallpaper (Tiled) and Set as Wallpaper (Centered). Save your image in Paint, and then choose either item to have your work of art appear as wallpaper. See Chapter 9 for more information about Paint; keep reading for information about Tiled and Centered wallpaper.

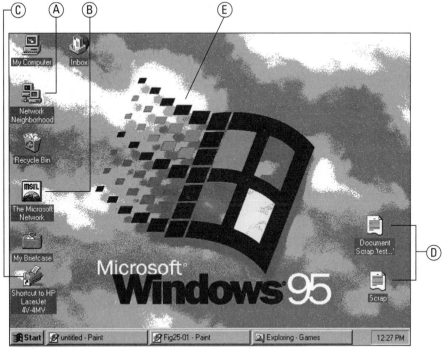

Figure 24-2
The Windows 95 background (Microsoft loyalist).
A. See Chapter 22 for more information about this. **B.** The Microsoft Network is talked about in Chapter 11. **C.** See Chapter 17 for information about pasting a printer on the desktop. **D.** Scrap files dragged or pasted to the desktop (see Chapter 8). **E.** This wallpaper file, named Win95, comes on the Windows installation CD.

Figure 24-3
A trendy image of a Judge Lance Ito background.
A. This is handy if you dink a lot; see Chapter 20. **B.** Pasted shortcuts to current work; see the section "Sticking stuff on the desktop" in Chapter 17. **C.** You can drag icons on the desktop just about anywhere. **D.** See Chapter 7, the section "Having Fun with the Loud Time." **E.** The Microsoft Office Menu (MOM), as discussed later in this chapter.

The first step in changing Windows' look

To change the way Windows looks, you have to access the Display Properties dialog box. Here are the steps:

1. Right-click the mouse on a blank part of the desktop.

   Click the mouse's right button on the desktop. This step makes the desktop's shortcut menu appear.

2. Choose Properties from the shortcut menu.

   The Display Properties dialog box appears, as shown in Figure 24-4.

3. Click on the proper tab to bring whichever panel forward.

   There are four panels, each of which adjusts something clever with the screen or desktop background.

The only panel not covered in this chapter is Screen Saver. See Chapter 26, the section "Saving the Screen from Boredom," for more information about it.

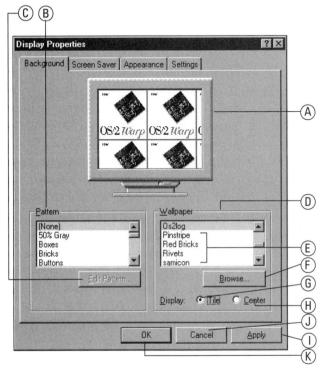

Figure 24-4
The Display Properties dialog box, with the Background
panel in the foreground.
A. The preview window, in which you can see how your choices affect the
screen. Right now, the exciting OS/2 Warp logo appears tiled on the screen.
B. Choose a pattern from this list to give the screen a cheap look. **C.** The
patterns are simply an arrangement of black-and-slate-colored squares. You
can edit them or create a new pattern by clicking this button. **D.** You must first
choose the None option at the top of this list to choose a pattern (on the other
side of the dialog box). **E.** Choose one of the various graphics bitmap files in
the Windows folder to preview how it will look on the little screen above.
F. You can click the Browse button to scope out a bitmap image file elsewhere
on your hard drive. However, I recommend saving in your Windows folder any
bitmap graphics file you may want to use as wallpaper. **G.** Smaller graphical
patterns should be tiled so that they fill the entire screen. **H.** Some graphics
should be centered: larger images and those that look better in the middle of
the screen. **I.** Click here to preview how the screen will look without making
any permanent changes. **J.** Click here to forget it. **K.** Click here when you've
chosen a new pattern and are ready to commit to it.

Choosing some fancy desktop patterns

Desktop patterns are boring. They're basically two-color graphics images that yawn with excitement. In fact, the only true advantage to picking a pattern for your desktop background is that it takes up less memory than wallpaper does and that it's faster to draw on the screen. So if you have a PC that's low on memory or with an ancient, sluggish graphics system, pick a pattern.

To choose a pattern, follow these steps:

1. Bring up the Display Properties dialog box, as discussed in the preceding section.

2. Click on the Background tab to bring that panel forward.

3. In the Wallpaper area, make sure that the None option is chosen.

4. Choose a pattern.

   Tulip is nice. It matches my paper towels. I don't understand Field Effect. Cargo Net is cool. Pick whatever pleases you. (Guys, you can always pick Daisies and tell your male friends that they're U-boat propellers.)

   Scroll through the list to find a pattern that thrills you.

   Click on the pattern once with the mouse to preview it in the monitor preview window.

   If you don't like the black-and-slate-colored background, you can change the slate color to something else. See the section "Making the Windows Color Scheme Match Your Office," later in this chapter. In the Display Properties dialog box Appearance panel, choose a new pattern color from the Color drop-down list.

5. Click on OK.

   This step locks in your pattern choice and returns you to the desktop to view your choice with pride.

Wallpaper without the glue

Wallpaper is much more exciting than the desktop patterns, primarily because they're colorful. Windows comes with a whole collection of them, and you can use any bitmap graphics image — even one you create yourself by using Paint — as wallpaper. You can let your creative juices flow to make your own, download an image by Michelangelo from the Internet, or use a scanner to scan in pictures of your kids to have as wallpaper.

To pick out wallpaper for the desktop, follow these steps:

1. Summon the Display Properties dialog box.

   Refer to the section "The first step in changing Windows' looks," earlier in this chapter, for directions.

2. Click on the Background tab to bring that panel forward if it isn't already.

3. In the Pattern area, make sure that the None option is chosen.

4. Choose a Wallpaper image.

   Scroll through the list, and click on each image name by using the mouse.

   Experiment with the Tile and Center buttons to see which method displays your image better.

   ⬅︎ If you don't see your graphics file here, click the Browse button to find it elsewhere on your computer. Refer to Chapter 17, the section "Working with folder trees in the Save As, Open, and Browse dialog boxes," for information about locating a file in a specific folder.

5. Click on OK.

   Your newly chosen background image appears on the screen, ready to impress the neighbors.

The Screen-Resolution Revolution

Here's a tip you'll never hear about on those infomercial real estate shows: It's possible to increase the size of your desktop without buying a larger monitor. Imagine your cozy 640-by-480-pixel lot enlarged to an 800-by-600 — or even a 1024-by-768-pixel ranch, all without buying a new monitor. This can be really nice, enabling you to see more windows on the screen, more icons on the desktop, more of everything without losing a penny.

To change your screen-size real estate, follow these steps:

1. Conjure up the Display Properties dialog box.

   Refer to the instructions in the section "The first step in changing Windows' looks," earlier in this chapter.

2. Click on the Settings panel to bring it forward.

   The Settings panel in the Display Properties dialog box is shown in Figure 24-5. You can goof around here all day if you like, using the preview window in the dialog box to see how the changes affect your system. Just click the Cancel button to chicken out and leave.

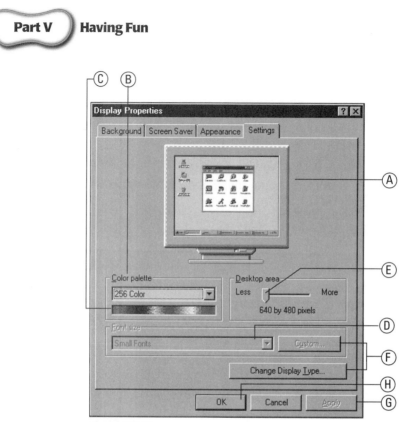

Figure 24-5

The Display Properties dialog box, with the Settings panel front and center. **A.** If you're having trouble visualizing what a new resolution will look like, gander here to see how your screen will be affected. **B.** Here you set the number of colors available. For kicks, change this value to 16, then to 256, and then to any higher values that are available. **C.** Look here to see how the number of colors affects what you see on the screen. The low values look truly gross. **D.** Here you can set the size of the text used by Windows. Small Fonts is okay most of the time, though at higher resolutions you'll probably want Large Fonts, to preserve your eyesight. **E.** Drag this real-estate-changing slider switch doojobbie with the mouse pointer to change the screen's resolution. Be sure to observe the preview window to see how things look. **F.** Don't bother. **G.** Click here if you're just testing. **H.** Click here to make the changes permanent.

3. Choose a new resolution from the Desktop area.

   Don't slam the slider all the way up to the highest value right away. Instead, first settle on the next highest resolution. For example, drag the slider until you see "800 by 600 pixels" displayed.

   If you choose a higher resolution, you may also want to choose Large Fonts from the Font size area. Or you can skip this option, run through the rest of the steps, and do it later if you really need to.

4. Choose a new color value from the Color palette.

   Click on the down arrow to drop down the drop-down list. Then pluck out a new color value.

   Don't pick 16! It's too stupid.

   The 256 value is okay. Anything higher is great for working on high-end graphics applications, such as Adobe Illustrator and those "morphing" programs, and seeing computer video.

5. Click on OK.

   At this point, Windows may wonder about your monitor type. Your monitor might not have been chosen during installation. See the nearby sidebar "Picking a monitor" for more information.

6. There is an off chance that Windows may want to restart itself now.

   This step depends on the options you chose. Normally, if you change only the resolution, Windows doesn't balk; skip to step 7. But if you change the font size or number of colors, Windows may request a reset. If so, click the Yes button when asked whether you want to reset now.

   Windows starts over again to test the new display options. Don't panic at anything you read on the screen! Log in. Read your tip-o-day. Enjoy your new screen resolution.

   Of course, you can't chicken out now. You have to start over again if you want to change back.

7. Read the Info dialog box.

   What it means is that Windows will try out the new resolution. After switching over, it gives you 15 seconds to say, "Yeah, this is cool." Otherwise, it switches back. If the new resolution doesn't work, you don't see anything on the screen, so just sit tight.

8. Click on OK.

   Psychedelic, eh?

9. You resized the desktop. Do you want to keep this setting?

   Click on Yes if it looks okay. Click on No if not. Or just sit stunned, and after 16 seconds Windows will switch back. Click on OK in the dialog box that's displayed if Windows switches back on you.

   If you do give up, be sure to close the Display Properties dialog box by clicking its × Close button.

By the way, you may notice that the text is teensy-tiny in those large resolutions. Better rework the preceding steps and choose Large Fonts when I told you to.

Picking a monitor

Here are the steps you have to go through if Windows suddenly remembers that it doesn't know which type of monitor is sitting on top of (or nearby) your computer:

1. **In the Change Display Type dialog box, locate the Monitor Type area.**

2. **Click on the Change button.** You see the Select Device dialog box.

3. **Choose your monitor's manufacturer from the list under Manufacturers.** If it says Gateway 2000 on your monitor, for example, choose Gateway from the list.

4. **Choose the monitor's model number from the list under Models.** For example, it says Crystal Scan 1024 NI on the monitor, in which case you choose that item from the list. You might also check the back of the monitor for a more detailed name.

   If your monitor make and model aren't visible, choose Standard monitor types from the Manufacturers' list, and then pluck out a model that matches the resolution you want, such as Super VGA 800 × 600. Cross your fingers.

5. **Click on OK.** The Select Device dialog box goes away.

6. **Click Close.** The Change Display Type dialog box sulks off.

7. **Continue changing the resolution.**

Pixel this!

Pixels are graphic dots on the screen. Each dot can be a different color, which is how you see an image on the monitor. The more dots, the higher the resolution and crisper the image.

An average resolution displays 640 pixels across and 480 pixels down, for a grid of 300,000-something dots on the screen. A higher resolution is 800-by-600 pixels, or even 1024-by-768 pixels, which can display very fine images. Some users prefer the higher resolutions because they can see more information on the screen.

After pixels comes the number of colors that can be displayed at one time. Typically, most Windows users want to see 256 colors at a time, which is pretty splashy. Cheaper PC video systems may not be able to handle 256 colors, so they display only 16 colors at a time. More advanced systems can display thousands of colors at one time. The actual number depends on your video system as well as on the resolution on the screen.

Of course, there is a minor speed penalty to pay for setting a high resolution, because Windows takes more time to deal with more pixels on the screen. But who cares! If you don't like the display, you can always change it back.

Making the Windows Color Scheme Match Your Office

If you've just done up your office or computer room in trendy earth tones (which are coming back, by the way), you may want Windows' drab on-screen colors to match. This is entirely possible. Just about every element on the screen can be changed to another color, font, size, what-have-you. Here's how:

1. Muster the Display Properties dialog box.

   Review the information in the section "The first step in changing Windows' looks," earlier in this chapter, to learn how this is done.

2. Click on the Appearance panel to move it center stage.

   Display the Properties dialog box. The Appearance panel looks something like Figure 24-6. It shows several of Windows' on-screen elements, colors, fonts, and whatnot. Each of these items can be changed, either individually or all at once by using some predefined schemes — like in a Miss Marple novel.

3A. Preview a bunch of color schemes.

   Use the drop-down list box below Scheme to display some of the color patterns dreamt up by the overly creative boys and girls at Microsoft — but don't do this if you have to drive or operate any heavy equipment later. The options aren't too exciting.

   After choosing an option, you'll see how it would affect things in the preview window.

   If you find a color arrangement you like (doubtful), move on to step 4.

3B. Make up your own color scheme.

   The Item drop-down list contains all the different elements of Windows you can tweak. However, it's easier to change something by just clicking the mouse on that element in the window in the top of the dialog box. For example, click on Active Window to change its colors, fonts, or size.

   If you toil a lot here, click the Save As button to give your new color scheme a name. That way, you can retain your choices for later.

   ➡ You can use the gizmos in this dialog box to adjust the various pieces parts. Still, note that this is one complex dialog box. See Chapter 29 for information about using the various gizmos and dealie-bobs herein.

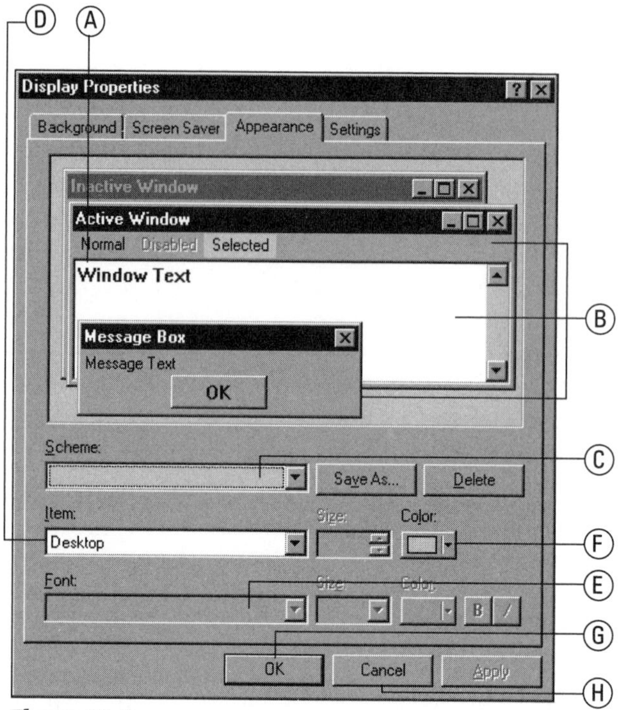

Figure 24-6

The Appearance panel in the Display Properties dialog box.
A. Your new colors are previewed in this window. **B.** You can click on individual items in this window to see how they're already set. As you click on different items, the settings in the dialog box reflect their color, size, font, and so on. **C.** You can choose a predefined color scheme from this drop-down list, although — trust me — all of them are pretty lame. **D.** This drop-down list describes each item in a window. You change its color, size, or fonts by using other buttons in the dialog box. **E.** Other stuff. **F.** You click this button to choose a new color for the desktop's pattern. **G.** Click here to save your new desktop color choices. **H.** No, thank you. I was just goofing around.

If you need help figuring out what anything in the dialog box does, click on the question-mark button in the upper right corner. Then click the mouse on whatever it is you're curious about. For example, the button with the / on it is used to make text appear *italicized*. I wouldn't have known that had I not question-mark-clicked on it. See Chapter 4, the sidebar "The weird ? button on some windows," for more information.

Some funky things you can change that have nothing to do with color

Three Icon entries are in the Item drop-down list. These entries aren't related to anything you can click on in the preview window, and they don't control colors or fonts. Choose each item listed here, and click the Apply button to see how they affect your desktop.

Icon: Sets the size of Windows icons, which means that you can make them appear larger or smaller. For example, change the value in the Size spinner to 48. Then click the Apply button to see what happens to the icons on your desktop. (They get huge!) If you want things normal, be sure to set the value back to 32 before you click on OK.

Icon Spacing (Horizontal): This value sets the distance that icons are placed from each other left and right. When you arrange icons on the desktop, Windows normally spaces them 43 pixels apart. You can make this value smaller to make things line up more snugly or make it larger to give yourself a wider icon grid on the desktop.

Icon Spacing (Vertical): This value sets the distance between icons up and down. You can change the value larger or smaller than 43 to make your desktop's icon grid taller or shorter.

You can preview your choices by clicking the Apply button. But be sure to reset these values before you click on OK or Cancel, especially if you're just goofing around.

4. Click on the Apply button.

   Unlike OK, the Apply button resets Windows with your changes but lets you chicken out. That way, you can preview how things will look without fully committing.

   If everything looks fine, click on OK to lock in your choices.

   If it looks horrid, go back a step and reset your choices. Then click on Cancel and be done with it.

Messing with the Taskbar

The taskbar is definitely a part of Windows' look. It's not the desktop. No, it's more like an annoying fat lip on the face of Windows. You can make some minor tweaks to that fat lip, by moving it, stretching it out, or even putting it away. But keep in mind that most people don't mess with the taskbar much. In fact, all Windows documentation, articles in magazines, and whatnot will show the taskbar the way it was when you first started Windows. Any changes you make will leave you on your own.

← Chapter 7 has lots and lots of information about the taskbar, primarily stuff that doesn't pertain to the way the taskbar looks. Flip back there to get the rest of the story.

Whipping about the taskbar

The taskbar isn't glued to the bottom of your screen. You can flip it up to either the right, left, or top edges of the screen, whichever you prefer. Here's how:

1. Point the mouse pointer at a blank part of the taskbar.

   If you can't see a blank part, point it at the Loud Time.

← And if you can't see the Loud Time, see Chapter 7, "But I can't see the clock!"

2. Press and hold down the mouse's button.

   Use the left button, the main one. Press and hold the button as though you're starting a mouse-drag operation — which is exactly what you're about to do.

   When you press and hold the mouse's button, you see a fuzzy outline appear around the taskbar.

➡ See Chapter 29 for more information about mouse-drag operations.

3. Drag the taskbar elsewhere.

   You can drag it to the left side of the screen, the right, bottom, or top. When you drag, the outline shows you where the taskbar will end up (see Figure 24-7).

4. Release the mouse button.

   Behold! The taskbar lives in a new place on the screen. Funky, huh? Now you have to remember that when this book or other documentation says, "The Start Thing's button is in the lower left corner of the screen," they're not talking about you, because you've moved the taskbar.

   To change it back, just repeat the preceding steps and move the taskbar back to the bottom of the screen (primary fat-lip position).

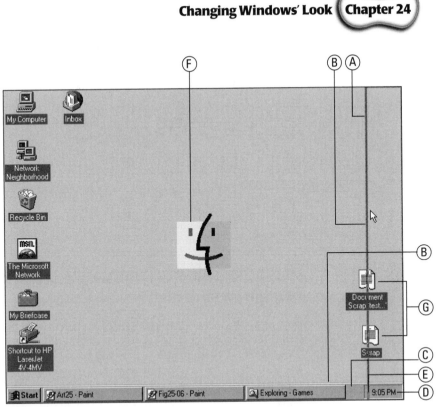

Figure 24-7
General taskbar-messing.
A. This outline shows where you can drag-move the taskbar. **B.** Drag on this inside edge to make the taskbar fatter. **C.** You should find a blank spot on the taskbar to click and drag. **D.** If there aren't any blank spots, you can drag by using the Loud Time. **E.** The speaker-volume thing doesn't show up if you don't have a sound card in your PC. **F.** This wallpaper is centered on the background. See the section "Wallpaper without the glue," earlier in this chapter. **G.** These icons adjust their positions after you release the mouse button.

Stretching the taskbar

You can adjust the taskbar's width by dragging it out to a larger size. Just click the mouse on the taskbar's inside edge to s-t-r-e-t-c-h. This comes in especially handy when the taskbar has too many buttons or if you choose a vertical taskbar orientation.

◀━ The fine details of performing this task can be found in Chapter 7, in the section "Too Many Buttons on the Taskbar!"

Tweaking the way the taskbar works

There are only two ways you can change the taskbar's operation:

✘ Force the taskbar to be always on top or treated like any other window on the screen. The taskbar normally is always on top, always visible. You can change this option so that the taskbar is covered by new windows as you open them.

✘ Employ the auto-hide option. The taskbar moves out of the way when something new pops up. However, you can always move the mouse pointer to the bottom of the screen, and it (rather annoyingly and often when you don't want it to) pops right back up.

My personal preference is to turn both options off, removing the little ✔ check mark from their check boxes. You're free to think otherwise, and follow these steps:

1. Call up the Taskbar Properties dialog box.

   Pop-up the Start Thing's menu (press Ctrl+Esc), and then choose Settings⇨Taskbar. This step brings up the Taskbar Properties dialog box.

2. Click on the Taskbar Options tab to bring that panel forward.

   It probably already is forward, but you can never trust computer software.

3. Click on Always on top to change that option.

   Put a ✔ check mark in the box if you always want the taskbar on top, no matter what. Click again to remove the ✔ and make the taskbar behave more like any other window.

   If you leave this option blank, you can always summon the taskbar by pressing Ctrl+Esc. Although that does pop up the Start Thing's menu, you can see the taskbar and poke at any buttons or tweak it if you like.

4. Click on Auto hide to change that option.

   Click once to put a ✔ check mark in the box, and again to remove the ✔. If this item is checked, the taskbar always sulks out of the way when something pops up over it. Dragging the mouse pointer to the bottom edge of the screen pops it back up, however.

   Sometimes, having this option on can be annoying. Whenever you move the mouse pointer to the bottom of the screen, for example, the taskbar pops up — "Here I am!" — like a lonely puppy dog wanting attention. You have to subtly move the mouse pointer away from the taskbar a bit to make it hide again. Major pain.

5. Click on OK.

Click on the OK button in the Taskbar Properties dialog box to lock in your changes.

◀▥ The other two options in the dialog box don't directly affect the taskbar. For information about Show small icons in Start menu, see the section "Radically Altering the Appearance of the Start Thing," in Chapter 6.

◀▥ The final option, Show Clock, is also covered in Chapter 7, in the sidebar "But I can't see the clock!"

Tweaking Your MOM

Just call her on the phone and say that she looks "frumpy" — that'll do it.

Seriously, MOM is an acronym that (I suppose) means Microsoft Office Menu, that little row of buttons riveted near the upper right corner of the screen (see Figure 24-8). It's how you start Microsoft Office programs, new documents, and so on. With Microsoft Office '95, you can make minor tweaks to the button bar — a.k.a. MOM — just as you can with Windows' own taskbar.

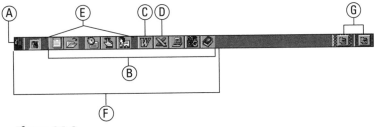

Figure 24-8
Moving your MOM.
A. The MOM icon. Click here to see the menu that controls MOM. **B.** These buttons enable you to do various things. Hover the mouse pointer over them long enough to see a bubble appear, telling you what's what. **C.** Start Word. **D.** Start Excel.
E. Click in one of these dark spaces to move MOM. Drag her to one side of the screen or another, or make her float out in the open — but not on Mother's Day.
F. Without the alternative toolbars, MOM is usually only this long. **G.** Click here to see an alternative toolbar pop up; see the section "Bar hopping," later in this chapter.

⬅ᴵᴵᴵ These tricks do not work with the older version of Microsoft Office. In that version, the buttons are stuck on the desktop and you can't move them. At least, I've never seriously given any thought to moving them, having accepted their position as kismet. Check out Chapter 10 for more information about Microsoft Office, though not much more.

Moving the Office Bar

It's a cinch to move the Microsoft Office toolbar. You just click the mouse in a dark place and drag it off — just as you did with the taskbar, in the section "Messing with the Taskbar," earlier in this chapter.

In addition to moving MOM to the four sides of the screen, you can also move her to a position in the middle of the screen. That sounds neat, but if you've set MOM to always be on top, the toolbar floats annoyingly in front of your applications.

My advice is to stick with tradition and keep your MOM at the top of the screen, near the upper right corner. By the way, on any other side of the screen, MOM arranges herself like the taskbar, long and thin, rather than like a riveted row of buttons.

Bar hopping

I don't go into too much detail on tweaking MOM here. That's really the subject of a book dedicated to Microsoft Office '95. Still, you can add some cool Windows things to MOM, making her even more useful. To check them out, follow these steps:

1. Bring up MOM's menu.

   Click the button on the MOM icon (see Figure 24-9). This step brings up her main menu.

2. Choose Customize.

   A Customize dialog box appears.

3. Click on the Toolbars panel to bring it forward.

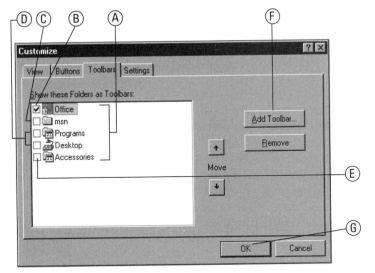

Figure 24-9
Your MOM's toolbar is customized here.
A. Various toolbars you can add to MOM. **B.** Keep the ✔ check mark here because you want to keep the Microsoft Office toolbar always. **C.** Click here to add a toolbar containing various Microsoft Network commands on a toolbar. **D.** There are other items whose commands or contents you can place on a toolbar. **E.** All the commands found in the Accessories folder on the Start Thing's menu can be added to the toolbar as well. **F.** You can click this button to create your own toolbar if you like. The commands in the toolbar should be programs off in some folder on your disk drive. **G.** Click here when you're done messing around.

4. Choose an additional toolbar for MOM.

For example, click on the Programs folder item. This step adds a second toolbar to MOM, one that contains all the folders and commands found in the Programs submenu off the Start Thing.

Choose as many toolbars as you want to add, or just click the Cancel button to ignore this option. (After all, junky desktops can be annoying.)

As you choose each new toolbar, a preview of what it looks like is displayed wherever MOM lies on your screen. Some of them can get long. Folders on a new toolbar represent windows that contain programs — just like in My Computer.

5. Click on OK.

   Click the OK button.

   The new toolbars appear alongside MOM.

   To choose a new toolbar, click on its icon on MOM.

You can remove the toolbars if they annoy you; just repeat the preceding steps, but in step 4, click one to remove the various ✔ check marks by the toolbar options. Remember to keep the Office toolbar visible so that you can run Microsoft Office.

Interesting, Weird, and Neat Stuff

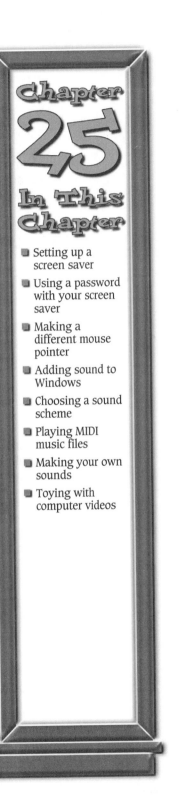

A Windows that's all work and no play would be almost as dull and boring as DOS used to be. I'm not talking about games: DOS has plenty of clever games to rule your days. Windows, on the other hand, dishes up such tasty treats as animated mouse pointers, screen savers, sounds, videos, and a host of other interesting and sweetly charming goodies — what I call the interesting, weird, and neat stuff.

Saving the Screen from Boredom

A screen saver is really nothing more than a toy. It's a tool that was originally intended to save the phosphor on older black-and-white (monochrome) monitors; if you left those monitors on too long, an image "burned" into their phosphor permanently. The screen saver prevented this burn-in by periodically darkening the screen.

Today's color monitors no longer need screen savers to prevent phosphor burn-in. Even so, a screen saver remains as a fun toy. It's neat

to have your computer's monitor turn blank and then see, for example, Mickey Mouse march across and start painting something. (For Mickey Mouse, you have to buy a third-party screen saver; he doesn't come with Windows.)

Screen savers also offer a form of security. First, with your screen darkened, someone can't wander by your office and see what you're doing when you're not there. Second, they also offer a form of password protection because only by typing the proper password can you return to Windows from the screen saver.

Has your screen been saved?

To activate a screen saver for your monitor, follow these steps:

1. Summon the Display Properties dialog box.

   Follow the steps outlined in the section "The first step in changing Windows' looks" in Chapter 24.

2. Click on the Screen Saver tab.

   This step brings forward the Screen Saver panel, similar to what you see in Figure 25-1. Work this box to set a screen saver for your monitor.

3. Pick a screen saver.

   Several are offered in the drop-down list (refer to Figure 25-1). Each of them turns your screen black with some type of busy graphic. Pick one to see in the Preview screen what it does.

   To have no screen saver, choose None from the list.

   For each screen saver, you should click on the Settings button to see what kind of adjustments you can make. There's nothing serious there — just fun.

   For the Scrolling Marquee screen saver, you should click on the Settings button to type your own special text. If you do this, click on the Preview button in the Display Properties dialog box to see how your text will look. That way, you can make editing changes right away, adjust the formatting and color, and so on.

4. Set the Wait time.

   The screen saver appears on your screen after a certain interval of laziness, anywhere from 1 to 60 minutes after you've last touched the keyboard or moved the mouse. Set the interval by using the spinner in the dialog box.

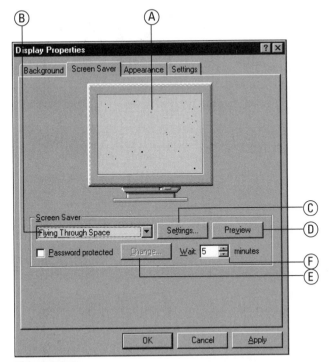

Figure 25-1
How shall thy screen be saved?
A. Preview your screen saver here. **B.** Pick a screen-saver type here. **C.** Adjust each screen saver. **D.** Preview full screen. **E.** Optional password. **F.** Set the time delay by using this spinner.

I prefer a time delay of about five minutes. That amount means that the screen saver automatically snaps on after I sit there looking at the screen, drooling for five minutes. It keeps me busy.

➡ See the next section for information about screen-saver passwords.

5. Click on OK.

Your screen saver is set in motion. The next time you return to your computer after a break, you see the screen saver on the screen rather than the overdue project in Excel. Just move the mouse a little, and the screen saver will flee.

Your computer still works while the screen saver is on. If your computer is on a network, the screen saver does not interfere with anything. (Heck, the network interferes with itself enough; it doesn't need a screen saver for that.)

Shhh! Using the password option

To set a password for your screen saver, click in the Password protected box to put a ✔ check mark there. That enables the Change button, allowing you to enter a screen-saver password. Here's how:

1. Click on the Change button.

    The Change Password dialog box appears.

2. Type your new password in the New password box.

    Make it short and brief. This is one password you don't want to casually forget.

    I might suggest a one-letter password, or maybe your initials. Something short is easier to remember than something long.

3. Type the same password again in the Confirm new password box.

    Clackity-clack-clack.

4. Click on OK.

    Windows tells you that the password has been changed successfully. Rah.

The screen blanks just as it did before, but when you try to reactivate it (by moving the mouse or pressing a key on the keyboard), you're greeted with a password box (see Figure 25-2). Type the proper password, and press the Enter key. Only then can you get back into your computer.

Ⓐ   Ⓑ   Ⓒ

Windows Screen Saver	✕
Type your screen saver password:	OK
[ ]	Cancel

Figure 25-2
Knock, knock. What's the password?
A. Screen saver running amok out here. **B.** Type the proper password here.
C. Click here to gain entry.

If you forget the password, you're seriously screwed. You have to reset your computer and then run through the steps in this section to reassign a password before the screen saver kicks in. (See, it's not very good security, but it does keep snoopers out of your PC.)

A More Lively Mouse Pointer

Nothing makes someone's jaw drop like seeing a mouse pointer that looks like a flapping Windows flag. "How'd you do that?" they'll ponder. The trick is really quite cinchy because all you have to do is switch mouse pointers from the cruddy old stationary models to something new and potentially different. Here's how:

1. Open a handy Control Panel near you.

   If you don't see the Control Panel's folder lying about, press Ctrl+Esc, S, C.

   Control Panel

2. Open the Mouse icon.

   Double-click on the little mouse guy. This step opens the Mouse Properties dialog box.

   Mouse

3. Click on the Pointers tab to bring it forward.

   You'll see the Pointers panel, as shown in Figure 25-3. This is where you can choose new mouse pointers to replace the standard ones used in Windows.

4. Click on a pointer to change it.

   For example, click on the Busy pointer, the hourglass.

5. Click on Browse.

   This step brings up a standard Browsing dialog box, in which you can hunt down a new pointer.

   Windows automatically shows you pointers in the Cursors folder (under your Windows folder). You might want to browse elsewhere, for example, if you've just downloaded a batch of new cursors from CompuServe or the Net.

   Double-click on a new pointer in the Browse dialog box to choose it and return to the Mouse Properties dialog box.

   If you don't like your new pointer, click on the Default button to restore it.

6. Repeat steps 4 and 5 for each pointer you want to change.

   Or if you really want to make an impact, choose a pointer scheme from the Scheme drop-down list. A *scheme* is merely a preset collection of pointers, all following some theme. For example, the Tarzan scheme has all sorts of jungle pointers in it. Unfortunately, Windows doesn't come with the Tarzan scheme.

7. Click on OK.

   When you're done making changes, click on OK.

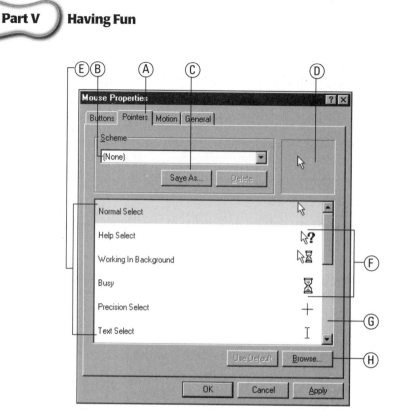

Figure 25-3
The Mouse Properties dialog box, Pointers panel.
A. Click here to bring this panel forward. **B.** Choose a whole pointer scheme from this list. **C.** You can save your own scheme if you like. **D.** Preview the current pointer. **E.** Names for various Windows pointers. **F.** Corresponding pointers. **G.** Scroll to see more pointers. **H.** Click here to go out and hunt for a new pointer.

You can click on Apply first if you like. That way, you can try out some of the cursors, but keep in mind that you can always change them back later if you don't like them.

A More Euphonious PC

Equipped with the proper hardware, your PC can really hoot it up. That feeble, little speaker can do much more than beep or twitter every time Windows tries to communicate with you. When your PC has the proper sound equipment, Windows can make wonderful music. Heck, just plowing through menus and opening windows can induce it to produce symphonic rhapsodies. Granted, this has nothing to do with getting work done, but that would go against the theme of this part of the book.

Making Windows noisy

Windows lets you associate any one of a number of things it does with a specific sound. Open a window, hear a bleep. Start a new program, hear a splat. Quit Windows, and hear a dozen people cheering. It makes it almost too fun.

To make noise happen, you have to fire up the Control Panel and play with the Sounds icon. Follow these steps:

1. Muster the Control Panel.

   Control Panel

   Open the Control Panel, which lurks in My Computer's main window, or you can snatch it from the Settings submenu off the Start Thing's main menu.

2. Open the Sounds icon.

   Sounds

   Double-click on the Sounds icon to open it up and mess with sound on your computer. The Sounds Properties dialog box appears, looking something like Figure 25-4.

3. Pick a Windows event from the Events list.

   A number of events are associated with Windows and several other programs. The events are fairly descriptive.

   Click on the event you want to associate with a sound.

4. Pick a sound from the Sound list.

   Choose from the drop-down list a sound to associate with that event.

   You may want to use the Browse button to look for a specific sound on your hard drive. Any standard "wave" sound file will work, such as those you can create yourself by using the Sound Recorder program (covered later in this chapter).

   Click on the Play button to hear the sound — a preview of sorts.

5. Continue assigning sounds to various Windows tasks.

   You can repeat steps 3 and 4 for just about everything Windows does.

    To assign a whole gang of sounds all at one time, you can choose a sound scheme, as described in the following section.

6. Click on OK when you're done.

   Click on the OK button to put the new sounds into play.

   Before clicking on OK, you can optionally click on the Save As button to save all your sounds as a sound scheme on disk.

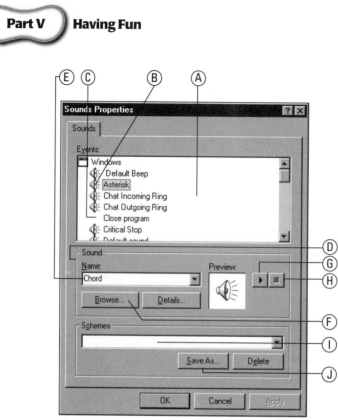

Figure 25-4
The Sounds Properties dialog box.
A. Various Windows events. **B.** Indicates that a sound has been assigned to an event. **C.** No sound for this event. **D.** Choose new sounds from this area. **E.** Pick a sound from this drop-down list. **F.** Use this button to go out and hunt for new sounds. **G.** Click here to preview the sound. **H.** Stop previewing. **I.** Choose all the sounds at once here. **J.** Create your own sound scheme.

Scheming sound schemes

A collection of sounds is called a *scheme*. Windows has a few of them available for you to choose from, each of which has its own collection of specific sounds that work together in a certain way — call it a sound motif, though you have to look up in your dictionary what *motif* means.

◀━ You may not have any sound schemes installed on your computer. If so, you have to set them up manually. Refer to the section "Adding the rest of Windows" in Chapter 13 for more information.

To use a preset sound scheme, choose one from the Schemes drop-down list in the Sounds Properties dialog box (see the preceding section).

My personal favorite sound scheme is Musica, though I like many of the Utopia sounds better.

Making music mit MIDI

Your PC's sound capabilities aren't limited to just playing back recorded sounds. Most PC sound systems have their own built-in synthesizer. Special programs on disk can tickle the keys on this synthesizer and play little ditties.

Turkish

The little ditties your PC can play are stored in *MIDI* files on disk. (Pronounce it "middy.") You double-click on one to play the MIDI music, which then launches a multipurpose program called the Media Player (see Figure 25-5). In the case of the MIDI file, the Media Player plays the musical instruments in your PC's synthesizer. In Figure 25-5, Mozart's Turkish march, "Rondo Alla Turca," is being played. (You can't hear it — this is a book.) The march doesn't come with Windows 95; I downloaded it from one of the online services.

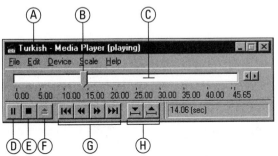

Figure 25-5
The Media Player pounds out Mozart at the computer keyboard.
A. The name of the MIDI song being played. **B.** Progress as indicated by a slider.
C. The slider can also be used to choose tracks when you play a CD. **D.** Play/Pause button. **E.** Stop button. **F.** Eject disk button. **G.** Buttons to move to different tracks, forward and back. **H.** Editing buttons you can cheerfully ignore.

There is really nothing more you can do with MIDI files other than play them. Special hardware and software are required in order to create these files. They do, however, make a refreshing musical break if you collect a bunch of them and want to entertain yourself; the MIDI songs play "in the background" while you do something else.

To play the music over and over again, choose Edit➪Options from the Media Player's menu. Then click on the Auto Repeat option to put a ✔ check mark there. The music plays over and over, really driving you nuts.

◀■ Another way your computer can play music is by sticking a musical CD in its CD-ROM player. Check out Chapter 14, the section "Playing a musical CD," for more information.

■▶ The Media Player can also play videos and CDs, depending on which file types you select when you choose its File➪Open command. See the section "Behold Computer Video!," later in this chapter, for another run at the Media Player.

◀■ You can embed a MIDI music file into any document that's OLE-friendly. See the section "An Episode with OLE" in Chapter 8 for more information.

Recording your own sounds for fun and profit

If your computer has sound capabilities plus a little hole for plugging in a microphone, you can record your own sounds in Windows. You do it with a little program called the Sound Recorder. (Clever names just ooze from the corporate offices of Microsoft.)

Here are some steps you can take to create your own sounds:

1. Hook up the microphone to your computer.

   Make sure that you plug it in to the microphone connector, not a "line in" connector. (One is amplified, and the other is not.)

   Likewise, you can plug in your stereo, VCR, or tape recorder and copy sounds from them. Just get to Radio Shack and get a cable to connect your stereo's line out with your computer's line in.

2. Run the Sound Recorder program.

   The Sound Recorder is shown in Figure 25-6. You'll find it lurking off the Start Thing's menu; Programs➪Accessories➪Multimedia➪ Sound Recorder is the way to get there.

◀■ You can also start the Sound Recorder, all prepped and ready by choosing New➪Sound from any of the various New menu commands that lurk all over Windows. See the section "Taking advantage of the numerous New menu commands" in Chapter 3 for more information about how they work.

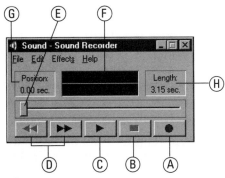

Figure 25-6
The Sound Recorder, poised to record something.
A. Click here to record a sound. **B.** Stop button. **C.** Play button **D.** Forward and Reverse buttons. **E.** This slider moves right as your sound plays. **F.** Graphical sound representation, à la "The Jetsons." **G.** Whatever. **H.** Uh-huh.

3. Choose File⇨New.

   The New Sound dialog box appears (see Figure 25-7). You can make various settings here to change the quality of the sound you record. The higher the quality, though, the larger the sound file on disk.

   If you've been messing around and haven't yet saved your sound to disk, you see a warning dialog box here that gives you a chance to save.

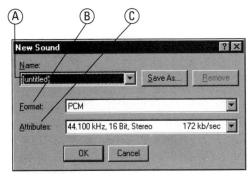

Figure 25-7
The New Sound dialog box.
A. Set the sound quality here, but it's okay to ignore. **B.** You can also ignore the format (though PCM sounds okay). **C.** Set the sound's clarity here; higher numbers mean clearer sound but larger sound files.

4. Click on OK to close the New Sound dialog box.

5. Clear your throat.

   A-hem. Test. One-two-three. Test. Test!

6. Click on the Record button, and begin speaking into the mic.

   Blah-blah-blah. "Here is what I had for lunch today." Blah-blah-blah.

7. Click on the Stop button when you're done recording.

   If you don't click on Stop, you'll have a really big sound file with carefully recorded sounds of you muttering and shifting position in your chair.

8. Optionally click on the Play button to hear your recording.

   This can be fun. It's almost like the time you got your first tape recorder.

   If you don't like what you hear (which probably happened with your first tape recorder as well), do steps 3 through 7 again. And again. And again. It takes a while to get things right.

9. Save your sound file to disk.

   Choose File⇨Save and find a proper place, and give a proper name to your sound file.

◄─⊪ You can make your sound file a part of Windows by assigning it to a specific Windows event. For example, have your kids scream "Bye-bye" when Windows quits. See the section "Making Windows noisy," earlier in this chapter, for more information.

Behold Computer Video!

Playing a video in Windows turns your $2,000 personal computer into a cheapy TV set, one that looks like it's picking up transmissions from Brezhnevian Russia. Okay, maybe it's not that bad, but watching a video in Windows can be really fun.

The first thing you have to do is find a video file. They're marked with a special icon, and you might have this type of file lurking in the Media folder off the Windows main folder. Just double-click on that file to start playing it. A window appears, such as the one shown in Figure 25-8, where your video plays.

Sunset
Blvd

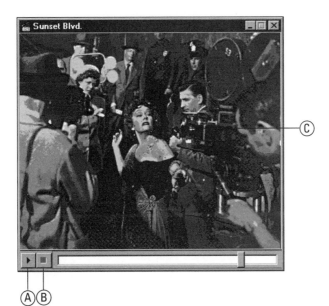

Figure 25-8
Norma Desmond is ready for her close-up.
A. Play/pause button. **B.** Stop button. **C.** She should have won the Oscar.

The only drawback to videos on the screen, aside from the fuzzy/jerky quality, is that they occupy a humongous amount of disk space. One little clip of Hannibal Lecter describing the ideal wine to have with liver will chew up some 4 megabytes of disk space. Other files take up even more space: A music video included with the Windows 95 beta test kit sucked up some 30 megabytes of space.

You obviously didn't buy a computer to watch TV. In most cases, you'll find videos used as accompaniment in multimedia products. For example, there are clips from *Star Wars* and *Sunset Boulevard* in Microsoft's Cinemania product. It's not the whole picture, but it's pretty fun to watch — yet another crazy thing Windows can do.

Part V   **Having Fun**

Fun, Games, and Frivolity

One thing about Windows being graphical and all that is that it opens the doors to some fun games. Just about everything you've ever played — in real life, in an arcade, or on any computer — has a Windows equivalent. Not only that, Windows itself comes with a handful of interesting games — wonderful toys to obsess over. So here's a chapter devoted to Windows games because, after all, you play them more than you should.

> "Look at me!
>
> Look at me!
>
> Look at me now!
>
> It is fun to have fun
>
> But you have to know how."
>
> — *The Cat in the Hat,* by Theodore Geisel (Dr. Seuss)

Games in Windows

A ton of Windows games are out there, games for all types. There are strategy games, blow-'em-up games, adventure games, card games, board games — you name it. Unfortunately, not all those come with Windows. But

look on the bright side: The games that do come with Windows can be fun and addicting, two of the highest qualifications of any computer game.

Finding the games

Windows keeps all its games in the same menu off the Start Thing. To start one or more of them, follow these steps:

1. Pop up the Start Thing's menu.

   Press Ctrl+Esc or click on the Start button on the taskbar.

2. Choose Programs.

   The Programs submenu appears.

3. Carefully wind the mouse over and click on Accessories.

   The Accessories submenu appears.

4. Even more carefully, roll the mouse pointer over to the Games item and click on it.

   The Games submenu appears, which may look like Figure 26-1. You see a list of the games installed with Windows plus maybe some additional games you've added.

5. Click on the game you want to start.

   Pluck out a game. Try Solitaire first. Minesweeper involves a great deal of mental energy that most people don't want to expend. Freecell is another frustrating card game. Both Hearts and Party Line (which may also be called Rumor) are network-based games.

Figure 26-1
Your typical Games submenu.
A. Windows games on the menu. **B.** Other games may also appear here. **C.** Network games.

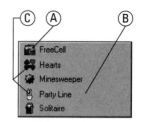

If you find one game severely addicting, consider adding it to the Start Thing's main menu. Refer to the section "Sticking something on the main Start Thing menu" in Chapter 6.

Another way to have instant access to a game is to drag a shortcut to the desktop. See Chapter 17, the section "Sticking stuff on the desktop."

Solitaire: The art of playing by yourself

Perhaps the most addicting computer game is Solitaire, like the card game of old (see Figure 26-2). But don't use that as an excuse to play it. Solitaire is a great way to learn how to use the mouse. You get to point, click, drag, and double-click. It's not fun, it's . . . *exercise.* Yeah. That's it.

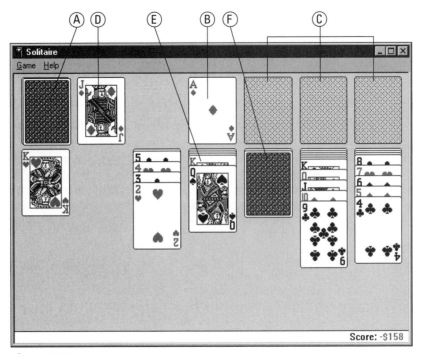

Figure 26-2
Old Sol can really get you going.
A. Click here to see the next card. **B.** Double-click on the ace to put it "up." **C.** Other aces go here. **D.** This Jack can go on the black Queen below. **E.** You can move a King to a blank spot. **F.** Click on this card to see what it is.

Start Solitaire according to the instructions offered in the section "Finding the games," earlier in this chapter.

You click on face-down cards to turn them over.

Drag cards from one column to another, and put red cards on black in sequence.

Double-click on cards to put them "up."

You can drag entire columns or just parts of columns.

Choose Game➪Options to play some variations.

Yes, there is a way to cheat, but you'd be so pitiful if you tried it that I think there's no point in even bothering.

◄▥ Remember that you can minimize a game when you're done playing, without quitting. That way, you can quickly resume later, such as after the boss comes in. Refer to the section "Done for the Day? To Quit or Put Away" in Chapter 4.

▥➤ Solitaire involves a great deal of mouse-ability. See Chapter 29 for more information about using the mouse.

Minesweeper, or how not to blow up Bob

Minesweeper is one of those old computer-logic puzzles. It goes like this: Suppose that you have a grid under which are several mines. You can look under any tile in the grid for a mine. If you find a mine — Boom! — you blow up (actually, Bob blows up). If you don't find a mine, you see a number that tells you how many tiles in the grid around you have mines under them. See? It's annoying.

For example, the nearby grid shows several uncovered tiles, but two of them have been flagged as mines. (That's because the 1 by each tile is touching only that one tile, meaning that there's a mine there.) The 2 right between the two flagged mines is already touching two mines, so the other blank tiles it's sitting next to are probably not mines. You can click the mouse on them to uncover their secret numbers, which tells you more about the rest of the tiles and so on until you've solved the puzzle. (Supposedly.)

To start a new game, click on Bob. Then begin clicking on blank tiles. Use your brain to determine where a mine lies based on the numbers you see (see Figure 26-3). Use cunning, guile, and your computer mouse.

When you think that you've found a mine, right-click on that tile. That marks the tile with a little flag, meaning "Mine here!"

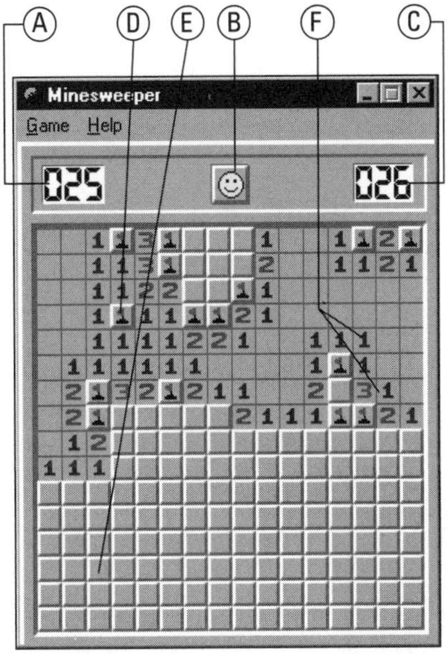

Figure 26-3
Sweep dem mines!
A. You have 25 mines left to find. **B.** Bob.
C. A timer (number of seconds elapsed).
D. Found and flagged mine. **E.** Unknown
territory. **F.** Numbers indicate the number
of bombs next door.

As you click on each tile to see what's underneath, Bob
gets nervous.

If you find a mine, all the hidden mines are shown, and —
regrettably — Bob dies.

You can set the size of the minefield by choosing various options from the
Game menu (Beginner, Intermediate, Expert, and Custom) to create your
own minefield. Each size is larger and has more mines to uncover.

If you win, Bob gets cool, and you get to enter your name in the high-
score sheet.

By the way, not to brag or anything, but my best times are Beginner, 9
seconds; Intermediate, 51 seconds; and Expert, 138 seconds. Use these
scores only for comparisons; your mileage may vary.

Freecell (another annoying Solitaire-like game)

A combination logic puzzle and solitaire card game, Freecell keeps you busy
for hours — after you unlock its secrets (see Figure 26-4). Perhaps the most
annoying part about Freecell is that every puzzle has a solution. Unlike
Solitaire, in which you can be zoinked out of success by a bad shuffle, every
single Freecell game has a solution, and sometimes several solutions. Now
that smells of a challenge!

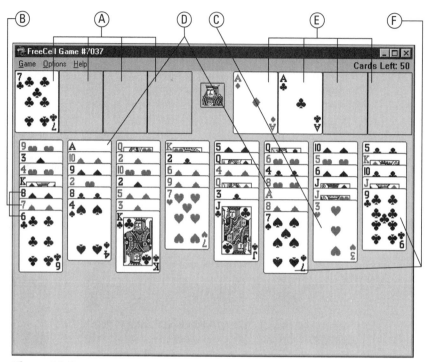

Figure 26-4

A typical, maddening Freecell game.

A. You can move one card at a time to these four "cells." **B.** Stack up cards here, alternating black and white in sequence. **C.** You can move cards as well; this 3 can go on the black 4 in the second column. **D.** Free the aces first; move them up to the cells on the right. **E.** Aces go here and then 2s, 3s, and 4s in their suit sequence. **F.** You can move stacks of cards back and forth, but only one card at a time.

Start yourself a Freecell game by following the instructions in the section "Finding the games," earlier in this chapter. Then just play. See what you can do. The game is smart and offers you suggestions about where cards can go and where they can't.

Unlike Solitaire, you do not drag cards with the mouse. Instead, you click on a card to select it and then click on where you want the card to move. The game tells you whether it's a valid move. If you can move a stack of cards, the game asks whether you want to move the entire stack or just the top card. Here are some of my own hints:

✗ Free up those aces first!

✗ Look for trouble spots, such as three of a kind in a row. That spells certain doom unless you can play all three cards.

✗ Try not to fill up the free cells, especially with high-suited cards, such as face cards.

✗ If you can clear one entire column, you're halfway to winning the game.

✗ Try to look several moves in advance.

Every puzzle has a solution. If you don't win the first time, try playing the same card layout again (it asks whether you want to when it announces that you've lost). I've done this hundreds of times and have yet to find a puzzle I can't defeat. Some of them are real boogers, though.

Party Line (also known as Rumor)

This isn't really a game, and it's actually kind of dumb, but it's included free with Windows and lives in the Games submenu, so I have to write about it here.

Basically, Party Line works like those "online chat" forums they have on CompuServe and America Online. You just type something, and that message is displayed on a number of other people's computers elsewhere on the network. No one knows who typed what, so it can get out of hand (which is the rollicking fun part, I suppose). Figure 26-5 offers a hint of some of the excitement Party Line dishes up.

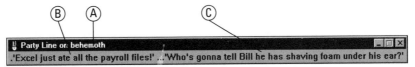

Figure 26-5
Party Line. Ha, ha.
A. Party Line's network host. **B.** Something some joker wrote. **C.** Something some other joker wrote.

Party Line is a network-only "game." Obviously, writing witty things only for yourself to read is called "Being an editorial writer for the *Washington Post.*"

When you first run Party Line (see the section "Finding the games," earlier in this chapter), you're asked whether you want to start your own party line or connect to a party line on another computer. If a party line is already swinging somewhere, type the computer's name and click on OK.

To add a message to the party line, press the F2 key and type the message. Oh, hardy-har.

The F3 key displays a dialog box with all the witty sayings collected in one place.

Just close the Party Line's thin window when you're sick of it.

Moving on . . . .

Hearts Attack

A better network game to play, and one that you can play on a nonnetworked computer as well, is Hearts (see Figure 26-6). It's the traditional game of Hearts, with the traditional rules (no cheating!). On a network, you can play with three of your nonworking co-workers, or you can just start your own game by choosing to be the "dealer" and then try to beat the pants off the computer.

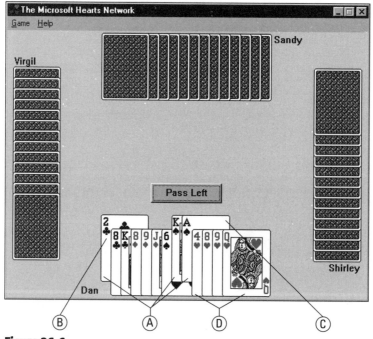

Figure 26-6
Hearts in action.
A. Click on a card to pass it. **B.** The 2 of clubs always leads. **C.** Pass these ugly suckers. **D.** Click on a card to play it (when the game is going).

Refer to the instructions in the section "Finding the games," earlier in this chapter, for information about starting Hearts. I won't bother going into any of the details of how to play or strategy here, though you can rest assured that if one of the computer players has the Queen, he or she will pass it to you. Here are some other hints:

✘ If you can't seem to play, you probably have the 2 of clubs; that card always "leads."

✘ Click on a card to pass or play.

✘ The computer always knows when you try to "run them," so don't, unless you really can and there's no way to stop you.

✘ Pass your clubs when you start.

By the way, in Figure 26-6, Shirley passed me the Queen on the first hand. Predictable.

Other games abounding

If you have a modem and access to an online service or the Internet, you have an open door to thousands of Windows games. Microsoft even makes Entertainment Packs, which contain all sorts of games (plus interesting wallpaper and fonts). There's even an Arcade Entertainment Pack that contains some classic old, early '80s arcade games you can play right in Windows (such as Tempest, Asteroids, Missile Command, BattleZone, and Centipedes).

Unfortunately, about the only type of game not available for Windows is the flight-simulator type, although I wouldn't be surprised if that type of game is available by the time you read this.

Wrestling with DOS Games

This is serious business. DOS games are perhaps some of the best, most sophisticated computer games ever devised. The reason is simple: DOS lets just about any program take complete control over the computer. DOS is easy to push around. So DOS games just shove it out of the way and, lo, soon the game has control over more computing power than existed on the planet Earth in the 1950s. That's pretty impressive.

To run a DOS game under Windows, you must properly configure Windows to sacrifice as much control as it can over to the DOS game. This is a tall order. In fact, most true Game Zanies start their computers in DOS mode only, bypassing Windows altogether. But Microsoft has made great strides in allowing greedy DOS games to run under Windows.

Excellent, if not self-promoting, books for using DOS

If you're serious about games, you have to understand DOS a little better than most and be prepared for some tweaking beyond that offered in any Windows book. Two books I recommend are *MORE DOS For Dummies* and *The Microsoft Guide to Managing Memory with MS-DOS,* both published by IDG Books. (Yeah, I wrote them both.)

Though it's a *Dummies* book, *MORE DOS For Dummies* contains ample information about using DOS and configuring your system. The *Managing Memory* book tells you how to optimize a DOS session for the most memory possible, a sore subject among game players.

Much of the configuring these books suggest can be entered directly into the Advanced Program Settings dialog box, shown later in this chapter, in Figure 26-7. Click on the Specify a new MS-DOS configuration option, and then click on the Configuration button to make the suggested settings for your game's MS-DOS mode. Good luck!

DOS games? Forget Windows!

There are those purists who insist that DOS games are best played in DOS, forget Windows. This is quite easy to do. You have three options, described in this section.

First, you can start your computer under DOS rather than under Windows. This is done right when the computer first starts, just after you see the "Starting Windows" message appear on the screen. You press the F8 key and then press 6 to choose the Command prompt only option from the menu. This option starts your computer in MS-DOS 7 mode, from which you can run your game without interference from Windows.

Second, you can just bolt from Windows and restart your computer in MS-DOS mode. Do this by choosing that option from the Shutdown dialog box when you shut down Windows; click on Restart the computer in MS-DOS mode, and you'll soon see a cheery DOS prompt awaiting your DOS game commands.

Third, you can configure your DOS game program to fly solo in Windows. This special, advanced option is discussed in the next section. Basically, it tells Windows to go away while your DOS program (such as a game) takes complete control over the computer.

All three of these methods achieve the same madness: Windows is shoved aside, and your game or DOS takes over the computer. That's always the safest, best way to play your DOS game in Windows.

➡ For more information about startup options for Windows, including starting your computer in DOS mode, see the section "Windows' special startup key commands" in Chapter 31.

⬅ See Chapter 1, the section "Quitting Windows and Turning Off Your PC," for more information about the Shutdown command.

Properly configuring a DOS game session in Windows

Suppose that you want to run that DOS game in Windows. If so, you have to be picky about how it runs. To be picky, you have to hunt down your DOS game by using My Computer or the Explorer and then bring up its Properties dialog box for some adjustments. Here's how:

1. Locate your DOS game by using My Computer or the Explorer.

2. Click on your game once using the mouse.

   This step highlights or selects the game for action. Don't double-click here; you want to make some adjustments before starting your game.

3. Bring up the program's Properties dialog box.

   Right-click on the program's icon, and choose Properties from the menu.

   The program's Properties dialog box appears.

⬅ See Chapter 12 for more information about dealing with a DOS program's properties. Most of the special stuff surrounding games is covered here, however.

4. Click on the Program tab to bring that panel forward.

5. Click on the Advanced button.

   This step brings up the Advanced dialog box (see Figure 26-7), where it all boils down to two choices: Should you attempt to run this program inside Windows, or do you want the program to shut down Windows and run by itself?

Figure 26-7
The Advanced Program Settings dialog box. **A.** Click here to run your game under Windows. **B.** Click here to shut down Windows and run your game by itself. **C.** Make sure that this thing here is checked. **D.** Ignore all this.

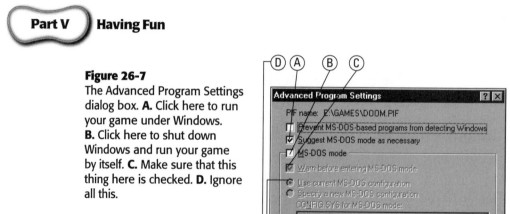

If you're daring, try running the game under Windows; leave the box by MS-DOS mode blank. This means that Windows will start up your game and try to run it in a window on the screen. Most of the time, this meets with success, though the game may run slowly and have to be run full-screen (as opposed to in its own window).

⬅ To run the game full-screen, press Alt+Enter. This and other DOS program secrets are unburied in Chapter 12.

If you find that your game runs too slowly in Windows, put a ✔ check mark in the box by MS-DOS mode. This tells Windows to shut itself down and run your game all by itself. Make sure that a ✔ check mark is in the box by Warn before entering MS-DOS mode. This directs Windows to display a proper warning dialog box (see Figure 26-8) before it dives in to your game-only mode.

Figure 26-8
The warning dialog box you see when your game is about to take over.

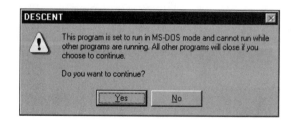

The warning in Figure 26-8 is kinda inaccurate. It makes it sound like Windows will merely close your programs, but in fact it really quits entirely. When you quit your game, Windows restarts.

My advice is to run all your DOS games in MS-DOS mode or just consider restarting your computer in MS-DOS mode (as described in the preceding section). That way, you're certain that your game won't interfere with Windows, and vice versa.

 **Part V** **Having Fun**

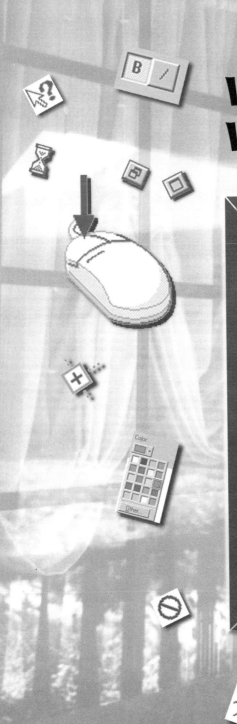

Part
VI

Windows Is As
Windows Does

In this part

■ Your basic Windows
  windows concepts

■ Trapped in a dialog box

■ Mousy concepts

■ Working with
  text and graphics

How do I...?

Change a window's size?

You change a window's size by stretching the window, grabbing one of its edges, and dragging the mouse to change the window's size.

➡ See the section "The joy of stretch" in Chapter 27.

➡ You can also use this technique to change the size of a graphics image pasted into a text document. See the section "Basic Messing with Graphics Stuff (Stretching)" in Chapter 30.

Work menus?

Menus can be controlled with either the mouse or the keyboard, though the mouse is better.

➡ See the section "Working the menus" in Chapter 27 and also the section "Working menus with your keyboard," later in the same chapter.

Find a lost window on the screen?

One of the most frustrating things to have happen is when a window wanders off into the zenith and you can't get it back. Don't uninstall Windows and start over again!

➡ See the section "Cleaning up stray windows" in Chapter 27 for instant lost-window recovery.

Work those frustrating gizmos in a dialog box?

The gizmos aren't really that frustrating, after you understand how each of them is supposed to work. That just takes a little courage and practice.

➠ See the section "All Them Gizmos" in Chapter 28, which covers the gizmos you may find in a dialog box, each in its own section.

Right-click the mouse?

A right-click is the same as a normal click, though you're clicking the right button, not the left one, on the mouse.

➠ See the section "Doing the right-click" in Chapter 29, but you might also want to check out "The Ubiquitous Pop-up Shortcut Menus" in Chapter 5 for more information about why you'd want to right-click.

Change the mouse to left-handed operation?

Southpaw, eh? Windows can comply, though be aware that this book, manuals, and the online Help assumes that you're using a right-handed mouse.

➠ Instructions for switch-hitting the mouse can be found in the sidebar "The left-handed mouse" in Chapter 29.

Your Basic Windows Windows Concepts

Chapter

27

In This Chapter

In Windows, information appears on the screen in a window. If the information had appeared in an envelope, Microsoft probably would have called its operating system Envelopes, but it doesn't, and they didn't. The philosophy is that it's easier to manage information when it appears in a contained space, especially if you're doing several things at a time. That way, each application runs in its own window, without elbowing others out of the way. Being able to control these windows is central to Windows' operation, which is why this chapter was written.

Windows' Windows (or "Pains of Glass")

All windows have two basic parts: the frame and the insides. There are subtle variations, but certain gizmos are common to all windows, and these gizmos work the same. Knowing what the gizmos are and how to work them brings you one step closer to feeling really in charge of your computer.

I've been framed!

Figure 27-1 shows a typical window on the screen. It has six basic elements.

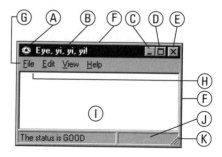

Figure 27-1

Fenestra Usitata.
A. Control menu has a minipicture of the application's icon. **B.** Title bar contains the document name, program name, username, or some other name. **C.** Minimize button shrinks the window down to a button on the taskbar. **D.** Maximize/Restore button zooms the window out to full size or not. **E.** Close, or go-away, button.
F. Window edges, which you can use to resize the window. **G.** Menu bar, where the menus are. **H.** Some windows may also have toolbars — this one doesn't. **I.** Get your work done here. **J.** Optional status bar area. **K.** Stretchy thing.

Control menu: Contains several commands for adjusting the window. Each of these commands is performed more easily by using the mouse and other window gadgets. And in case your mouse is ever broken, the keyboard equivalent for this menu is Alt+spacebar.

Title bar: Everything must have a name.

Minimize button: Click this button to shrink the window down to a button on the taskbar. Thwoop! The button even looks like a shrunken-down window. Kinda.

Restore/Maximize button: The Restore button looks like two overlapping windows. Click on it to restore the window to its size and position after maximizing. The Maximize button lets you zoom out the window to full-screen size, which is the preferred mode of operation for most applications.

Close button: Click here to make window go bye-bye. Other ways to do that include choosing Close from the Windows Control menu; choosing Exit, Quit, or Close from the application's File menu; pressing Alt+F4 or Alt+spacebar, C on the keyboard; and double-clicking on the Control-menu icon. They really want to give you ample opportunities to stomp a window into the dirt.

Edges. You can "grab" any edge of the window by using the mouse and drag the window to a new size. If you drag a window's corner, you can resize a window in two directions at a time.

⟹ See the section "The joy of stretch," later in this chapter, for more information about changing a window's size by pulling its edges around.

⟸ Another button that may appear on dialog-box windows is the question-mark button. For more information, see the sidebar "The weird ? button on some windows," in Chapter 4.

Inside information

A window's contents depend on what the window does. There are four common things you may find inside any window:

Menu bar: A list of commands going from left to right just under the window's title bar

Toolbars: A row of buttons, command shortcuts, and other gizmos that may appear below the menu bar

Work area: Where it happens

Status bar: A strip of helpful information about a program, typically lying low toward the bottom of the window

⟸ Refer to Figure 27-1 to find out where these things are, but keep in mind that not every window will sport them.

Adjusting a Window's Position and Size

It seems like whenever you start an application, its window appears on the screen at some random position and size. Sometimes that's just great. Other times, you'd like to rearrange the window's position and size, which is really cinchy to do, providing you know how to stretch a window to another size.

The joy of stretch

Windows on the desktop can change their size because their edges are made of rubber. To move a window's edge, you grab it with the mouse and stretch it to a new position. The following steps tell you how, and you can look at Figure 27-2 as well:

1. Point the mouse pointer at one of the window's edges you want to move.

   When the mouse pointer is positioned correctly, it changes into an up-down or left-right pointy arrow. This arrow shows you in which direction you can move the window's edge.

2. Drag the window's edge to a new position.

   Press and hold down the left mouse button, and then move the mouse in or out to make the window larger or smaller along that one edge. (This process is called "grabbing a window.")

   As you drag the mouse around, you'll see a fuzzy bar showing you approximately where the window's edge will end up.

3. Release the mouse button when you're pleased.

   The window snaps to the new edge and changes its size larger or smaller.

Figure 27-2
Stretching a window.
A. Grab one of the window's edges or corners with the mouse.
B. The mouse pointer changes to reflect which ways you can move the window's edge. **C.** Stretch it out or in to make the window a new size. **D.** The fuzzy bar tells you where the window's new position will be. **E.** Release the mouse button to resize the window.

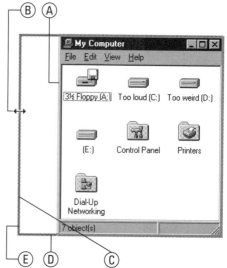

It's also possible to move two of the window's edges at a time. You do this by grabbing one of the window's corners and not an edge. Here's how:

1. Point the mouse pointer at one of the window's corners.

   Any of the four corners will do, though the most popular corner to grab is the lower right (don't ask me why — just try it).

   The mouse pointer changes to a diagonally pointing arrow when it's positioned correctly. Like dragging a window's edge, this arrow shows you in which direction you can move.

2. Drag the corner to a new position.

You can drag the corner in two directions at a time, making the window taller, wider, shorter, or narrower.

Note that there is a minimum size for every window on the screen.

If you drag the window too small, the menu bar "wraps" itself down to a second or third line.

Toolbars disappear when a window is too narrow. The moral? Don't make your window too narrow if you have a toolbar displayed.

While dragging the mouse around, you can use the fuzzy window outline to give you an idea of how the window will size up when you're done.

3. Release the mouse button.

The window snaps to its new size.

The wonder of Maximize and Restore

If you want to resize the window to fill the entire screen, you click on the Maximize button. This makes the window full size no matter what size or shape your screen.

After you click on the Maximize button, it changes to another button, the Restore button. This button returns your window to the size and position it was in before maximizing.

Look out for the stretchy thing in the lower right corner

Some windows may not stretch in the traditional way. You'll notice them because they sport what I call the stretchy thing in their lower right corner — like a ribbed triangle. With those types of windows, often the only way to have to change their size is to drag them by their stretchy thing. These windows usually can be dragged in only one direction or another, or they must maintain some minimum size so that you can see their contents.

Note that most status bars have a stretchy thing in their lower right corner. This may or may not mean that that's the only way to stretch the window.

You can also maximize and restore any window by double-clicking on its title bar. This is actually an old Macintosh trick, one that Microsoft probably borrowed from Apple a long time ago and never got sued over.

You cannot stretch a window when it's maximized. In fact, you can't even see the window's edges that make that possible.

Moving windows

Just as cartoons used to show cavemen dragging women around by their hair, you drag a window around using its hair. But because most windows are bald, you must use their title bar instead.

To drag a window around, follow these steps (also shown in Figure 27-3):

1. Point the mouse pointer at the window's title bar.

2. Grab the title bar with the mouse pointer.

   This is actually the start of a drag operation: Press and hold down the mouse's left button.

3. Move the mouse — and the window — to a new position.

   As you drag the mouse pointer on your desktop, an outline of the window on the screen mimics those movements. This gives you a rough idea of where your window will fit.

4. Release the mouse button.

   Plop! The window falls into place.

Cleaning up stray windows

Sometimes a window wanders off to the side of the screen and slips out of mouse reach. When that happens, it can be darned hard to reach the window and next-to-impossible to read anything the window may be seeing.

Who knows why windows stray off? But their doing so is no reason to turn off your computer or painfully reinstall Windows. Instead, you can try a quick trick to get the wandering window back:

1. Get rid of any extra windows.

   Close or minimize any windows on the screen, except for the one you can't get to (of course). You want your stray window to be the only one "open."

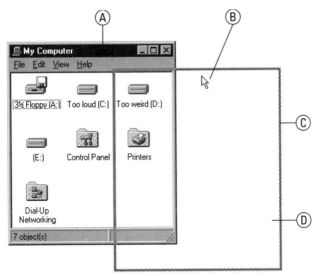

Figure 27-3
Dragging a window around by its head.
A. Point the mouse pointer at the title bar. **B.** Drag the mouse pointer to a
new position. **C.** A fuzzy outline of the window lets you know how it will look.
D. Release the mouse button – the window has moved.

2. Bring up the taskbar's shortcut menu.

   Right-click the mouse in a blank spot on the taskbar.

   If you can't find a blank spot on the taskbar, right-click on the current
   time, shown on the far right side of the taskbar. That shortcut menu
   looks a little different, but it still contains the vital command you need.

3. Choose Cascade from the menu.

   The window is instantly resized and placed in the upper left corner
   of the screen.

Now you can get at it, change its size, read its contents, whatever. Whew!
Aren't you lucky?

◄··· Also check out the section "Oh, lordy, I have too many windows open!" in
Chapter 2 for more information about arranging windows on the desktop.

To Deal with Scrollbars

What you see in a window is merely a small representation of something that can be much bigger. For example, a chapter in your Great American Novel can be several pages long, but you can see only 23 lines or so on the screen at a time. To see the rest of the document, you have to scroll.

⬅ꜜ You can make a window's scrollbars disappear, providing you can stretch the window out to a larger size. See the section "The joy of stretch," earlier in this chapter. (By the way, I once saw a PC hooked up to a special "virtual" monitor, where some computer geeks had stretched out a window to 32 feet by 32 feet in size. Talk about a slow day . . . .)

Scrolling for dollars

Scrolling is done in two directions: up and down and left and right. To control how you scroll and which parts of your document you can see, you use a vertical or horizontal scrollbar.

Left and right is horizontal — like the horizon. Think about the horizon. It goes left and right; a straight line (minus mountains) going left and right is horizontal.

Up and down is vertical. There is no cute way to remember that.

Working a scrollbar (scrollin', scrollin', scrollin')

You use the scrollbar to see a different part of the image inside a window. But the scrollbar doesn't really move the image; instead, it moves the window. To see the *left* side of your document, for example, you click on the *left* arrow on the horizontal scrollbar. But that moves your document to the *right*. This confuses some beginners, but you can get used to it snappy-quick.

Figure 27-4 shows a typical scrollbar, which can be either a vertical or horizontal scrollbar, but it's horizontal here because that's what fits best on the page. Note that there are several ways to use the scrollbar, not just the arrows at the end.

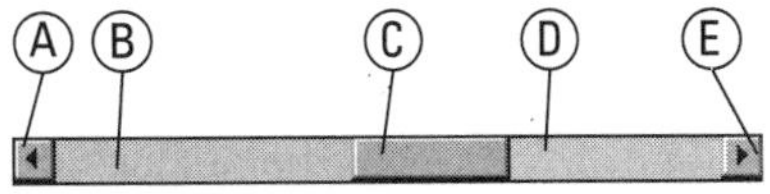

Figure 27-4
Mr. Jolly Scrollbar.
A. Scroll left arrow; click here to move the
window left one smidgen. **B.** Click here to move the window left one "page," or a
bigger chunk than a smidgen. **C.** The elevator box, or thumb tab. **D.** Click here to
move the window right one "page." **E.** Scroll right arrow, which you click to move
the window right a smidgen.

The most curious part of the scrollbar is the elevator box, or thumb tab.
First, its position gives you a vague idea of what the window is looking at
in relationship to the entire document. For example, if the elevator box is at
the top of the vertical scrollbar, you know that you're looking at the start of
your document.

Second, the elevator box's size lets you know how much of the document
you can see at one time. If it's really long, your document is relatively short,
and you can see most of it in the window at once. If it's squat, you have a
hefty document.

Third, you can drag the elevator box with the mouse to scroll anywhere in
your document at once.

Chasing Menus

A key part of most application windows is their menu bar. This bar is where
the commands which control that application live. What the commands do
and how they work depends on the application. The following sections tell
you how the menus operate.

Many menu commands are common to all Windows applications. Refer to
Chapter 4 for more information about those common menu commands.

Working the menus

The best way to work Windows menus is with your mouse. It involves a
great deal of pointing and clicking and occasionally some dragging. Before
doing so, gawk at Figure 27-5 to glean some menu terminology knowledge.

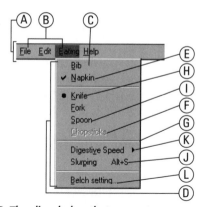

Figure 27-5

Menu pieces parts.

A. The menu bar itself. **B.** Menu titles (the names of various menus). **C.** A menu all dropped down and ready to play. **D.** Menu items or commands. Each of these relates somehow to the menu title. Here you see various eating commands. **E.** A check mark by a command means that that option is currently on. **F.** A dimmed command is currently unavailable. You must do something in the application or set some condition before the command can be used. **G.** The dimple bar that separates different types of commands. **H.** A dot appears by one of several commands, indicating which one of the group is active. **I.** The underlined letter is the keyboard shortcut key. **J.** Key command shortcut. **K.** A submenu lurks here. **L.** This command opens a dialog box in which you can choose more options.

Menus consist of titles and the menu itself. You click on the menu name on the menu bar to see the menu.

Located on each menu are various commands. The commands are often divided into groups on longer menus, separated by dimple bars.

A ✔ check mark next to a menu command means that that option is on. Choosing the command again removes the ✔, turning it off. Choose the command a third time to switch it on again.

Sometimes only one of several menu items can be selected at one time. In Figure 27-5, for example, you can choose either Knife, Fork, or Spoon (the Chopsticks item is unavailable). Whichever item you pick from the group has a • dot by it.

When a menu item isn't available, it appears "dimmed" on the menu. You can't choose that item no matter what; typically, you have to rework some part of the program to make it available as an option (such as choosing Chinese food).

A ▶ triangle next to a command indicates a submenu. Choosing that command displays the submenu, which pops up on the screen. Sometimes there are sub-submenus, such as the disaster that naturally befalls the Start Thing's menu.

Finally, some commands have ellipses, or three dots (...), after their names. That means that the command opens a dialog box in which you can set more options. This isn't a hard and fast rule, however. Lots of the commands that should have dots after them don't, and some that don't should have.

Beware the instant menu!

Watch out for some "instant" menu titles. These really aren't titles but are, in fact, commands on the menu bar. Some programmers are nice and let you know that they're really commands by putting an exclamation point after them. So your menu bar may look like this:

Here, the Schedule! menu is really a command. This isn't a hard and fast rule either, so just be on the lookout for certain

menu titles that are commands and that offer you no clue about it either way.

Working menus with your keyboard

Every menu item and command has a key equivalent. This means that you can get at any menu by using the keyboard, often faster than you can by using the mouse. The key is to look for the underlined letter in the menu. Press the Alt key plus that letter to activate that menu or command.

For example, the Edit menu has an underlined E. If you press Alt+E, you drop down the Edit menu. You can then choose any item in that menu by pressing the underlined letter: T for Cut, C for Copy, P for Paste, and so on. You don't have to press the Alt key after you have the menu open.

You can also press each key separately. For example, just press and release the Alt key. This activates the main menu. From that point on, you have to press only the underlined letter to make something happen: Alt, E, T for Edit⇨Cut, for example.

◀■■ Some people find these keyboard shortcuts much faster than working the mouse, especially when you're using a word processor or any application where your fingers are already on the keyboard. Also check out the sidebar "Common quick-key shortcuts" in Chapter 4 for some command equivalents to certain common menu items.

The Old Multi-Document Interface Gag

Some sophisticated applications let you work on multiple documents at a time. To handle that situation, each document appears in its own window inside the application's main window. It's windows within windows within Windows! It's called the *multi-document interface,* which can be abbreviated to "multi-document interface."

The key to knowing whether your application supports the multi-document interface is to find a menu labeled Window. This usually indicates that the application can support having multiple document windows open at a time.

Like the application's window, the document windows have basic pieces parts (see Figure 27-1); each document window has a Minimize, Maximize/ Restore, and Close button, for example.

When the document window is maximized, as shown in Figure 27-6, its buttons appear right under the application's buttons on the menu bar.

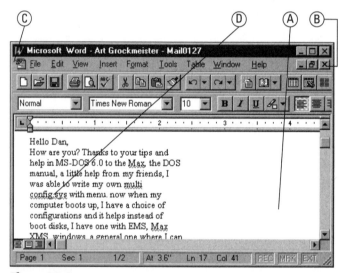

Figure 27-6
A document window "maximized" inside an application.
A. This is actually a document window. **B.** Here are the document window's Minimize, Restore, and Close buttons. **C.** The document's Control menu is similar to the main application's Control menu. This is something you can ignore.
D. The "red" underlined words are flagged by Word as misspelled, part of its new on-the-fly spell-checking — which can be annoying. See Chapter 10 for more information about Word.

When the document window is minimized, it appears like a button on the taskbar, but the button floats in the bottom of the application's work space (see Figure 27-7).

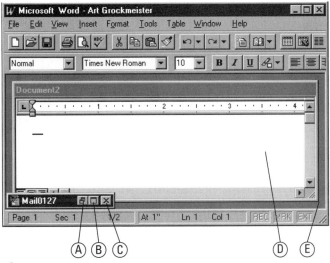

Figure 27-7
A minimized document window.
A. Click here to put the window back up on the screen the way it was before.
B. Click here to maximize the window. **C.** Click here to close. **D.** Another document window, floating in limbo. **E.** This is the fabric of the universe here, the strange background in an application's workspace window (the same *void* they talk about in Genesis 1:2).

◀ When the document window floats in the application's work space, you can change its size or position just like a window on the desktop. See the section "Adjusting a Window's Position and Size," earlier in this chapter. The instructions there apply also to document windows.

◀ You can also arrange document windows in a cascading or tiled pattern. This works by choosing the proper arrangement command from the application's Window menu; Window⇨Tile, Window⇨Cascade, or Window⇨Arrange. See the section "Oh, lordy, I have too many windows open!" in Chapter 2 for more information about how this works on the desktop. The same rules apply for arranging document windows.

Part VI **Windows Is As Windows Does**

Trapped in a Dialog Box

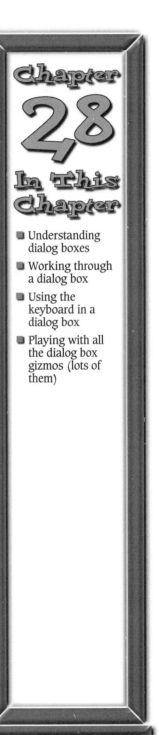

Chapter 28

In This Chapter

- Understanding dialog boxes
- Working through a dialog box
- Using the keyboard in a dialog box
- Playing with all the dialog box gizmos (lots of them)

When Windows wants your opinion, it asks. Then it ignores you. But when it needs information, it presents you with a dialog box. That's a special window on the screen, like an information sheet. You fill in various options, set various settings, and generally goof around until you think that you have everything set just right. Then you tell Windows that it's all OK or you chicken out and Cancel.

Dialog boxes are useful in that they let you set numerous options without having to fuss with a bunch of menus. On the down side, Windows tosses up dialog boxes on the screen like dough in a pizza parlor on a Saturday night. Some dialog boxes are so complex that they make you think that you've just sat down in the space shuttle cockpit: Things can get confusing. The purpose of this chapter is to tell you how a dialog box works so that the gizmos and gadgets you encounter there will actually help you get something done, hopefully something you want.

➡ You have to use a mouse to work any dialog box, though keyboardy ways of doing things are also possible. See Chapter 29 for more information about the mouse terminology used in this chapter.

Anatomy of a Dialog Box

Dialog boxes range from the utterly simple to a variation on a Boeing 747 cockpit. Even so, all of them tend to look and work the same.

The most basic of all dialog boxes is the "info" dialog box. One of these types is shown in Figure 28-1, the About Windows dialog box. It contains basic information, some blah-blah text, and an OK button.

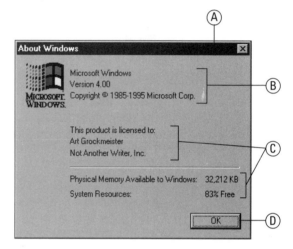

Figure 28-1
Windows! Read all about it!
A. Choose Help⇨About Windows 95 from the My Computer window to see this dialog box.
B. Information about Windows. La-de-da. **C.** Good-to-know stuff, but nothing you can do about it.
D. Click here when you've been impressed enough.

Another simple dialog box is the warning dialog box (see Figure 28-2), which lets you know that something is amiss and may even give you a chance to remedy the situation.

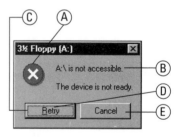

Figure 28-2
Oops. Musta taken a wrong turn.
A. The "Warning" icon. Other icons include a question mark (?) for a question, an exclamation point (!) for "what the huh?," and maybe even more that I haven't seen yet. **B.** A rude way of telling you that there is no disk in drive A. **C.** This line of ants around the Retry button means that it has the "focus" — it's the current item in the dialog box. **D.** Stick the disk in the drive, and click here. **E.** Or forget the whole deal.

Basic pieces parts

Every dialog box has three main elements: the title bar, contents, and a button. The title bar gives the dialog box a name, the contents are the "dialog" part for the computer, and the button is your dialog part.

Oftentimes, the button says "OK" when in fact it should say "Oh well."

Don't confuse the buttons in the dialog box with the main dialog-box control buttons. There are typically one to three main control buttons, all of which you find at the bottom of the dialog box.

The more complex dialog boxes sport a question-mark button, next to the × Close button in the upper right corner of the dialog box (see Figure 28-3). Click on this button, and the mouse pointer changes to a mouse pointer/question-mark thing. Then you can click on any other gadget in the dialog box to get pop-up help.

Figure 28-3
A sample dialog-box.
A. Dialog-box title.
B. Question-mark button; click here, and then point and click at something else in the dialog box to get pop-up help.
C. Close button; same as Cancel button. **D.** Click on one of these tabs to bring its panel forward. **E.** A panel, or page, associated with a tab. Some dialog boxes can have a dozen or more tabs and panels. **F.** A dimple line marks an area in the dialog box. **G.** Area title. **H.** This button has the line of ants, or the "focus." Press the Tab key to move the focus to another part of the dialog box. Also, pressing the Enter key is the same as choosing the focused item. **I.** Main control buttons, which you click on when you're done with the dialog box.

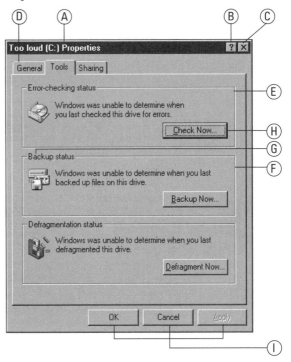

Another way to get pop-up help is to right-click on something in a dialog box. This usually displays the What's This? shortcut menu. Click on What's This? to get some bubble help.

Panels, pages, and tabs

Some dialog boxes have more than one face. The faces, also called panels or pages, are each connected to a tab, like the tab on a file folder. Click on the tab, and that panel moves forward in the dialog box.

Areas, regions, asylums

Within each dialog box you may find various areas or regions. These are groupings of gadgets within the dialog box, usually controlling some related item.

Areas are each given a title and then surrounded by a dimple line. Although this serves to look cool, it also keeps those related items together. And if you're hunting for something inside one of those 747-cockpit dialog boxes, it can make finding that something easier.

Working the Dialog Box

Some dialog boxes just give up and tell you something (see Figure 28-4). Most others are there to get information from you. That's done primarily through the gizmos, covered later in this chapter. But certain rules apply to using all dialog boxes, which are covered in the next few, brief sections.

Figure 28-4
The briefest of dialog boxes.
A. Start up here. **B.** Read things, make choices (which isn't apparent in this dialog box). **C.** Confirm your decisions. **D.** Change your mind.

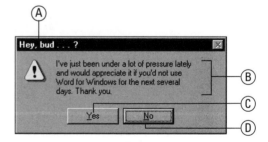

The mousy way of using a dialog box

The best way to control the stuff in a dialog box is by using the mouse; dialog boxes are very mouse-friendly. You need a keyboard in order to type various text items in a dialog box, which the mouse is lousy at. Otherwise, it's point and click, drag, click-click, and so on.

The keyboardy way of using a dialog box

Keyboards and dialog boxes can go together, but normally it's rather awkward. To use a keyboard to control a dialog box, you have to know about the line of ants and understand how the Tab key works.

The focal point of every dialog box is in the line of ants, a dotted rectangle that surrounds the current item in a dialog box. As shown in Figure 28-1, for example, it's the OK button that has the focus; as shown in Figure 28-2, it's the Retry button; as shown in Figure 28-3, it's the Check Now button; in Figure 28-4, the No button has the focus.

You can move the focus by either clicking the mouse on another gadget in the dialog box or pressing the Tab key. The line of ants jumps from item to item each time you press the Tab key.

Pressing the Enter key selects the gizmo that has the line of ants around it. This is the same as clicking the mouse on that item.

To switch from one panel to another, press the Tab key until the current panel's tab is highlighted. Then press the left- and right-arrow keys to switch to another tab.

You can instantly choose any gizmo in a dialog box by using a keyboard shortcut. You'll notice that various items in the dialog box have one letter

Backup Now...

underlined. If you press the Alt key plus that letter, you choose that item — similar to clicking on it. For example, as shown in Figure 28-3, you can choose the Backup Now button by pressing Alt+B in that dialog box.

The universal "cancel" key in any dialog box is Esc. Pressing that key is the same as clicking the mouse on the Cancel button.

Time to commit to something

Nothing you do in a dialog box happens until you tell Windows that it's OK. So after making your selections and settings, you have to click on OK to make it happen. Or if you change your mind, you can click on the Cancel button.

A third button, Apply, may appear in some dialog boxes. This button enables you to preview your settings without leaving the dialog box. It's the same as clicking on OK, but the dialog box's window doesn't close. That way, you can take a peek at how your decisions affect the rest of Windows, make minor tunes and tweaks — or toss the whole thing out — and then click on OK to confirm.

All Them Gizmos

What makes a dialog box work are all the doodads and gizmos you find lurking inside it. The following sections discuss how to use the various gadgets you may find lurking in a dialog box near you.

This list may not be complete; programmers can create new gadgets every day, including some truly intuitive and creative stuff. Don't be afraid of them! Nothing you do in a dialog box has serious consequences unless you click on the OK button. So feel free to goof around if some gadget seems like a fun toy.

◀▥ For example, the Time Zone gadget in the Date/Time Properties dialog box is a fun one to play in. Goof around there, but click on Cancel when you leave — unless you're in the process of moving, of course. See Chapter 7, the section "Fooling with the time (or, setting the time on your PC)."

Buttons

Buttons aren't a typical dialog box gizmo. They usually perform their actions immediately, such as a Save As button opening up another dialog box.

Buttons work by clicking the mouse on them. This instantly selects whichever option is attached to the button. The name on the button should give you some hint about what happens next.

You can activate a button by using the keyboard in two ways: First, you can find an underlined letter in the button's name and then press the Alt key plus that letter. Second, you can press the Tab key until the line of ants surrounds that button's name and then press the Enter key. (It's obviously better to use the mouse.)

⟫➡ Also see the section "On/off buttons," later in this chapter, for information about another type of button.

Check boxes

Check boxes are used when an option can be either on or off. A check mark (✔) in the box means that the option is on; an empty box means that the option is off.

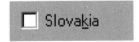

You put a ✔ check mark in the box and also remove it by clicking the mouse on that option, either in the box or on the option's name. Click once to put a ✔ there and again to remove it.

Using the keyboard, you press the Alt key plus the underlined letter in the command name, such as Alt+K to activate Slova*k*ia.

Computer geeks call this type of gizmo a *toggle;* choose it once to turn it on, and choose it again to turn it off. See? It toggles back and forth like the togs of old.

The collapsible tree-structure thing

The collapsible tree-structure thing appears frequently in Windows. It's used to display something that has a *hierarchical structure* — for example, an outline or the way folders are organized on a hard drive.

The idea is that some items in the tree structure contain other items, just like one folder on the hard drive can contain other folders. The collapsible tree-structure thing comes in handy because it enables you to hide the contents of folders so that you don't see everything at once. In the outline example, it's possible to view only the major headings in your outline. Then you can open each heading to see the details as you want. This is truly less boggling than seeing everything at once.

An icon in a tree structure with a plus (+) by it contains more branches in the tree. Click once on the + to open up the branches and take a look. But stand back! Sometimes this opens a whole can of worms, often much more stuff than can be displayed in the window at one time.

After being opened, the + plus thing changes into a – minus thing.

An icon with a minus (–) by its name is already open. To close this part of the tree, click on the – once with the mouse.

When you close a branch of the tree, the – minus thing changes to a + plus thing.

A missing plus or minus thing means that there are no more branches inside of it (nothing more to be opened).

◀▥ Icons appear by the plus or minus signs in a collapsible tree structure. In the Explorer, the icons are of little folders; pluses have closed folders by them, and minuses have open folders. See Chapter 17, the section "Climbing the Folder Tree" for more information.

◀▥ The collapsible tree-structure thing appears in several other places in Windows, most often in the Control Panel. I can tell you quite assuredly, if you ever see one of these beasts and it's not in the Explorer, *don't mess with it!* Usually that tree structure controls advanced aspects of Windows that are best left untouched. See Chapter 20 for more information about the Control Panel.

Drop-down lists

Operating Systems:

OS/2 Warp ▼

OS/2 Warp ▲
Macintosh System 8
Power PC Operating system (???)
TRS-DOS
CP/M
DOS, yes, good old DOS. Thanks ▼

A drop-down list displays a bunch of fill-in-the-blanks options. These you either typed earlier or they're preset options you can't change. Either way, the drop-down list works the same.

You activate a drop-down list by clicking on the down-arrow button to the right of the list. This displays the list like a menu.

If the list is long, you can use its scrollbar to browse through the options.

When you see the option you want, click on it once using the mouse. The drop-down list disappears, and your choice appears in the list's text box.

These things are a bear to work by using the keyboard alone. Basically, you set the focus on the list box by pressing the Tab key or by pressing the Alt key plus the underlined letter in the list box's title. Then press Alt+↓ (the down-arrow key) to drop down the list. Press the up- or down-arrow keys to find an item in the list, and then press the Enter key. (Or just use the mouse.)

By the way, sometimes when the dialog box hovers at a low altitude on the screen, the list box drops "up." That's just so that you can see all the options; nothing's wrong with your computer.

➡ Some list boxes don't drop down. See the section "List boxes," later in this section.

Drop-down palettes

A drop-down palette works like a drop-down list box. The difference is that a small table of selections appears rather than a scrolling list. Most often you see this used in the Color palette, from which you choose a color for some-such operation.

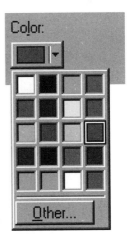

To pick an item, click on it with the mouse.

Unfortunately, you can't manipulate this one by using the keyboard.

In the Color drop-down palette, there's a button for Other, which lets you custom-create your own color. Clicking on it brings up the interesting and fun Color dialog box, in which you can custom-create your own color. It's an enormous time-waster, so I won't bother describing how it works in this book.

Input boxes

File name: Blech-o-matic

An input box is merely an area in a dialog box where you can type something. It contains editable text and can even be edited using common word-processor commands.

To activate an input box, click on it with the mouse. Then just start typing.

If you want to replace the text in an input box, double-click on it with the mouse. This selects all the text, and whatever you type replaces it.

Always remember to press the Tab key when you're done typing text. In most dialog boxes, pressing Enter is the same as selecting some other option, such as the OK button, which probably isn't what you want.

You can select portions of the text in an input box by using the mouse; see Chapter 30 for more information about working with text, including the various text-editing commands you can use in a text input box.

You can also cut, copy, and paste text in an input box. I amazed a co-worker once when I selected a phone number from one application and then pasted it into an input box in another application's dialog box. You save a great deal of typing that way, and you're assured that the number is entered exactly. See Chapter 8, the section "The three amigos: Cut, Copy, Paste," for more information about cut, copy, and paste.

List boxes

A list box is a scrolling list of options, though sometimes there aren't enough to them to warrant a scrollbar. Unlike a drop-down list box, most of these items are visible at one time.

You pick an item by clicking on it with the mouse. You can use the scrollbar to scroll the list up or down to see more options.

With the keyboard, you can press the up- or down-arrow keys to choose an item. First select the list box by pressing the Alt key plus the underlined letter in the list box's name, such as Alt+D for Eating Disorder.

On/off buttons

You mostly see on/off types of buttons on toolbars. They work like check boxes; when the button looks pushed in, that option is on. When the button is left sticking out (an "outtie"), then the option is off.

To turn on an on/off button, click on it once with the mouse. Click on it again to turn that option off.

Keyboard equivalents for these types of buttons are rare because they appear mostly on toolbars, and toolbars are very nonkeyboard things.

Radio buttons

Radio buttons are on/off buttons, very similar to check mark boxes. The difference is that radio buttons are grouped in "families" of two or more. Only one radio button in the family may be chosen at any one time. This works like the buttons on old car radios: You could punch up only one station at a time, unless you were four years old.

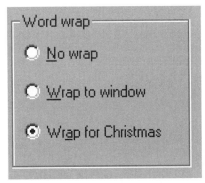

To choose one radio button in a family, click on it with the mouse. The circle grows a dot in it, indicating that that's the item you've chosen. To unselect that item, you must click on a different radio button in that family.

With the keyboard, simply choose the key shortcut for the radio button by pressing the Alt key plus the underlined key in the command, such as Alt+A for Wrap for Christmas.

More than any other group of commands, you see radio buttons in various areas roped off by a dimple line. That keeps one family of radio buttons separate from any other radio buttons that may live in the same dialog box. Without that dimple line, heck, it'd be the Hatfields and the McCoys all over again.

Sliders

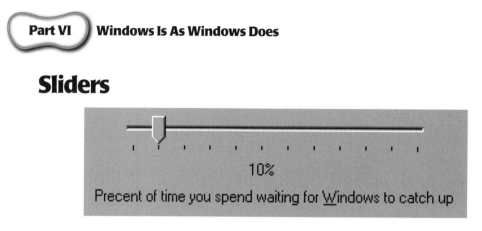

A slider can be one of a number of controls, each of which you manipulate by grabbing the control with the mouse and moving it to a new position. Numbers nearby the slider usually tell you what the new position does.

With a mouse, you have to point at the slider control and then drag the slider to a new position; hold down the mouse button, move the mouse to move the slider, and then release the mouse button when you're done. This works similarly to a scrollbar.

With the keyboard, you press the Alt-key equivalent, such as Alt+W, and then press the left- and right-arrow keys to adjust the slider. Some sliders may have a text-input box, in which case you can use it to enter a precise value.

Spinners

Spinners are delightful little gadgets that adjust a value up or down, such as setting the time of day, the year, or your weight in kilograms after a hearty meal.

To adjust the value, you click on the tiny arrows — the spinner — by using the mouse. Click on the up arrow to make the value larger, and click on the down arrow to make the value smaller.

When you have multiple values, as with the time of day, you should double-click the mouse on the hour, minute, or seconds value to first select it. Then use the spinner to adjust the time.

The keyboard alternative to using a spinner is to just type the proper value. Most spinners' text boxes can be edited. If not, try pressing the up or down arrows to adjust the value.

Mousy Concepts

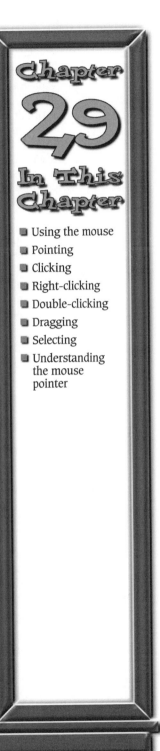

- Using the mouse
- Pointing
- Clicking
- Right-clicking
- Double-clicking
- Dragging
- Selecting
- Understanding the mouse pointer

Y ou're fooling yourself if you think that you can use Windows without a mouse. You need a mouse in order to use Windows. You must have one. Not only that, you have to understand how the mouse works and how to perform some common mouse tricks. This is all really simple stuff but something you should practice a bit to get used to. Think of the mouse as your fuzziless little friend. The happy rodent. Heck — Mickey! After all, it's not called the computer *rat,* you know.

"Here I Come to Save the Day!" (Using Mr. Mouse)

You don't have to have your hand on the mouse all the time you use your computer. You have to grab it only when something mousy is required, which isn't that often.

The mouse points away from, with its tail trailing off toward the rear of your desk, back into the bowels of your computer somewhere. So you grab the mouse with its head facing toward you. Remember: The tail points *away* from you.

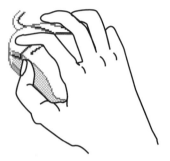

When it comes time to grab the mouse, gently rest your hand on it. It doesn't have to be the palm of your hand. Instead, open up your hand and lay it on the mouse with your index finger on the left button and your middle finger on the right button. Your thumb and other fingers rest off to the side, and your wrist lies limply on your tabletop.

Some mice have three buttons; ignore the middle button for now.

➡ If you're left-handed, you put your index finger on the right button and your middle finger on the left. See the sidebar "The left-handed mouse," later in this chapter.

The mouse gets going thanks to elbow movement on your behalf; do not roll the mouse with your wrist or use your elbow to help glide Mr. Mouse around on your tabletop. The mouse controls a pointer or mouse cursor on the screen that mimics the movements of the mouse on your tabletop. Move the mouse wildly in a circle, and the pointer on the screen follows suit.

It's best to roll your computer mouse on a soft, fuzzy mouse pad. This pad enables the mouse's rubber ball underneath to get some traction, and it makes for smoother mouse operations.

Another item you can buy is a wrist pad, which helps elevate your wrist when you use the mouse. This pad supposedly lessens the chance of mouse injury while using a computer. (Mouse wrist is the tennis elbow of the '90s.)

The best way to learn about the mouse

Alas, Windows doesn't come with a mouse tutorial. Maybe it will someday, but for some reason, Microsoft is afraid that you'll master the mouse without any extra help to be offered by any software. Fortunately, there is a program you can use to help you understand how the mouse works: the Solitaire game!

When you play Solitaire, you use the mouse to click on menus, double-click on cards, and drag cards to certain positions. All the mouse techniques are used to play the game, which makes it an ideal mouse tutorial — providing that you like playing Solitaire.

See Chapter 26 for more information about wasting time with the Solitaire game.

Know These Mouse Terms

There are five things you can do with the mouse, and five terms used to describe them: point, click, double-click, drag, and select, or highlight. Each of these terms is elaborated on in the following sections, and a brief description is offered in Table 29-1.

Table 29-1	Things You Can Do with a Computer Mouse
Mouse Action	**Description**
Point	Move the mouse pointer on the screen so that it's hovering over some object, a button or what-have-you.
Click	To press and release the mouse's main button, the one on the left.
Double-click	Two quick clicks in a row, both pointing at the same spot.
Drag	To press and hold the mouse button down and then move the mouse around. In Windows, this technique is used to move objects around on the screen. The drag ends when you release the mouse button.
Select	To click on something, highlighting it.

Behavior Patterns Common to the Computer Mouse

The following sections contain descriptions of the various things you can do with a computer mouse. This is not required reading. Look here only if you have trouble with a mouse concept or need a little extra help.

Getting to the point

When you're told to point the mouse at something, you move the mouse pointer or cursor over to that something. In Figure 29-1, for example, the mouse is pointing at the drive C icon in My Computer.

Figure 29-1
Getting to the point.
A. The mouse pointer. **B.** The mouse pointer is pointing here. **C.** This is where Dr. Cornelius has hidden the microfilm.

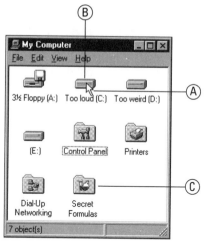

Remember that you move the mouse pointer on the screen by rolling the mouse around on your tabletop. The movements of the mouse pointer on the screen mimic those of the mouse on your table.

When you're told to point at something, point right at it. Do not point below it or off to the right. Hover the mouse right over that sucker to point at it.

A point is usually followed by a click.

Some things just click

Clicking the mouse requires that you press and release its button. But which button? Button, button, who's got the mouse button?

The main mouse button is the one you click: the index-finger button, the left button. When you see instructions to click the mouse, that's the button you click.

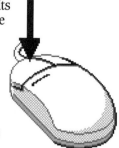

➡ Of course, if you're left-handed, you click the right button, which is the button your index finger is on. See the nearby sidebar "The left-handed mouse."

If your hearing hasn't gone to hell, you can hear the clicking sound the mouse makes when you click its button. This is where this mouse technique got its name.

Most often you click the mouse to activate some graphical goody-goody on the screen, such as a button, menu, or other interesting object.

The left-handed mouse

If you're one of the lucky few southpaws in this world, you can choose to use your mouse on the right side of your computer — like the rest of us — or use your mouse on the left side, where it's more intuitive for you. Heck, even some right-handers like a left-handed mouse. My friend Wally Wang, co-author of IDG Books' *Illustrated Computer Dictionary For Dummies,* is one such righty who uses a lefty mouse.

To make your mouse left-hand-friendly, follow these steps:

1. **Pop up the Start Thing.** Press Ctrl+Esc.

2. **Choose Settings⇨Control Panel.**

3. **Double-click on the Mouse icon to open it up.** You see the Mouse Properties dialog box (see Figure 29-2).

Figure 29-2
The Mouse Properties dialog box.
A. Click here to set a right-handed mouse. **B.** Click here to set a left-handed mouse.
C. These instructions (both sides) tell you which button does what in Windows. **D.** The double-click speed slider, where you can adjust how sensitive Windows is to your mouse double-clicking. **E.** Slide it over here if you're not clicking fast enough. **F.** Double-click here.

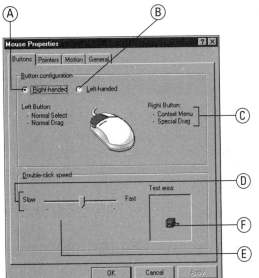

4. **Click on the Left-handed radio button.** You see the button highlight on the demo mouse shift from the left side to the right — where you want it.

5. **Click on OK.** This step closes the Mouse Properties dialog box. Then close the Control Panel's window as well.

You've just switched mouse buttons, so from here on in, you use the *right* button to click, double-click, and open things. You use the *left* mouse button to pop up shortcut menus. Remember that!

Doing the right-click

The *right-click* is used in Windows to bring up various shortcut menus. To do a right-click, you just click the mouse's right button. This works the same as the normal click does, though it's called a right-click in this book and in Windows.

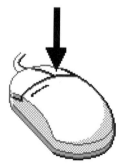

Yes, and if you're using a lefty mouse, you do a left-click. But keep in mind that this book uses the term "right-click" throughout. Don't get confused (as if can openers, doorknobs, and bottle caps haven't driven you insane already).

◀▬ See Chapter 5, the section "The Ubiquitous Pop-up Shortcut Menus," for more information about the various shortcut menus that infest Windows.

The double-quick double-click

A *double-click* is two quick clicks of the mouse in a row *and* in the same spot. Both clicks must be at the same spot on the screen or else it doesn't work (and that describes most of your problems with a double-click).

You double-click most often to "open" something up, such as a new program or document. "Double-click," said the manual. "Click, click" went the mouse. Run, run did the program.

There's a great place to practice your double-clicks in Windows. It's located in the Mouse Properties dialog box. There you can double-click on a tiny little jack-in-the-box icon to test your double-clicking skills. Follow these steps:

1. Call up the Start Thing.

   Press Ctrl+Esc to summon that fun-loving pop-up menu.

2. Choose Settings➪Control Panel.

   ◀▬ This step opens the Control Panel's window, full of goodies for controlling your computer. See Chapter 20 for the details.

3. Double-click on the Mouse icon.

   This step displays the Mouse Properties dialog box.

Mouse

4. Click on the Buttons panel to bring that panel forward if it isn't already.

   What you see will be similar to Figure 29-2. Look for the Test area in the lower right corner of the Buttons panel.

5. Double-click the mouse on the jack-in-the-box.

    Point the mouse right at the ugly, purple thing. Then click the button twice while trying to keep the mouse steady. It helps if you gently hold the mouse in your hand; if you have a death grip on the sucker, a double-click will never work.

    If you're successful, a clown pops up. Egads! Try double-clicking again to put him away.

6. Adjust the double-click speed if you find double-clicking difficult.

    If you find that you can't click fast enough to make Mr. Jack-in-the-box pop up, adjust the slider in the dialog box, moving it to the Slow end of the scale. Then do step 5 again.

    If you think you're Bill Gates, slide the slider all the way over toward Fast. You *really* have to double-click fast to get the jack-in-the-box up.

    If you're like me, you'll leave the slider in the middle, where most folks are happy with the double-click speed.

7. Click OK to close the Mouse Properties dialog box.

8. Close the Control Panel window.

    Click on its X Close button in the upper right corner.

Moving can be such a drag

Dragging is the most complex mouse action to describe. It's essentially a combined click-and-move at the same time. Here are the steps you take:

1. Point the mouse at something you want to drag.

    In Windows, it can be an icon, a graphical object, a window, the edge of a window, or any of a number of draggable things.

2. Press and hold down the mouse button.

    Just like you would click, except that you're keeping the button held down.

    Normally you press and hold the main mouse button — the one on the left. However, there is a "right-drag" operation in Windows, in which case you press and hold the right mouse button instead.

    Southpaws, as usual, reverse the buttons in the preceding paragraphs.

3. Move the mouse to a new position on the screen.

    This is the drag part. Still keeping the button down (which isn't that hard), you move the mouse on the screen. This step typically moves something on the screen so that you get immediate visual feedback about what you're doing.

4. Release the mouse button.

When the mouse pointer is pointing at the new position, release the mouse button. You're done dragging.

Selective service

Selecting isn't really an official mouse operation. It's actually just pointing and clicking at something. The difference is that the thing you clicked on becomes highlighted or selected. For example, you click on an icon to select it, and the icon becomes highlighted.

To select more than one object, you press and hold the Ctrl (Control) key while clicking. This process is officially known as a Ctrl+click (Control+click). Each item you Ctrl+click becomes selected. If you don't Ctrl+click, only the last item you clicked on is selected.

◄— You can also select a group of items by dragging the mouse around them. This technique is covered at the end of Chapter 16, in the section "Calf-ropin' files."

The Ever-Changing Mouse Pointer

The mouse pointer doesn't always look like an arrow. No, it changes. Depending on what you're doing in Windows at the time, the mouse pointer can take on a number of different personas. A few of the more popular ones are shown and described in Table 29-2.

The hourglass "Busy" pointer is your worst enemy. It means that you have to sit and wait until Windows is done spinning its wheels before you can do something else. Sometimes this can be a long, long time. Other times, it's even longer.

The "Working in Background" pointer doesn't spell true death. You can actually click on things while Windows is working, but everything moves slowly.

Pointer	Name	Function
	Table 29-2	**Different Mouse Pointers You May Find Loitering About**
	Normal Select	Your typical mouse pointer.
	Busy	Tells you that Windows is off doing something. Wait.
	Working in Background	You can still work, but Windows is busy doing something you just asked for.
	Text Select	Used when editing text to position the cursor or select text.
	Help Select	Means that you can click on something to see help about it.
	Unavailable, don't bother	Whatever you're trying to do, or "Uh-uh."

⬅ The mouse pointer doesn't have to look the way it does in Table 29-2. There are other styles or schemes you can use, each replete with its own stock of pointers. See Chapter 25 for the details.

Working with Text and Graphics

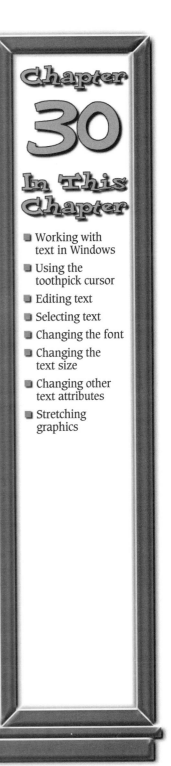
Chapter

30

In This Chapter

- Working with text in Windows
- Using the toothpick cursor
- Editing text
- Selecting text
- Changing the font
- Changing the text size
- Changing other text attributes
- Stretching graphics

Part of Windows' common approach is that it treats any text or graphics in any application the same way. There is a definite way to edit text, to change its size and style, and so on. This is a constant, something done the same whether it's in a big program such as Microsoft Word or in a tiny text field in a dialog box. (Though Word has more features, there are basic text-editing techniques.) The same holds true with graphics on the screen, though there's not as much you can do with them. This chapter covers the basic tenets of working with text and graphics just about anywhere in Windows.

Basic Messing with Text Stuff

Even though Windows is graphical, there is a great deal of text involved. You still need a keyboard, along with your mouse, to make things happen. In fact, I'd say that a goodly chunk of your time spent working with Windows will be typing text, either in an application or in a dialog box somewhere. No matter what, you can always rely on Windows' consistent rules for dealing with text.

◄▥ See Chapter 28, the section "Input boxes," for information about typing text in a dialog box.

All hail the flashing toothpick cursor

Windows uses two dealies when you play with text. The first is the Text Selection pointer, which is what the mouse pointer turns into when you hover it over text. This pointer says that you can use the mouse to select text and position the flashing toothpick cursor on the screen.

The flashing toothpick cursor is used to help you edit your text. It marks the position on the screen where new characters appear as you type them. New text appears behind the toothpick cursor, and the toothpick cursor moves to the right as you type.

You can move the toothpick cursor by clicking the mouse at a new spot in the text. This works whether you're working in a word processor or toiling away in some tiny text input box in some obscure dialog box. You can also move the toothpick cursor with your keyboard's arrow keys, as covered in the next section.

Basic text-editing stuff

To create new text, type away. If you make a mistake, you can use the Backspace key to back up and erase your text. Unlike on a typewriter, a computer's Backspace key backs up and erases.

When you're done typing a line of text, you press the Enter key.

In a dialog box, when you're done filling in an input box, you press the Tab key.

While you're working with text, you use several special keys on the key-board to edit as you go. These keys are listed in Table 30-1.

◄▥ Word processors offer additional key combinations to let the toothpick cursor do other, amazing things. See Chapter 9 for information about WordPad; see Chapter 10 for information about Microsoft Word.

Table 30-1	Common Windows Editing Keys
Key	*What It Does*
Backspace	Backs up the toothpick cursor and deletes the preceding character
Delete	Deletes the next character, the one after the toothpick cursor
Ctrl+Delete	Deletes all text from the toothpick cursor until the end of the line
Home	Moves the toothpick cursor to the beginning of the line or the first character in an input box
End	Moves the toothpick cursor to the end of the line or the last character in an input box
Tab	Moves the toothpick cursor to the next input box in a dialog box
Enter	Ends a line or paragraph of text (use only in a word processor)
←	Moves the toothpick cursor back one character
→	Moves the toothpick cursor forward one character
↑	Moves the toothpick cursor up one line
↓	Moves the toothpick cursor down one line
Ctrl+←	Moves the toothpick cursor back one word
Ctrl+→	Moves the toothpick cursor forward one word

Making text feel special by selecting it

All text in Windows, whether it's in a word processor or some lowly text in a dialog box, can be edited by using the Cut, Copy, and Paste commands, even if there isn't an Edit menu hanging around nearby. What you use instead are the keyboard shortcuts for those commands: Ctrl+X for Cut, Ctrl+C for Copy, and Ctrl+V for Paste. Also available is Ctrl+Z, the Undo command.

Before you can cut or copy text, it first must be selected. There are several ways to do this in Windows.

The best way to select text is to drag over it with the mouse's Text Selection pointer, as shown in Figure 30-1. Start the drag at the beginning of your text, and then drag to select and highlight. Release the mouse button when you've selected the necessary text.

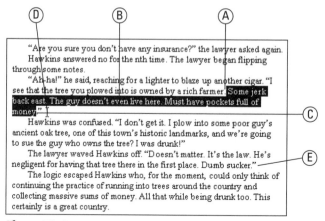

Figure 30-1
Text is selected.
A. Start dragging the mouse here. **B.** This text is selected, ready for cutting or copying. **C.** Release the mouse button here. **D.** The Text Selection mouse pointer design. **E.** This was edited so as not to offend lawyers.

To select all the text in a dialog box's input box, double-click on that box. This highlights all the text.

You can also select text by using the Shift key while moving the toothpick cursor. For example, Shift+← selects one character to the left of the toothpick cursor. Keep pressing Shift+← to select more characters.

After the text is selected, you can use the Cut or Copy commands on it to cut or copy the text; press Ctrl+X to cut and Ctrl+C to copy.

You can also press the Delete key to delete all the selected text.

Press Ctrl+V to paste previously copied text.

Press Ctrl+Z, the Undo command, to give up and undo whatever editing changes you've made.

← Refer to Chapter 8 for more information about the Cut, Copy, Paste, and Undo commands. They apply to any selected text in Windows, even text in a dialog box.

← Refer to Chapter 29 for more help with using the mouse to drag and select text.

Changing the Way Text Looks

The appearance of text in most applications can be changed. This doesn't apply to dialog boxes, where the text is pretty boring. But in a word processor or similar application, you can change the way the text looks.

There are two major things you can change about text: the font, or typeface, which is the text style, and the size of the text. You can also change various attributes of the text, making it **bold**, *italicized,* underlined, or a number of other effects, depending on what your software offers and how well your creative juices are flowing.

A font of typefaces

The way text appears, its style, is called a *typeface.* This is the official, typesetter's term. The unofficial computer term is a *font,* which isn't exactly a typeface, but no one's watching, and there really are no professionals in the room.

Fonts are changed in one of two ways. The first is from a Font menu item. The second is by using a Font drop-down list on a toolbar. In both cases, you fetch a new style for your text by scrolling through a list of fonts installed on your computer.

The new font you choose affects any selected text in your document, or, if no text has been selected, it affects any new text you type.

◀▬ Refer to Chapter 21 for more information about fonts, lovely fonts, so many things to do there. La-de-da.

Text sizes from petite to full-figured

The size of your text can also be changed, from teensy-tiny to relatively huge. The value used is *points,* which is another typesetter term. A point is essentially a tiny piece of a letter, about as big as an ant can eat in one bite.

Text typically appears on the screen in 8-, 10-, or 12-point sizes. The larger the point value, the bigger the text. If you set the point size to about 72, you get text about one inch high. Or if you're in Canada, if you set the point size to about 28, you get text a hair over one centimeter in height.

As with the font, setting a new point size is typically done with a drop-down list box, either on a toolbar or hidden in a menu. You can usually type a size value in addition to selecting it from a list.

The new point size affects any selected text in your document, or, if no text is selected, it affects anything new you type. Figure 30-2 illustrates how this works.

Figure 30-2
Text of different point sizes in WordPad.
A. Here is WordPad's Format bar. Choose View⇨Format Bar to see it. **B.** Pick a font from this drop-down list. The current font is boring Times New Roman (Western). Yee-ha! **C.** Choose the font size from this drop-down list. **D.** This text here was typed at 72 points, an American inch. **E.** This feeble text here was typed at 28 points, a Canadian centimeter. **F.** Toothpick cursor. **G.** Text attributes are set here: bold, italic, underline, and artist. (Actually, the last button sets the text color.)

Other funky things to do with text (attributes)

Text attributes control basically four different things: bold, italic, underline, and text color. The first three are set either in a text dialog box or using on/off buttons on a toolbar, as shown in Figure 30-2.

To change text attributes, select the text you want to change and then choose the new attribute. Or you can choose an attribute and then type some new text, in which case that new text will be affected by that attribute.

Use **bold text** for strong emphasis or in titles. Go sparingly with it; too much bold text can make your reader want to read something else.

In most cases, you should use *italic text* for emphasis. For example, use italics whenever you were told to underline something in your typewriter class. For example, italicize book titles, films, foreign words and phrases, and stuff you *really* want to emphasize.

Underline? Ha! No one uses it.

If you want to create a blank line for input, such as if you're creating a form, use the underline key on your keyboard. Just press and hold down the key to make a nice, long underline for fill-in-the-blanks type stuff.

Text color is another attribute you can set. It looks nice on the screen and can make your documents rainbow-beautiful. But if you don't have a color printer, you're really wasting your time.

I use underline around my office for comments and to emphasize text that I think needs reworking. For example, I color text blue if I'm not sure about something; red if it needs reworking, or green if it's a comment to me, not to be printed. If you try this approach, just remember to go back and remove the comments or fix the text before you print.

Basic Messing with Graphics Stuff (Stretching)

Playing with graphics isn't as extensive as playing with text in Windows. Most high-end graphics programs use their own techniques for drawing and creating images. Still, there is one thing you can do to most graphical images, especially those pasted into another program.

Suppose that you plop a map of Mississippi into your report on Sam Clemens. After pasting the map into your word processor, you realize that it's Missouri you really want, so you create a graphical bitmap of that and paste it into your word processor instead. The graphic you see may look like Figure 30-3.

Figure 30-3
Missouri awaits you.
A. Click on the graphic object once to select it. The "handles" appear only when it's selected. **B.** Click and drag here to make the graphic wider. **C.** Click and drag here to make the graphic taller. **D.** Click on any corner to change the graphic's size in two directions at one time.

← Click on the graphic once to select it. You'll see tiny handles appear on its sides and corners, just as shown in Figure 30-3. You can "grab" any of the graphic handles to stretch or shrink the graphic — just like you can resize a window on the screen (see Chapter 27).

If you hold the Shift key while you drag one of the handles, the image maintains its same dimensions. So if you want a larger Missouri all around, press the Shift key and then grab one of the corners with the mouse. Drag the mouse outward, and Missouri will still look like Missouri as it's resized.

← For more information about copying and pasting objects between two applications, see Chapter 8, the section "Sharing Information."

← See the section "The joy of stretch" in Chapter 27 for instructions on resizing a window. These same techniques apply to resizing a graphics image on the screen.

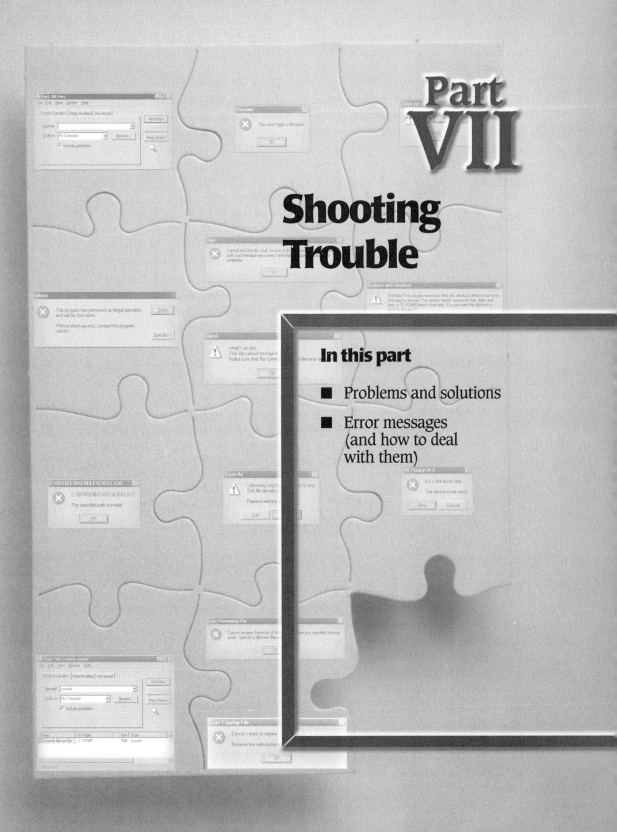

Part VII

Shooting Trouble

In this part

- Problems and solutions

- Error messages (and how to deal with them)

How do I . . . ?

Get my printer to work?

Hardware problems can be frustrating, but working through Windows Troubleshooter takes care of everything — and it can be a bit of fun as well.

➡ See Chapter 31, the section "The All-Purpose Amazing, Spectacular, Windows Troubleshooter," for more information about using the Troubleshooter.

Find long-lost files?

Even though you may lose a file, Windows hopefully never loses track of it. The Find command, available all over, can be used to hunt down wayward files and folders.

➡ See Chapter 31, the section "File? File? Here, File! C'mon, Boy! Where'd You Go?," for more information and a how-to.

Understand this bizarre error message?

Windows, despite all its friendliness, can dish up some doozies when it comes to baffling error messages. Why can't it just say, "Hey, type that filename again!"?

➡ A whole baker's dozen error messages are cussed and discussed in Chapter 32.

Problems and Solutions

Providing that you do the routine maintenance covered in Chapter 18, nothing should ever go wrong with your computer. Oh, it will eventually wear out. Time will pass, and new technology will make your PC seem slower. And your hard disk will fill up, but you can always buy a second one. But the only time something strange happens (aside from anything on the network) is when you add new hardware or software. If anything strange goes on in your computer, it will probably happen after one of those two events.

The biggest problem with computer catastrophes is not knowing what to do next. There are generally two things you can do. The first is to troubleshoot, which is easily accomplished using Windows' fancy Troubleshooter software. The second thing you can do is to start your computer with an Emergency Boot Disk and work repairs from there. This chapter covers it all.

The All-Purpose, Amazing, Spectacular, Windows Troubleshooter

Whenever your computer acts funny, you should set out to use the Troubleshooter. This is actually part of the Windows Help system. It's a series of dialog boxes that ask you simple questions. Eventually the questions lead you to an answer or at least the proper dialog box, where amends can be made.

➟ If you can't get at the Troubleshooter or your computer seems hopelessly lost, read through the section "Mayday! Mayday! Stick in that Emergency Boot Disk!" later in this chapter.

A walk through the Troubleshooter

To work through the Troubleshooter, follow these steps:

1. Start Help.

   Press Ctrl+Esc to pop up the Start Thing's menu, and then choose the Help command.

   Help may write in its little book for a while. Please wait.

   Eventually you see the Help dialog box (see Figure 31-1).

2. Bring the Index panel forward.

   Click the mouse on the Index tab to bring that panel forward.

3. Type **trouble** in the first input box.

   This step looks up the word *Troubleshooting* in the index and displays a banquet of options for getting your PC repaired.

4. Find your chosen subject.

   Twenty or so different items are listed under "Troubleshooting" in the Help index. Pick the one that irks you presently.

   If your hard disk seems sluggish, for example, click on "disk performance." This step brings up a dialog box (see Figure 31-2) that explains why your disk may be working so sluggishly. It also contains a link to the proper program to fix it.

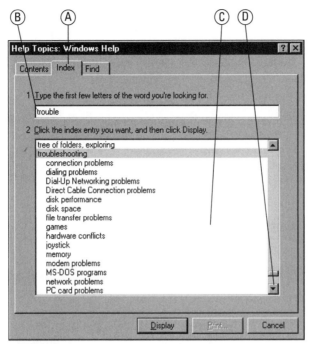

Figure 31-1
Here comes trouble!
A. Click on this tab to bring this panel forward. **B.** Type the word **trouble** here.
C. Your options banquet. **D.** Scroll down through the list to see more options.

Figure 31-2
The Troubleshooter suggestions for a sluggish hard drive.
A. Starts the Defragmenter program (see Chapter 18).
B. Click the mouse on this word to see a definition.
C. Step-by-step instructions.
D. Other info. **E.** Click here and choose the Print Topic command to get a hard copy of the information.

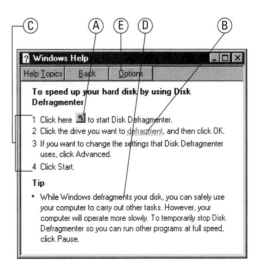

When you see help displayed, as shown in Figure 31-2, it's a good idea to click on the Options button and choose the Print Topic command from the menu. That way, you'll have a hard copy of the instructions the Troubleshooter is suggesting. That helps, especially if your PC crashes and you forget which step to take next.

5. Continue to work through the Troubleshooter.

   Sometimes the Troubleshooter asks you a series of questions. Suppose that you choose Printing Problems from the list. The Troubleshooter wants you to narrow down the problem, as shown in Figure 31-3. Simply choose whichever item best reflects your situation. The Troubleshooter may even want to know more information, as shown in Figure 31-4.

Figure 31-3
The Troubleshooter wants more information.
A. Read this first. **B.** Then choose one of these options.

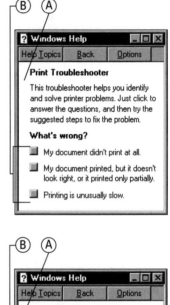

Figure 31-4
Even more questions are asked.
A. Here is your original problem. **B.** The Troubleshooter wants even more information.

Eventually you encounter either a written explanation of what's wrong or one of those "go to" buttons that takes you to a part of Windows where the problem can be solved. The Troubleshooter is sincere; it may even want to be sure that your problem is solved by asking you even more questions (see Figure 31-5).

Figure 31-5
The problem is, hopefully, resolved.
A. Moves you into the Printers folder.
B. Instructions for when you get there. **C.** This window "floats" on top of the screen so that you can still see the instructions. **D.** Windows wants to know whether it helped.

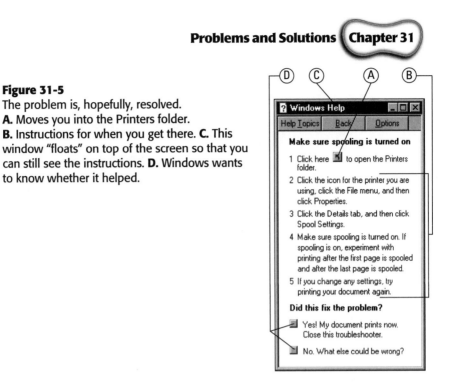

Dealing with annoying hardware conflicts

Sometimes your problem may involve some new gadget you installed, one that refuses to work. Windows even asks you, after you run the Add New Hardware wizard, whether it works correctly. If not, you troubleshoot hardware.

To start the hardware conflict troubleshooter, follow these steps:

1. Choose "hardware conflicts" from the Help system.

   Waltz through the steps in the preceding section, and choose "hardware conflict" in step 4.

   A help dialog box is displayed, with two button-options.

2. Choose Start the Hardware Conflict Troubleshooter.

   Another dialog box is displayed; click on the go-to button to display the Device Manager. This step displays the Device Manager tab in the System Properties dialog box (the one I told you to ignore way back in Chapter 20; see Figure 31-6).

3. Click the button by Click here to continue.

4. Work through the questions.

   The Troubleshooter continues to ask you questions and walk you through any modifications that need to be made in the Device Manager.

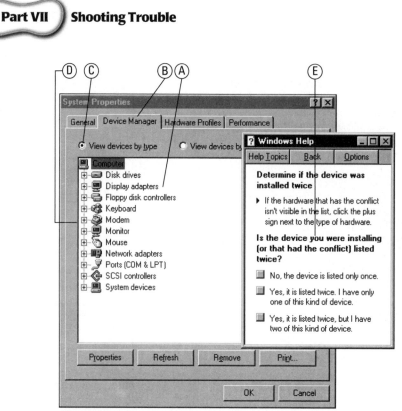

Figure 31-6
Working through the Device Manager to resolve hardware conflicts.
A. The Device Manager lists hardware attached to your computer. **B.** Click here to make sure that this tab is forward. **C.** Make sure that the dot is in this radio button. **D.** It's a collapsible tree-structure thing. **E.** Continue answering questions and following the step-by-steps.

The Device Manager is scary stuff, so pay special attention to everything you read; don't *assume* anything!

If you're asked to "double-click the hardware that has a conflict," expand the part of the tree that deals with that piece of hardware. If it's a sound card that's not doing well, for example, expand the "Sound, video and game controllers" part of the tree to see your sound card. *Then* double-click on your sound card. You see its special Properties dialog box, which contains the "Device usage" section (toward the bottom) that the Troubleshooting text refers to.

There is an off chance that you may have to reinstall your hardware. This process may be required in order to reset a "jumper" to a new "IRQ" setting. (This happens only with older PC cards, not with the newer Plug-and-Play-happy cards.) If so, turn off your computer and reinstall the device, configured as the Troubleshooter suggests.

Eventually, and hopefully, your hardware conflict will be solved — or at least you'll have the problem narrowed down and know what to tell tech support if the problem persists.

Special Ways to Start Your Computer

Sometimes you may have to start Windows in a special way: in "safe" mode, for example. Or maybe you just want to skip over Windows and start your PC by using DOS or with a special Emergency Boot Disk. All this may be part of your troubleshooting strategy, or maybe you just want to forgo Windows for now and play a DOS game. Whatever, the following sections tell you how.

See Chapter 26 for more information about playing DOS games (though I don't divulge any hints or offer any shortcuts).

Windows' special startup key commands

When your computer first starts, or after you reset, you see the following message on the screen:

Starting Windows 95...

If you sit there and drool while this message appears, Windows starts, hopefully as it always does. But if you're quick, you can stab the F8 key on your keyboard. That displays a special startup menu with several options for starting Windows, all described in Figure 31-7.

Choose an option as described in the menu.

If you want to start your computer in DOS mode for playing DOS games, type **5** and press the Enter key.

If you're having trouble starting Windows, type **3** and press Enter. That at least gets Windows started, and from there you can run the Troubleshooter, as described earlier in this chapter.

If you choose 1, Windows starts as it always does.

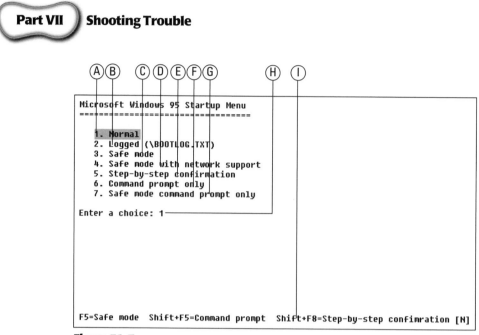

Figure 31-7
Windows' special startup menu.
A. This option is the same as if you didn't press the F8 key. **B.** Don't know what this means. **C.** Use only if you're having problems starting Windows (a minimum Windows configuration). **D.** Same as C, but the network gets hooked up.
E. Windows asks you Yes or No for each of its startup options. This is good for troubleshooting startup problems. **F.** MS-DOS mode, great for playing games. You can get there right away by pressing Shift+F5 rather than F8 after the "Starting Windows 95" message. **G.** Same as F, but in safe mode. **H.** Type a number here, and then press Enter. **I.** Ignore.

"I see strange messages on the screen!"

These messages appear when you accidentally press the Esc key when Windows starts. What that does is switch you over to "text mode," where you see various startup files run and display their confusing text messages. You just have to remember not to press the Esc key next time to return to the happy Windows-in-the-blue-sky startup screen.

Mayday! Mayday! Stick in that Emergency Boot Disk!

If all hell does break loose and you can't start Windows at all, you can always use the handy Emergency Boot Disk (created in Chapter 14, in the section "Creating a disk to start your computer: The fun yet useful Emergency Boot Disk"). This disk will definitely start your computer when Windows stubbornly refuses to boot.

To use the Emergency Boot Disk, follow these steps:

1. Place the Emergency Boot Disk in your drive A.

   It must be drive A.

2. Reset or turn on your computer.

   Remember that this is a desperate situation; I'm assuming that you can't get your PC to start any other way. *Never* reset with Windows on the screen unless it tells you that it's okay to do so.

3. The Emergency Boot Disk starts.

   Because the Emergency Boot Disk is in drive A, it starts your computer rather than Windows on your hard drive. You see something like the following displayed in — yech! — ugly text mode:

   Starting Windows 95...

   Microsoft ® Windows 95

   (C)Copyright Microsoft Corp 1981-1995.

   A:\>

   That last thing there is a DOS prompt. Welcome to 1981! Before you break out your copy of *DOS For Dummies,* there are really only a few things you can do here.

When Windows built your Emergency Boot Disk, it copied over a few handy files, each of which plays a special role in getting your computer back into shape. All the files are listed in Table 31-1, along with their function and a reference to where you can read more about them elsewhere in this book.

Table 31-1	Commands and Programs Available on the Emergency Boot Disk
Command	**What It Does**
ATTRIB	Grants access to read-only files; use only if directed to by technical support.
CHKDSK	Quickly scans a disk for errors; use ScanDisk instead.
DEBUG	A programmer's tool used to inspect memory, disks, and your PC's guts. Not for the faint-hearted.
EDIT	Starts a text editor, which you can use to mess with the CONFIG.SYS and AUTOEXEC.BAT files on your hard drive (but only if tech support tells you so).
FDISK	Initializes a hard drive, which also erases the drive. Don't use this turkey.
FORMAT	Formats disks, typically used after FDISK when you're setting up a hard drive for the first time. Don't bother.
REGEDIT	Grants access to Windows' registry files, which may aid in disk recovery. Use only under the direction of Microsoft tech-support personnel.
SCANDISK	At last! One you can use yourself. Run this program to examine and optionally fix disk boo-boos. Instructions are offered in Chapter 18.
SYS	A program to copy Windows boot files from the floppy disk back to the hard drive. This may be required, but do so only under the direction of Microsoft tech-support personnel.

To run one of these commands, carefully type its name at the A:\> prompt. Press the Backspace key to back up and erase. Then press the Enter key. For example:

A:\>**scandisk**

In the preceding line, the ScanDisk program's name was typed. Press the Enter key, and ScanDisk runs.

Be aware that the programs are run in text-only mode. They look and work in a manner similar to their Windows graphical counterparts, but they may not be operated in the same manner. Also, the suggestions given in this book are best suited only to those daring enough to try these solutions on their own. If you're one of those people, great. Otherwise, my best advice is to dial up Microsoft technical support and beg them for assistance. (The phone numbers are listed in your Windows manual, and, yes, it will probably cost you money — at least for the phone call.)

◀ᴵᴵᴵ There is really only one cure for total hard disk disaster: Have a good backup handy. I cannot urge you strongly enough to back up. Refer to Chapter 18, where I beat the concept into the dirt.

File? File? Here, File! C'mon, Boy! Where'd You Go?

Things come and go. Sometimes a file was just here, and then it's gone. It happens to everyone, but most likely the reason you do lose files is that you didn't store them in the proper folder. That's a sin. Fortunately, Windows makes it easy to find your lost file, providing you know a few details about it — like its name, for one.

◀ᴵᴵᴵ Refer to Chapter 17, the section "Setting Up Folders Just So," for more information about organizing your work so that you don't lose files all the time.

"I want to find my file now. No messing around!"

Follow these steps, Mr. Inarush:

1. Open up My Computer or the Explorer.

2. Press the F3 key.

   This step brings up the Find: All Files dialog box (see Figure 31-8 when you have time).

3. Type the name of the file you're looking for.

   Be as precise as possible, if you can.

   If you know only part of the filename, just type that part.

   If you aren't sure of some letters, replace them with the question-mark character:

   POR???B

4. Choose My Computer from the Look in drop-down list.

5. Make sure that the Include subfolders item is checked.

6. Click Find Now.

   Windows looks for your file.

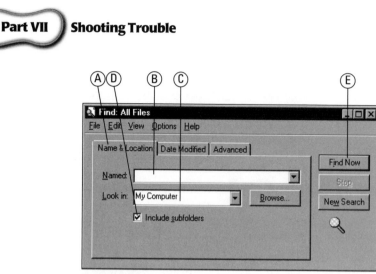

Figure 31-8
The file-finding dialog box.
A. Make sure that the Name & Location dialog box is forward. **B.** Type all or part of your filename here. **C.** Choose the disk drive to look in here, or choose My Computer to look everywhere. **D.** Always check this. **E.** Click here to start.

7. The results are displayed in the bottom of the dialog box.

   Double-click on the file to open it, or you can do whatever you want with it. The file has been found.

A bit more relaxed explanation, if you're not in a hurry

Howdy!

To look for a long-lost file anywhere on your computer, follow these steps:

1. Open up My Computer or the Explorer.

   My Computer is my favorite here. If you open up the main My Computer window, you save yourself the trouble of going through step 4.

    See Chapter 2 for more information about using My Computer.

2. Press the F3 key.

   This step brings up the Find: All Files dialog box (refer to Figure 31-8).

   You can also summon the Find: All Files dialog box from My Computer's shortcut menu, as well as from the Start Thing's menu: Press Ctrl+Esc, F, F (think "find files").

3. Type the name of the file you're looking for.

   You can type all or only part of the filename. If you're looking for the file called Sounds like an Elephant who ate too many beans, for example, you have to type only **Sounds** or **Elephant**, and Windows finds the rest. (Actually, it finds all files matching the words you type.)

   If you aren't sure of some of the letters, you can replace them with question marks, thusly:

   SOU??S

   Windows still searches for the proper matches.

4. Choose My Computer from the Look in drop-down list.

   This step ensures that Windows looks on every hard drive in your computer. If you're certain that the file is on one hard drive or another, you can limit the search by just choosing that drive from the drop-down list.

   Any network drives attached to your computer can also be chosen for searching.

   If you pressed the F3 key while in a folder deep down in My Computer, that folder also appears on the list. Although this is a great way to narrow the search to one folder (or one branch of your hard disk "tree"), I still recommend choosing My Computer. After all, the file is *lost,* you know.

5. Make sure that the Include subfolders item is checked.

   Put a ✔ check mark in the box. That way, Windows looks everywhere.

6. Click the Find Now button.

   Windows looks for your file everywhere you suggested. This takes some time, though as each potential match is located, it's displayed in a list at the bottom of the dialog box (see Figure 31-9).

   By the way, Windows does not look for any lost files in the Recycle Bin. If you suspect that your lost file was deleted, you have to browse the Recycle Bin by yourself. See Chapter 5, the section "A quick, odorless peek into the Recycle Bin to restore something."

7. The results are displayed at the bottom of the dialog box.

   You can double-click on the file to open it, or you can drag it out to the desktop or into a folder, where you won't lose it again. (This moves the file from wherever it was hiding, by the way.)

See Chapter 16, the section "Deeply Moving Files," for more information about moving files.

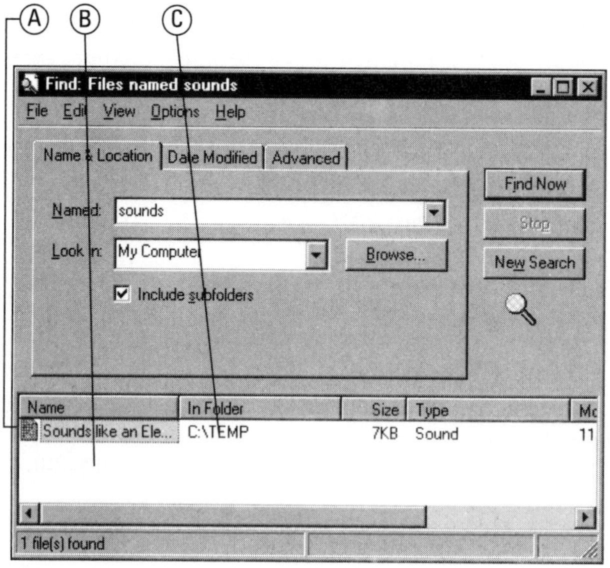

Figure 31-9
The file is found!
A. The results of the search. **B.** Other files that may have matched also appear in this list (sometimes). **C.** The file's pathname, which tells you where it's located.

◀▪▪▪ Refer to Chapter 17, "Beating a pathname to a file's door," for more information about what a pathname is and how it can help you find your file's location.

Other options you may want to try in the Find dialog box

If you click on the Advanced tab in the Find files dialog box, you can look for files of a specific type or that contain certain text. If you're looking only for sound files, for example, you can choose the Sound type from the list — and then leave the filename blank. Windows finds all your sound files for you.

If you want to find a file that contains a specific snippet of text, type that text in the Containing text box in the Advanced panel. If you leave the filename blank, Windows hunts only for files that contain that bit of text.

If you do look for a file that contains text, try to choose the type of text file you're looking for: Word, Rich Text, Text Document, and so on. Again, this helps speed up the search by directing Windows to skip over nontext files.

Error Messages (and How to Deal with Them)

Chapter

32

In This Chapter

- Understanding various error messages
- Solving the problems causing error messages

Error messages are a pain in the rump. Not really because they pop up there and spoil your rhythm, but because it's just real darn hard to understand them. Even with all that the scriveners at Microsoft tried to do to make Windows easier to use, they just can't remove the terms *invalid, default, specified,* and *illegal operation.* Yikes! It makes particle physics sound elementary.

The following sections divvy up some error messages, explaining why they happened and what, if anything, you can do to fix the problem.

← Some error messages, or really warning dialog boxes, are not covered here. When you try to delete a program, for example, Windows slaps a warning on the screen. That's covered in Chapter 5.

← General file warning messages are covered in Chapter 4.

Cannot Find the File

What happened: You typed the name of a program to run, and Windows couldn't find it (see Figure 32-1). This usually happens when you type the name of a program by using the Start Thing's Run command.

How to fix it: Use the Browse button in the Run command's dialog box to hunt for the file. Or you can refer to the section "File? File? Here, File! C'mon, Boy! Where'd You Go?" in Chapter 31 to try to hunt down the file elsewhere on your system.

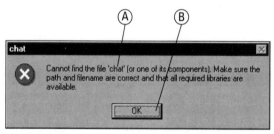

Figure 32-1
This program refuses to run.
A. The name of the program you tried to run. **B.** Click here. Oh, well.

Cannot Find This File

No, this isn't the same type of error as in the preceding section, though they both have insidiously similar dialog boxes.

What happened: You tried to open a file in WordPad or some other application by typing that file's name (see Figure 32-2). Tsk, tsk, tsk.

How to fix it: Use your mouse to pluck out the file from the scrolling list. Browse! Or you can edit the filename and try typing it again.

Figure 32-2
Check-your-typing-and-try-again error.
A. Bizarre way to say you mistyped a filename. **B.** Oh, well.

Cannot Rename

What happened: You tried to give a file a new name, and a file with that same name already exists in the same folder (see Figure 32-3).

How to fix it: Give the file another name.

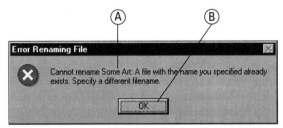

Figure 32-3
The try-to-rename-the-file-again warning dialog box.
A. The file you tried to rename. **B.** Oh, well.

The Device Is Not Ready

What happened: You tried to access a disk drive, and, for some reason, Windows wasn't able to do so (see Figure 32-4). Pray that it's a floppy disk; if it's a hard drive, there may be something horribly wrong with the drive.

How to fix it: For a floppy disk, stick a formatted disk in the drive. Either you don't have a disk in the drive, the drive's door latch isn't closed, or the disk isn't formatted.

If it's a hard drive, you have to do some troubleshooting. Refer to the section "The All-Purpose, Amazing, Spectacular, Windows Troubleshooter" in Chapter 31 for more information.

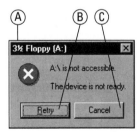

Figure 32-4
"I'm not ready yet!"
A. The disk drive (device) that's not ready. **B.** You can click here after putting a proper disk in the drive. **C.** Click here to give up.

The Disk in the Destination Drive Is Full

What happened: You tried to move or copy something to a disk, and, lo, there just isn't enough room there for it (see Figure 32-5).

How to fix it: For a floppy disk, you can replace the disk and try again. For a hard drive, you have to delete some files to free up space.

← A great way to free up space on a hard drive is to adjust the amount of disk space the Recycle Bin eats up. See the section "Tweaking the Recycle Bin" in Chapter 5 for more information.

Figure 32-5
No room at the inn.
A. Follow these instructions. **B.** Click after you insert a new disk. **C.** Click to give up.

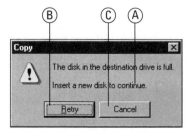

The Disk Is Write-Protected

What happened: You tried to alter a file on a write-protected disk (see Figure 32-6). A write-protected disk cannot be written to, and the information saved on that disk cannot be changed or deleted.

How to fix it: You can either use another disk or remove the write-protection from that disk. To change the write-protect status on a floppy disk, slide the tile so that it covers up the hole. (On the older 5¼-inch disks, you have to remove the sticker over the disk notch.)

Figure 32-6
Write-protection has stopped you cold.
A. The file you tried to copy or alter. **B.** Do this. **C.** Then click here and try again.

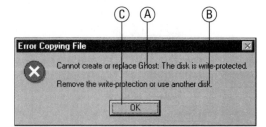

Read-Only File Cannot Be Changed and Saved

What happened: You tried to save a file that's been marked "read-only" by Windows (see Figure 32-7). This type of file cannot be altered or even deleted.

How to fix it: My best advice is not to fix it; read-only files are made that way for a reason. Obviously someone doesn't want you altering the file. If you're persistent, you can open up the file's Properties dialog box and in the Attributes section click on Read-only to remove the ✔ check mark from the box.

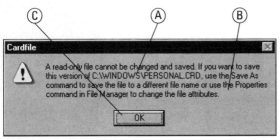

Figure 32-7
"Don't mess with me!"
A. Here is the name of the read-only file. **B.** Yes, you can always try to save the file by using a different name. **C.** Oh, well.

Replace Existing File?

What happened: You've tried to save a file to disk, but a file with that same name already exists (see Figure 32-8).

How to fix it: Click on No unless you're absolutely sure that you want to replace the already existing file. Keep in mind that if you save, you cannot recover the original file — no matter what. Just type a different name when you try to save the file again.

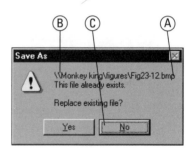

Figure 32-8
You shouldn't overwrite existing files.
A. The name of the file you're about to overwrite. **B.** A file elsewhere on the network; see Chapter 22. **C.** Click here.

Save Changes?

What happened: You were working on a document and decided to close it or open a new document, but the document has not been saved to disk (see Figure 32-9). Omigosh!

How to fix it: Nothing to fix, really. Just click on Yes to save the file.

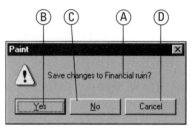

Figure 32-9
Save your files before it's too late!
A. The name of the file you've been working on. **B.** Click here, definitely. **C.** Click here and you lose any editing or changes you've made. **D.** Clicking here cancels everything and returns you to your document for more messing around.

The Item This Shortcut Refers to Has Been Changed or Moved

What happened: Shortcuts can get you there quickly, and they can get you lost. Sometimes the file a shortcut points to may be moved or deleted. Windows catches most of that, but sometimes it misses a file or two. When that happens, you're warned, but Windows also tries to make amends by finding the file (see Figure 32-10).

How to fix it: See whether the match suggested in the following dialog box is okay. If so, click on Yes. Otherwise, you may want to scour the Recycle Bin for the original file. And if it can't be found, just delete the shortcut; it doesn't point to anything anyway.

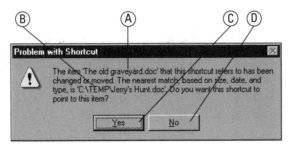

Figure 32-10
Missing shortcuts can get Windows lost.
A. The shortcut file you tried to access. **B.** Windows' suggestion for a matching file
(wrong, in this case). **C.** Click here to go ahead with Windows' suggestion. **D.** Click
here otherwise.

The Specified Path Is Invalid

What happened: You tried to run a program from the Start Thing's menu,
and Windows couldn't find it (see Figure 32-11).

How to fix it: You can follow the steps in the section "File? File? Here,
File! C'mon, Boy! Where'd You Go?" in Chapter 31 to try to find the file on
your disk.

← This error message may follow another error message warning you that
some of the program's pieces parts are missing. In that case, you probably
have an installation problem. Consider reinstalling the software. See
Chapter 13 for more information about installing software.

← If the program lives on the Start Thing's menu, you may consider
removing it. See Chapter 6, the section "Zapping a program from a Start
Thing submenu."

Figure 32-11
Windows can't find this program.
A. The long, boring pathname to the file.
B. The filename part (this is Excel here).
C. Oh, well.

This Filename Is Not Valid

What happened: You tried to save a file to disk and typed a forbidden filename character (see Figure 32-12).

How to fix it: Retype the filename, but don't use any of the following characters:

" * / : < > ? \ |

← Also see Chapter 16, the sidebar "Basic file-naming rules and regulations."

Figure 32-12
You can't name a file that!
A. The offending filename. **B.** Contains the slash character. Heavens! **C.** Oh, well.

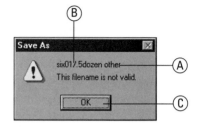

This Program Has Performed an Illegal Operation

What happened: This is a scary one. For some reason, the program you were using "crashed." It died. It's gone. Who knows why this happened? The dialog box suggests contacting whoever developed the software to let them know about it (see Figure 32-13). Sounds like a good idea.

How to fix it: You can't. Click the Close button to close down the offending application. Furthermore, I advise saving everything you're working on and restarting your computer. In some rare cases, you may not be able to do that, but try anyway.

← Stubborn programs that refuse to be shut down can be killed off in Windows by using the Ctrl+Alt+Delete key combination. See the section "The drastic way to quit" in Chapter 3.

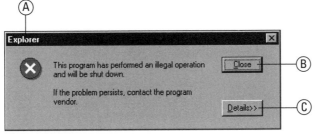

Figure 32-13
The big OOPS has happened!
A. The program that died (probably because my version of Windows was an early "beta" test). **B.** Click here. **C.** This doesn't tell you much.

You Must Type a Filename

What happened: You tried to rename a file but didn't type a name (see Figure 32-14). Foolishly, you just pressed the F2 key and then Enter. All files must have a name, silly.

How to fix it: Try again. This time, type a name for the file.

← For more information, see Chapter 16, the section "Blessing a File with a New Name."

Figure 32-14
Gotta name that file.
A. The Rename program caused this error.
B. Like, duh. **C.** Oh, well.

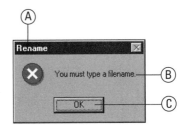

Part VII **Shooting Trouble**

Index

H

handles, on graphics, 544
hard disks/drives
advantages of buying
second, 365
compressed, 366
Defragment utility, 350,
363–364
described, 268
DriveSpace (compression)
utility, 350, 365–369
recommendation on
organization, 274
recommendations on
maintenance, 274,
349–350
removable, 268
ScanDisk utility, 350,
359–362
sharing on networks,
424–426
storage capacities, 266
warning against
formatting, 274
hardware
installing, 435
and Plug and Play feature,
393, 435–436,
552–553
troubleshooting problems
with, 547–557
Hardware Conflict
Troubleshooter,
551–553
Hearts game, 484, 490–491
Help system, 68, 81–88
About Windows
command, 516
Find panel, 86–87
Index, 84–85
in Microsoft Office,
211–212
MS-DOS Program
Troubleshooter,
249–250

printing or copying from,
88, 549–550
with problems from
Troubleshooter,
548–551
quitting, 84
returning to application
from (Escape key), 82
tooltips, 37, 148
Hide Variations command
(View menu), 400
hiding
scrollbars, 508
taskbar, 464–465
hierarchical structure of
folders, 126, 332–335,
521–522
Home key, 539
host drives, 366
hot keys, 68
hourglass icons, 534
Household Inventory
document (tutorial),
180
"How Do I" sections, 5–6
how to use, 2
HyperTerminal, 222–229

I

I-beam (toothpick) text
selection pointer,
535, 538
icon handling
aligning, 40, 97, 309,
342, 461
copying and pasting, 97
finding by name, 36
opening, 29
rearranging file icons by
delete date, 104
rearranging file icons by
type, 342
renaming, 304
sizing, 461
sorting, 39

viewing files as, 38
viewing in Start menu,
136–137
icons
Accessibility Options,
387–388
Add New Hardware, 393
Add Printer, 441
Add/Remove
Programs, 393
Control Panel, 385
Date/Time, 394
Display, 394
Do It!, 4
Entire Network, 417
Fax, 147
Fax-Modem, 150, 151
Fonts, 394
hourglass, 534
Inbox, 429
Joystick, 388
Keyboard, 388–391
Mail and Fax, 396
Microsoft Mail
Postoffice, 396
Modems, 391–392
Mouse, 395, 473, 532
Multimedia, 397
Network, 395, 408–409
Network Neighborhood,
408, 414
New Hardware, 436
ODBC, 397
Passwords, 395, 413
Printers, 372, 396
Question Mark, 460
Regional Settings, 397
Scrap, 167
"serving/sharing hand,"
29, 424
Sounds, 396, 475
System, 397
Telephony, 397
"warning" X, 516
See also taskbar

Title	Author	ISBN	Price
INTERNET / COMMUNICATIONS / NETWORKING			12/20/94
CompuServe For Dummies™	by Wallace Wang	1-56884-181-7	$19.95 USA/$26.95 Canada
Modems For Dummies™, 2nd Edition	by Tina Rathbone	1-56884-223-6	$19.99 USA/$26.99 Canada
Modems For Dummies™	by Tina Rathbone	1-56884-001-2	$19.95 USA/$26.95 Canada
MORE Internet For Dummies™	by John R. Levine & Margaret Levine Young	1-56884-164-7	$19.95 USA/$26.95 Canada
NetWare For Dummies™	by Ed Tittel & Deni Connor	1-56884-003-9	$19.95 USA/$26.95 Canada
Networking For Dummies™	by Doug Lowe	1-56884-079-9	$19.95 USA/$26.95 Canada
ProComm Plus 2 For Windows For Dummies™	by Wallace Wang	1-56884-219-8	$19.99 USA/$26.99 Canada
The Internet For Dummies™, 2nd Edition	by John R. Levine & Carol Baroudi	1-56884-222-8	$19.99 USA/$26.99 Canada
The Internet For Macs For Dummies™	by Charles Seiter	1-56884-184-1	$19.95 USA/$26.95 Canada
MACINTOSH			
Macs For Dummies®	by David Pogue	1-56884-173-6	$19.95 USA/$26.95 Canada
Macintosh System 7.5 For Dummies™	by Bob LeVitus	1-56884-197-3	$19.95 USA/$26.95 Canada
MORE Macs For Dummies™	by David Pogue	1-56884-087-X	$19.95 USA/$26.95 Canada
PageMaker 5 For Macs For Dummies™	by Galen Gruman	1-56884-178-7	$19.95 USA/$26.95 Canada
QuarkXPress 3.3 For Dummies™	by Galen Gruman & Barbara Assadi	1-56884-217-1	$19.99 USA/$26.99 Canada
Upgrading and Fixing Macs For Dummies™	by Kearney Rietmann & Frank Higgins	1-56884-189-2	$19.95 USA/$26.95 Canada
MULTIMEDIA			
Multimedia & CD-ROMs For Dummies™, Interactive Multimedia Value Pack	by Andy Rathbone	1-56884-225-2	$29.95 USA/$39.95 Canada
Multimedia & CD-ROMs For Dummies™	by Andy Rathbone	1-56884-089-6	$19.95 USA/$26.95 Canada
OPERATING SYSTEMS / DOS			
MORE DOS For Dummies™	by Dan Gookin	1-56884-046-2	$19.95 USA/$26.95 Canada
S.O.S. For DOS™	by Katherine Murray	1-56884-043-8	$12.95 USA/$16.95 Canada
OS/2 For Dummies™	by Andy Rathbone	1-878058-76-2	$19.95 USA/$26.95 Canada
UNIX			
UNIX For Dummies™	by John R. Levine & Margaret Levine Young	1-878058-58-4	$19.95 USA/$26.95 Canada
WINDOWS			
S.O.S. For Windows™	by Katherine Murray	1-56884-045-4	$12.95 USA/$16.95 Canada
MORE Windows 3.1 For Dummies™, 3rd Edition	by Andy Rathbone	1-56884-240-6	$19.99 USA/$26.99 Canada
PCs / HARDWARE			
Illustrated Computer Dictionary For Dummies™	by Dan Gookin, Wally Wang, & Chris Van Buren	1-56884-004-7	$12.95 USA/$16.95 Canada
Upgrading and Fixing PCs For Dummies™	by Andy Rathbone	1-56884-002-0	$19.95 USA/$26.95 Canada
PRESENTATION / AUTOCAD			
AutoCAD For Dummies™	by Bud Smith	1-56884-191-4	$19.95 USA/$26.95 Canada
PowerPoint 4 For Windows For Dummies™	by Doug Lowe	1-56884-161-2	$16.95 USA/$22.95 Canada
PROGRAMMING			
Borland C++ For Dummies™	by Michael Hyman	1-56884-162-0	$19.95 USA/$26.95 Canada
"Borland's New Language Product" For Dummies™	by Neil Rubenking	1-56884-200-7	$19.95 USA/$26.95 Canada
C For Dummies™	by Dan Gookin	1-878058-78-9	$19.95 USA/$26.95 Canada
C++ For Dummies™	by Stephen R. Davis	1-56884-163-9	$19.95 USA/$26.95 Canada
Mac Programming For Dummies™	by Dan Parks Sydow	1-56884-173-6	$19.95 USA/$26.95 Canada
QBasic Programming For Dummies™	by Douglas Hergert	1-56884-093-4	$19.95 USA/$26.95 Canada
Visual Basic "X" For Dummies™, 2nd Edition	by Wallace Wang	1-56884-230-9	$19.99 USA/$26.99 Canada
Visual Basic 3 For Dummies™	by Wallace Wang	1-56884-076-4	$19.95 USA/$26.95 Canada
SPREADSHEET			
1-2-3 For Dummies™	by Greg Harvey	1-878058-60-6	$16.95 USA/$21.95 Canada
1-2-3 For Windows 5 For Dummies™, 2nd Edition	by John Walkenbach	1-56884-216-3	$16.95 USA/$21.95 Canada
1-2-3 For Windows For Dummies™	by John Walkenbach	1-56884-052-7	$16.95 USA/$21.95 Canada
Excel 5 For Macs For Dummies™	by Greg Harvey	1-56884-186-8	$19.95 USA/$26.95 Canada
Excel For Dummies™, 2nd Edition	by Greg Harvey	1-56884-050-0	$16.95 USA/$21.95 Canada
MORE Excel 5 For Windows For Dummies™	by Greg Harvey	1-56884-207-4	$19.95 USA/$26.95 Canada
Quattro Pro 6 For Windows For Dummies™	by John Walkenbach	1-56884-174-4	$19.95 USA/$26.95 Canada
Quattro Pro For DOS For Dummies™	by John Walkenbach	1-56884-023-3	$16.95 USA/$21.95 Canada
UTILITIES / VCRs & CAMCORDERS			
Norton Utilities 8 For Dummies™	by Beth Slick	1-56884-166-3	$19.95 USA/$26.95 Canada
VCRs & Camcorders For Dummies™	by Andy Rathbone & Gordon McComb	1-56884-229-5	$14.99 USA/$20.99 Canada
WORD PROCESSING			
Ami Pro For Dummies™	by Jim Meade	1-56884-049-7	$19.95 USA/$26.95 Canada
MORE Word For Windows 6 For Dummies™	by Doug Lowe	1-56884-165-5	$19.95 USA/$26.95 Canada
MORE WordPerfect 6 For Windows For Dummies™	by Margaret Levine Young & David C. Kay	1-56884-206-6	$19.95 USA/$26.95 Canada
MORE WordPerfect 6 For DOS For Dummies™	by Wallace Wang, edited by Dan Gookin	1-56884-047-0	$19.95 USA/$26.95 Canada
S.O.S. For WordPerfect™	by Katherine Murray	1-56884-053-5	$12.95 USA/$16.95 Canada
Word 6 For Macs For Dummies™	by Dan Gookin	1-56884-190-6	$19.95 USA/$26.95 Canada
Word For Windows 6 For Dummies™	by Dan Gookin	1-56884-075-6	$16.95 USA/$21.95 Canada
Word For Windows For Dummies™	by Dan Gookin	1-878058-86-X	$16.95 USA/$21.95 Canada
WordPerfect 6 For Dummies™	by Dan Gookin	1-878058-77-0	$16.95 USA/$21.95 Canada
WordPerfect For Dummies™	by Dan Gookin	1-878058-52-5	$16.95 USA/$21.95 Canada
WordPerfect For Windows For Dummies™	by Margaret Levine Young & David C. Kay	1-56884-032-2	$16.95 USA/$21.95 Canada

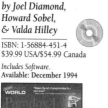

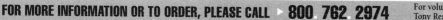

Order Center: **(800) 762-2974** *(8 a.m.–6 p.m., EST, weekdays)*

12/20/94

Quantity	ISBN	Title	Price	Total

Shipping & Handling Charges

	Description	First book	Each additional book	Total
Domestic	Normal	$4.50	$1.50	$
	Two Day Air	$8.50	$2.50	$
	Overnight	$18.00	$3.00	$
International	Surface	$8.00	$8.00	$
	Airmail	$16.00	$16.00	$
	DHL Air	$17.00	$17.00	$

*For large quantities call for shipping & handling charges.
**Prices are subject to change without notice.

Ship to:

Name _____

Company _____

Address _____

City/State/Zip_____

Daytime Phone _____

Payment: ☐ Check to IDG Books (US Funds Only)

☐ VISA   ☐ MasterCard   ☐ American Express

Card # _____ Expires _____

Signature _____

Subtotal _____

CA residents add
applicable sales tax _____

IN, MA, and MD
residents add
5% sales tax _____

IL residents add
6.25% sales tax_____

RI residents add
7% sales tax_____

TX residents add
8.25% sales tax_____

Shipping_____

Total _____

Please send this order form to:

IDG Books Worldwide
7260 Shadeland Station, Suite 100
Indianapolis, IN 46256

Allow up to 3 weeks for delivery.
Thank you!